AGING IN AMERICA

AGING IN AMERICA

VOLUME 1
Psychological Aspects

John C. Cavanaugh and Christine K. Cavanaugh, Editors
Jane Berry and Robin West, Advisory Editors

Praeger Perspectives

PRAEGER
An Imprint of ABC-CLIO, LLC

A B C ⬥ C L I O

Santa Barbara, California • Denver, Colorado • Oxford, England

Library of Congress Cataloging-in-Publication Data

Aging in America / John C. Cavanaugh ... [et al.].
    v. ; cm. — (Praeger perspectives)
  Includes bibliographical references and index.
    Contents: Vol. 1. Psychological aspects — vol. 2. Physical and mental health —
vol. 3. Societal issues.
    ISBN 978-0-313-35093-1 (set : alk. paper) — ISBN 978-0-313-35095-5
(vol. 1 : alk. paper) — ISBN 978-0-313-35097-9 (vol. 2 : alk. paper) —
ISBN 978-0-313-35099-3 (vol. 3 : alk. paper) — ISBN 978-0-313-35094-8 (set ebook) —
ISBN 978-0-313-35096-2 (vol. 1 ebook) — ISBN 978-0-313-35098-6 (vol. 2 ebook) —
ISBN 978-0-313-35100-6 (vol. 3 ebook)
  1. Older people—United States.   2. Older people—Care—United States.
3. Aging—United States.   I. Cavanaugh, John C.
  HQ1064.U5A35   2009
  305.260973—dc22   2009030407

14   13   12   11   10   1   2   3   4   5

This book is also available on the World Wide Web as an eBook.
Visit www.abc-clio.com for details.

Praeger
An Imprint of ABC-CLIO, LLC

ABC-CLIO, LLC
130 Cremona Drive, P.O. Box 1911
Santa Barbara, California 93116-1911

This book is printed on acid-free paper (∞)
Manufactured in the United States of America

CONTENTS

PREFACE

The aging of the population of the United States and the rest of the industrialized world is a well-known fact. But knowing this and fully understanding its implications are two different things. Such understanding was the genesis of this three-volume set on the implications of aging for our society. Our goal was to provide a foundation for individuals who do not necessarily have deep background in gerontology, but who have a working knowledge of key general principles in related fields. We also provide those more grounded in gerontology with fresh perspectives on topics that have received considerable treatment over the years. In this way, we strive to offer a learning opportunity to all interested readers.

Understanding what is known and, more importantly, what is not known about aging is essential for understanding one of the most important societal challenges we will face in the 21st century: how society should respond to rapidly increasing numbers of older adults. Only by knowing more about the processes underlying aging and how to differentiate between normative and abnormal aging will we be able to respond to the needs of older adults appropriately.

All aspects of society are already and will be increasingly affected by the growing numbers of older adults. The front edge of the baby boom generation became eligible for early Social Security payments in 2008 and will become eligible for Medicare in 2011. As the century progresses, the face of the older adult population will change dramatically as the number of minority older adults, especially Latinos, increases very rapidly. How well society responds to these demographic changes depends critically on the knowledge we have about the basic processes of aging.

The volumes are organized around three themes. Volume 1 focuses on basic psychological processes. Volume 2 considers topics in physical and mental health. Volume 3 takes a wider view on issues impacting society more broadly.

Volume 1 includes chapters on basic cognitive processes (cognitive neuroscience, attention, memory, language and communication, and everyday problem solving), personality and social psychological processes (personality and emotion, stereotypes, and personal control), environmental influences, end-of-life issues, and successful aging. Volume 2 takes a close look at basic biological and physiological processes (longevity and morbidity, and behavioral genetics), issues in physical health (health promotion and disease prevention, and stress), the interface between physical and mental health, issues in mental health (assessment, mental health and adjustment), and treatment and intervention issues (rehabilitation, medication adherence, and caregiver health). Volume 3 examines issues confronting society, including the demographics of aging using Hispanic Americans as an example, labor force participation, family structure and social networks, elder abuse, lifestyle, housing, spirituality, politics, hospice, and technology.

Like any complex project, this set of books was a collaborative effort. We especially thank Drs. Jane Berry, Robin West, Sara Qualls, and Lisa McGuire for serving as advisory editors. Their insights and comments on the chapters ensured the high quality of the chapters. Elizabeth Potenza at Praeger shepherded the project from start to finish.

We also thank our parents, John T. and Barbara Cavanaugh and William and Mary Kamenjar, for providing us with outstanding examples of how to grow older. Their acceptance of some and fight against other age-related changes constantly reminds us that life is always to be lived to the fullest, no matter what our bodies may say. We both hope to carry on their legacy.

John C. and Christine K. Cavanaugh

Chapter 1

Neuroscience and Aging

Fredda Blanchard-Fields

The 21st century has been described as the century of the brain. This is partly due to numerous recent technological advances, such as the development of functional magnetic resonance imaging (fMRI) and diffusion tensor imaging (DTI). Such procedures have facilitated the study of brain structure and functions using noninvasive methods. Because of these advances we can now more systematically examine the neuronal correlates of behavior in living beings. Of particular importance to the graying of America, neuroscientific approaches are being widely applied to research questions that deal with both cognitive and social-emotional aging. Although the lion's share of neuroscience and aging research has focused on cognitive aging, recently researchers have used these techniques to investigate processing preferences for emotional compared to neutral information in older adults (see Mather et al., 2004). Similarly, research in the emerging field of social cognitive neuroscience has shown associations between neural structures and a variety of social cognitive tasks such as person perception, stereotypes, and theory of mind (Amodio & Frith, 2006; Ochsner & Lieberman, 2001). One of the challenges for adult development theories will be to incorporate these models and techniques into our conceptual understanding of the aging process.

There are distinct advantages to taking a neuroscientific approach to the study of aging. For example, a particularly beneficial outcome of this approach to research is the fact that the neuroscience approach has taken intervention research to new pinnacles. Interventions that are important in enhancing the quality of life of older adults can now be evaluated beyond simply observing behavioral change by including evaluation at the neurological level (e.g., Colcombe et al., 2003). In particular, the neuroscience approach offers a new level of analysis to understanding cognitive and social-emotional functioning.

This latter point relates to a life span–related thread that runs throughout this chapter: Behavior and development are multiply determined. At the simplest level, age is not the best predictor of behavior. Instead, behavior across the life span is determined by multiple forces, some of which are age-related, such as biological changes, differing opportunity structures in society, and changes in motivational orientations and emotional functioning. For example, researchers now acknowledge that cognitive change in older adulthood is influenced at multiple levels of analysis, including declines in brain volume and density, the positive and negative effects of stereotyping, as well as deploying attention away from negative stimuli. As indicated previously, the investigation of these multiple forces on development has become more tractable as new technologies and research methods have evolved, such as brain imaging.

This chapter provides an overview of contemporary theories and recent empirical findings of neuroscience and aging, while at the same time outlining future challenges that need to be addressed. We begin by discussing the general neuroscience approach and the availability of new methods of measurement that result in the emergence of new phenomena. Next, the chapter focuses on cognitive neuroscience and aging, including age-related change in brain structure, neurochemical properties, and brain function. Two contemporary areas of research are explored, including neural plasticity in later adulthood and culture, brain, and aging. Next, we explore more recent developments in the area of social neuroscience and aging. In particular, there are intriguing findings that delineate the neurological underpinnings of spared emotional processing in older adulthood as compared to declines in cognitive processing. Finally, in elucidating each of the neuroscience approaches, we outline how these new technological advances and empirical phenomena can provide challenges for our understanding of adult development.

NEUROSCIENCE APPROACHES

There are three general methods that researchers take in the neuroscience of aging: The neuropsychological, the correlational, and the activation imaging approach (see Cabeza, 2004). The *neuropsychological approach* compares brain-related psychological functioning of healthy older adults with adults displaying various pathological disorders in the brain. In this approach, researchers are interested in whether patients with damage in specific regions of the brain exhibit similar cognitive deficits to those exhibited by older adults. If this is the case, then one could conclude that decline in cognitive functioning as we grow older may be related to unfavorable changes in the same specific regions of the brain observed in the brain-damaged patients. This type of comparison is typically made between healthy older adults and those patients exhibiting frontal lobe damage. For example, Parkinson's disease is accompanied by dopaminergic deficits that affect the frontostriatal system, which results in a decrease in processing speed (resembling what is observed in healthy older adults). Another important objective of research using this approach is to isolate the neural mechanisms that are associated with both normal and pathological decline in cognitive functions. These findings stimulate theoretical development by identifying influential factors that warrant theoretical explanation as to how and why these factors may cause cognitive decline as we age.

The *correlational approach* attempts to link measures of cognitive performance to measures of neural structure or functioning. For example, a researcher may be interested in the correlation between cognitive-behavioral data, such as executive functioning, with neural structural measures, such as white matter deterioration or brain volume (Raz, 2000). This example focuses on the role of brain structure in explaining cognitive decline (see Raz, 2000). Instead of direct measures of brain structure or functioning, some researchers investigate the correlation between behavioral tests that are associated to the function of specific brain regions (e.g., frontal lobe tests). However, this latter approach is more speculative in that there can be much uncertainty as to whether the tests accurately reflect anatomical and functional authenticity of the specific brain region under investigation.

Finally, the *activation imaging approach* attempts to directly link functional brain activity with cognitive-behavioral data. This approach allows the in vivo investigation of changes in brain function as they affect cognitive performance within older adults. For example, studies using this approach found that young adults' brains show unilateral activation (i.e., activation in only one hemisphere of the brain) when they perform specific cognitive tasks, whereas older adults' brains tend to show increased activation in both brain hemispheres when performing the same tasks (see Cabeza, 2002). As we discuss later, this differential activation in young and older adult brains may provide neurological evidence that older adults undergo compensatory changes to adapt to the inevitable decline of specific areas of the brain.

Overall, these neuroscientific approaches to studying cognitive aging provide theoretical development within the field of adulthood in several ways. First, theories can be further tested using these approaches. For instance, the idea of selective allocation of attention can be further validated by relating varying allocations of behavioral attention to event-related potentials measuring differential activation of specific brain regions (Wood & Kisley, 2006). Second, age-related changes in performance can be associated with both functional and structural brain variables to explain how the brain influences performance. This is not only applicable to change processes in older adults' brains, but also could be investigated in the maturing brains of adolescents and children. Third, research methods that focus on the age-related changes in the architecture and functioning of the brain can help to explain why certain cognitive functions, such as well-practiced tasks, vocabulary, and wisdom, can be preserved into old age while other functions, such as processing speed, decline rapidly as people age.

However, we need to note that neuroscientific methods also have their limitations (Cabeza, 2004). For instance, documenting activities in different brain regions does not necessarily imply that different psychological processes are involved (decline in sensory motor functioning, vision, and hearing may be similar processes but different regions of the brain). Nevertheless, advances in the field of neuroscience have a major impact on our understanding of cognitive age because they reveal new findings that psychological theories have to account for and be consistent with.

NEUROSCIENCE AND COGNITIVE AGING

A major thrust of adult development and aging research has focused on cognitive aging. The development of classic theories of cognitive aging has been primarily based on behavioral data (see Salthouse, 1996; Schaie, 1996). More recently, the availability of neuroscientific methods such as those described previously has stimulated research that allows us to study cognitive processes—and changes in these processes—in the living brain using noninvasive brain imaging techniques, such as magnetic resonance imagery (MRI) and fMRI.

MRI is a noninvasive technique that employs a powerful magnet (i.e., the MRI scanner) and radio waves to produce images of the brain. Whereas an MRI focuses on the structure of the brain, the fMRI focuses on the function of the brain. The MRI scanner has the ability to monitor the blood flow to different regions of the brain as the participants in a particular study respond to specific stimuli, such as an image of a face, words, or sounds. The difference between MRI and fMRI is that the more conventional MRI provides snapshots of specific brain structures, whereas the fMRI monitors activities in the brain that are time-locked to behavioral performance. The fMRI approach relies on the fact that oxygenated blood flows to specific regions of the brain as these areas are activated. The iron in the blood distorts the magnetic field enough for the scanner to identify the activity. A similar method to fMRI is positron emission tomography (PET) which measures local blood flow changes that correspond to neuronal activity (Logothetis, 2003).

These techniques and others offer new opportunities to test models of cognitive aging. Neuroscience has become increasingly more relevant to cognitive aging research as the focus has shifted from studying pathologies of the aging brain, such as Alzheimer's or Parkinson's disease toward investigating normal and healthy aging. In addition, neuroscientific data are more informative for models of cognitive aging and usher in increased progress in the field by testing established theories using cutting-edge methods. Furthermore, examination of the structure and function of the brain have become even more informative for cognitive aging research as the focus shifts from *describing* brain activation patterns toward *explaining* them. However, to be sure, it is easy to be seduced by these novel and available methods of neuroscience investigation. The field of neuroscience and aging must base empirical studies on a solid theoretical foundation. The field of cognitive aging is a good example of an area that has profited from major advances in neuroimaging techniques, revealing findings that have enhanced our understanding of normal and pathological aging, yet require theoretical explanations (see Cabeza, 2004; Hedden & Gabrieli, 2004; Kramer, Fabiani, & Colcombe, 2006).

The Structure of the Brain

It may be useful at this point to provide a very brief overview of the anatomy of the human brain. Neuroanatomy is fundamental to the discipline of neuroscience, and we refer to a number of brain regions that exhibit age-related changes in both structure and function. The brain consists of both gray and white matter. Gray matter corresponds mainly to nerve cell bodies, whereas the white matter corresponds mainly to axons or nerve fibers emanating from cell bodies in the gray matter. One component of the gray matter forms the cortex. The cerebral cortex is the area to which neuroscience has dedicated most of its effort. In this area there are two major hemispheres, right and left, which are linked via a thick bundle of neurons (or nerve cells) called the corpus callosum. Each region of the brain has distinguishing features. For example, language processing is associated primarily with the left hemisphere, whereas recognizing nonspeech sounds, emotions, and faces is associated with the right hemisphere. As we shall see in the following sections, the frontal cortex is a focal area for research. This area is intimately involved in intentional behavior such as the ability to make and carry out plans and executive functioning, among other critical cognitive processes. In addition, there is the cerebellar cortex, which contains the cerebellum. The other major component of gray matter forms nuclei containing the caudate, putamen, and pallidum located deep in each hemisphere as well as the amygdala among other areas. In the following section, details regarding the functional aspects of the various regions of the brain are discussed more fully with respect to age-related change.

Age-Related Changes in the Structure of the Brain

The majority of studies examining structural changes in the brain as we grow older have applied a correlational approach by employing postmortem analyses or cross-sectional and longitudinal in vivo imaging techniques, such as scanning the brain using structural MRI. In these studies, different regions of the brain are examined in terms of thinning and shrinkage in volume and density. Other structural deficiencies can also be detected, such as the declining health of the white matter of the brain or white matter hyperintensities (WMH). WMH is determined by the observation of high signal intensity or a bright spotty appearance, which indicates brain pathologies such as myelin loss or neural atrophy (Nordahl et al., 2006).

Overall, postmortem and neuroimaging studies demonstrate that considerable shrinkage occurs in the aging brain. However, this shrinkage is selective and differential (Raz & Rodrigue, 2006). For example, the association cortices (e.g., the prefrontal cortex), the neostriatum, the hippocampus, and the cerebellum show profound shrinkage (Raz & Rodrigue, 2006). The sensory cortex, such as the visual cortex, shows relatively little shrinkage. Although the hippocampus shows shrinkage, this is accelerated by vascular disease such as hypertension. Finally, such age-related shrinkage in the cortex may actually reflect a decrease in size and density at the cellular level of the neuron.

The white matter is also an area that shows deterioration with increasing age. This area is composed of axonal bundles beneath the cortical structures of the brain. A method called diffusion tensor imaging (DTI) assesses the rate and direction that diffuses through the white matter. This results in an index of density or structural health of the white matter (Park & Reuter-Lorenz, 2008). By using DTI, studies examining WMH tend to demonstrate that such disruptions of white matter integrity may represent a mechanism for prefrontal cortex dysfunction in older adults (Nordahl et al., 2006). As we discuss later, this has important implications for cognitive functioning in older adulthood. Of particular importance is the fact that WMH are linked to cerebrovascular disease (e.g., hypertension), which is preventable and can be treated through changes in lifestyle or medication. The critical issue is that it may be possible that some of the age-related cognitive decline we observe can be treated or even prevented (Nordahl et al., 2006).

In order to understand the impact of these deteriorating structural changes in the aging brain, it is important to determine how they relate to cognitive functioning. With increasing age, many facets of information processing become less efficient, including speed of processing, executive function, and declarative long-term memory. Memory and executive function have received a preponderance of attention in the cognitive neuroscience and aging literature. Executive functioning includes processes such as inhibitory control or the ability to control the contents of the conscious mind using working memory. Subsequent executive function failures in older adults include erroneous selection of irrelevant information to process in working memory, the inability to divert attention away from irrelevant information to the task in question, and attentional dysregulation such as inefficiency in switching tasks, among others (Park & Reuter-Lorenz, 2008).

There is some evidence that suggests that volume shrinkage in the brain is linked to poor cognitive performance. For example, WMH in nondemented older adults was linked to lower cognitive test scores and decreased executive functioning (de Groot et al., 2002; Madden et al., 2004). Poor performance on executive functioning tasks has also been linked with decreased volume of the prefrontal cortex (Raz & Rodrigue, 2006). Studies also show observed reductions in cortical volume in the hippocampal regions are also related to memory decline (Rosen et al., 2003). It should be noted that the role of frontal volume as a predictor of cognitive function has yielded some inconsistent findings. Whereas some studies find prefrontal volume linked to working memory performance (Salat, Kaye, & Janowsky, 2002), others do not (Gunning-Dixon & Raz, 2003). However, overall, it appears that age-related change in frontal regions of the brain correlate with executive dysfunction and memory decline (Buckner, 2004). Similar to the point made earlier regarding WMH, Buckner believes that age-related decline in vascular functioning may affect white matter structures that underlie frontal-striatal areas important to executive functioning. Finally, decline in other areas of cognitive performance has been differentially linked to specific brain regions. Skill acquisition has been linked to shrinkage of the striatum, prefrontal cortex, and cerebellum; spatial memory has been linked to hippocampal volume (Raz & Rodrigue, 2006).

The neuropsychological approach has also shed light on the link between structural changes in the aging brain and cognitive functioning. For example, there is a proliferation of research examining the medial temporal influences on memory by examining Alzheimer's disease patients. For example, brain atrophy, cellular pathology, and cell loss are observed in this region of the brain in Alzheimer's patients, who also show profound memory impairment (Buckner, 2004). As Buckner points out, this has raised challenges to aging research asking whether Alzheimer's disease is reflective of an acceleration of normal aging processes as opposed to a disease process. Indeed research on nondemented older adults found correlations between medial temporal lobe atrophy and poor memory performance (Rodrigue & Raz, 2004), although again, it is not straightforward with studies that do not find such an association (Van Petten, 2004).

In a recent review, Raz and Rodrigue (2006) point out that much of the conflicting findings in this area could be a result of the sample composition— whether cross-sectional differences or longitudinal change are being examined, whether different subregions are under investigation, and whether different cognitive tests are used. One way to assuage some of these concerns is to provide converging evidence from both cross-sectional and longitudinal studies of brain structure changes. For example, Raz and Rodrigue point to converging evidence that suggests age-related increases in white matter lesions. In addition, the prefrontal cortex, neostriatum, hippocampus, and cerebellum appear to be aging-sensitive. With respect to structure-cognitive performance linkages, longitudinal studies indicate a stronger relationship between brain structure and cognitive performance. By examining individual differences in change, longitudinal studies converge with cross-sectional studies showing that increases in WMH are associated with reduced performance on executive functioning tasks (Cook et al., 2004).

Age-Related Changes in Neurochemical Properties

There have also been advances in techniques measuring neurochemical changes in the aging brain. This has been particularly evident in studies implicating brain dopamine (DA) in performance on various cognitive tasks (Bäckman, Nybert, Lindenberger, Li, & Farde, 2006). Such studies have used postmortem analyses, neuropsychological patient studies, computational modeling, and molecular imaging (that specifically examines dopamine receptor densities). Bäckman et al. (2006) draw several conclusions regarding this research. First, there is increasingly clear evidence that the overall efficacy of the dopaminergic system declines in normal aging. Furthermore, dopaminergic receptors are strongly related to higher-order cognitive functioning, especially in the regulation of attention and the modulation of responses to contextual stimuli (Park & Reuter-Lorenz, 2008).

For example, Bäckman and colleagues (2000) found a relationship between declines in the striatal dopamine system and declines in episodic memory and speed tasks. Other researchers have found a link between decreases in DA density and age-related deficits in working memory, word fluency (Erixon-Lindroth et al., 2005), and memory (Yang et al., 2003). However, Bäckman et al. (2006) point out that although the evidence is quite compelling, there are areas that need further research. For example, we do not know about the relationship between age-related changes in DA and age-related changes in task-related brain activity. Another question raised is whether there are age-related differences in the release of DA during performance of cognitive tasks. If there is diminished DA release during performance in older adults as compared to young adults, this would shed light on the impact of age-related decline in modulation of neural activity with increasing age. This stands in stark contrast to simply examining the resting state of DA in older adults. In other words, we can observe DA release in action.

Overall, the brief review of studies using molecular methods to examine dopamine changes with increasing age suggest that dopaminergic receptors are implicated in cognitive aging. These studies expand our understanding of the neurochemical processes affected by increasing age that influence structural and cognitive changes.

Age-Related Changes in Brain Activity

We have just reviewed the literature addressing structural and neuro-chemical changes in the brain as we grow older and how deteriorative structural changes relate to decreases in cognitive functioning. We now explore other brain-related factors that might explain age differences in cognitive functioning: age-related changes in brain activity. Functional imaging using, for example, fMRI or PET, examines how changes in brain activity occur in correspondence to changes in task demands and the type of cognitive functioning under investigation. In other words, we are interested in examining the functional consequences of age-related deterioration in specific brain structures. A second aim of these types of studies is to identify cortical recruitment patterns in older adults that may occur in service of compensation when tasks pose a distinct difficulty. In other words, do older adults in comparison to young adults recruit different regions of the brain in order to perform cognitive tasks? On one hand, this could reveal neurological under-pinnings of the cognitive decline observed in older adults. On the other hand, perhaps these changes reflect adaptive accommodations that the brain makes in order to assist older adults to adjust to the neurological insults that occur with increasing age, thus allowing them to function adaptively in everyday life.

Functional Consequences of Brain Deterioration

The major theoretical approach reviewed previously focuses on age-related changes in brain function and is typically labeled the *frontal lobe theory of aging* (Buckner, 2004; Raz, 2000; West, 1996). This theoretical approach suggests that the many age-related declines in cognitive functioning are a function of insults to the frontal lobes, both structurally and neurochemically. Functional neuroimaging examines the neural substrates of cognitive decline. The typical finding that corroborates this approach is reduced activation in older adults as compared to young adults in prefrontal and medial-temporal areas supporting cognitive functioning, such as memory (Grady et al., 1995; Logan, Sanders, Snyder, Morris, & Buckner, 2002). Interestingly, there are studies that also show increased prefrontal activity during cognitive tasks, specifically memory, in older adults as compared to young adults (Cabeza, Anderson, Locantorre, & McIntosh, 2002; Grady, Bernstein, Siegenthaler, & Beig, 2002; Gutchess et al., 2005). We discuss this point later.

An example of the first finding is a fairly recent study that demonstrated age-related differences in activation of the anterior cingulate cortex during a verbal working memory task (Otsuka, Osaka, Morishita, Kondo, & Osaka, 2006). As indicated earlier, working memory is linked to executive functioning and involves temporary storage and processing of information, which supports higher-order cognitive functioning. In particular, it serves an attentional role by controlling attentional resources for performance on cognitive tasks. The anterior cingulate cortex is a concomitant of the prefrontal cortex and has been implicated in executive control (Bunge, Klingberg, Jacobsen, & Gabrieli, 2000). The overall finding is that reduced working memory performance was related to decreased activation of the anterior cingulate cortex in older adults as compared to young adults (Otsuka et al., 2006). Other research further supports this type of finding, suggesting that reduced brain activation or *under-recruitment* of the prefrontal cortex occurs during intentional cognitive processing (Buckner, 2004). Furthermore, Buckner points out that reduced frontal recruitment in aging is context dependent. For example, research demonstrated that older adults who showed reduced activation or recruitment of the appropriate frontal regions for intentional memory encoding recruited these regions almost to the same degree as young adults when a supportive memory encoding task was offered (Logan et al., 2002). They conclude that this may be a matter of decreased flexibility on the part of older adults to produce effective retrieval strategies. However, other studies show that young and older adults display comparable frontal activity or recruitment, for example, when examining memory retrieval (Schacter, Alpert, Savage, Rauch, & Albert, 1996). As we discuss in the next section, an increase in frontal recruitment could serve adaptive functioning purposes in older adults.

Compensation and Prefrontal Bilaterality

One of the most significant findings in the cognitive aging neuroscience literature is the observed discontinuity of neural activation patterns when comparing young and older adults' brain activity during the performance of cognitive tasks. As indicated previously, it is not simply that older adults show reduced activation in regions associated with a particular cognitive task. Initial studies focusing on verbal working memory and long-term memory presented evidence for focal, unilateral activity in the left prefrontal region in young adults and bilateral activation (i.e., in both the left and right prefrontal areas) in older adults when performing the same tasks (Buckner, 2004; Cabeza, 2002; Reuter-Lorenz, 2002). These findings ushered in a flurry of discussion as to its meaning for the aging brain. Is the older brain working harder to compensate for deterioration in these focal regions related to the cognitive task? Or is inefficient operation of inhibitory mechanisms rendering the activation as interference to optimal functioning (Park & Reuter-Lorenz, 2008)?

In a recent review of this literature, Park and Reuter-Lorenz (2008) note that there is now a growing body of evidence indicating that this bilateral activation in older adults may serve a functional and supportive role in their cognitive functioning. Findings include the association between bilateral activation in older adults and higher performance (not found in young adults) in a number of tasks, including category learning tasks, visual field tasks, and various memory tasks (Cabeza et al., 2002; Reuter-Lorenz et al., 2001; Rypma & D'Esposito, 2001). Furthermore, a number of studies showed evidence for increased frontal bilaterality and decreased hippocampal activity in older adults across numerous tasks, including attention, working memory, and long-term memory (Cabeza et al., 2004), suggesting the global nature of this phenomenon. Longitudinal data also confirms this pattern in that older adults who showed the greatest shrinkage in hippocampal volume also had the poorest memories in addition to increased activation in the right prefrontal cortex (Persson et al., 2006). In sum, additional age-related neural activation (especially in prefrontal areas) may be functional and adaptive for optimal performance. Researchers now suggest that these activation patterns may reflect an adaptive brain that functionally reorganizes (Park & Reuter-Lorenz, 2008).

A number of models have attempted to explain these findings, including the HAROLD Model by Cabeza (2002), the CRUNCH Model developed by Reuter-Lorenz and her colleagues (Reuter-Lorenz, 2002; Reuter-Lorenz & Mikels, 2006), and, most recently, the STAC model (Park & Reuter-Lorenz, 2008). Again, these models make the assumption that the primary reason for greater activation in different brain regions, as well as bilaterality, is the need for the recruitment of additional brain regions in order to successfully execute cognitive functions.

As indicated previously, numerous studies document the fact that young adults show unilateral brain activation when performing various cognitive tasks. In contrast, older adults' brains tend to show increased activation in both brain hemispheres. This finding resulted in various theoretical developments, including the formation of the HAROLD model: *Hemispheric Asymmetry Reduction in Older Adults* (Cabeza, 2002). The HAROLD model elegantly explains the empirical findings of reduced lateralization in prefrontal lobe activity in older adults. It suggests that the function of the reduced lateralization is compensatory in nature, that is, additional neural units are being recruited to increase attentional resources, processing speed, or inhibitory control.

According to the *compensation-related utilization of neural circuits hypothesis* (CRUNCH) developed by Patricia Reuter-Lorenz and her colleagues (Reuter-Lorenz, 2002; Reuter-Lorenz & Mikels, 2006), the aging brain adapts to neurological decline by recruiting additional neural circuits (in comparison to young adults) to perform tasks adequately. This model incorporates bilaterality of activation, but also suggests that the older brain uses two main mechanisms to perform tasks: "more of the same" and "supplementary processes." When task demands are increased, more activation can be found in the same brain region relative to easier tasks. This effect can be found in young adults as well as in older adults. Neural efficiency declines in older adults, therefore, additional neuronal circuits are recruited earlier than in young adults. "Supplementary processes" are taking place when different brain regions are activated to compensate for lacking processing resources. Reduced lateralization is one way of recruiting additional resources. In addition, however, compared to young adults' brains, older adult brains also show overactivation in different brain regions, suggesting that compensation can take different forms in the aging brain.

These findings have stimulated scientific debates on the mechanisms and functional adaptiveness of reduced lateralization. Whereas Cabeza and Reuter-Lorenz and colleagues interpret their findings in the light of a compensational framework, other researchers have challenged this interpretation by suggesting a cortical decline interpretation of the findings (see Kramer et al., 2006; Logan et al., 2002). Both with respect to theoretical work and empirical data, the field of neurocognitive science is still in its early stage of development. Therefore, definitive conclusions about the adaptiveness and functionality of the observed patterns of increased brain activation cannot be drawn at this point in time.

More recently, Park and Reuter-Lorenz (2008) have proposed the *Scaffolding Theory of Cognitive Aging* (STAC). They maintain that one needs to push the envelope regarding the compensatory role of bilateral activation and over-recruitment. In other words, what aspects of cognitive functioning does the compensation serve? For example, there is growing evidence that the increase in frontal activity in older adults may be a response to the decreased efficiency of neural processing related to perceptual areas of the brain (Park & Reuter-Lorenz, 2008). Interesting findings have also emerged when examining the default network of the brain. This refers to baseline functioning when the individual lies quietly in the magnet and fixates on a symbol against a blank screen. It represents a resting state for all regions of the brain (Raichle et al., 2001). When an individual begins a demanding cognitive task, this default network is suppressed. A number of researchers found that older adults display less suppression of the default network than young adults do (Grady, Springer, Hongwanishkul, McIntosh, & Winocur, 2006), and this is related to lower cognitive performance (Persson, Lustig, Nelson, & Reuter-Lorenz, 2007). Thus, this failure to shift from a resting state to a more active state to engage in cognitive processing may be another reason for increased frontal activity in older adults (Reuter-Lorenz & Cappell, 2008; Reuter-Lorenz & Lustig, 2005).

The STAC model (Park & Reuter-Lorenz, 2008) suggests that older adults continue to perform at high levels despite neuronal deterioration because of compensatory scaffolding. This is the recruitment of additional circuitry to bolster functional decline. A difference between this model and others is that compensation is not simply a neural response to brain insults as we grow older, but the brain's response to challenge in general. Thus, you may see this occurring when young adults are learning a new task. Learning moves from effortful processing to overlearning. The neurological shift is from a broader dispersed network (the scaffold) to a more focal and optimal circuit of neural regions. However, Park and Reuter-Lorenz point out that the initial scaffolding remains available as a secondary circuitry that can be counted on when performance is challenged. This is what older adults may be doing. However, scaffolded networks are less efficient than the honed, focal ones. For older adults, the focal networks become less efficient, therefore, they engage the scaffolded circuits, which may be less efficient and associated with poorer performance. Without the scaffolding, however, performance would be even worse because older adults would have to rely on the more focal areas. The elegance of this model is that older adults' performance can be understood in terms of factors that impact decline and those that impact compensation. As Park and Reuter-Lorenz argue, this integrative approach embraces a lifelong potential for plasticity and the ability to adapt to age-related changes.

Neural Plasticity and the Aging Brain

As indicated previously, models explaining age-related changes in brain functions as a form of compensation embrace the notion of neural and cognitive plasticity across the adult life span. Plasticity is a multifaceted concept. For example, as illustrated previously, it can refer to the ability to compensate for declining performance from a behavioral perspective or reorganization of neural circuitry as a form of compensation from a neuroscience perspective. There have been many attempts to assess the potential for plasticity in cognitive functioning by focusing on the potential to improve cognitive performance following training. One of the more prominent behavioral findings in the literature can be found in P. Baltes and colleagues' attempts to examine the range of plasticity in older adult cognitive performance (e.g., Baltes & Kliegl, 1992; Willis, Bliezner, & Baltes, 1981). They found that whereas older adults are able to improve cognitive ability in memory tasks through tailored strategy training beyond the level of untrained young adults, it is highly task-specific, and the ability-level gains were very narrow in focus.

More recently from a behavioral perspective, research suggests that basic cognitive processes affected by aging can improve through training and transfer to multiple levels of functioning as long as the basic functions are shared across tasks (e.g., Dahlin, Neely, Larsson, Bäckman, & Nyberg, 2008). From a neural plasticity perspective, more recent work on animal models of plasticity has revealed compelling evidence that demonstrates the effects of experience on various aspects of brain functioning in adulthood and aging (see Jessberger & Gage, 2008). There is now growing evidence of these types of effects in human brains. For example, new learning has been linked to structural changes in the brain. Draganski and colleagues (2004) demonstrated an increase in gray matter in individuals who were novices at juggling to begin with in comparison to learning the skill after a period of 3 months. Similarly, evidence indicates that hippocampal volume increased in medical students after extensive studying for an exam (Draganski et al., 2006). These types of findings extend to older adults as well, although they are limited in nature. For example, biochemical changes, such as increased creatine and choline signals in the hippocampus, in healthy older adults were observed after 5 weeks of training using Method of Loci mnemonic strategies to improve memory (Valenzuela et al., 2003). In a PET study, Nyberg and colleagues (2003) further investigated brain activation comparing young and older adults after the Method of Loci training. They found that young adult brains' showed increased activity in the left dorsolateral prefrontal cortex when applying the Method of Loci, but this activity was not observed in older age groups. However, both young and older adults that showed a benefit from the method displayed increased left occipito-parietal activity. Another group of unimproved older adults showed no increase in activity of either brain areas. Nyberg and colleagues conclude that at a neural level, although neural plasticity is present across the adult life span, there are age-related reductions in plasticity or the potential for improvement.

There are limited studies on neural plasticity in humans. With advancements in histological and molecular techniques of human postmortem samples along with in vivo noninvasive methods, such as MRI, fMRI, PET and others, future research may be able to close the apparent gap between animal and human research in the context of adulthood and aging neural plasticity.

Culture, Neuroimaging, and Aging

A final area that is receiving growing attention is the interplay between culture and neurobiological aging as it affects the mind. Denise Park has spearheaded this approach by asking questions such as, where are we likely to find neurocultural differences in the aging brain? She became particularly interested in the ventral visual cortex, which is the perceptual region of the brain. This is a highly specialized region that shows little shrinkage with age. Interestingly, there are some areas of age-related changes in perceptual processing that do not show cultural differences, whereas other areas do show cultural differences (Goh et al., 2004). For example, older adults from Western cultures showed significantly greater object-processing adaptation in the lateral occipital complex, which is involved in visual processing, than did older East Asians, who showed almost no adaptation (Goh et al., 2004). This finding provides neuroimaging evidence for cultural biases in perceptual processing of objects. Overall, however, age-related change seems to have a more profound effect on changes in brain functioning than culture.

Conclusion

Overall, one of the most significant issues in the theoretical discussion of the implications of cognitive neuroscientific findings is the relationship between brain patterns and behavior. Does the overactivation found in older adult brains relative to young adults reflect successful compensation, or does it reflect greater cognitive deficits? Longitudinal research may be necessary to investigate the time course of neurological decline and additional recruitment of resources. Also, studying the effect of cognitive training on lateralization and over-recruitment could provide important insights into the functional meaning of brain activation changes.

In addition, this discussion of neuroscientific methods has demonstrated that cognitive functioning can be understood at new levels. Advances in methods allow us to adequately test conditions under which age-related structural change is associated with decline, compensation, or even improvement in functioning. Rather than using general biological deterioration as the default explanation for cognitive changes, we can now identify specific biological mechanisms reflected in different structures of and activation patterns in the brain. In addition to regions of the brain that decline, these techniques have also allowed us to differentiate preserved areas of the brain, such as the amygdala, from areas that are more prone to decay, such as specific areas in the prefrontal cortex. These respective areas relate to preserved emotional processing on the one hand, and decline in other more effortful cognitive processes on the other. The following section explores these areas in the context of social-emotional neuroscience and aging.

NEUROSCIENCE AND SOCIOEMOTIONAL AGING

The emerging field of social cognitive neuroscience has also taken advantage of advancements in technologies to investigate the neural underpinnings of social cognitive and emotional processing. For example, Lieberman, Gaunt, Gilbert, and Trope (2002) have outlined a social cognitive neuroscience approach to attributional inferences. They identify social cognitive processes, such as the relatively automatic X-system, which is a social categorization process driven by chronic accessibility (easily activated, well-practiced categories of information), priming (easily evoked by cues in the environment), and the degree to which the input is ambiguous (thus it will more likely be assimilated automatically based on a person's past experience and current goals instead of focusing on the online characteristics of the information; Lieberman et al., 2002). Furthermore, they present compelling evidence for the existence of this system in neuroanatomy. Areas such as the lateral temporal cortex, amygdala, and basal ganglia are often associated with automatic social cognition (Adolphs, 1999; Knutson, Adams, Fong, & Hommer, 2001). Lieberman et al. also identify the C-system, which is the more deliberative form of social cognitive judgments employing symbolic logic and reflective awareness. The neural basis of this system appears to reside in the prefrontal cortex, anterior cingulate, and hippocampus (Goel & Dolan, 2000; Lieberman et al., 2002). Interestingly, the amygdala and the basal ganglia are areas that show less deterioration in the aging brain, whereas the prefrontal cortex shows more severe deterioration. The basal ganglia and, more specifically, the amygdala are linked to emotional processing, which appears to be relatively spared in the aging adult. Furthermore, both behavioral and neuroscience research has demonstrated a dissociation between cognitive aging and emotional aging. Thus, the area of emotional processing has witnessed a proliferation in both theoretical conceptualizations and corresponding empirical work. For the purposes of this chapter, the neural underpinnings of socioemotional processing with increasing age is the focus of the remainder of this section.

Emotional Processing, the Brain, and Aging

Given the dissociation between cognitive and emotional aging, a number of questions have served to guide contemporary research in the area of emotional processing. Such questions include: What declines? What is preserved? and What improves? In addition, it is important to identify the conditions under which we observe decline, preservation, and improvement. The neuroscience approach takes a step further in identifying the specific biological mechanism reflected in the structure and activation patterns of the brain associated with, for example, preserved emotional processing.

As we saw in the cognitive neuroscience section, neuroimaging allows us to identify brain regions of activation that underlie successful information processing, for example, activation of the prefrontal cortex (PFC) during encoding relates to better memory. There is much behavioral work indicating that if information has emotional significance we will more likely remember this emotional information, more so than information that is more neutral in nature. A number of researchers have been interested in uncovering the neural circuitry that is most responsible for this enhanced memory for emotional information. Kensinger and colleagues (Kensinger, 2006; Kensinger & Corkin, 2004) propose two distinct cognitive and neural processes that contribute to emotional memory enhancement for arousing information versus valenced, nonarousing information. They primarily examine memory of negatively valenced information. Processing of negative high arousal stimuli for memory is relatively automatic in nature and is linked to activation of the amygdala as it interacts with hippocampal areas in the brain. For the processing of negative low arousal stimuli, activation of the prefrontal cortex–hippocampus network is implicated for memory processing. This area is associated with controlled self-generated encoding processes (Kensinger & Corkin, 2004). Kensinger (2006) argues that emotional enhancement in memory for detail is a result of more engagement in emotion-specific processes, which are linked to these distinct neural processes. Thus, when one accurately remembers negative high arousal items, this corresponds to increased activation of the amygdala and orbitofrontal cortex. Other studies support this in that if the amygdala is damaged, individuals do not attend to arousing stimuli. How do structural and functional changes in the brain affect these processes?

Behavioral Evidence for Age-Related Differences in Emotional Processing

First, let's briefly examine the behavioral literature in this area. Similar to the behavioral research on young adults, there is growing research indicating that older adults also detect emotional information (e.g., in visual search tasks: Kensinger & Leclerc, 2009; Leclerc & Kensinger, 2008) and remember emotional information (e.g., remembering emotional words: Kensinger, 2008) better than nonemotional information. However, despite this emotional enhancement effect on information processing, evidence suggests that young and older adults can display differential effects of the emotional valence on memory performance. There has been an abundance of research examining a positivity effect in older adults (e.g., Carstensen, Isaacowitz, & Charles, 1999). This effect stems from a developmental motivational shift where perceived constraints on one's temporal horizon cause older adults to value emotional goals more so than individuals who hold an expansive temporal horizon, such as those found in young adults. Consequently, older adults are more motivated to derive emotional meaning from life and to maintain positive affect. From an information processing perspective, older adults are more likely than young adults to attend to the emotional meaning of information or on how such information makes them feel (Carstensen & Mikels, 2005). Findings indicate that young adults have a tendency to attend to and remember more negative information relative to positive information, and older adults display a tendency to attend to and remember more positive information relative to negative information (e.g., Mather & Carstensen, 2005). More recently, researchers suggest that older adults process this positive information in a more self-referential manner (Gutchess, Kensinger, & Schacter, 2007).

Interestingly, Kensinger (2008) finds that the positivity effect in memory with older adults is qualified in that a positivity effect is *not* revealed for arousing words (i.e., both young and older adults remember positive and negative arousing words better than neutral words). However, the positivity effect occurs for older adults with nonarousing words. Young adults remember negative nonarousing words better than positive nonarousing words, whereas older adults remember positive nonarousing words better than negative nonarousing words.

Neurological Recruitment Underlying the Positivity Effect in Memory

We begin this section by examining what we know about the emotional memory network and the degree to which corresponding brain structures decline or are preserved with increasing age. Interestingly, the regions implicated in emotional processing, such as the ventromedial prefrontal cortex (VMPFC), undergo relatively modest structural changes with aging, and the amygdala is relatively structurally preserved with aging (Raz, 1996). In contrast, other regions of the PFC undergo a more rapid and earlier pace of decline, such as the dorsolateral regions of the PFC (Raz, 1996). Even more importantly, it is necessary to examine the function (i.e., activation) of emotion processing regions of the brain across the adult life span.

LaBar and Cabeza (2006) describe a core emotional memory network, which consists of the amygdala, hippocampus, and lateral orbitofrontal cortex. Activation in these areas relates to the successful encoding of emotional information in general. Again, these regions are well preserved in emotional memory as one grows older. Indeed, for both young and older adults, activation of the amygdala and lateral orbitofrontal cortex corresponds to memory performance for both positive and negative items (Kensinger & Schacter, 2008). There are also areas in the brain beyond this emotional core that are more valence-dependent. For example, for both young and older adults, the occipito-temporal regions (more specifically the fusiform gyrus) are more likely to be recruited during successful encoding of negative information, whereas anterior prefrontal regions are activated during successful encoding of positive information (Mickley & Kensinger, 2008).

Neuroimaging studies reveal differential age-related activation of neural substrates that might help us understand the neurological mechanisms underlying the positivity effect. For example, older adults show activation of the medial prefrontal cortex and regions of the cingulate gyrus when responding to positive stimuli, whereas young adults do not display this phenomenon (Kensinger & Schacter, 2008). Similarly, older adults showed greater amygdala activation for positive pictures than for negative ones; young adults did not (Mather et al., 2004). Such findings indicate that it may not be overall decline in functioning of the amygdala that causes age-related response of emotional stimuli, but a shift in the type of emotional stimuli to which the amygdala is most responsive (Kensinger & Leclerc, 2009; Leclerc & Kensinger, 2008).

Kensinger and colleagues argue, overall, that the arousal component of responding in the dorsal medial PFC is similar in both young and older adults. In contrast, the activation of positive versus negative information in the VMPFC does show age-related patterns of activation. What are the implications for the positivity effect? Two studies (Kensinger & Leclerc, 2009; Leclerc & Kensinger, 2008) demonstrated age-related reversals within the VMPFC (i.e., greater activity for young adults for negative versus positive emotional images and greater positive versus negative images in this area for older adults). It may be that this reversal in valence-based responding leads to changes in the allocation of attention to emotional stimuli. This could lead to young adults' preferential focus to negative stimuli and to older adults' positivity effect.

Finally, another intriguing possibility is raised in the literature that the positivity effect may arise from changes in controlled emotional processing or emotion regulation (Kensinger & Leclerc, 2009; Leclerc & Kensinger, 2008; Mather & Knight, 2005). It is proposed that the positivity effect is behaviorally based on the degree to which cognitive control resources are limited. If they are limited, this reduces the ability to regulate responses to emotional information, and older adults who are low in resources show no positivity effect (Mather & Knight, 2005). Similarly, two studies by Kensinger and Leclerc (2009; Leclerc & Kensinger, 2008) argue that the ventromedial PFC is implicated in controlled stages of emotional process and, thus, provides neurological support in that the age-related neural-based reversal in valence-based responding described previously is the neurological counterpart to the behavioral evidence for a positivity effect. Finally, self-referential processing regions of the brain become more active for positive than negative information for older adults only (Kensinger & Leclerc, 2009; Leclerc & Kensinger, 2008).

Research conducted in different domains of emotional processing have also demonstrated age-related differences in brain activation. For example, fMRI studies have found age differences in brain activation when viewing faces with negative emotional expressions (e.g., Anderson, Christoff, Panitz, De Rosa, & Gabrieli, 2003). Young adults show increased activity in the amygdala when viewing negative emotional expressions, whereas activity in the amygdala is reduced in older adults when viewing these faces. Interestingly over-recruitment of areas such as the anterior cingulate gyrus is increased in older adults when viewing these faces (Gunning-Dixon et al., 2003). This is quite reminiscent of the compensation models discussed in the context of cognitive aging and neuroscience perspectives.

Overall findings in this line of research have revealed that the core emotional memory network is preserved with aging. Age-related differences are most evident in the successful encoding of positive information as opposed to processes corresponding to the memory for negative information. Thus, with increasing age, the structural preservation of various regions in the cortex is associated with the preservation of emotional processing, especially in arousal-based influences on attention and memory, and show changes in valence-based influences.

CONCLUSIONS

Advances in neuroscientific methods have stimulated a vast amount of research in cognition and aging as well as socioemotional aging. New findings describing linkages between behavioral and brain data require theoretical explanations. For example, is the functional dissociation between emotional processing and cognitive processing compensatory in nature? Does it reflect a neurological deficiency, or is it a result of a shift in motivational preferences? Is the extra recruitment observed in older adults' brain activation a function of the same mechanism, or does it reflect the addition of differential preferences?

A new challenge for this field is to determine whether the same behavior can be related to different neuronal activation patterns. Are they functionally equivalent or biologically different? In addition, more theoretical and empirical work is needed to investigate whether different changes in the brain may be associated with identical or differential mechanisms. Another challenge is to study changes in the brain longitudinally to investigate causal relationships. For instance, it may well be that certain brain patterns or changes in brain patterns can predict longitudinal behavioral changes. This, in turn, may have implications for pathologies of aging.

Another challenge to this line of research is taking into consideration the fourth age (individuals beyond the age of 85 years). This challenge is one that all areas of research will have to face in the future. For example, in very old adults, there may be limitations in the degree to which the aging brain can compensate through recruitment of alternative areas of the brain. Finally, another challenge for brain research is the issue of variability, both inter- and intraindividual variability. Is aging associated with uniform patterns of changes, or are older adults compensating differentially for declines? How variable is the recruitment of additional brain resources within an individual? For example, one of the few studies examining the neurological underpinnings of intraindividual variability in cognitive performance finds that behavioral intraindividual variability in performance is associated with poorer performance and corresponding lower activation in the left prefrontal cortex and anterior cingulate (MacDonald, Nybert, Sandblom, Fischer, & Bäckman, 2008).

In conclusion, neuroscience and aging research has allowed further understanding of what is preserved and what declines as a function of increasing age. Importantly, we now have a better understanding of how to preserve or enhance cognitive and socioemotional functioning in older adulthood.

Understanding aging involves multiple levels of analyses converging on important age-related research questions including behavioral, neurological, as well as neurochemical levels. There is an outstanding need for more theoretical models integrating the surge of empirical findings in this area. HAROLD, CRUNCH, and STAC models represent a good beginning, especially in elucidating the compensatory capabilities of the aging adult. The advent of more sophisticated techniques will further the mission of understanding the components that facilitate quality of life in older adulthood.

REFERENCES

Adolphs, R. (1999). The Human Amygdala and Emotion. *The Neuroscientist*, *5*, 125–137.

Amodio, D. M., & Frith, C. D. (2006). Meeting of minds: The medial frontal cortex and social cognition. *Nature Reviews Neuroscience*, *7*, 268–277.

Anderson, A. K., Christoff, K., Panitz, D. A., De Rosa, E., & Gabrieli, J.D.E. (2003). Neural correlates of the automatic processing of threat facial signals. *Journal of Neuroscience*, *23*(13), 5627–5633.

Bäckman, L., Nybert, L., Lindenberger, U., Li, S-C., & Farde, L. (2006). The correlative triad among aging, dopamine, and cognition: Current status and future prospects. *Neuroscience and Behavioral Reviews*, *30*, 791–807.

Bäckman, L., Ginovart, N., Dixon, R. A., Wahlin, T.-B. R., Wahlin, Å, Halldin, C., et al. (2000). Age-related cognitive deficits mediated by changes in striatal dopamine system. *American Journal of Psychiatry*, *157*, 635–637.

Baltes, P. B., & Kliegl, R. (1992). Further testing of limits of cognitive plasticity: Negative age differences in a mnemonic skill are robust. *Developmental Psychology*, *28*, 121–125.

Buckner, R. L. (2004). Memory and executive function in aging and AD: multiple factors that cause decline and reserve factors that compensate. *Neuron*, *44*(1), 195–208.

Bunge, S. A., Klingberg, T., Jacobsen, R. B., & Gabrieli J. D. (2000). A resourse model of the neural basis of executive working memory. *Proceedings of the National Academy of Sciences USA*, *97*(7), 3573–3578.

Cabeza, R. (2002). Hemispheric asymmetry reduction in older adults: The HAROLD model. *Psychology of Aging*, *17*(1), 85–100.

Cabeza, R. (2004). Commentary: New frontiers of cognitive aging: Approaches to cognitive neuroscience of aging. In R. A. Dixon, L. Bäckman, & L. G. Nilsson (Eds.), *New Frontiers in Cognitive Aging* (pp. 179–196). Oxford, UK: Oxford University Press.

Cabeza, R., Anderson, N. D., Locantore, J. K., & McIntosh, A. R. (2002). Aging gracefully: compensatory brain activity in high-performing older adults. *Neuroimage*, *17*(3), 1394–1402.

Cabeza, R., Prince, S. E., Daselaar, S. M., Greenberg, D., Budde, M., Dolcos, F., et al. (2004). Comparing the neural correlates of autobiographical and episodic memory with a new fMRI paradigm. *Journal of Cognitive Neuroscience*, *9*, 1583–1594.

Carstensen, L. L., Isaacowitz, D. M., & Charles, S. T. (1999). Taking time seriously: A theory of socioemotional selectivity. *American Psychologist*, *54*, 165–181.

Carstensen, L. L., & Mikels, J. A. (2005). At the intersection of emotion and cognition: Aging and the positivity effect. *Current Directions in Psychological Science,* *14,* 117–121.

Colcombe, S., Erickson, K., Rax, N., Webb, A., Cohen, N., McAuley, E., et al. (2003). Aerobic fitness reduces brain tissue loss in aging humans. *Journal of Gerontology, Biological Sciences, Medical Sciences, 58,* M176–M178.

Cook, I. A., Leuchter, A. F., Morgan, M. L., Dunkin, J. J., Witte, E., David, S., et al. (2004). Longitudinal progression of subclinical structural brain disease in normal aging. *American Journal of Geriatric Psychiatry, 12*(2), 190–200.

Dahlin, E., Neely, A. S., Larsson, A., Bäckman, L., & Nyberg, L. (2008). Transfer of learning after updating training mediated by the striatum. *Science, 320,* 1510–1512.

de Groot, J. C., de Leeuw, F-E., Oudkerk, M., van Gijn, J., Hofman, A., Jolles, J., et al. (2002). Cerebral white matter lesions and cognitive decline. The Rotterdam Scan Study. *Annals of Neurology, 52,* 335–341.

Draganski, B., Gaser, C., Busch, V., Schuierer, G., Bogdahn, U., & May, A. (2004). Changes in grey matter induced by training. *Nature, 427,* 311–312.

Draganski, B., Gaser, C., Kempermann, G., Kuhn, H. G., Winkler, J., Büchel, C., et al. (2006). Temporal and spatial dynamics of brain structure changes during extensive learning. *Journal of Neuroscience, 26,* 6314–6317.

Erixon-Lindroth, N., Farde, L., Robins Wahlin, T. B., Sovago, J., Halldin, C., & Bäckman, L. (2005). The role of the striatal dopamine transporter in cognitive aging. *Psychiatry Research Neuroimaging, 138,* 1–12.

Goel, V., & Dolan, R. (2000). Anatomical segregation of component processes in an inductive inference task. *Journal of Cognitive Neuroscience, 12*(1), 1–10.

Goh, J.O.S., Siong, S. C., Park, D., Gutchess, A., Hebrank, A., & Chee, M.W.L. (2004). Cortical areas involved in object, background, and object–background processing revealed with functional magnetic resonance adaptation. *Journal of Neuroscience, 24,* 10223–10228.

Grady, C. L., Bernstein, L., Siegenthaler, A., & Beig, S. (2002). The effects of encoding task on age-related differences in the functional neuroanatomy of face memory. *Psychology and Aging, 17,* 7–23.

Grady, C. L., McIntosh, A., Horwitz, B., Maisog, J., Ungerleider, L., Mentis, M., et al. (1995) Age-related reductions in human recognition memory due to impaired encoding. *Science, 269*(5221), 218–221.

Grady, C. L., Springer, M. V., Hongwanishkul, D., McIntosh, A. R., & Winocur, G. (2006.) Age-related changes in brain activity across the adult lifespan. *Journal of Cognitive Neuroscience, 18,* 227–241.

Gunning-Dixon, F. M., Gur, R. C., Perkins, A. C., Schroeder L., Turner, T., Turetsky, B. I., et al. (2003). Age-related differences in brain activation during emotional face processing. *Neurobiology of Aging, 24*(2), 285–295.

Gunning-Dixon, F. M., & Raz, N. (2003). Neuroanatomical correlates of selected executive functions in middle-aged and older adults: A prospective MRI study. *Neuropsychologia, 41*(14), 1929–1941.

Gutchess, A. H., Kensinger, E. A., & Schacter, D. L. (2007). Aging, self-referencing, and medial prefrontal cortex. *Social Neuroscience, 2,* 117–133.

Gutchess, A. H., Welsh, R. C., Hedden, T., Bangert, A., Minear, M., Liu, L. L., et al. (2005). Aging and the neural correlates of successful picture encoding: frontal activations compensate for decreased medial-temporal activity. *Journal of Cognitive Neuroscience, 17*(1), 84–96.

Hedden, T., & Gabrieli, J.D.E. (2004). Insights into the aging mind: A view from cognitive neuroscience. *Nature Reviews, 5,* 87–97.

Jessberger, S., & Gage, F. H. (2008). Structural and functional plasticity of the aging hippocampus. *Psychology and Aging, 23,* 684–691.

Kensinger, E. A. (2006). Remembering emotional information: Effects of aging and Alzheimer's disease. In E. M. Welsh (Ed.), *Progress in Alzheimer's Disease Research* (pp. 213–226). Hauppauge, NY: Nova Science Publishers, Inc.

Kensinger, E. A. (2008). Age differences in memory for arousing and nonarousing emotional words. *Journal of Gerontology: Psychological Sciences, 63,* P13–P18.

Kensinger, E. A., & Corkin, S. (2004). The effects of emotional content and aging on false memories. *Cognitive, Affective & Behavioral Neuroscience, 4,* 1–9.

Kensinger, E. A., & Leclerc, C. M. (2009). Age-related changes n the neural mechanisms supporting emotion processing and emotional memory. *European Journal of Cognitive Psychology, 21,* 192–215.

Kensinger, E. A., & Schacter, D. L. (2008). Neural processes supporting young and older adults' emotional memories. *Journal of Cognitive Neuroscience, 20,* 1161–1173.

Knutson, B., Adams, C. S., Fong, G. W., & Hommer, D. (2001). Anticipation of monetary reward selectively recruits nucleus accumbens. *Journal of Neuroscience, 21,* RC159.

Kramer, A. F., Fabiani, M., & Colcombe, S. J. (2006). Contributions of cognitive neuroscience to the understanding of behavior and aging. In J. E. Birren & K. W. Schaire (Eds.), *Handbook of the Psychology of Aging* (6th ed., pp. 57–83). Amsterdam: Elsevier.

LaBar, K. S., & Cabeza, R. (2006). Cognitive neuroscience of emotional memory. *Nature Reviews Neuroscience, 7,* 54–64.

Leclerc, C. M., & Kensinger, E. A. (2008). Age-related differences in medial prefrontal activation in response to emotional images. *Cognitive, Affective, and Behavioral Neuroscience, 8,* 153–164.

Lieberman, M. D., Gaunt, R., Gilbert, D. T., & Trope, Y. (2002). Reflection and reflexion: A social cognitive neuroscience approach to attributional inference. *Advances in Experimental Social Psychology, 34,* 199–249.

Logan, J. M., Sanders, A. L., Snyder, A. Z., Morris, J. C., & Buckner, R. L. (2002). Under-recruitment and nonselective recruitment: Dissociable neural mechanisms associated with aging. *Neuron, 33,* 827–40.

Logothetis, N. K. (2003). The Underspinnings of the BOLD Functional Magnetic Resonance Imaging Signal. *The Journal of Neuroscience, 23*(10), 3963–3971.

MacDonald, S.W.S., Nyberg, L., Sandblom, J., Fischer, H., & Bäckman, L. (2008). Increased response-time variability is associated with reduced inferior parietal activation during episodic recognition in aging. *Journal of Cognitive Neuroscience, 20*(5), 779–786.

Madden, D. J., Whiting, W. L., Huettel, S. A., White, L. E., MacFall, J. R., & Provenzale, J. M. (2004). Diffusion tensor imaging of adult age differences in cerebral white matter: Relation to response time. *NeuroImage, 21*(3), 1174–1181.

Mather, M., Canli, T., English, T., Whitfield, S., Wais, P., Ochsner, K., et al. (2004). Amygdala responses to emotionally valenced stimuli in older and younger adults. *Psychological Science, 15*, 259–263.

Mather, M., & Carstensen, L. L. (2005). Aging and motivated cognition: The positivity effect in attention and memory. *Trends in Cognitive Sciences, 9*, 496–502.

Mather, M., & Knight, M. (2005). Goal-directed memory: The role of cognitive control in older adults' emotional memory. *Psychology and Aging, 20*, 554–570.

Mickley, K. R., & Kensinger, E. A. (2008). Neural processes supporting subsequent recollection and familiarity of emotional items. *Cognitive, Affective, and Behavioral Neuroscience, 8*, 143–152.

Nordahl, C. W., Ranganath, C., Yonelinas, A. P., Decarli, C., Fletcher, E., & Jagust, W. J. (2006). White matter changes compromise prefrontal cortex function in healthy elderly individuals. *Journal of Cognitive Neuroscience, 18*(3), 418–429.

Nyberg, L., Sandblom, J., Jones, S., Neely, A. S., Petersson, K. M., Ingvar, M. I., et al. (2003). Neural correlates of training-related memory improvement in adulthood and aging. *Proceedings of the National Academy of Sciences, USA, 100*, 13728–13733.

Ochsner, K. N., & Lieberman, M. D. (2001). The emergence of social cognitive neuroscience. *American Psychologis, 56*, 717–734.

Otsuka, Y., Osaka, N., Morishita, M., Kondo, H., & Osaka, M. (2006) Decreased activation of anterior cingulate cortex in the working memory of the elderly. *Neuroreport, 17*(14), 1479–1482.

Park, C. D., & Reuter-Lorenz, P., (2008). The adaptive brain: Aging and neurocognitive scaffolding. *Annual Review of Psychology, 60*, 21.1–21.24.

Persson, J., Lustig, C., Nelson, J. K., & Reuter-Lorenz, P. A. (2007). Age differences in deactivation: a link to cognitive control? *Journal of Cognitive Neuroscience, 19*(6), 1021–1032.

Persson, J., Nyberg, L., Lind, J., Larsson, A., Nilsson, L. G., Ingvar, M., et al. (2006). Structure-function correlates of cognitive decline in aging. *Cerebral Cortex, 16*(7), 907–915.

Raichle, M. E., MacLeod, A. M., Snyder, A. Z., Powers, W. J., Gusnard, D. A., & Shulman, G. L. (2001). A default mode of brain function. *Proceedings of the National Academy of Sciences, USA, 98*(2), 676–682.

Raz, N. (1996). Neuroanatomy of aging brain: Evidence from structural MRI. In E. D. Bigler (Ed.), *Neuroimaging II: Clinical Applications* (pp. 153–182). New York: Academic Press.

Raz, N. (2000). Aging of the brain and its impact on cognitive performance: integration of structural and functional findings. In F. Craik & T. A. Salthouse (Eds.), *The Handbook of Aging and Cognition* (pp. 1–90). Hillsdale, NJ: Lawrence Erlbaum Associates.

Raz, N., & Rodrigue, K. M. (2006). Differential aging of the brain: Patterns, cognitive correlates and modifiers. *Neuroscience and Biobehavioral Reviews, 30*, 730–748.

Reuter-Lorenz, P. A. (2002). New visions of the aging mind and brain. *TRENDS in Cognitive Science, 6*, 394–400.

Reuter-Lorenz, P. A., & Cappell, K. A. (2008). Neurocognitive aging and the compensation hypothesis. *Current Directions in Psychological Science, 17*(3), 177–182.

Reuter-Lorenz, P. A., & Lustig, C. (2005). Brain aging: Reorganizing discoveries about the aging mind. *Current Opinion in Neurobiology, 15*(4), 245–251.

Reuter-Lorenz, P. A., Marshuetz, C., Jonides, J., Smith, E. E., Hartley, A., & Koeppe, R. (2001). Neurocognitive ageing of storage and executive processes. *European Journal of Cognitive Psychology, 12*, 257–278.

Reuter-Lorenz, P. A., & Mikels, J. A. (2006). The aging mind and brain: Implications of enduring plasticity for behavioral and cultural change. In P. B. Baltes, P. A. Reuter-Lorenz, & F. Rösler (Eds.), *Lifespan Development and the Brain: The Perspective of Biocultural Co-constructivism* (pp. 255–276). New York: Cambridge University Press.

Rodrigue, K. M., & Raz, N. (2004). Shrinkage of the entorhinal cortex over five years predicts memory performance in healthy adults. *Journal of Neuroscience, 24*(4), 956–963.

Rosen, A. C., Prull, M. W., Gabrieli, J. D., Stoub, T., O'Hara, R., Friedman, L., et al. (2003). Differential associations between entorhinal and hippocampal volumes and memory performance in older adults. *Behavioral Neuroscience, 117*(6), 1150–1160.

Rypma, B., & D'Esposito, M. (2001). Age-related changes in brain-behaviour relationships: evidence from eventrelated functional MRI studies. *European Journal of Cognitive Psychology, 13*(1–2), 235–256.

Salat, D. H., Kaye, J. A., & Janowsky, J. S. (2002). Greater orbital prefrontal volume selectively predicts worse working memory performance in older adults. *Cerebral Cortex, 12*(5), 494–505.

Salthouse, T. A. (1996). The processing-speed theory of adult age differences in cognition. *Psychological Review, 103*(3), 403–428.

Schacter, D. L., Alpert, N. M., Savage, C. R., Rauch, S. L., & Albert, M. S. (1996). Conscious recollection and the human hippocampal formation: Evidence from positron emission tomography. *Proceedings of the National Academy of Sciences, USA, 93*, 321–325.

Schaie, K. W. (1996). Intellectual development in adulthood. In J. E. Birren, K. W. Schaie, R. P. Abeles, M. Gatz, & T. A. Salthouse (Eds.), *Handbook of the Psychology of Aging* (4 ed., pp. 266–286). San Diego, CA: Academic Press.

Valenzuela, M. J., Jones, M., Wen, W., Rae, C., Graham, S., Shnier, R., et al. (2003). Memory training alters hippocampal neurochemistry in healthy elderly. *Synaptic Transmission, 14*, 1333–1337.

Van Petten, C. (2004). Relationship between hippocampal volume and memory ability in healthy individuals across the lifespan: review and meta-analysis. *Neuropsychologia, 42*, 1394–1413.

West, R. L. (1996). An application of prefrontal cortex function theory to cognitive aging. *Psychological Bulletin, 120*, 272–292.

Willis, S. L., Blieszner, R., & Baltes, P. B. (1981). Intellectual training research in aging: Modification of performance on the fluid ability of figural relations. *Journal of Educational Psychology, 73*, 41–50.

Wood, S., & Kisley, M. A. (2006). The negativity bias is eliminated in older adults: Age related reduction in event-related brain potentials associated with evaluative categorization. *Psychology & Aging, 21*, 815–820.

Yang, Y. K., Chiu, N. T., Chen, C. C., Chen, M., Yeh, T. L., & Lee, I. H. (2003). Correlation between fine motor activity and striatal dopamine D2 receptor density in patients with schizophrenia and healthy controls. *Psychiatry Res, 123*(3), 191–197.

Chapter 2

Aging, Attention, and Mobility

Joan M. McDowd and Diane L. Filion

INTRODUCTION

Experimental psychologists have long been interested in attention as a fundamental mechanism in the control of behavior. Studies of attention in its varied modes have identified task parameters that promote and impede selective attention, divided attention, switching attention, and sustained attention in young and old adults (for a general overview, see McDowd, 2007). A number of authors have provided recent reviews that synthesize the existing experimental literature (e.g., Kramer & Kray, 2006; Kramer & Madden, 2008; McDowd & Shaw, 2000). In this chapter, we focus our review on studies that relate age differences in attention in everyday behaviors. These *translational* studies seek to understand aging in an everyday context, but also make use of laboratory techniques to enrich that understanding. We will consider three mobility-related tasks: balance, walking, and automobile driving. Although the role of attention in driving has long been recognized, balance and walking have typically been thought of as relatively automatic and noncognitive. However, there is increasing evidence indicating that attentional processes are critical to balance and gait performance. We examine this "penetration of cognition into action control" in the context of these everyday tasks (Heuninckx, Wenderoth, Debaere, Peeters, & Swinnen, 2005, p. 6787). In addition, we briefly review recent theoretical developments in the area of attention and aging, including supporting evidence from the neurosciences.

ATTENTION IN MOTOR BEHAVIOR

Many everyday activities involve a motor or movement component, which is a domain of function typically thought to be separate from the cognitive domain. However (although not a totally new idea, cf., Binder, Storandt, & Birge, 1999; Carlson et al., 1999; Welford, 1958), there is a growing literature documenting interactions between cognitive and motor processes. Instead of constituting a domain completely independent from cognition, it is increasingly recognized that motor behavior requires cognitive processes such as the integration of a variety of sources of information and "that attentional and executive cognitive processes may be implicated in the integration process" (Li & Dinse, 2002, p. 729). In addition, there is accumulating evidence that the role of attention in motor behavior is even greater for older adults than young adults (e.g., Heuninckx et al., 2005; Lee, Wishart, & Murdock, 2002; Sparrow, Parker, Lay, & Wengier, 2005; Wishart, Lee, Murdoch, & Hodges, 2000).

One example of the relation between attention and motor behavior is given in the study by Heuninckx et al. (2005). They used fMRI to examine interlimb coordination in young and old adults. They found that brain activation during the coordination tasks was greater and more widespread for older adults than young adults (similar findings in other cognitive domains have been reported by Buckner, 2004; Cabeza, 2002; Reuter-Lorenz, 2002); older adults recruited more brain areas to support task performance, including areas not typically associated with motor behavior. These additional areas included several frontal regions commonly linked with attention. Heuninckx, Wenderoth, and Swinnen (2008) found a similar pattern of results showing that performance of the interlimb coordination task resulted in activation of the classic motor coordination regions but also in the sensorimotor and frontal regions. More importantly, they found that the level of activation in those "extra" regions was significantly correlated with motor task performance. The finding of sensorimotor and frontal activation during these tasks led the authors to conclude that "aging is associated with a shift along the continuum from automatic to more controlled information processing for movement, as reflected by more pronounced intersensory processing and integration of information, and increased attentional effort" (Heuninckx et al., 2005, p. 6794). We now examine evidence for this view, indicating a significant role for attention in the motor processes of posture and balance.

Attention in Posture and Balance

One area of research in which the notion of an age-related increase in attentional effort required for motor tasks has been a particularly important focus is in the area of balance. One of the most common problems in aging is the problem of falls (e.g., Kannus, Sievanen, Palvanen, Jarvinen, & Parkkari, 2005) and the associated risks of cuts, bruises, broken bones, and even head injuries. In addition, falls in older adults often lead to required hospitalizations and can negatively impact a person's ability to live independently. For these reasons, there is great interest in the role of balance and gait in fall prevention and on understanding the circumstances in which falls occur. A number of studies have examined balance and gait in older adults in the context of an attention deficit model (see Woollacott & Shumway-Cook, 2000, for a review). These studies demonstrate divided attention deficits when cognitive tasks are combined with motor tasks, such as postural stability and balance tasks, or walking. Findings from these studies are generally interpreted in terms of reduced attentional resources among older adults. For example, Stelmach, Zelaznik, and Lowe (1990) induced a balance perturbation in young and older adults, with and without a secondary task, and then measured the amount of time taken to regain balance stability. They asked young and old adults to swing their arms while standing in place (which produced a balance perturbation as measured by foot center of pressure on a force plate). After swinging their arms for several seconds, participants engaged in a secondary task: either squeezing a force transducer in time with a metronome, or mentally counting correct math problems presented over a speaker. The measure of interest was the length of time it took for balance parameters (foot center of pressure) to return to baseline levels, which the authors referred to as the recovery of balance. Because older adults were slower than younger adults to recover balance in the dual task condition involving the math task, the authors concluded that recovery from the perturbation while engaged in the math tasks exceeded the attentional capacity of old but not young adults. (Performing the squeeze task while recovering balance did not exceed the capacity of either age group.) Stelmach et al. further suggest that because of age changes in sensitivity to proprioceptive and vestibular input, more attention had to be devoted to those inputs in order to maintain balance. Thus, maintaining balance required more attentional resources for older adults, and when those resources were stretched in a challenging dual task situation, balance suffered.

In a similar study, Teasdale, Bard, LaRue, and Fleury (1993) asked young and old adults to maintain a stable upright posture, with and without performing an auditory secondary task. They performed these two tasks with eyes open or eyes closed and while standing on a firm surface or standing on a foam surface. The sensory manipulations were designed to see if the attentional demands of postural control were greater when less sensory information was available. Based on greater slowing of secondary reaction times in old than young adults, the authors reported that as the postural task became more challenging, more attentional capacity was required of old than young adults. In this case, the age-related deficit in performing two tasks at once had negative consequences for balance among older adults.

A similar pattern was observed by Maki, Zecevic, Bateni, Kirshenbaum, and McIlroy (2001). These investigators asked young and older adults to perform a continuous visuomotor pursuit-tracking task while standing on a platform that exhibited small unpredictable movements that altered the participant's balance. The investigators assumed that large tracking errors would occur in response to the platform movements. Such errors would indicate that attention had been momentarily switched away from the tracking task to the balance recovery task, providing the investigators with a sensitive index of the time required for the participant to switch the allocation of attentional resources to the balance recovery task. The results indicated that older adults were significantly slower to switch their attention to the balance recovery task and that their delay in allocating attention to the balance task was significantly correlated with the timing of their postural response. These results suggest that age-related changes in *attentional dynamics*, including the time course of attentional allocation, the prioritization of tasks for attentional allocation, and the flexibility to switch allocation priorities rapidly, may play an important role in age-related changes in balance, posture, and fall susceptibility (see also Doumas, Smolders, & Krampe, 2008; Jamet, Deviterne, Gauchard, Vancon, & Perrin, 2007).

The dual task methodology has been useful in understanding age differences in balance beyond findings such as those just described showing that postural control is more attention demanding for older adults than for young. This added utility comes from examining balance parameters (in addition to changes in secondary task performance) under dual task conditions. For example, Huxhold, Li, Schmiedek, and Lindenberger (2006) observed that in dual task conditions, the postural control of older adults decreased significantly as the attention demands of the cognitive task increased. In other studies, it has been observed that in dual task situations, older adults frequently take a step to recover balance sooner than younger adults (Rankin, Woollacott, Shumway-Cook, and Brown, 2000). However, as noted by Brown, Shumway-Cook, and Woollacott (1999), stepping is itself a capacity-demanding task that may actually be dangerous if attentional resources are not available to ensure a reliable step (see also Melzer & Oddsson, 2004).

The negative impact of divided attention on maintaining posture and balance has also been translated into beneficial intervention strategies. For example, Silsupadol, Siu, Shumway-Cook, and Woollacott (2006) reported a series of three case studies of older adults with balance impairments. They describe three strategies for training balance: single task only, dual task with fixed priority instructions (i.e., equal attention to both tasks), and dual task with variable priority instructions (i.e., told to prioritize balance on some trials and the cognitive task on other trials). Although all three strategies resulted in improved balance, the patient who received dual task training with variable priority instructions improved the most and, according to normative data, enjoyed the greatest reduction in fall risk. This finding suggests that training on balance tasks in simulated real life situations where one is almost always engaged in multiple tasks and where task priorities are likely variable is the most beneficial to balance performance.

Attention in Walking

Although walking has long been considered an automatic motor task for adults, recent work has demonstrated that walking is actually a complex (and nonautomatic) task involving important cognitive functions. In walking, "numerous sensory and conscious inputs and competing objectives (for example, upright posture versus locomotion) are seamlessly integrated across hierarchical systems, all while subtle real-time decisions and adjustments are being made" (Hausdorff, Yogev, Springer, Simon, & Giladi, 2005, p. 542). To illustrate this complexity, Hausdorff and colleagues compared walking to two motor tasks: a simple finger tapping task, considered to be relatively automatic, and a computerized "catching" game requiring attentional involvement. The tapping task required that participants tap a key with a single finger at a regular interval. The catching task required that a rectangular object falling from the top of the computer screen be "caught" by a mouse-controlled paddle before the object reached the bottom of the screen. The catching task required rapid responses, visual scanning, and good hand-eye coordination. Results from a sample of 43 older adults showed that walking performance (walking speed, stride time variability) was related to catching task performance (time to start moving paddle, accuracy, misses) but not to tapping performance (tap intervals, tap interval variability). Hausdorff et al. also demonstrated that a selective attention task (the Stroop Test) was correlated with both walking and the catching task, but not to the tapping task. This pattern of results indicates that walking is not simply an automatic motor task, but requires the complex integration of both motor and cognitive functions.

Dual task methodology has also been applied to identifying and understanding age differences in walking. For example, Lindenberger, Marsiske, and Baltes (2000) asked participants to walk on a track while memorizing a list of words using the Method of Loci. They reported that the requirement to divide attention had a larger impact on older adults than young adults; both memory accuracy and speed of walking were more negatively affected by divided attention for old than young adults (see also Li, Lindenberger, Freund, & Baltes, 2001, for a follow-up study with similar findings). Based on this finding, Lindenberger et al. (2000) suggest that adult aging is characterized by "the age-associated permeation of behavior with cognition. According to this view, which is reminiscent of Alan Welford's early observations (e.g., Welford, 1958, pp. 186–187), sensory and motor aspects of performance are increasingly in need of cognitive control and supervision because of frailty, sensory losses, and lower level problems in sensorimotor integration and coordination" (p. 434). This creates something of a 'double-whammy' for older adults; lower level processes need more cognitive "supervision" at the same time that supervisory or executive processes also undergo some negative age-related changes (e.g., Allain et al., 2007; Treitz, Heyder, & Daum, 2007). Thus, it is hardly any surprise that older adults are at a greater risk for gait and balance impairments and falls.

Springer and colleagues (2006) examined dual task effects on gait variability in young adults, healthy older adults, and older adults defined as *idiopathic fallers* (one or more falls in a 6-month period with no known cause). Gait variability is an index of balance control while walking; increased variability has been associated with increased fall risk (e.g., Hausdorff, Rios, & Edelberg, 2001; Maki, 1997). Springer et al. predicted that dual task effects would be greater among the fallers than the healthy older adults and that the dual task effects would be related specifically to executive function. To measure executive function, they used computerized versions of the Stroop task and a Go/No Go response inhibition task. They also included a paired associated recognition test as a cognitive control.

Gait parameters were examined under four conditions while participants walked at their usual speed along a 25-meter long, 2-meter wide instrumented hallway. The four conditions were usual walking, usual walking while counting backward by sevens, usual walking while listening to a text on which there would be a quiz, and usual walking while listening to a text on which there would be a quiz and also keeping track of the occurrence of certain target words. Gait parameters included average step time, as well as step time variability. When comparing step variability between healthy older adults and young adults, no differences in variability were observed in any of the dual tasks. However, when comparing step variability between healthy older adults and older adult fallers, the fallers had greater variability than nonfallers in each of the dual task conditions. Overall gait speed and average step speed did not differ between the two older groups; only the variability measure showed the dual task effect. The relation between the other cognitive tasks and gait variability was mixed and generally weak. It was reported that performance on the Stroop tasks correlated significantly with dual task conditions involving the simple listening task and the counting backward task for fallers but not nonfallers. (The Go/No Go task apparently did not correlate with any of the walking tasks, as it is not mentioned.) As expected, the recognition memory task did not correlate with gait variability on any of the walking tasks. This pattern of findings may be due to limited power from relatively small sample sizes (17 fallers and 24 nonfallers). Alternatively, it may be that not all types of attention influence gait parameters. The findings with regard to performance under dual task conditions are consistent with a number of other studies, but inhibitory processes such as those measured by the Go/No Go task are not well studied in the context of gait. Another limiting factor for interpretation is that there are not well-developed models of motor performance in aging that would specify which attentional functions should and should not have a role. Work to develop such models would seem to be a productive avenue for future research. One promising development is the model of Mahboobin, Loughlin, and Redfern (2007). They modeled attention as a limited resource whose availability can speed or slow sensory integration processes in support of postural control and balance. The next steps would seem to be extending such models to walking and further specification of the mechanisms of attention that facilitate performance (see following discussion of resource models of attention).

Walking speed has received significant attention recently as a marker for age-related frailty (Brach, Studenski, Perera, VanSwearingen, & Newman, 2007; Walston et al., 2006). In an effort to understand this association, Holtzer, Verghese, Xue, and Lipton (2006) examined the relationship between a range of cognitive variables and gait velocity in 186 healthy older adults who are a part of the Einstein Aging Study. The investigators administered a neuropsychological battery that assessed speed of processing, attention, memory, language, and executive function. They submitted the test scores to a factor analysis that yielded three primary factors: verbal IQ, speed/executive attention, and memory. They then tested those three factors as predictors of gait velocity under two conditions: one that involved simple walking with no other cognitive task and one that involved walking while reciting alternate letters of the alphabet. Results revealed that all three of the cognitive factors were significant predictors of gait velocity in the walking-only condition, but only the speed/executive attention and memory factors were significant predictors of gait velocity in the dual task condition, with the speed/executive attention factor being the strongest predictor.

Extending this work to the prediction of falls, Holtzer et al. (2007) examined the same three cognitive factors in a sample of 172 older adults from the Einstein Aging Study sample as predictors of self-reported history of falls within the past year. Results revealed that lower scores on the speed/executive attention factor and the memory factor were both significant predictors of single falls but that only the speed/executive attention factor significantly predicted both single falls and recurrent fall history.

The role of attention in walking speed was also examined by Ble and colleagues (2005) in the InCHIANTI study of aging. They used the Trail-Making Test (TMT) as the measure of attention. The TMT test is a paper and pencil "connect the dots" task with two parts. In the first part (TMT-A), as quickly as possible the participant must connect 25 numbered dots that are sprinkled around on a page. This measure assesses visual search ability and motor speed. The second part (TMT-B) involves a sheet with numbered dots 1–13 along with dots identified with alphabetic letters A–L. The participant's task is to connect the dots, alternating between numbers and letters (i.e., 1–A–2–B–3–C). TMT-B measures visual search, motor speed, and the ability to keep track of a sequence and alternate between sets of items. To isolate just the functions of keeping track and switching attention, Ble et al. calculated the difference in completion times between the two task conditions and used this difference to identify those with good and poor attention. Based on norms, they created a group of poor TMT performers, an intermediate performance group, and a good performance group.

To assess walking speed, Ble et al. (2005) created two walking courses: a 4-meter course requiring walking at usual pace along a straight path, and a 7-meter obstacle course that required participants to use a fast pace and to step over two foam obstacles, one 6 cm tall and one 30 cm tall. They measured the time taken to complete each course, and then looked at this time as a function of TMT performance group. They expected the fast paced obstacle course to make greater demands on attention, motor control, and motor planning, and indeed that's what they found. Walking speed in the 4-meter course did not differ as a function of TMT group. However, walking speed on the 7-meter obstacle course was significantly faster for the Good TMT group than either the Intermediate or Poor TMT groups. In a calculation of the odds ratio for walking speed in the three TMT groups, participants in the Poor TMT group were found to be 4.2 times more likely to have a 7-meter walking speed in the lowest 1/3 of the group than the Good TMT performance group. The authors interpret these findings as indicating a significant role for attention in complex motor tasks such as negotiating even a simple obstacle course.

Coppin and colleagues (2006) reported another study of attention in walking speed, pulling from the same population as reported in the Ble et al. (2005) study described previously. In addition to negotiating an obstacle course, participants in the Coppin et al. study walked a 7-meter course on which they had to pick up an object from the floor, walked a 7-meter course while carrying a light large package, walked a 7-meter course while also talking, and walked a 60-meter course while wearing a weighted vest. They also administered the Trail-Making Test and created TMT performance tertiles described as good, intermediate, and poor attentional function. They found relations between attention group and gait speed for the walking while picking up an object, wearing a weighted vest, and the walking over obstacles tasks. Walking while talking and carrying a package did not differ as a function of TMT performance group. This task-related variation in the role of attention is interpreted by the authors as due to "the degree of locomotor and sensorial adaptation required for the performance of complex walking tasks" (Coppin et al., 2006, p. 621).

Ble et al. (2005) concluded that "the age-related decline in executive function described by many observational studies is not without consequences for the health of older individuals" (p. 414). This statement implies that an intervention might be appropriate. Coppin et al. (2006) are more explicit about the need for intervention research, stating: "Further research is needed to determine whether improvement in executive function abilities translates to better physical function and performance on selected complex walking tasks" (p. 622). In order to develop interventions, it will be important to be able to target relevant processes for remediation or training. Ble et al. and Coppin et al. both acknowledge that they used only a single measure of the complex set of abilities called "executive function," but they don't address the particular cognitive processes underlying TMT performance. In these studies it seems that mental updating and attention switching are important for challenging gait tasks. Royall and colleagues (2007) also make the point about identifying specific cognitive processes that may account for disability or functional status. They note the need for additional research to identify "the dimension(s) of cognition which is/are most relevant to functional outcomes" (p. 260). As in the case of the Ble et al. and Coppin et al. studies, some of that information may be already in the literature but is in need of "translation" from a neuropsychological level of analysis to a process level.

Atkinson and colleagues (2007) also advocated for research to lead to potential treatments. In an effort to understand changes in gait speed over time, they used data from the Health, Aging, and Body Compositions Study. Baseline cognitive testing of 2,349 individuals occurred using the Modified MiniMental Status Examination (MMSE), CLOX 1, and the EXIT 15. The Modified MMSE contains additional items not included in the original MMSE that measure verbal fluency, delayed recall, and abstract reasoning. The CLOX 1 is a clock drawing test in which participants are instructed to draw a clock with the hands set at 1:45. The EXIT 15 is an interview measure that assesses executive functions such as inhibition, word and design fluency, and sequencing ability. Participants also walked at their usual pace along a 20-meter hallway; time to walk the 20 meters was measured as gait speed.

Analyses to examine the relation between the cognitive measures and change in gait speed over a 3-year span showed that the Modified MMSE and the CLOX 1 test were significantly related to gait speed decline, even after demographics, health habits, comorbid conditions, risk factors, and other health events were taken into account. Although initially a significant predictor of decline, when CES-D depression was included as a comorbid condition, the EXIT 15 was no longer significant. This finding was unexpected but may have been due to ceiling effects in performance, or it may be that the EXIT as a composite measure includes aspects of cognition that may be less related to motor performance or more influenced by other aspects of health. The authors concluded that "future research should focus on which aspects of cognitive function are most associated with physical decline and clarification of the mechanisms underlying the association. Further investigation of the complex relationships between cognitive function, physical performance decline, and comorbidities may point to new pathways for the treatment of physical decline associated with diminished cognitive function" (Atkinson et al., 2007, p. 849).

Selective attention (the ability to focus on task-relevant information and ignore irrelevant information) has also been examined in relation to mobility. Inzitari and colleagues (2007) compared the contribution of global cognition, memory, and selective attention to declines in motor performance across a 3-year period. Global cognition was assessed using the MMSE. Episodic memory was assessed using the Babcock Story Recall Test, summing immediate and delayed recall. Selective attention was measured with the Digit Cancellation Test (DCT), which required participants to cross out a target digit among lines of digits; this test is scored in terms of the number correctly cancelled in 45 seconds. Motor performance was indexed with a series of six tasks: time to stand from a chair without using the arms, number of times one could step up and down from a 23-cm step in 10 seconds, number of errors while walking along a 5 cm wide line for 2 meters, length of time one could stand on one leg, usual walking speed across 5 meters, and the number of steps required to complete a 180° turn. All 1,052 participants had normal baseline motor performance. Two measures of decline were calculated: the mean difference between performance at baseline and at follow up, and a decliner/nondecliner grouping. Decliners were those with difference scores greater than the 75th percentile for the sample. This definition identified 166 of the 1,052 participants as decliners.

Of the three predictors of decline, only DCT performance independently predicted decline in motor performance, even after accounting for age, gender, education, and diagnoses of dementia or cognitive impairment and no dementia. The risk of being a "decliner" increased across quartiles of DCT performance, independent of age, gender, education, marital status, Basic Activities of Daily Living (BADL) and Instrumental Activities of Daily Living (IADL) losses, MMSE, and Babcock Recall task performance: participants in the lowest quartile of DCT performance had greater than two times the risk of being a decliner compared to those in the highest quartile. By comparison, risk did not vary as a function of performance quartile for either the MMSE or the Babcock memory task. In an examination of the individual motor performance tasks, DCT score was significantly lower for the decliners in all tasks except the time to stand from a chair. Scores on the MMSE and Babcock test were not different between decliners and nondecliners for any of the motor subtasks. To summarize, baseline selective attention performance predicted declines in motor performance 3 years later. This association was not due to general cognitive declines because neither MMSE nor episodic memory showed a similar association. The authors also suggest that measuring selective attention with the DCT may be clinically useful for predicting motor performance decline and then, presumably, for predicting intervention and care needs.

Yogev-Seligman, Hausdorff, and Giladi (2007) have also commented on the utility of attention measures in clinical settings. They state that tests measuring dual task ability and executive function "can provide the clinician with important information about gait disturbances and the risk of falling that might not be seen during a routine exam" (pp. 335–336). They suggest some tasks that can be easily used in the clinic to assess the impact of a dual task on gait, such as walking while talking, walking while counting backward, walking and carrying a tray with a glass of water, or walking while performing a verbal fluency task. Use of these measures can provide the clinician with "valuable insight into the degree to which the patient walks safely while encountering common everyday 'dual tasks' and may assist in the prescription of therapeutic interventions and clinical recommendations about how to handle such situations" (p. 336).

Summary: Attention in Balance and Gait

The studies reviewed in this section represent two general approaches to understanding the role of attention in balance and walking for young and old adults. The first involves applying the dual task method. Findings from this approach indicate that dividing attention during balance and walking tasks generally puts older adults at a disadvantage (relative to young adults) in terms of more negatively affecting performance on both the motor and attention tasks. This pattern of results is taken to indicate that balance and walking are not automatic for adults, particularly for older adults. This pattern also suggests that walking under divided attention conditions is particularly risky for older adults; because dual tasks are more disruptive to walking, older adults may be at a greater risk for falls under such conditions.

The second approach involves predicting parameters of walking performance from performance on various attention tasks. In the studies reviewed, selective attention and attention switching were identified as predictors of walking performance. These findings seem most informative and useful as researchers work to develop models of motor–cognition interactions that can explain walking behavior and predict the circumstances under which falls are most likely to occur.

Finally, the studies reviewed highlight the need for clinical assessments to detect attention deficits. If such deficits can be detected on an individual basis, then it would be possible to intervene and perhaps prevent disability that may come from restricted mobility or from the sequelae of a fall. As noted previously, a number of researchers are thinking along these lines, though it remains to be seen whether the need for intervention research will be addressed in the near future.

Attention in Driving

Automobile driving is a complex task requiring a variety of cognitive processes, including attention. Understanding the changing attention skills of older adults in the context of driving has been a topic of great interest for its implications for both personal independence and public safety. A variety of types of attention have been examined, particularly selective attention and divided attention. This work has been carried out using real-life, on-road assessments as well as laboratory assessments.

An example of laboratory work is given in Hoffman, McDowd, Atchley, and Dubinsky (2005). They administered a series of visual and cognitive tasks in an effort to predict performance among older adults on a low fidelity driving simulator. The cognitive tasks included the Useful Field of View Test (UFOV®) and DriverScan. The UFOV is based on a computerized visual target discrimination task. The discrimination task is performed on centrally presented targets, either by itself, along with a peripheral localization task (divided attention), or both tasks and a display that also includes a random arrangement of distracting triangles (selective attention). Performance is assessed by varying display duration to find the duration at which a person can achieve 75% accuracy in each subtest.

DriverScan is a change detection task developed with driving scenes and using the methods of item response theory (Hoffman, Yang, Bovaird, & Embretson, 2006). Pairs of photographs of driving scenes are presented in a rapidly alternating sequence. The two members of each pair differ by only one component (e.g., a street sign, pedestrian, building, etc.), and the task is to detect the difference as rapidly as possible. Thus, DriverScan measures the ability to detect rapidly occurring, driving relevant changes via visual selective attention.

Results of structural equation modeling to account for driving simulator performance showed that DriverScan and the divided attention subtest of the UFOV account for unique variance in simulator driving after controlling age, visual impairment, and processing speed. DriverScan was the strongest predictor of simulator driving, perhaps because of its use of real-life driving scenes. In any case, visual search and divided attention ability as measured in these tasks were significantly related to driving performance. Hoffman et al.

(2005) encouraged the continued investigation of such measures, their relation to each other and to driving impairment, as a way to better understand both attention and driving abilities.

Caird, Edwards, Creaser, and Horrey (2005) also used a change detection test to assess drivers' abilities to identify changes in rapidly changing views of busy intersections. Their task was modified from the typical change detection task. In this modified task, rather than detecting the change between pictures, the participant was asked to decide whether the intersection was safe for a left turn, right turn, or for proceeding straight ahead. Then two images were rapidly alternated for 5 or 8 seconds; in one image the intersection was clear, and in the other image there was a vehicle or pedestrian or traffic signal that would bear on whether the intersection was safe for the relevant maneuver. The participant was seated in a simulated vehicle consisting of a steering wheel, brake, and accelerator. After each trial, participants were to step on the gas pedal if the intersection was safe, or the brake if it was not safe for the relevant maneuver. Performance was scored in terms of accuracy of decision about the intersection.

Four groups of participants completed this task: young, middle-aged, young-old, and old-old adults. Analyses of overall accuracy indicated that young adults (M = 74%) and middle-aged (M = 74%) performed better than the young old (60%) and old old (54%). Follow-up analyses to examine possible effects of object size and contrast in relevant picture areas indicated that these factors did not affect accuracy. Exposure time (pictures alternating for 5 or 8 seconds) was not a significant factor in the accuracy analysis. Follow-up qualitative analysis of individual trials (intersections) indicated that older adults seem to base decisions on traffic lights and do not modify these decisions in the presence of other factors, such as pedestrians or other cars. The search window that older adults employ appears to be smaller than that used by young adults, and because of this restricted search, older adults miss critical aspects of the scene. The authors suggest that over-reliance on the most obvious guides to intersection behavior (traffic signals) may be a compensatory strategy adopted by older adults with impaired attentional search abilities. They further suggest that training older adults in more successful compensatory strategies may be one way to reduce intersection accidents among older adults.

Underwood, Phelps, Wright, van Loon, and Galpin (2005) addressed a similar question as Caird et al. (2005), but they came to a different conclusion. Underwood et al. used eye tracking technology to monitor eye movements as people watched film clips created from a driver's point of view. The task was to watch the clips for driving hazards (e.g., animals, pedestrians, slow vehicles, objects in the road) and press a response button as soon as a hazard was detected. Results showed few age differences. Young and old adults noted the hazards equally quickly, and both age groups detected approximately 90%

of the intended hazards. Eye fixations to road environment (e.g., buildings, intersections, signs, etc.), roadway (the road itself), and road users (cars, pedestrians, cyclists, etc.) were calculated in terms of proportion of time spent in each zone, before and during the hazard. Attention to the different zones differed in the presence of hazards, but this difference did not vary with age. The breadth of eye scan paths in the horizontal plane was also examined, and no age effects were noted. The authors conclude that their study provided no evidence that there are "functional differences in the distributions of attention of the younger and older drivers—scan paths, inspection times and the spread of search are remarkably consistent" (Underwood et al., 2005, p. 354). It is difficult to know why these results differ from the more negative picture of aging drivers reported by Caird et al. (2005). The Underwood et al. task is perhaps more true to life because it involves film clips of driving scenes rather than rapidly alternating still pictures. On the basis of their findings, Underwood et al. conclude that "the majority of older drivers are safe drivers" (p. 355). However, it would appear that the evidence on that is quite mixed, and it is difficult to resolve discrepancies between findings because task demands can vary widely.

Underwood et al. (2005) also noted that in their task participants only had to notice hazards; no reactions or driving maneuvers to avoid the hazards were required. One possibility is that age-related slowing of response times may prevent older adults from responding to the hazard in time to avoid an accident. Zhang and colleagues (2007) examined "brake reaction speed (BRS)" in a large sample of older adults aged 67 to 87 years (p. 216). Participants sat before a computer monitor with floor-mounted brake and accelerator pedals at their feet. The computer display showed a traffic signal that was initially green. Participants started the trial by pressing the accelerator to the green light. After a variable period of time (average 30 seconds), the light went from green to red, and the participant's task was to release the accelerator and press on the brake pedal, using the same foot. Total BRS was separated into two components: initial reaction time (IRT)—time from the signal turning red to the foot beginning to release the accelerator pedal; and physical reaction time (PRT)—time from the foot leaving the accelerator pedal until the brake pedal was fully depressed. In addition to the BRS test, other assessments were made, including: visual acuity and contrast sensitivity tests; physical comorbidities likely to affect driving, such as pain in feet and legs, arthritis, etc.; the Trails A (visual search) test; and the Brief Test of Attention (an auditory selective attention task).

Zhang et al. (2007) first transformed response times to a rate measure (1/time). Analyses showed that age was significantly related to total brake response rate (BRR), confirming that older adults are slower to respond to a traffic signal, even within a range of older adults. In addition, Zhang et al. had expected that the physical health measures would be related to the physical response rate (PRR), and the attention measures would be related to the initial response rate (IRR). Contrary to these expectations, their results showed that the attention and physical comorbidity measures were significantly related to both the IRR and the PRR. Thus, overall, those who showed better attention skills also had quicker braking responses to the signal display. Interpretation of this finding is somewhat complicated, however. Because the attention measures correlated with both response components, it may be that speed of processing accounts for the relations, rather than attention. In addition, motivation for the particular choice of attention measures is unclear. The Trails A task is basically a visual search task, and the braking task did not involve visual search. The Brief Test of Attention is an auditory task, and the braking task was visual. What we do know, however, is that braking behavior is slowed in the aging adult, which may compound the driving risk when accompanied by even subtle attentional impairments.

Other experimental work on aging and visual attention has used the inhibition of return (IOR) test to examine visual search processes. Bédard and colleagues (2006) examined the relation between IOR performance and driving. IOR is an empirical phenomenon purported to reflect a basic mechanism in attentional search. The empirical phenomenon is the finding that people are slower to locate a target that is presented in a location that has just been searched than if it is presented in a new location. This finding is interpreted as reflecting an efficiency in visual search that prevents repeatedly searching the same location. Bédard et al. suggested that IOR is very important in good driving, which requires continuous visual scanning. Impaired IOR might lead to greater driving risk.

Bédard et al. (2006) administered a standard driving test to 41 adults aged 55–84 years. The course was similar to a licensing exam test and was administered by a certified driving instructor. The test lasted about 35 minutes and was scored on a 0–100 scale. They also administered an IOR test. They found that age was related to driving test score, with older adults doing worse. Regression analyses showed that location-based IOR was a significant factor in driving test score, in addition to age. Together, age and IOR accounted for just under 30% of the variance, suggesting that although the results may be promising about the role of IOR in driving, there is more to be explained. Even so, the findings suggest that "reflexive mechanisms of visual attention may support safe driving" (p. 132), and their impairment may increase driving risk.

The use of road tests is increasing as a method for assessing age differences in driving performance. Perryman and Fitten (1996) developed a standardized road test for use on the grounds of the Sepulveda, California, VA Medical Center. The Sepulveda Road test is 2.7 miles long and has a variety of intersections, road signs, traffic signals, and speed bumps. Young and old drivers drove a specially instrumented car along a specific traffic-controlled route. Six traffic events were presented to each participant, and steering, braking acceleration, and eye movements and visual search were measured. The eye movement data are most relevant to the assessment of attention; older adults made fewer lateral eye movements, suggesting decreased visual search activity. This is in contrast to the findings of Underwood et al. (2005) described previously, who found no age differences in eye movements in their hazard detection task. Perhaps the added task of actually driving, as required in the Perryman and Fitten study, affects the ability to maintain a broad visual search window. In any case, the latter authors suggest that age changes in visual search ability may be a fundamental cause of age-related declines in the ability to skillfully operate a motor vehicle.

McKnight and McKnight (1999) combined a structured road test with a set of computerized cognitive measures and records of motor vehicle accidents in their study of aging and driving ability. They tested 407 older drivers divided into two groups: those who were reported to the DMV for driving incidents and a volunteer control group. Attentional assessments included measures of selective attention, divided attention, and vigilance using the Automated Psychophysical Test (APT; McKnight & McKnight, 1994). Aggregate standardized scores for the attention measures were significantly correlated ($r = 0.46$) with reported number of incidents of unsafe driving across all 407 participants. However, the attention measures were also correlated with sensory, perceptual, psychomotor, and memory measures, so it is difficult to know which ability may be underlying the association. Multiple regression or other analyses that may have helped sort out this issue were not reported. The standardized road test did not help shed light on this question either; the road test was deemed less reliable because there were examiner and site differences that limited the utility of the data collected. In general, they did find that lower scores on the attention tasks were associated with more errors on the road test.

Other studies with smaller samples and single data collection sites have reported more success in reliably assessing driving ability among older adults. Richardson and Marottoli (2003) examined visual attention and driving using experimental and neuropsychological assessments and a driving assessment that included parking lot, highway, urban, and suburban driving. Their goal was to identify the driving situations in which age-related attention deficits were most likely to be manifested. They predicted that older adults' driving errors would be most likely to occur during highway merging or other high-traffic intersections, in situations requiring speed regulation and estimating distance, and in the realm of vehicle positioning. The course was 20 miles long and took about an hour to complete. Drivers drove in a special vehicle fit with a dual braking system, accompanied by a primary examiner in the front seat and a secondary examiner in the back seat. Tests took place on week days, at the same time of day. Thirty-five older adults (mean age 80 years ± 3 years) who were participating in a larger study agreed to the on-road test. The test had 36 items that were scored on a 3-point scale: 0 = major errors or unsafe; 1 = minor errors; 2 = no errors. Cognitive measures included memory and spatial ability and processing speed. In addition, a number cancellation test was included as a measure of visual attention, and Trails B (described earlier) was included as an executive function measure.

Driving test performance was correlated (after partialling out distance acuity) with number cancellation ($r = .43$), visual reproduction ($r = .40$), and Trails B ($r = -.38$). However, rather than having a role in only the more challenging driving maneuvers, the number cancellation test was related to 25 of the 36 driving test items. The visual memory test was associated with 16 individual maneuvers, and the Trails B task was associated with 17 items. Most of the items in these latter two groups were a subset of the items that correlated with visual attention. Thus, the authors suggest that visual attention may be an important target for intervention to improve driving safety among older drivers. They note that the participants in this study were typical older drivers and not those referred for driving assessment or training. They also suggest that their approach of identifying specific cognitive variables (attention) along with specific difficult driving situations may provide the framework for developing intervention training programs. In their data, however, the attention variable correlated with almost all of the driving behaviors, preventing any specificity for targeted driving training.

Other researchers have also been interested in developing measures to identify safe and unsafe drivers. Ball and colleagues (2006) conducted a prospective cohort study using physical, cognitive, speed of processing, and mobility measures to predict at-fault automobile accidents. Participants included 1,910 adults over the age of 55 who presented themselves at one of three motor vehicle administrations in Maryland between November 1998 and October 1999. Initially, 3,970 such adults were invited to participate; approximately 48% agreed and were enrolled in the study. They were followed for 4–5 years with regard to the incidence of at-fault driving accidents. Baseline measures included a short assessment of physical abilities (walking speed, foot tapping, upper limb mobility, and head/neck rotation), cognitive abilities (cued and delayed recall, visual scanning, visual perception, Trails A and B), and a composite measure of visual attention and processing speed. The latter measure was subtest 2 of the Useful Field of View (UFOV) test, which measures divided attention. In the UFOV test, each participant has to identify a central target and locate a peripheral target simultaneously. Display duration is manipulated until the participant reaches 75% accuracy. The dependent variable is thus the amount of time required for a participant to achieve this level of performance in the divided attention condition.

There were 91 participants involved in at-fault accidents in the subsequent follow-up period (4–5 years); 1,808 were not involved in an accident across the same period of time. Among the set of predictor measures, only the UFOV and the visual perception task were different between these two groups. A series of univariate logistic regression analyses revealed that the following were associated with future at-fault auto accidents: older age, male sex, a fall in the previous 3 years, poorer Trails B, visual perception, and UFOV performance. Follow-up multivariate analyses that first entered age, sex, and number of miles driven revealed that visual perception and the UFOV were unique predictors of accidents, but Trails B was not. These data demonstrate that deficits in divided attention predict a person's likelihood of having an automobile accident. The authors suggest that the UFOV, as a computerized test, may be feasible as a driving assessment to identify drivers who may be in need of additional training to improve safety, or be advised to stop driving. The authors also note that training on the UFOV has been shown to increase driving safely and shows great promise as an intervention to support independence among older adults as drivers.

Divided attention has also been examined by other investigators in the context of driving tasks. McPhee, Scialfa, Dennis, Ho, and Caird (2004) asked young and old adults to search for traffic signs on a computer display involving varying degrees of visual clutter. Participants performed the search task either by itself, or while simultaneously listening to and answering questions about a brief prose passage. They found that older adults were more impaired by the requirement to divide attention, both in terms of search speed and accuracy, and concurrent memory task accuracy. They liken this situation (visual search + auditory listening task) to driving while talking on a cell phone. Their results indicate that combining tasks such as these can be extremely risky, particularly for older adults.

A more limited age-related divided attention effect was reported by Chaparro, Wood and Carberry (2005) who took their participants out on a driving course. Driving performance was scored in terms of accuracy in identifying road signs, avoiding hazards, staying in a lane, and time to complete the 5.1 km course. In addition to the driving tasks, participants were to add pairs of single digit numbers and report the sums out loud. The numbers were presented either auditorily via speakers, or visually via a dash-mounted monitor. Although older drivers did worse than young drivers on almost every measure, only time to complete the course showed an age-related divided attention effect. One possible account of this limited effect was the ease of the secondary task (adding single-digit numbers); accuracy was very high (99%) and there were no age differences in number of responses made. Even so, there were dual task effects on every measure, but overall young and old were similarly affected. Perhaps practice with the complex nature of real world driving allowed older adults to integrate the added math task by simply slowing down a bit.

Wikman and Summala (2005) argued that "proper time sharing is a necessary precondition of safe driving" and that "in time sharing, it is the properly timed attention shift from one target to another that is critical for safety" (p. 716). In this context, they designed a study to examine attention switching in a dual task situation: Attention had to be switched between a driving task and a visual search task using a display mounted on the dashboard. The 350 km driving task consisted of divided four-lane highway and undivided two-lane highway that differed in pavement type, lane width, shoulder width, and speed limit. The car was specially instrumented with video cameras, dual brakes, and an LED display used for the secondary visual attention task. That display consisted of eight LED lights arranged in a generally circular fashion. Single digits were presented on each of the LEDs. In one version of the task, the participant had to read off the numbers that were displayed. In the second version, the participant was required to push the LED buttons in numerical order. In both cases, as soon as one sequence of eight was completed, another sequence was presented. Both tasks were administered for portions of the course on both the divided and undivided highways.

Young, middle-aged, and older adults participated in the Wikman and Summala (2005) driving study, accompanied by an experimenter who administered the visual task while the participant was driving. Analysis of data from the visual digit task revealed that older adults spent more time looking away from the road than either of the other two groups and did not compensate for this by slowing their speed (no effect of age on driving speed). They were also more likely than the other groups to have "long" glances, defined as glances away from the road longer than 2 seconds. Older adults also showed less good control of lane location, especially on the button press task. Thus, the facility with which older adults could switch back and forth between tasks was impaired, resulting in periodic unsafe driving performance. Particularly troubling were the long glances, indicating an impairment in switching attention from one task to another in an efficient manner.

Wikman and Summala (2005) also tested the relative contributions of visual acuity measures and visual search ability (measured with the Trails A test) to driving safety (time eyes were off the road, number of long glances). They found that the visual search task mediated the relationship between age and driving safety measures, whereas the visual acuity measures did not. Interestingly, they apparently did not administer Trails B, which might be even more closely related to attention switching performance and would serve as an accurate predictor of safe driving in the present task. In any case, the authors conclude that older adults should avoid time-sharing while driving, and they caution the auto industry about planning in-vehicle technology for older drivers. Navigation devices, for example, may be a particular challenge to safe driving if the driver glances at the visual map rather than just following the verbal directions.

Summary

Studies of attention in driving have included both laboratory measures and on-road driving tests. Each approach has its associated strengths and weaknesses, and these methodological differences may have contributed to some of the differences in findings reported in this chapter. Even in light of these differences, the complexity of the driving task is attested to by the various aspects of attention found to be related to driving: selective attention, visual search, attention switching, and divided attention. Age differences in each of these measures have been found to be related to poorer driving ability, indicating that attentional ability is fundamental to driving and, perhaps, a primary target for intervention to improve and maintain the skills of older drivers.

Some research effort has also been devoted to identifying those drivers most at risk for accidents. This endeavor will become critically important as the number of older drivers increases over the next decades. Equally important will be the development of interventions that can support safe driving among older adults. Driving can provide both a sense of independence and also real practical independence for the older adult. Identifying drivers at risk and developing successful interventions will be key to supporting this independence for as long as possible.

THEORETICAL AND EMPIRICAL DEVELOPMENTS IN UNDERSTANDING ATTENTION

The studies reviewed here indicate an important role for attention in the performance of mobility tasks. Even so, the concept of attention is quite broad: Attention can operate in selective, divided, switching, and sustained modes (McDowd & Shaw, 2000). One might ask whether these are different "attentions" (e.g., Logie, Cocchini, Della Sala, & Baddeley, 2004), or whether they should be treated as different modes of the same fundamental mechanism. One model of attention proposing a single attention entity is resource theory (Craik & Byrd, 1982; Kahneman, 1973).

Resource Theory of Attention

Resource theory is based on the observation that individuals have a limited information processing capacity. Attentional resources are the limited supply of cognitive processing fuel that allows tasks to be performed. An individual's task performance remains efficient as long as task demands do not exceed the supply of resources. When demand does exceed supply, as may be the case for complex or multicomponent tasks, then performance on one or more component tasks will decline or fail.

The notion of attentional resources has great intuitive appeal and, perhaps for that reason, has enjoyed continued presence in the literature. Indeed, much of the literature on balance and gait reviewed previously has been conducted in the context of a resource model—aging increases the attentional resource demands of physical performance such that secondary task performance suffers. However, resource theory has long had its critics. One fundamental criticism is that no one can quite say what resources are, in terms of nervous system function; this criticism argues that the term *resources* merely describes observed behavior and doesn't constitute a theoretical explanation. Navon (1984) referred to the concept of resources as a "theoretical soupstone," that is, an unnecessary construct for explaining behavior.

Two recent papers suggest that the concept of resources may indeed have form in the nervous system. Sarter, Gehring, and Kozak (2006) introduced a new view of the notion of "attentional effort," which corresponds to the application of attentional resources to a task. It is likely a common experience to have to "pay more attention" to tasks that are more difficult (e.g., listening in a noisy environment compared to a quiet environment; executing a new dance step compared to a well-learned one). Sarter et al. argue that rather than the task driving the application of additional resources, the motivations of the individual to perform well results in the application of additional attentional effort. This top-down view of attentional effort emphasizes the central role of a person's goals, intentions, and motivations in maintaining adequate task performance. As an individual's motivation to perform well kicks in, neural resources are recruited in order to support performance.

Sarter et al. (2006) argue that if an individual is challenged by a task and is motivated to perform well, then cortical, mesolimbic, and cholinergic systems are recruited to maintain performance levels. Sarter et al. review a significant amount of literature showing that these brain systems contribute to increasing the efficiency of processing incoming information, strengthening the filtering of irrelevant information, and ensuring that processing activities focus on the most relevant information. In the context of capacity models of attention, it is possible that these brain systems are the neural material of which attentional resources are made. Thus, the Sarter model may represent significant progress toward translating the metaphors of attentional resources into observable brain activity.

It is also possible to extend the Sarter et al. (2006) model to account for age differences in attentional performance that have been interpreted as a reduction in resources. They assume that the "activation and orchestration of such top-down mechanism [*sic*] . . . underlie the ability to stabilize or regain attentional performance under challenging conditions" (p. 148). According to Sarter et al., this "orchestration" is carried out by "supervisory attentional systems" (Norman & Shallice, 1986; Stuss,

Shallice, Alexander, & Picton, 1995) or a "central executive" (Baddeley, 1986), two constructs that are consistent with models of executive function that have been shown to decline with age (see previous review). The outcome of such a decline in executive function might be to prevent older adults from adequately marshalling the top-down systems to help support performance.

An alternative account would involve the aging brain and, in particular, aging of the mesolimbic and cholinergic systems. Perhaps the strategy of bringing additional brain systems to bear on task performance is intact, but those brain systems are no longer able to provide the attentional supports required for task performance. At this point these possibilities are purely speculative and, although they show some promise, require additional empirical work to be validated.

Although not intended to provide a tangible account of the construct of attentional resources, recent work on glycogen in the brain seems very relevant. Gailliot (2008) has suggested that glucose stored in the brain as glycogen provides a significant energy source for cognitive executive function. This energy source is also limited; one piece of evidence reviewed by Gailliot shows that performance on an executive function task is worse if it had been preceded by another executive function task, suggesting that the preceding task had depleted the energy resource, causing the subsequent task to be impaired. He presents a variety of evidence in support of his claim that executive function depends on limited brain glycogen supplies and that factors affecting brain glycogen supplies also affect executive function. The details of this evidence are quite compelling and interesting in their own right. Of particular interest for the data on physical functioning reviewed previously is the finding that physical exercise also consumes brain glycogen, making it difficult to combine intense physical tasks with complex cognitive tasks or executive function. (Although purely speculative, it might follow that walking as physically taxing for older adults may use up brain glycogen, possibly explaining dual costs in older adults while walking and memorizing, for example.) If glycogen is depleted in the aging brain (especially under mild to moderate physical exertion), that could account for the significant interference observed when combining motor and cognitive tasks. However, for present purposes, the relevant point is that the evidence regarding brain glycogen may provide some substance to the concept of attentional resources.

Together, these studies indicate that although to date the staying power of the construct of attentional resources may be related to its intuitive appeal, recent work suggests that the construct may have real neural analogues. If this potential is borne out, it might be possible to develop direct measures of resources, adding to the explanatory power of the theory. Additional empirical work is needed to address these possibilities.

Resources, or the Control of Resources?

As reviewed previously, one explanation for age-related performance differences is that attentional resources decline. An alternative view is that aging is associated with a decline in the ability to *control the allocation* of attentional resources, rather than a decline in amount of resources per se. In particular, the inhibitory deficit hypothesis (IDH; e.g., Hasher & Zacks, 1988) suggests that age-related declines in cognition may be largely explained by declines in the ability to inhibit the allocation of attentional resources to information that is distracting or irrelevant to the current task goals. This view has some support from a body of empirical work that has shown older adults to be disadvantaged on tasks requiring active inhibition of irrelevant information. However, the IDH has been controversial, both empirically and theoretically. The empirical issues have been reviewed elsewhere (e.g., Gorfein & MacLeod, 2007; McDowd, 1997); for present purposes we will consider a fundamental theoretical issue.

The IDH was initially postulated to explain age differences in working memory capacity (Hasher & Zacks, 1988). Working memory (WM) is made up of temporary memory stores that hold and process activated information and a central executive process that controls access to those temporary stores (Baddeley & Hitch, 1974). In this view, working memory capacity is measured as the number of items that can be held in the stores while simultaneously processing other task relevant information. According to IDH, reduced working memory capacity observed in older adults was a result of faulty inhibitory processes that "cluttered" working memory space with irrelevant or no-longer-relevant information, functionally reducing working memory capacity (Zacks & Hasher, 1994). In this view, inhibitory function is a *cause* that determines working memory capacity by protecting working memory stores from irrelevant information.

In contrast, Engle and colleagues (e.g., Engle, 2002; Kane, Bleckley, Conway, & Engle, 2001; Redick, Heitz, & Engle, 2007) have articulated a different view of WM and of inhibition in WM. In their view, "WM capacity is not about individual differences in how many items can be stored per se but about differences in the ability to control attention to maintain information in an active, quickly retrievable state. . . . WM capacity is not directly about memory—it is about using attention to maintain or suppress information . . . Greater WM capacity does mean that more items can be maintained as active, but this is a result of greater ability to control attention, not a larger memory store" (Engle, 2002, p. 20). Thus, inhibition of irrelevant information is a *consequence* of working memory capacity rather than its cause.

In support of this view, Engle and colleagues have shown that working memory capacity predicts performance on a variety of complex cognitive tasks that one might not expect to be related to a memory task (e.g., visual selective attention tasks and the antisaccade task; see Redick et al., 2007, for a review). These results are interpreted as demonstrating that working memory capacity reflects an ability that is "fundamentally important to higher-order cognition" (Engle 2002, p. 22), the ability to efficiently allocate attentional resources in order to meet one's goals. This view of the importance of efficient attention allocation is also reflected in the Sarter et al. (2006) model on motivated performance reviewed previously. Returning to the issue of understanding age differences in performance, Engle's conceptualization of working memory suggests the following: Observed age differences in working memory capacity may have new relevance for understanding age differences in attentional functioning. Indeed, age-related declines in working memory capacity suggest that the age differences in performance described in this review may be due to age changes in the control of attention, rather than a reduction in resources per se. Future work to address this question directly would represent a significant advance in understanding the mechanisms of age differences in performance.

Progress in understanding the mechanisms of age differences in performance is particularly important because even in Engle's model of working memory, the substance of executive attention is not specified. Recent work by O'Reilly and colleagues (e.g., Hazy, Frank, & O'Reilly, 2006) may be relevant in this regard. The goal of this work is described as "banishing the homunculus" in working memory by working to "elucidate the precise computational and neural mechanisms underlying working memory and 'executive' function" (Hazy et al., 2006, p. 105). They have developed a computational model of working memory function based on a neural system involving the posterior cortex, the prefrontal cortex/basal ganglia system, and the hippocampus. The posterior cortex handles most routine processing of sensory and motor information. The hippocampal system supports rapid learning of associations, which may be relevant for subsequent controlled information processing. The prefrontal cortex works in concert with the basal ganglia. It maintains relevant information in an active state; which information remains active is updated by the basal ganglia. In this model, working memory is "an emergent property of the interaction between these three brain areas . . . Information is distributed in a relatively stable configuration throughout the cortex, and . . . working memory amounts to the controlled activation of these representations" (p. 106). This model seems most consistent with Engle's view of working memory; Hazy et al.'s view is "that working memory and executive function are really two sides of the same coin" (p. 106).

Interestingly, Hazy et al. (2006) also believe that this neural system underlying working memory "may represent a kind of phylogenetic extension of the same kinds of mechanisms that underlie all forms of complex motor coordination and planning" (p. 107). If so, their model may provide a parsimonious account of the relationship between motor and attentional function. In any case, work such as this modeling approach provides a means to test hypotheses about neural mechanisms underlying performance and to identify the mechanisms of age differences.

SUMMARY, CONCLUSIONS, AND FUTURE DIRECTIONS

In this chapter, we have reviewed a variety of studies examining cognitive influences on motor behavior related to mobility. We believe these data are interesting in several ways. First, they illustrate the interrelatedness of cognitive and motor functions, reflecting evolving views of brain architecture and brain-behavior relations. Going forward, models of cognitive functions will have to incorporate this interrelatedness, as will models of motor functions. Second, the studies reviewed here illustrate the application of experimental measures of attention to understanding real world behaviors. A variety of methods and measures have been used in efforts to explain mobility-related behavior, and their utility in this regard has been documented.

We have also tried to point out directions for future research, both in terms of refining empirical approaches and elaborating theoretical models to incorporate both attention and motor processes. The promise of this work is to provide the knowledge essential for promoting independence among older adults. Mobility is critical to independence, and the extent to which research findings can be translated into interventions to support mobility reflects the extent to which this work can support good quality of life for older adults.

REFERENCES

Allain, P., Berrut, G., Etcharry-Bouyx, F., Barre, J., Dubas, F., & Le Gall, D. (2007). Executive functions in normal aging: An examination of script sequencing, script sorting, and script monitoring. *The Journal of Gerontology: Psychological Sciences*, *62B*, 187–190.

Atkinson, H. H., Rosano, C., Simonsick, E. M., Williamson, J. D., Davis, C., Ambrosius, W. T., et al. (2007). Cognitive function, gait speed decline, and comorbidities: The Health, Aging and Body Composition Study. *Journal of Gerontology: Medical Sciences*, *62A*(8), 844–850.

Baddeley, A. D. (1986). *Working Memory*. Oxford, UK: Clarendon Press.

Baddeley, A. D., & Hitch, G. (1974). *Working Memory*. In G. H. Bower (Ed.), *The Psychology of Learning and Motivation: Advances in Research and Theory* (vol. 8, pp. 47–89). New York: Academic Press.

Ball, K. K., Roenker, D. L., Wadley, V. G., Edwards, J. D., Roth, D. L., McGwin, G. J., et al. (2006). Can high-risk older drivers be identified through performance-based measures in a Department of Motor Vehicles setting? *Journal of the American Geriatrics Society*, *54*, 77–84.

Bédard, M., Leonard, E., McAuliffe, J., Weaver, B., Gibbons, C., & Dubois, S. (2006). Visual attention and older drivers: The contribution of inhibition of return to safe driving. *Experimental Aging Research, 32,* 119–135.

Binder, E. F., Storandt, M., & Birge, S. J. (1999). The relation between psychometric test performance and physical performance in older adults. *Journal of Gerontology: Medical Sciences, 54*(8), M428–32.

Ble, A., Volpato, S., Zuliani, G., Guralnik, J. M., Bandinelli, S., Lauretani, F., et al. (2005). Executive Function Correlates with Walking Speed in Older Persons: The InCHIANTI Study. *Journal of the American Geriatric Society, 53,* 410–415.

Brach, J. S., Studenski, S. A., Perera, S., VanSwearingen, J. M., & Newman, A. B. (2007). Gait variability and the risk of incident mobility disability in community-dwelling older adults. *Journal of Gerontology A: Biological Sciences and Medical Sciences, 62*(9), 983–988.

Brown, L. A., Shumway-Cook, A., & Woollacott, M. H. (1999). Attentional demands on postural recovery: The effects of aging. *Journal of Gerontology: Medical Sciences, 54A*(40), M165–M171.

Buckner, R. L. (2004). Memory and executive function in aging and AD: Multiple factors that cause decline and reserve factors that compensate. *Neuron, 44,* 195–208.

Cabeza, R E. (2002). Hemispheric asymmetry reduction in old adults: The HAROLD model. *Psychology and Aging, 17,* 85–100.

Caird, J. K., Edwards, C., Creaser, J., & Horrey, W. J. (2005). Older driver failures of attention at intersections: Using change blindness methods to assess turn decision accuracy. *Human Factors, 47*(2), 235–249.

Carlson, M. C., Fried, L. P., Xue, Q., Bandeen-Roche, K., Zeger, S. L., & Brandt, J. (1999). Association between executive attention and physical functional performance in community-dwelling older women. *Journal of Gerontology: Social Sciences, 54B*(5), S262–S270.

Chaparro, A., Wood, J. M., & Carberry, T. (2005). Effects of age and auditory and visual dual-tasks on closed road driving performance. *Optometry and Vision Science, 82*(8), 747–754.

Coppin, A. K., Shumway-Cook, A., Saczynski, J. S., Patel, K. V., Ble, A., Ferucci, L., et al. (2006). Association of executive function and performance of dual-task physical tests among older adults: Analyses from the InChianti study. *Age and Ageing, 35,* 619–624.

Craik, F.I.M., & Byrd, M. (1982). Aging and cognitive deficits: The role of attentional resources. In F.I.M. Craik & S. Trehub (Eds.), *Aging and Cognitive Processes* (pp. 191–211). New York: Plenum.

Doumas, M., Smolders, C., & Krampe, R. Th. (2008). Task prioritization in aging: Effects of sensory information on concurrent posture and memory performance. *Experimental Brain Research, 187,* 275–281.

Engle, R. W. (2002). Working memory capacity as executive attention. *Current Directions in Psychological Science, 11,* 19–23.

Gailliot, M. T. (2008). Unlocking the energy dynamics of executive functioning. *Perspectives on Psychological Science, 3*(4), 245–263.

Gorfein, D. S., & MacLeod, C. M. (Eds.). (2007). *Inhibition in Cognition.* Washington, DC: American Psychological Association.

Hasher, L., & Zacks, R. T. (1988). Working memory, comprehension, and aging: A review and a new view. In G. H. Bower (Ed.), *The Psychology of Learning and Motivation* (vol. 22, pp. 193–225). New York: Academic Press.

Hausdorff, J. M., Rios, D. A., & Edelberg, H. K. (2001). Gait variability and fall risk in community-living older adults: A 1-year prospective study. *Archives of Physical Medicine and Rehabilitation, 82*(8), 1050–1056.

Hausdorff, J. M., Yogev, G., Springer, S., Simon, E. S., & Giladi, N. (2005). Walking is more like catching than tapping: Gait in the elderly as a complex cognitive task. *Experimental Brain Research, 164*, 541–548.

Hazy, T. E., Frank, M. J., & O'Reilly, R. C. (2006). Banishing the homunculus: Making working memory work. *Neuroscience, 139*, 105–118.

Heuninckx, S., Wenderoth, N., Debaere, F., Peeters, R., & Swinnen, S. P. (2005). Neural basis of aging: The penetration of cognition into action control. *Journal of Neuroscience, 25*(29), 6787–6796.

Heuninckx, S., Wenderoth, N., & Swinnen, S. P. (2008). Systems neuroplasticity in the aging brain: Recruiting additional neural resources for successful motor performance in elderly persons. *The Journal of Neuroscience, 28*, 91–99.

Hoffman, L., McDowd, J. M., Atchley, P., & Dubinsky R. A. (2005). The role of visual attention in predicting driving impairment in older adults. *Psychology and Aging, 20*(4), 610–622.

Hoffman, L., Yang, X., Bovaird, J. A., & Embretson, S. E. (2006). Measuring attention in older adults: Development and psychometric evaluation of DriverScan. *Educational and Psychological Measurement, 66*, 984–1000.

Holtzer, R., Friedman, R., Lipton, R. B., Katz, M., Xue, X., & Verghese, J. (2007). The relationship between specific cognitive functions and falls in aging. *Neuropsychology, 21*(5), 540–548.

Holtzer, R., Verghese, J., Xue, X., & Lipton, R. B. (2006). Cognitive processes related to gait velocity: Results from the Einstein Aging Study. *Neuropsychology, 20*(2), 215–223.

Huxhold, O., Li, S-C., Schmiedek, F., & Lindenberger, U. (2006). Dual-tasking postural control: Aging and the effects of cognitive demand in conjunction with focus of attention. *Brain Research Bulletin, 69*, 294–305.

Inzitari, M., Baldereschi, M., Di Carlo, A., Di Bari, M., Marchionni, N., Scafato, E., et al. (2007). Impaired attention predicts motor performance decline in older community-dwellers with normal baseline mobility: Results from the Italian Longitudinal Study on Aging (ILSA). *Journal of Gerontology: Medical Sciences, 62A*(8), 837–843.

Jamet, M., Deviterne, D., Gauchard, G. C., Vancon, G., & Perrin, P. P. (2007). Age-related part taken by attentional cognitive processes in standing postural control in dual-task context. *Gait & Posture, 25*, 179–184.

Kahneman, D. (1973). *Attention and Effort.* Englewood Cliffs, NJ: Prentice-Hall.

Kane, M. J., Bleckley, K. M., Conway, A.R.A., & Engle, R. W. (2001). A controlled-attention view of working-memory capacity. *Journal of Experimental Psychology: General, 130*, 169–183.

Kannus, P., Sievanen, H., Palvanen, M., Jarvinen, T., & Parkkari, J. (2005). Prevention of falls and consequent injuries in elderly people. *Lancet, 366*, 1885–1893.

Kramer, A. F., & Kray, J. (2006). Aging and attention. In F.I.M. Craik & E. Bialystock (Eds.), *Lifespan Cognition: Mechanisms of Change* (pp. 57–69). Oxford, UK: Oxford University Press.

Kramer, A. F., & Madden, D. J. (2008). Attention. In F.I.M. Craik & T. A. Salthouse (Eds.), *The Handbook of Aging and Cognition* (3rd ed., pp. 189–250). New York: Psychology Press.

Lee, T. D., Wishart, L. R., & Murdoch, J. E. (2002). Aging, attention, and bimanual coordination. *Canadian Journal on Aging, 21*, 549–557.

Li, K.Z.H., Lindenberger, U., Freund, A. M., & Baltes, P. B. (2001). Walking while memorizing: Age-related differences in compensatory behavior. *American Psychological Society, 12*(3), 230–237.

Li, S. C., & Dinse, H. (Eds.). (2002). Aging of the brain, sensorimotor, and cognitive processes. *Neuroscience and Biobehavioral Reviews, 26*, 729–867.

Lindenberger, U., Marsiske, M., & Baltes, P. B. (2000). Memorizing while walking: Increase in dual-task costs from young adulthood to old age. *Psychology and Aging, 15*(3), 417–436.

Logie, R. H., Cocchini, S., Della Sala, S., & Baddeley, A. (2004). Is there a specific capacity for dual task co-ordination? Evidence from Alzheimer's Disease. *Neuropsychology, 18*(3), 504–513.

Mahboobin, A., Loughlin, P. J., & Redfern, M. S. (2007). A model-based approach to attention and sensory integration in postural control of older adults. *Neuroscience Letters, 429*(2–3), 147–151.

Maki, B. E. (1997). Gait changes in older adults: Predictors of falls or indicators of fear. *Journal of the American Geriatric Society, 45*(3), 313–20.

Maki, B. E., Zecevic, A., Bateni, H., Kirshenbaum, N., & McIlroy, W. E. (2001). Cognitive demands of executing postural reactions: Does aging impede attention switching? *Cognitive Neuroscience and Neuropsychology, 12*, 3583–3587.

McDowd, J. M. (1997). Inhibition in attention and aging. *Journal of Gerontology: Psychological Sciences, 52*(6), P265–P273.

McDowd, J. M. (2007). An overview of attention: Behavior and brain. *Journal of Neurological Physical Therapy, 31*, 98–103.

McDowd, J. M., & Shaw, R. J. (2000). Attention. In F.I.M. Craik & T. A. Salthouse (Eds.), *The Handbook of Aging and Cognition* (2nd ed., pp. 221–292). Hillsdale, NJ: Lawrence Erlbaum Associates.

McKnight, A. J., & McKnight, A. S. (1994). The automated psychophysical test (APT) for assessing age-diminished capabilities. *Behavioral Research Methods, Instruments, and Computers, 26*(2), 187–191.

McKnight, A. J., & McKnight, A. S. (1999). Multivariate analysis of age-related driver ability and performance deficits. *Accident Analysis and Prevention, 31*(3), 337–346.

McPhee, L. C., Scialfa, C. T., Dennis, W. M., Ho, G., & Caird, J. K. (2004). Age differences in visual search for traffic signs during a simulated conversation. *Human Factors, 46*(4), 674–685.

Melzer, I., & Oddsson, L.I.E. (2004). The effect of a cognitive task on voluntary step execution in healthy elderly and young individuals. *Journal of the American Geriatric Society, 52*, 1255–1262.

Navon, D. (1984). Resources—A theoretical soup stone? *Psychological Review, 91*, 216–234.

Norman, D., & Shallice, T. (1986). Attention to action: Willed and automatic control of behavior. In R. Davidson, G. Schwartz, & D. Shapiro (Eds.), *Consciousness and Self Regulation: Advances in Research and Theory* (vol. 4, pp. 1–18). New York: Plenum.

Perryman, K. M., & Fitten, L. J. (1996). Effects of normal aging on the performance of motor-vehicle operational skills. *Journal of Geriatric Psychiatry and Neurology, 9*(3), 136–141.

Rankin, J. K., Woollacott, M. H., Shumway-Cook, A., & Brown, L. A. (2000). Cognitive influence on postural stability: A neuromuscular analysis in young and older adults. *Journal of Gerontology: Medical Sciences, 55A*(3), M112–M119.

Redick, T. S., Heitz, R. P., & Engle, R. W. (2007). Working memory capacity and inhibition: Cognitive and social consequences. In D. S. Gorfein, & C. M. MacLeod (Eds.), *Inhibition in Cognition* (pp. 125–1420). Washington, DC: American Psychological Association.

Reuter-Lorenz, P. (2002). New visions of the aging mind and brain. *Trends in Cognitive Science, 6,* 394–400.

Richardson, E. D., & Marottoli, R. A. (2003). Visual attention and driving behaviors among community-living older persons. *Journal of Gerontology: Medical Sciences, 58*(8), M18–M22.

Royall, D. R., Lauterbach, E. C., Kaufer, D., Malloy, P., Coburn, K. L., & Black, K. J. (2007). The cognitive correlates of functional status: A review from the committee on research of the American Neuropsychiatric Association. *Journal of Neuropsychiatry and Clinical Neuroscience, 19,* 249–265.

Sarter, M., Gehring, W. J., & Kozak, R. (2006). More attention must be paid: The neurobiology of attentional effort. *Brain Research Reviews, 51,* 145–160.

Silsupadol, P., Siu, K., Shumway-Cook, A., & Woollacott, M. H. (2006). Training of balance under single and dual task conditions in older adults with balance impairment: Three case reports. *Physical Therapy, 86,* 269–281.

Sparrow, W. A., Parker, S., Lay, B., & Wengier, M. (2005). Aging effects on the metabolic and cognitive energy cost of interlimb coordination. *Journal of Gerontology: Biological Sciences, 60A,* 312–319.

Springer, S., Giladi, N., Peretz, C., Yogev, G., Simon, E., & Hausdorff, J. M. (2006). Dual-tasking effects on gait variability: The role of aging, falls, and executive function. *Movement Disorders, 21*(7), 950–957.

Stelmach, G. E., Zelaznik, H. N., & Lowe, D. (1990). The influence of aging and attentional demands on recovery from postural instability. *Aging, 2,* 155–161.

Stuss, D. T., Shallice, T., Alexander, M. P., & Picton, T. W. (1995). A multidisciplinary approach to anterior attentional functions. *Annals of the New York Academy of Science, 769,* 191–211.

Teasdale, N., Bard, C., LaRue, J., & Fleury, M. (1993). On the cognitive penetrability of posture control. *Experimental Aging Research, 19,* 1–13.

Treitz, F. H., Heyder, K., & Daum, I. (2007). Differential course of executive control changes during normal aging. *Aging, Neuropsychology, and Cognition, 14,* 370–393.

Underwood, G., Phelps, N., Wright, C., van Loon, E., & Galpin, A. (2005). Eye fixation scanpaths of younger and older drivers in a hazard perception task. *Ophthalmic and Physiological Optics, 25*(4), 346–356.

Walston, J., Hadley, E. C., Ferrucci, L., Guralnik, J. M., Newman, A. B., Studenski, S. A., et al. (2006). Research agenda for frailty in older adults: Toward a better understanding of physiology and etiology: Summary from the American Geriatrics Society/National Institute on Aging Research Conference on Frailty in Older Adults. *Journal of the American Geriatric Society, 54*(6), 991–1001.

Welford, A. T. (1958). *Ageing and Human Skill.* London: Oxford University Press.

Wikman, A.-S., & Summala, H. (2005). Aging and time sharing in highway driving. *Optometry and Vision Science, 82*(8), 716–723.

Wishart, L. R., Lee, T. D., Murdoch, J. E., & Hodges, N. J. (2000). Effects of aging on automatic and effortful processes in bimanual coordination. *Journal of Gerontology: Psychological Sciences, 55B,* P84–P94.

Woollacott, M., & Shumway-Cook, A. (2000). Attention and the control of posture and gait: A review of an emerging area of research. *Gait and Posture, 16,* 1–14.

Yogev-Seligman, G., Hausdorff, J. M, & Giladi, N. (2007). The role of executive function and attention in gait. *Movement Disorders, 23*(3), 329–342.

Zacks, R. T., & Hasher, L. (1994). Directed ignoring: Inhibitory regulation of working memory. In D. Dagenbach & T. H. Carr (Eds.), *Inhibitory Mechanisms in Attention, Memory, and Language* (pp. 241–264). New York: Academic Press.

Zacks, R. T., Hasher, L., & Li, K.Z.H. (2000). Human memory. In F.I.M. Craik & T. A. Salthouse (Eds.), *The Handbook of Aging and Cognition* (2nd ed., pp. 293–357). Mahwah, NJ: Lawrence Erlbaum Associates.

Zhang, L., Baldwin, K., Munoz, B., Munro, C., Turano, K., Hassan, S., et al. (2007). Visual and Cognitive predictors of performance on Brake Reaction Test: Salisbury Eye Evaluation Driving Study. *Ophthalmic Epidemiology, 14*(4), 216–222.

CHAPTER 3

LANGUAGE AND COMMUNICATION

Elizabeth A. L. Stine-Morrow, Matthew C. Shake, and Soo Rim Noh

Language is an essential capacity for human activity. It enables knowledge acquisition, affords entry into worlds that may be otherwise inaccessible, and is a conduit of human relationships. Communicative effectiveness depends on both the ability to derive meaning from the written word (orthography) and acoustic stream (phonology) and the ability to formulate a message and translate it into a surface form that is comprehensible by others. Communication, then, is a skilled activity that derives from the fluid execution of component processes in a(n implicit or explicit) social context. Aging brings multidimensional change in cognition (Baltes, Staudinger, & Lindenberger, 1999), as well as motivational changes that may alter the roles for cognition in everyday life (Carstensen, Mikels, & Mather, 2006). Our goal in this chapter is to discuss how such adult developmental changes impact language processing and communicative effectiveness.

The study of cognitive aging is rich and nuanced (see chapters 1, 2, and 11 in this volume). At the risk of oversimplifying, aging brings both increases in knowledge and "crystallized abilities" that hinge on the acquisition of culture, but declines in sensory function and "mental mechanics" that require controlled attention and transformation of input. Declines in mental mechanics driven in part by age-graded change in neural integrity of the brain, primarily frontal lobe function (Dennis & Cabeza, 2008), have been conceptualized alternatively as a slowing in information processing (Salthouse, 1996), a decrease in working memory capacity (Wingfield, Stine, Lahar, & Aberdeen, 1988), reduced attentional resources (Craik & Jennings, 1992), less effective executive function (Braver & West, 2008), and a decrease in inhibitory control

(Zacks, Hasher, & Li, 2000). Interestingly, the fundamental neural mechanisms underlying sentence processing appear to remain intact (Dennis & Cabeza, 2008), with age differences primarily arising in the processing of complex forms (Wingfield & Grossman, 2006). Sensory declines are rooted not only in the peripheral auditory and visual systems, but perhaps also in brain function. There is evidence that with age sentence processing evokes relatively less activation of (posterior) areas of the brain that are responsible for sensory processing and relatively more activation of the frontal areas that are responsible for executive control. This phenomenon has been observed for cognitive performance outside of language processing as well, and has been dubbed "the posterior-anterior shift in aging" (PASA). The PASA effect may be exaggerated among older adults who show good comprehension when they are processing more complex linguistic forms (Wingfield & Grossman, 2006), suggesting that effective communication in later adulthood may require higher levels of attentional engagement (see chapter 2, this volume). Growth in knowledge-based systems—such as vocabulary, world knowledge, and particularized knowledge within one's domain of expertise—is also possible late into adulthood, depending on one's long-term engagement with activities that build these systems.

In the sections that follow, we consider how these changes impact language comprehension and memory and language production in both spoken and written communication. In the final section, we consider the implications of the age effects on comprehension, memory, and production for communication in the context of everyday life.

LANGUAGE COMPREHENSION AND MEMORY

In contemporary theories of language processing, it is generally accepted that in reading or understanding spoken language, individuals recode the surface form (i.e., the verbatim sound or print information) at multiple levels (e.g., Graesser, Millis, & Zwaan, 1997; Kintsch, 1998; Stine-Morrow, Miller, & Hertzog, 2006; Zwaan & Rapp, 2006). This involves representing the meanings of individual words, the ideas given directly by the text (called the "textbase"), the situation implied by the discourse (the "situation model"), and the structural form of the discourse (e.g., narrative form). At the textbase level, relationships among concepts are identified to construct propositions (idea units) and integrate them into a semantic representation. At the discourse level, processes are geared toward building a situation model, an elaborated representation in which the propositional content of speech or text is integrated with information from one's prior knowledge (Kintsch, 1998). Thus, the result of language comprehension is a multifaceted mental representation. Aging does not affect the construction of all of these facets similarly. We consider each in turn.

Decoding the Surface Form and Understanding Words

Older adults have more trouble understanding speech in everyday life than younger adults, whether or not they have clinically significant hearing loss. Age-related declines in auditory processing have been well documented (for recent reviews see Burke & Shafto, 2008; Schneider, Daneman, & Pichora-Fuller, 2002). With age, the peripheral auditory system shows declines in sensitivity, especially for high-pitched sounds (presbycusis), which can impact the ability to distinguish among certain speech sounds. Declines also occur in the central auditory pathways, which makes temporal perceptual process-ing slower, which may contribute to difficulty with phoneme discrimination. Moreover, the structural integrity of speech-responsive brain regions (i.e., the temporal lobes) declines with advancing age, which makes speech recognition more effortful for older adults by forcing them to rely on other brain regions, such as the frontal lobe, to support speech recognition (Eckert et al., 2008). Due to these age-related changes in hearing, older adults find it especially difficult to follow rapid speech or to understand speech when there is back-ground noise (e.g., conversations at a cocktail party; Schneider et al., 2002).

The Effects of Speech Rate and Noise

Unlike reading, in which one can review and control the speed of processing, listeners have to handle spoken information as it is presented, often at a fast rate. Some studies have investigated age-related difficulties in understanding fast speech by using time-compressed speech, which removes the desired amount of time from the speech signals while preserving the quality of the speech (Schneider, Daneman, & Murphy, 2005; Wingfield, Poon, Lombardi, & Lowe, 1985). These studies have found that recognition of words in rapid speech is more difficult for older listeners, and older adults recognize words more poorly than their younger counterparts when the speech rate is accelerated, even when the hearing thresholds are matched across age (Burke & Shafto, 2008; Schneider et al., 2005). There is some evidence that this age-related difficulty in word recognition in fast speech can be attributed to older adults' particular difficulty in processing brief consonant cues (identifying stop-consonant gaps such as slit vs. split; Gordon-Salant & Fitzgibbons, 2001). Gordon-Salant, Fitzgibbons, and Friedman (2007) further investigated age differences in the negative impact of speech rates by restoring the time-compressed speech by inserting pauses and expanding the duration of phonemes (even though the speech itself remains faster than a normal rate). These investigators found that older listeners (and listeners with hearing impairments) showed a greater improvement in word recognition for the speech in the time expansion condition relative to baseline performance. This age-related benefit of selective time expansion was greater when applied to consonant segments than to vowels. This suggests that elderly listeners, especially those with hearing loss, may require more time to process the spoken message as well as more deliberate articulation of consonants by speakers. By contrast, time restoration at clause boundaries, while still helpful, is less beneficial for older listeners relative to younger ones (Wingfield, Tun, Koh, & Rosen, 1999), suggesting that temporal processing of speech sounds is a critical bottleneck to comprehension that cannot be easily reconstructed downstream—unless (as we discuss later) a strong semantic context constrains the possibilities.

As mentioned earlier, listening to speech when there is background noise is particularly challenging for older listeners. When conversing in a cocktail party situation, listeners distinguish many sounds as they occur simultaneously, including when various sounds start and stop and how they differ. It has been suggested that an age-related loss of neural synchrony may result in internal jitter when there is a competing signal, therefore, older listeners often perceive words as unclear and are inaccurate in identifying individual words when there is noise (Burke & Shafto, 2008; Schneider et al., 2002).

The Interaction of Perception and Cognition

Because the auditory system is challenged, older adults have to devote resources to perceptual processing that would otherwise be available for higher-level cognitive operations, such as comprehension and memory; this has been called the *effortfulness* hypothesis (Burke & Shafto, 2008; Wingfield, Tun, & McCoy, 2005). The effortfulness hypothesis emphasizes the importance of the interaction of sensory and cognitive functions to understand age differences in spoken language. Wingfield and colleagues (2005) showed that after listening to lists of unrelated words that were stopped at random points, older adults with hearing loss could recall the most recent word in the list as well as those with normal hearing. However, older listeners with hearing loss were substantially poorer at recalling the two words prior to the most recent. The ability of the older adults with hearing loss to recall the final words suggests that their difficulty in remembering the previous two words was not due to a failure in the perception of the words, but to the increased effort that was required to identify the words, which would otherwise have been available for encoding (see also Pichora-Fuller, Schneider, & Daneman, 1995).

Data from brain imaging also support the effortfulness hypothesis. Eckert and colleagues (2008) demonstrated that while younger listeners showed frontal lobe engagement when words were less perceivable, elder listeners showed this pattern when words were more perceivable, even though there were no age-related changes in word recognition. Another interesting finding in that study was that declines in hippocampal gray matter responsive to word recognition predicted brain activity in the frontal lobe (an example of PASA), suggesting that word recognition in speech becomes more effortful with the loss of speech region integrity, such that word recognition in speech requires more cognitive control for older adults.

Contextual Facilitation

There is evidence that older adults compensate for declining recognition of speech sounds by relying on contextual support. For example, older adults are more likely to rely on visual cues in speech communication, such as looking at the speakers' lips or facial expressions to support their comprehension (Helfer, 1998; Thompson, 1995). Older adults also tend to be better at using language context than younger adults, especially when listening conditions are challenging (Wingfield et al., 1985; Stine & Wingfield, 1987), at least as long as the constraining context is available prior to the ambiguous speech sound (Wingfield, Alexander, & Cavigelli, 1994). After listening to sentences and recalling the last words, older adults show a greater contextual advantage in accuracy of word recognition than do younger adults, when words are highly predictable from the sentence context (e.g., stir your coffee with a spoon) than when they were not (e.g., Jane was thinking about the spoon), even under high degrees of noise (Schneider et al., 2002). Older adults also benefit more from the supporting context for word recognition when listening to rapid speech (Schneider et al., 2005; Wingfield et al., 1985). Thus, this age-related increased in reliance on contextual support suggests that it is important to provide a variety of cues in order to help older listeners.

Visual Word Recognition

Visual word processing, involving orthographic decoding and word recognition, appears to be well-preserved with advancing age (Thornton & Light, 2006), although declines are observed in very old age (older than 75; Schaie, 1996; Singer, Verhaegen, Ghisletta, Lindenberger, & Baltes, 2003). This suggests that increased reading experience, along with cumulative verbal knowledge, may result in greater automaticity of word processing; this could explain why older adults' visual word processing performance is comparable to younger adults' performance, or even better (Lien et al., 2006; Thornton & Light, 2006). For example, Lien and her colleagues showed that older adults could recognize words (word/nonword discrimination) while their central attention was devoted another task, but younger adults could not. This is an exceptional finding in cognitive aging, given that age-related deficits in a dual-task situation are well documented. Similarly, while aging has a detrimental impact on the processing of auditory speech at a fast rate, this is not true for visual word recognition (e.g., speeded-spelling tasks; Humes, Burk, Coughlin, Busey, & Strauser, 2007).

There is also evidence that older adults are more likely than their younger counterparts to rely on lexical (e.g., word frequency) than on perceptual characteristics (e.g., word length or "neighborhood density," the degree of overlap in spelling patterns) to recognize words (Rayner, Reichle, Stroud, Williams, & Pollatsek, 2006; Spieler & Balota, 2000; see also Whiting et al., 2003). In a word naming task, naming latency was more likely to be predicted by word frequency than by word length and neighborhood density among older adults compared to younger adults (Spieler & Balota, 2000). Similarly, using eye-tracking, Rayner and his colleagues (2006) demonstrated that older adults fixated relatively longer on low-frequency words than on high-frequency words while reading sentences. Thus, the fact that older adults are comparatively less affected by word length and neighborhood density may suggest that they require less attention to the perceptual features of words because they rely on accumulated vocabulary knowledge to process words more holistically. Holistic processing may also reflect an adaptation to declines in visual sensory processing. Whiting et al. (2003) reported that older adults' frequency effects during a lexical decision task (word/nonword discrimination) were related to increased activation of those visual cortex areas that support lexical functions, but this was not true for younger adults. They argued that visual sensory declines may reduce the analysis of visual stimuli in older adults so that they rely more on lexical level features.

Although older adults' visual word recognition is relatively well preserved, there is some evidence of age-related difficulties in decoding when orthography is disrupted, as in when words are embedded in visual noise or presented in less familiar fonts (Old English vs. Times New Roman) or in mixed case type (Allen, Madden, Weber, & Groth, 1993; Rayner et al., 2006; Speranza, Daneman, & Schneider, 2000). However, older adults exhibit greater or similar contextual facilitation of word recognition in visual noise when words are highly predictable from the sentence context (Humes et al., 2007; Speranza et al., 2000), as has been demonstrated in auditory word recognition.

Understanding Word Meanings

As documented previously, vocabulary knowledge shows little or no decline over the life span such that older adults often demonstrate superior performance on vocabulary tests when compared to their younger counterparts (Verhaeghen, 2003). Even though age-related stability or growth in word understanding is the norm, there are exceptional cases when age-related problems occur. One example is inferring the meanings of unfamiliar words from context, as demonstrated by McGinnis and her colleagues (McGinnis, Goss, Tessmer, & Zelinski, 2008; McGinnis & Zelinski, 2000, 2003). When they asked younger and older adults to produce a definition as specific as possible for an unfamiliar word after reading a short text (e.g., *dippoldism*—the beating of school children), older adults showed a tendency to produce a generalized (rather than an exact) definition (cruelty or meanness for *dippoldism*; McGinnis & Zelinski, 2000). This effect was especially true among the older old (over age 75). Adults in this age group were also more likely to endorse definitions that reflected the overall story theme as well as irrelevant definitions, even though there were choices available that were closer to the precise meaning of the word (McGinnis & Zelinski, 2000, 2003). The investigators suggested that age deficits in understanding unfamiliar words could be due to older adults' difficulty in remembering text elements important for inferring the exact definition after reading the passage, which in turn was attributable to declines in processing resources such as working memory; as a consequence, they rely on a more gist-based representation of the word meaning. McGinnis and Zelinski note that such age deficits could be due to semantic impairments associated in part with disease-related neurodegeneration.

Another aspect of word-level processing that becomes more challenging with age is proper name learning. For example, in a study by James (2004), younger and older adults were presented with pictures of new faces paired with both surnames and occupations and were later asked to recall the name and the occupation paired with each picture. Although there was no age difference in remembering occupations, older adults showed greater difficulty remembering names than young adults, even when the names and occupations were the same words (a farmer vs. Mr. Farmer). The age-related decline in name learning ability has been attributed to the fact that names lack semantic associations to support their retrieval (James, 2004).

Similarly, Noh et al. (2007) showed that after reading a passage about various unique Australian animals, older adults recalled fewer specific names of the animals relative to the young. Both young and old were more likely to remember the animal than its specific name (e.g., referring to the Leafy Seadragon as "the Leafy something" or "the fish with the pretty tail"). With repeated exposure to the names through rereading, older adults were especially likely to remember the animals rather than their exact names. Younger readers, however, took differential advantage of rereading to learn the specific animal names. Collectively, these findings suggest that older readers may often learn and be able to retrieve key concepts from text, even if the way they refer to these concepts might differ substantially from the original text.

Representing and Remembering the Meaning Given by the Text (Textbase)

Of course, language comprehension involves more than simply understanding and retaining individual words. Concepts must be integrated to provide a semantic representation of ideas. In fact, there is some debate with respect to the extent and locus of age differences in deriving the meaning from sentences. On the one hand, core processes underlying sentence understanding (e.g., instantiating the meanings of familiar words in context, canonical syntactic processing) appear to remain robust (Burke & Shafto, 2008). Some researchers have focused on the substantial preservation of "on-line obligatory, unconscious processes that assign the structure and the literal, preferred, discourse-congruent meaning of sentences" (Waters & Caplan, 2005, pp. 403–404). However, older adults require more time to encode simple ideas from text (Hartley, Stojack, Mushaney, Annon, & Lee, 1994) and often show poorer memory for the content expressed by the text (Johnson, 2003). Evidence from cognitive neuroscience also suggests that sentence meaning may be computed somewhat more slowly and perhaps not as thoroughly: The N400 component of the evoked potentials, which is somewhat larger at the introduction of a word that is anomalous within the sentence context (e.g., "Dan was so happy to meet his . . . shoe"), shows a somewhat reduced response that also occurs somewhat later relative to younger adults—although to be clear, older adults certainly do show a brain response to anomaly (Federmeier & Kutas, 2005). Age differences in text-base memory can actually be exaggerated when the goal for recall accuracy is emphasized (Stine-Morrow, Shake, Miles, & Noh, 2006), further suggesting that older readers have particular difficulty encoding the content (ideas) given directly by the text (see also Shake, Noh, & Stine-Morrow, 2009).

Perhaps as a swing of the pendulum away from the emphasis on automaticity and obligatory demands of language processing, a number of papers over the last few years have considered individual variability in the thoroughness with which linguistic computations are conducted (Christianson, Hollingsworth, Halliwell, & Ferreira, 2001; Sanford & Graesser, 2006; Sanford & Sturt, 2002; Stine-Morrow, Miller, et al., 2006), the take-home message here being that sometimes (and perhaps even often) readers create underspecified representations of the language input. In some ways, this reflects the larger zeitgeist of cognitive science that acknowledges the here-and-there quality of attentional control (Kane et al., 2007; Raichle et al., 2001). Readers "zone out" and do not always conduct full analysis of language input (Hannon & Daneman, 2004; Smallwood, Schooler, & McSpadden, in press).

Research on comprehension in the face of syntactic ambiguity illustrates this point nicely. For example, Christianson et al. (2001) found that in encountering sentences such as, "When Anna dressed the baby spit up," readers are likely to affirm that Anna dressed the baby *and* that the baby spit up. Thus, readers activate both meanings (baby as the object of being dressed and as the agent of spitting up), and even though the final correct parse forbids one interpretation, it appears nevertheless to linger, resulting in less than full understanding of the ideas expressed by the sentence (e.g., missing that Anna actually dressed herself and inappropriately retaining the idea that she dressed the baby). This is an example of *underspecification* in language understanding, that is, the tendency to not fully resolve the meaning in discourse (Hannon & Daneman, 2004; Sanford & Sturt, 2002). Much grade school humor exploits this principle (e.g., If a plane crashed in the Pyrenees between France and Spain, where will the survivors be buried? How many animals did Moses take on the ark?).

Little research has specifically examined age differences in such underspecification though some of the research described earlier is certainly consistent with this notion (e.g., age differences in N400 response; Federmeier & Kutas, 2005). Also, given arguments in the memory literature about age differences in the distinctiveness of processing (e.g., Craik & Jennings, 1992), one might expect older adults to be particularly vulnerable to such effects. In fact, existing research presents a somewhat conflicting picture. In the arena of syntactic underspecification, as in the example with Anna (not) dressing the baby, older adults do show exaggerated underspecification (Christianson, Williams, Zacks, & Ferreira, 2006). Similarly, based on allocation of reading time, some researchers have argued that older adults are less likely to encode the specific ideas from text as thoroughly (e.g., Radvansky, Zwaan, Curiel, & Copeland, 2001; Stine-Morrow, Gagne, Morrow, & DeWall, 2004). However, other research has shown quite the opposite.

Daneman, Hannon, and Burton (2006) asked younger and older adults to read a series of short passages, some of which contained an anomalous phrase, and then to answer a question. For example, in a story about Amanda staying up all night drinking coffee to study, she is bouncing off the walls because she had taken too many tranquilizing stimulants, and participants were asked what Amanda should do. College-aged readers are notoriously bad at noticing such anomalies (Barton & Sanford, 1993). Daneman et al. showed that older adults are as good as (or as bad as) younger adults in detecting such anomalies, but no worse. In fact, in tracking the eye movements of participants, these researchers showed that older adults who detected these anomalies spent longer on the anomalous phrase (i.e., tranquilizing stimulants). When the anomalous phrase was internally coherent (but still inconsistent with the passage; e.g., tranquilizing sedatives), older readers were actually likely to notice the anomaly sooner than the young (on first-pass fixations, rather than in looking back to reread).

In another investigation of age differences in underspecification, Price and Sanford (2008) presented sentences such as, "Simon sat down on the chair near the beach hut," and then presented them again in the same form or with a slight change (e.g., Simon sat on a seat or rock instead), asking participants to indicate whether the sentence was changed. Older adults were no less likely to notice the change (after a short delay) relative to the young, suggesting that they did not necessarily encode the idea of the sentence in a more shallow way. Interestingly, when the focus of the sentence was altered with a cleft construction (e.g., "What Simon sat on was the rock" vs. "It was Simon who sat on the rock"), older listeners were relatively more affected by the focus condition (i.e., especially good at recognizing the change when the syntactic construction put the critical concept in focus and especially bad at recognizing the change when the syntactic construction put the focus on another concept). This is interesting because it suggests that older adults may be particularly adept at using cues to direct attention to concepts and ideas that are more important. Thus, older adults may not simply encode textbase ideas less thoroughly (Radvansky et al., 2001; Stine-Morrow et al., 2004), but rather be more selective in which ones receive attention.

Collectively, studies of age differences in processing the explicit content given by the text are clear in demonstrating that older adults' memory for text at this level is poorer than that of younger adults (Johnson, 2003). This difference may ultimately derive in part from age differences in strategies of encoding (Stine-Morrow, Miller, et al., 2006), which may be a consequence of more selective processing as a means of coping with more limited processing resources.

Representing Discourse Structure and the Discourse Situation

In contrast to the representation of particular ideas given by the text, representations of the discourse situation, as well as of the larger discourse structure (e.g., narrative arc, line of argument in an expository text), appear to be fairly resilient through adulthood (Radvansky & Dijkstra, 2007; Stine-Morrow, Miller, Gagne, & Hertzog, 2008; Stine-Morrow, Miller, & Leno, 2001). Older readers can take good advantage of structure strategy training (i.e., identifying and focusing on components of discourse structure) to improve text memory (Meyer & Poon, 2001).

The situation model, which has received considerable attention recently, is conceptualized in different ways in the literature. In the Kintsch (1998) approach, the situation model is a representation in which ideas explicitly given by the text are integrated with ideas from the knowledge base. For example, interactions between text coherence and knowledge (i.e., the finding that high-knowledge readers show better memory for low-coherence texts while low-knowledge readers learn from more coherent texts) have been explained in terms of the rich situation model that high-knowledge readers generate through inference. The event-indexing model by Zwaan, Magliano, and Graesser (2005), on the other hand, assumes that the reader tracks a narrative protagonist along five specific dimensions (space, time, goals, intentions, emotion). Finally, the situation model has been described as a representation that is grounded in experience so that reading stimulates a perceptual simulation of events described by the text (Barsalou, 2008). For example, readers slow down in the face of spatial and temporal discontinuities (Morrow, Bower, & Greenspan, 1989; Therriault, Rinck, & Zwaan, 2006), presumably because they are tracking the spatiotemporal position of the protagonist in the narrative. Readers are faster at verifying pictures (e.g., an eagle with spread wings rather than folded wings) that are consistent with an implied shape of an object in a sentence (e.g., "The ranger saw the eagle flying in the sky" vs. ". . . perched in the tree"), presumably because the reader is simulating perception of the event described in the sentence (Zwaan, Stanfield, & Yaxley, 2002). Such findings are broadly consistent with the view that construction of the situation model depends on a generative simulation of experience.

The general consensus in the literature is that the ability to conceive of the situation suggested by the discourse is well preserved with age among literate adults. Older readers are perfectly capable of rejecting statements as false when they are inconsistent with the situation suggested by the text they have just read (Radvansky et al., 2001). In think-aloud protocols, older adults generate similar patterns of inferences about the narrative situation (McGinnis, Goss, Tessmer, & Zelinski, 2008). They slow down to reconcile discontinuities in the situation (Morrow, Stine-Morrow, Leirer, Andrassy, & Kahn, 1997; Noh et al., 2007; Radvansky et al., 2001; Stine-Morrow, Morrow, & Leno, 2002; Stine-Morrow et al., 2004), and they show strong perceptual simulation effects, as in the eagle example (Copeland & Radvansky, 2007; Dijkstra, Yaxley, Madden, & Zwaan, 2004). Also, older readers appear to follow larger discourse structures (e.g., speeding up within episodes as the narrative plot unfolds, slowing down when a new line of argument is presented in expository text; Stine-Morrow, et al., 2001; Stine-Morrow et al., 2008).

The one case where older readers may have difficulty creating a mental representation of the situation from text is when there is some demand to temporarily hold information in memory that is not yet bound together into a situation model. Copeland and Radvansky (2007) illustrated this point by presenting participants with passages such as, "The rose is above the lily. The tulip is above the orchid. The lily is to the left of the orchid." Participants then had to select the correct arrangement of items (in this case, flowers) as an indicator that they had understood the spatial situation implied by the text. In this example, the concepts were described in an AB-CD-BD arrangement so that rose and the lily (AB) had to be held in mind and the tulip and orchid (CD) had to be held in mind before their relative spatial relationship could be disambiguated by the final statement describing the arrangement of the lily and orchid (BD). In this task, older adults had much more difficulty than the younger adults conceiving the situation suggested by the text. Interestingly, older adults were at no special disadvantage when statements were presented so as to enable continuity in situation construction (e.g., an AB-BC-DC arrangement in which each statement creates incremental change in the situation). The fact that older adults did relatively well in the continuous condition suggests that they did not have difficulty in representing the spatial situation per se—and as such, jibes with the finding that older readers appear to be quite good at tracking a character through space in reading narratives (Morrow, Leirer, Altieri, & Fitzsimmons, 1994; Stine-Morrow et al., 2002). This is an interesting finding that hints that there may boundary conditions on the principle of situation model resilience, for example, when the textbase must be retained in working memory over some distance in the text before the situation is resolved.

By contrast, a well-developed situation model can make it easier to understand and remember the specific ideas presented in the text. An everyday example is when one tries to assemble something in a kit from written instructions (e.g., a grill); it is sometimes easier to understand individual steps when one first studies the diagram of the completed object to know how the pieces fit together as a whole. Similarly, there is some facilitation in understanding ideas when they are embedded in discourse (Stine-Morrow et al., 2008), and older readers take particularly good advantage of situational context to facilitate their understanding of the textbase (Miller, Cohen, & Wingfield, 2006; Miller & Stine-Morrow, 1998).

LANGUAGE PRODUCTION

The ability to produce language is an essential aspect of communication. Despite the relative ease with which individuals often convey information through speech, the process does vary considerably as we age; some components of the language production system show susceptibility to aging, while others appear to remain relatively intact into old age. Methods used to examine aspects of language production typically involve presenting participants with pictures of objects or written probes and asking them to generate an appropriate word or phrase (e.g., to identify an item or describe an event).

Word Finding and Naming

Although it is well documented that older adults have generally greater vocabularies (Verhaeghen, 2003), this advantage in the richness of available language does not always translate to smooth and effortless retrieval and production of words and, in turn, conversational fluency. Older adults are likely to make more errors in producing a word to name a given object (Feyereisen, 1997), particularly in very old age. Connor, Spiro, Obler, and Albert (2004) tracked naming performance among healthy adults for a period of 20 years; they found that the ability to accurately name objects declined fairly consistently with age at a rate of about 2% per year, but the most marked declines only occurred after age 70. Interestingly, individuals who had high initial levels of performance showed less decline with age. The source of such production difficulties remains a question of considerable debate, although it does not appear to be due to age differences in semantic access; as noted earlier, the ability to access word meaning seems to remain relatively intact. Rather, age-related changes in phonological access seem to be the more likely culprit of older adults' word production problems (Burke & Shafto, 2008; James & MacKay, 2007; LaGrone & Spieler, 2006; Mortensen, Meyer, & Humphreys, 2006).

The most convincing evidence for this explanation comes from the widely documented tip-of-the-tongue (TOT) phenomenon, which occurs when an individual is temporarily unable to retrieve a word but has a strong sense that he or she knows it. This common experience has been shown to increase in frequency with age, both in experimental studies and in studies of daily life using personal diary reports (Heine, Ober, & Shenaut, 1999; James & Burke, 2000; White & Abrams, 2002). TOT states are especially more likely in the old for low-frequency words and those with unusual grammatical class (Abrams, Trunk, & Merrill, 2007; Vitevitch & Sommers, 2003), and unusual or uncommon words are also more difficult for older adults to produce, particularly proper names lacking descriptiveness (Fogler & James, 2007; James, 2006). This increase in TOT is an experience frequently cited by older adults as being particularly frustrating (Schweich et al., 1992).

As mentioned, considerable research has been aimed at identifying the source of these deficits. The two components of lexical access (lemma selection, i.e., identifying the word and its syntactic form; and phonological form retrieval, i.e., identifying the phonemes needed to produce the word in speech) are both plausible culprits; a third possibility is some degradation in the connection between lemma selection and retrieval of the phonological form (Mortensen et al., 2006). Phonological form retrieval seems unlikely to be the sole source of the deficit, however, given that TOTs are generally age-equivalent when subjects are given a phonemic cue (e.g., a word sharing phonemes with the target word; James & Burke, 2000); although in very old age, this may not be solely enough to eliminate the TOT effect (Au et al., 1995; White & Abrams, 2002). Some researchers have interpreted the evidence thus far as best supporting the idea that degradation in the connections between the two processes is the primary source, that is, a delay in the ability to map the word unit (lemma selection) onto its phonological form (Burke & Shafto, 2008; Mortensen et al., 2006). Recent neuroscience evidence has also identified left insula atrophy as a neural correlate of the TOT deficit (Shafto, Burke, Stamatakis, Tam, & Tyler, 2007). Finally, deficits in production are also found in spelling. Accuracy seems to decline with age (especially past the age of 75; MacKay & Abrams, 1998), although the age deficits may only be present in poor spellers, suggesting age is not the only factor (Margolin & Abrams, 2007).

Producing the Coherent Utterance

Davidson, Zacks, and Ferreira (2003) examined syntactic planning in younger and older adults and found that younger and older adults were equivalent in speed and fluency when generating a sentence. However, other evidence suggests older adults have difficulty when the syntax to be produced is complex. Kemper, Herman, and Lian (2003; see also Kemper, Herman, & Liu, 2004) found that older adults showed performance similar to the young when two or three words were included in the sentence generation task, but performed more poorly when there were four words. Their sentences were also less grammatically complex than the young adults' sentences (even when their sentence production was syntactically correct and fluent), and older adults had particular difficulty with complex syntax involving verb usage. Kemper and colleagues have attributed this age deficit to declines in working memory capacity (see also Altmann & Kemper, 2006).

Beyond the Sentence: Producing Discourse

There has been an interesting body of research examining the complexity of language production across age, both in written and oral format. This research seems to show consistently that the complexity of discourse tends to decline with age, for example, in autobiographies (Kemper, Thompson, & Marquis, 2001) and in verbal samples (Kemper & Sumner, 2001). Interestingly, declines in complexity of discourse production in early adulthood are predictive of mortality rates and risk for Alzheimer's disease later in the life span (Snowdon et al., 1996).

Off-Target Verbosity

Some studies suggest older adults produce more off-topic speech (Gold & Arbuckle, 1995), although the reason for this is not entirely clear. Some have argued it is due to (1) reduced ability to inhibit the expression of irrelevant thoughts and/or (2) poorer verbal fluency (Arbuckle & Gold, 1993; Bortfeld, Leon, Bloom, Schober, & Brennan, 2001). A third alternative, however, is that increased off-topic speech is more reflective of a shift in conversational goals with age (or cohort differences in expectations for social interactions), such that older adults emphasize more personally relevant information (even if not relevant to the task or question at hand as defined by others). This idea has been borne out by data suggesting off-topic verbosity only shows age differences for personally relevant speech (e.g., during personal interviews or autobiographic questions) and not when the generation context is well-defined and task-oriented, for example, in descriptions of pictures (James, Burke, Austin, & Hulme, 1998) or in referential communication tasks (Arbuckle, Nohara-LeClair, & Pushkar, 2000).

Dysfluencies and Speech Errors

These same studies that indicate older adults are more verbose also tend to find that aging increases the frequency of some dysfluencies and speech errors, including slips of the tongue (MacKay & James, 2004), nonlexical fillers (e.g., "uh" or "um"), word repetitions, and syntactic reformulations (Bortfeld et al., 2001). The increased dysfluency may be tied to more basic word retrieval issues such as the ones discussed earlier. For example, Le Dorze and Bedard (1998) found that while young and old adults retrieved similar numbers of ideas and words about pictures they were describing, the older speakers needed more time to produce them (i.e., a lower number of unique ideas produced per minute). This reduced efficiency was related to age increases in both word repetition and self-reports of word-finding problems. It should be noted, however, that not all studies have reported age-related increases in speech dysfluencies; whether or not they occur is likely due to the type of dysfluency being examined (Schmitter-Edgecombe, Vesneski, & Jones, 2000).

Synopsis

Overall, it appears that naming ability stays relatively intact into the 70s, at which point more marked declines occur. The evidence suggests older adults tend to have more dysfluencies and speech errors when producing language but that the source of these problems may be due specifically to word-finding difficulties. These word-finding difficulties, as expressed in phenomenon such as the TOT experience, do not appear to be due to declines in the ability to access the meanings of words, but rather to difficulty in accessing information about surface features.

Communication in Context

Language understanding is self-regulated in the sense that there is some choice in the degree to which different facets of the representation are elaborated as a function of the goals of the reader or listener (Stine-Morrow, 2007; Stine-Morrow, Miller, et al., 2006). We have certainly all had the experience of discussing something we have read or a movie we have seen with a friend, only to discover that what we each remember from the text or movie is very different. Depending on what our interests are, what we already know about the topic, and what our immediate purpose is, the thoroughness of different sorts of processing can vary. The fact that there is the opportunity for knowledge growth through adulthood (Ackerman & Rolfus, 1999) and the suggestion that age-related changes in time perspective may drive change in the role of cognition (Carstensen et al., 2006) are important factors to consider in creating opportunities for communicative contexts that will be effective across the life span.

One implication of the aging demographic is that venues such as classrooms, workplace training sites, and community meetings are more likely to be populated by older adults, a factor that needs to be taken into account to create contexts for effective communication, learning, and decision making. Text design needs to take into account older readers. Though clichéd, reminders to avoid small print and reverberating sound systems are nevertheless valid, not only because they limit processing of the surface form, but also because they detract from one's ability to allocate attention effectively to the meaning of the message. Similarly, a fast speech rate can be particularly problematic for older adults; recall from our review that age differences in text memory are often minimized when older adults can control the pacing.

At the same time, older adults learning in a domain in which they already have established knowledge structures may show a level of facility to rival young learners (Miller & Stine-Morrow, 1998; Miller et al., 2006). Older adults who are knowledgeable in a domain may be particularly likely to focus their attention on the most relevant parts of a problem and productively elaborate it (Miller, Stine-Morrow, Kirkorian, & Conroy, 2004; Morrow et al., 2008).

Even though, as we have seen, older adults are typically found to encode fewer text ideas, this is usually demonstrated in an experimental context in which there may be little intrinsic reason to exert effort except to demonstrate one's competence to an experimenter that one is likely never to see again. Age differences in text memory have been found to be substantially reduced by a context (in this case, retelling a story to a child instead of recalling it to an experimenter) that provides a socioemotional motivation for attending to the textbase (Adams, Smith, Pasupathi, & Vitolo, 2002).

The implication of viewing language processing as at least in part self-regulated (Stine-Morrow et al., 2008; Stine-Morrow, Miller, et al., 2006) is that there is substantial choice in how one faces any communicative endeavor. The landscape of adult development requires that we adapt our communicative strategies so as to be effective in different contexts.

A final note: Even though certain age-related changes can make engagement in reading, conversation, and other communicative contexts somewhat more challenging, it may be that these are the very activities that will help to maintain cognitive vitality. For example, there is some evidence that habitual reading may slow cognitive decline in the early stages of Alzheimer's disease (Wilson et al., 2000). One provocative line of research in recent years suggests that bilingualism (and even more so, multilingualism) has cognitive benefits that are more pronounced as one grows older, particularly in the area of executive control (Bialystok, Craik, & Freedman, 2007; Bialystok, Craik, & Luk, 2008; Kavé, Eyal, Shorek, & Cohen-Mansfield, 2008). These findings have been explained in terms of the constant linguistic requirement of managing two language systems in which one is fluent (e.g., selective activation of lexical items in one language while suppression corresponding information from the other language). Such research is a reminder of the two-way street of investing effort as one grows older: Cognitive activities sometimes require a greater investment of resources to maintain one's earlier level of effectiveness, but this investment can pay off in increased capacity with which to meet subsequent challenges.

REFERENCES

Abrams, L., Trunk, D. L., & Merrill, L. A. (2007). Why a superman cannot help a tsunami: Activation of grammatical class influences resolution of young and older adults' tip-of-the-tongue states. *Psychology and Aging, 22,* 835–845.

Ackerman, P. L., & Rolfhus, E. L. (1999). The locus of adult intelligence: Knowledge, abilities, and nonability traits. *Psychology and Aging, 14,* 314–330.

Adams, C., Smith, M. C., Pasupathi, M., & Vitolo, L. (2002). Social context effects on story recall in older and younger women: Does the listener make a difference? *Journal of Gerontology: Psychological Sciences, 57B,* P28–P40.

Allen, P. A., Madden, D. J., Weber, T. A., & Groth, K. E. (1993). Influence of age and processing stage on visual word recognition. *Psychology and Aging, 8,* 274–282.

Altmann, L. P., & Kemper, S. (2006). Effects of age, animacy, and activation order on sentence production. *Language and Cognitive Processes, 21,* 322–354.

Arbuckle, T. Y., & Gold, D. P. (1993). Aging, inhibition, and verbosity. *Journal of Gerontology: Psychological Sciences, 48,* 225–232.

Arbuckle, T. Y., Nohara-LeClair, M., & Pushkar, D. (2000). Effect of off-target verbosity on communication efficiency in a referential communication task. *Psychology and Aging, 15,* 65–77.

Au, R., Joung, P., Nicholas, M., Obler, L. K., Kaas, R., & Albert, M. L. (1995). Naming ability across the adult life span. *Aging and Cognition, 2,* 300–311.

Baltes, P. B., Staudinger, U. M., & Lindenberger, U. (1999). Lifespan psychology: Theory and application to intellectual functioning. *Annual Review of Psychology, 50,* 471–507.

Barsalou, L. W. (2008). Grounded cognition. *Annual Review of Psychology, 59,* 617–645.

Barton, S. B., & Sanford, A. J. (1993). A case study of anomaly detection: Shallow semantic processing and cohesion establishment. *Memory & Cognition, 21,* 477–487.

Bialystok, E., Craik, F.I.M., & Freedman, M. (2007). Bilingualism as a protection against the onset of symptoms of dementia. *Neuropsycholgia, 45,* 459–464.

Bialystok, E., Craik, F.I.M., & Luk, G. (2008). Cognitive control and lexical access in younger and older bilinguals. *Journal of Experimental Psychology: Learning, Memory, and Cognition, 34,* 859–873.

Bortfeld, H., Leon, S. D., Bloom, J. E., Schober, M. F., & Brennan, S. E. (2001). Disfluency rates in conversation: Effects of age, relationship, topic, role, and gender. *Language and Speech, 44,* 123–149.

Braver, T. S., & West, R. (2008). Working memory, executive control, and aging. In F.I.M. Craik & T. A. Salthouse (Eds.), *The Handbook of Aging and Cognition* (3rd ed., pp. 311–372). New York: Psychology Press.

Burke, D. M., & Shafto, M. A. (2008). Language and aging. In F.I.M. Craik & T. A. Salthouse (Eds.), *The Handbook of Aging and Cognition* (3rd ed., pp. 373–443). New York: Psychology Press.

Carstensen, L. L., Mikels, J. A., & Mather, M. (2006). Aging and the intersection of cognition, motivation, and emotion. In J. E. Birren & K. W. Schaie (Eds.), *Handbook of the Psychology of Aging* (6th ed., pp. 343–362). New York: Academic Press.

Christianson, K., Hollingsworth, A., Halliwell, J., & Ferreira, F. (2001). Thematic roles assigned along the garden path linger. *Cognitive Psychology, 42,* 368–407.

Christianson, K., Williams, C. C., Zacks, R. T., & Ferreira, F. (2006). Younger and older adults' "good-enough" interpretations of garden-path sentences *Discourse Processes, 42,* 205–238.

Connor, L. T., Spiro, A., Obler, L. K., & Albert, M. L. (2004). Change in object naming ability during adulthood. *Journal of Gerontology: Psychological Sciences, 59B,* 203–209.

Copeland, D. E., & Radvansky, G. A. (2007). Aging and integrating spatial situation models. *Psychology and Aging, 22,* 569–579.

Craik, F.I.M., & Jennings, J. M. (1992). Human memory. In F.I.M. Craik & T. A. Salthouse (Eds.), *The Handbook of Aging and Cognition* (pp. 51–110). Hillsdale, NJ: Lawrence Erlbaum Associates.

Daneman, M., Hannon, B., & Burton, C. (2006). Are there age-related differences in shallow semantic processing of text? Evidence from eye movements. *Discourse Processes, 42,* 177–203.

Davidson, D. J., Zacks, R. T., & Ferreira, F. (2003). Age preservation of the syntactic processor in production. *Journal of Psycholinguistic Research, 32,* 541–566.

Dennis, N. A., & Cabeza, R. (2008). Neuroimaging of healthy cognitive aging. In F.I.M. Craik & T. A. Salthouse (Eds.), *The Handbook of Cognitive Aging* (3rd ed., pp. 1–54). New York: Psychology Press.

Dijkstra, K., Yaxley, R. H., Madden, C. J., & Zwaan, R. A. (2004). The role of age and perceptual symbols in language comprehension. *Psychology and Aging, 19,* 352–356.

Eckert, M. A., Walczak, A., Ahlstrom, J., Dennslow, S., Horwitz, A., & Dunbo, J. R. (2008). Age-related effects on word recognition: Reliance on cognitive control systems with structural declines in speech-responsive cortex. *Journal of the Association for Research in Otolaryngology, 9,* 252–259.

Federmeier, K. D., & Kutas, M. (2005). Age in context: Age-related changes in context use during language comprehension. *Psychophysiology, 42,* 133–141.

Feyereisen, P. (1997). A meta-analytic procedure shows an age-related decline in picture-naming: Comments on Goulet, Ska, & Kahn. *Journal of Speech and Hearing Research, 40,* 1328–1333.

Fogler, K. A., & James, L. E. (2007). Charlie Brown versus Snow White: The effects of descriptiveness on young and older adults' retrieval of proper names. *Journals of Gerontology: Psychological Sciences, 62,* 201–207.

Gold, D. P., & Arbuckle, T. Y. (1995). A longitudinal study of off-target verbosity. *Journal of Gerontology: Psychological Sciences, 50,* 307–315.

Gordon-Salant, S., & Fitzgibbons, P. J. (2001). Sources of age-related recognition difficulty for time-compressed speech. *Journal of Speech, Language, and Hearing Research, 44,* 709–719.

Gordon-Salant, S., Fitzgibbons, P. J., & Friedman, S. A. (2007). Recognition of time-compressed and natural speech with selective temporal enhancements by young and elderly listeners. *Journal of Speech, Language, and Hearing Research, 50,* 1181–1193.

Graesser, A. C., Millis, K. K., & Zwaan, R. A. (1997). Discourse processing. *Annual Review of Psychology, 48,* 163–189.

Hannon, B., & Daneman, M. (2004). Shallow semantic processing of text: An individual-differences approach. *Discourse Processes, 37,* 187–204.

Hartley, J. T., Stojack, C. C., Mushaney, T. J., Annon, T.A.K., & Lee, D. W. (1994). Reading speed and prose memory in older and younger adults. *Psychology and Aging, 9,* 216–223.

Heine, M. K., Ober, B. A., & Shenaut, G. K. (1999). Naturally occurring and experimentally induced tip-of-the-tongue experiences in three adult age groups. *Psychology and Aging, 14,* 445–457.

Helfer, K. S., (1998). Auditory and auditory-visual recognition of clear and conversational speech by older adults. *Journal of the American Academy of Audiology, 9,* 234–242.

Humes, L. E., Burk, M. H., Coughlin, M. P., Busey, T. A., & Strauser, L. E. (2007). Auditory speech recognition and visual text recognition in younger and older adults: Similarities and differences between modalities and the effects of presentation rate. *Journal of Speech, Language, and Hearing Research, 50,* 283–303.

James, L. E. (2004). Meeting Mr. Farmer versus meeting a farmer: Specific effects of aging on learning proper names. *Psychology and Aging, 19,* 515–522.

James, L. E. (2006). Specific effects of aging on proper name retrieval: Now you see them, now you don't. *Journal of Gerontology: Psychological Sciences, 61,* 180–183.

James, L. E., Burke, D. M. (2000). Phonological priming effects on word retrieval and tip-of-the-tongue experiences in young and older adults. *Journal of Experimental Psychology: Learning, Memory, and Cognition, 26,* 1378–1391.

James, L. E., & Burke, D. M., Austin, A., & Hulme, E. (1998). Production and perception of "verbosity" in younger and older adults. *Psychology and Aging, 13,* 355–367.

James, L. E., & Mackay, D. G. (2007). New age-linked asymmetries: Aging and the processing of familiar versus novel language on the input versus output side. *Psychology and Aging, 22,* 94–103.

Johnson, R. E. (2003). Aging and the remembering of text. *Developmental Review, 23,* 261–346.

Kane, M. J., Brown, L. H., McVay, J. C., Silvia, P. J., Myin-Germeys, I., & Kwapil, T. R. (2007). For whom the mind wanders, and when: An experience-sampling study of working memory and executive control in daily life. *Psychological Science, 18,* 614–621.

Kavé, G., Eyal, N., Shorek, A., & Cohen-Mansfield, J. (2008). Multilingualism and cognitive state in the context of the oldest old. *Psychology and Aging, 23,* 70–78.

Kemper, S., Herman, R., & Lian, C. (2003). Age differences in sentence production. *Journal of Gerontology: Psychological Sciences, 58,* 260–268.

Kemper, S., Herman, R., & Liu, C. J. (2004). Sentence production by young and older adults in controlled contexts. *Journal of Gerontology: Psychological Sciences, 59,* 220–224.

Kemper, S., & Sumner, A. (2001). The structure of verbal abilities in young and older adults. *Psychology and Aging, 16,* 312–322.

Kemper, S., Thompson, M., & Marquis, J. (2001). Longitudinal change in language production: Effects of aging and dementia on grammatical complexity and propositional content. *Psychology and Aging, 16,* 227–239.

Kintsch, W. (1998). *Comprehension: A Paradigm for Cognition.* New York: Cambridge University Press.

LaGrone, S., & Spieler, D. H. (2006). Lexical competition and phonological encoding in young and older speakers. *Psychology and Aging, 21,* 804–809.

Le Dorze, G., & Bedard, C. (1998). Effects of age and education on the lexico-semantic content of connected speech in adults. *Journal of Communication Disorders, 31,* 53–71.

Lien, M-C., Allen, P. A., Ruthruff, E., Grabbe, J., McCann, R. S., & Remington, R. W. (2006). Visual word recognition without central attention: Evidence for greater automaticity with advancing age. *Psychology and Aging, 21,* 431–447.

Mackay, D. G., & Abrams, L. (1998). Age-linked declines in retrieving orthographic knowledge: Empirical, practical, and theoretical implications. *Psychology and Aging, 13,* 647–662.

Mackay, D. G., & James, L. E. (2004). Sequencing, speech production, and selective effects of aging on phonological and morphological speech errors. *Psychology and Aging, 19,* 93–107.

Margolin, S. J., & Abrams, L. (2007). Individual differences in young and older adults' spelling: Do good spellers age better than poor spellers? *Aging, Neuropsychology, and Cognition, 14,* 529–544.

McGinnis, D., Goss, R. J., Tessmer, C., & Zelinski, E. M. (2008). Inference generation in young, young-old, and old-old adults: Evidence for semantic architecture stability. *Applied Cognitive Psychology, 22,* 171–192.

McGinnis, D., & Zelinski, E. M. (2000). Understanding unfamiliar words: The influence of processing resources, vocabulary knowledge, and age. *Psychology and Aging, 15,* 335–350.

McGinnis, D., & Zelinski, E. M. (2003). Understanding unfamiliar words in young, young-old, and old-old adults: Inferential processing and the abstraction-deficit hypothesis. *Psychology and Aging, 18,* 497–509.

Meyer, B.J.F., & Poon, L. W. (2001). Effects of structure strategy training and signaling on recall of text. *Journal of Educational Psychology, 93,* 141–159.

Miller, L.M.S., Cohen, J. A., & Wingfield, A. (2006). Contextual knowledge reduces demands on working memory during reading. *Memory & Cognition, 34,* 1355–1367.

Miller, L.M.S., & Stine-Morrow, E.A.L. (1998). Aging and the effects of knowledge on on-line reading strategies. *Journal of Gerontology: Psychological Sciences, 53B,* P223–P233.

Miller, L.M.S., Stine-Morrow, E.A.L., Kirkorian, H., & Conroy, M. (2004). Age differences in knowledge-driven reading. *Journal of Educational Psychology, 96,* 811–821.

Morrow, D. G., Bower, G. H., & Greenspan, S. L. (1989). Updating situation models during comprehension. *Journal of Memory and Language, 28,* 292–312.

Morrow, D. G., Leirer, V., Altieri, P., & Fitzsimmons, P. (1994). Age differences in updating situation models from narratives. *Language and Cognitive Processes, 9,* 203–220.

Morrow, D. G., Miller, L.M.S., Ridolfo, H. E., Magnor, C., Fischer, U. M., Kokayeff, N. K., et al. (2008). Expertise and age differences in pilot decision making. *Aging, Neuropsychology, and Cognition, 16,* 33–55.

Morrow, D. G., Stine-Morrow, E.A.L., Leirer, V. O., Andrassy, J. M., & Kahn, J. (1997). The role of reader age and focus of attention in creating situation models from narratives. *Journal of Gerontology: Psychological Sciences, 52B,* P73–P80.

Mortensen, L. M., Meyer, A. S., & Humphreys, G. W. (2006). Age-related effects on speech production: A review. *Language and Cognitive Processes, 21*, 238–290.

Noh, S. R., Shake, M. C., Joncich, A. D., Parisi, J. M., Morrow, D. G., & Stine-Morrow, E.A.L. (2007). Age differences in learning from text: The effects of content pre-exposure on reading. *International Journal of Behavioral Development, 31*, 133–148.

Pichora-Fuller, M. K., Schneider, B. A., & Daneman, M. (1995). How young and old adults listen to and remember speech in noise. *Journal of the Acoustical Society of America, 97*, 593–608.

Price, J. M., & Sanford, A. J. (2008, April). *Focus Effects in Healthy Aging: Ease of Reference and Shallow Processing.* Paper presented at the Cognitive Aging Conference, Atlanta, GA.

Radvansky, G. A., & Dijkstra, K. (2007). Aging and situation model processing. *Psychonomic Bulletin and Review, 14*, 1027–1042.

Radvansky, G. A., Zwaan, R. A., Curiel, J. M., & Copeland, D. E. (2001). Situation models and aging. *Psychology and Aging, 16*, 145–160.

Raichle, M. E., MacLeod, A. M., Snyder, A. Z., Powers, W. J., Gusnard, D. A., & Shulman, G. L. (2001). A default mode of brain function. *Proceedings of the National Academy of Sciences, 98*, 676–682.

Rayner, K., Reichle, E. D., Stroud, M. J., Williams, C. C., & Pollatsek, A. (2006). The effect of word frequency, word predictability, and font difficulty on the eye movements of young and older readers. *Psychology and Aging, 21*, 448–465.

Salthouse, T. A. (1996). The processing-speed theory of adult age differences in cognition. *Psychological Review, 103*, 403–428.

Sanford, A. J., & Graesser, A. C. (2006). Shallow processing and underspecification. *Discourse Processes, 42*, 99–108.

Sanford, A. J., & Sturt, P. (2002). Depth of processing in language comprehension: Noticing the evidence. *Trends in Cognitive Sciences, 6*, 382–386.

Schaie, K. W. (1996). *Intellectual Development in Adulthood: The Seattle Longitudinal Study.* Cambridge, UK: Cambridge University Press.

Schmitter-Edgecombe, M., Vesneski, M., & Jones, D.W.R. (2000). Aging and word-finding: A comparison of spontaneous and constrained naming tests. *Archives of Clinical Neuropsychology, 15*, 479–493.

Schneider, B. A., Daneman, M., & Murphy, D. R., (2005). Speech comprehension difficulties in older adults: Cognitive slowing or age-related changes in hearing? *Psychology and Aging, 20*, 261–271.

Schneider, B. A., Daneman, M., & Pichora-Fuller, M. K. (2002). Listening in aging adults: From discourse comprehension to psychoacoustics. *Canadian Journal of Experimental Psychology, 56*, 139–152.

Schweich, M., Van der Linden, M., Bredart, S., Bruyer, R., Nelles, B., & Schils, J. P. (1992). Daily-life difficulties in person recognition reported by young and elderly subjects. *Applied Cognitive Psychology, 6*, 161–172.

Shafto, M. A., Burke, D. M., Stamatakis, E. A., Tam, P. P., & Tyler, K. K. (2007). On the tip-of-the-tongue: Neural correlates of increased word-finding failures in normal aging. *Journal of Cognitive Neuroscience, 19*, 2060–2070.

Shake, M. C., Noh, S. R., & Stine-Morrow, E.A.L. (2009). Age differences in learning from text: Evidence for functionally distinct text processing systems. *Applied Cognitive Psychology, 23*, 561–578.

Singer, T., Verhaeghen, P., Ghisletta, P., Lindenberger, U., & Baltes, P. B. (2003). The fate of cognition in very old age: Six-year longitudinal findings in the Berlin Aging Study (BASE). *Psychology and Aging, 18*, 318–331.

Smallwood, J., Schooler, J. W., & McSpadden, M. (in press). When attention matters: The curious incident of the wandering mind. *Memory & Cognition.*

Snowdon, D. A., Kemper, S., Mortimer, J. A., Greiner, L. H., Wekstein, D. R., & Markesbery, W. R. (1996). Cognitive ability in early life and cognitive function and Alzheimer's disease in late life: Findings from the Nun study. *Journal of the American Medical Association, 275*, 528–532.

Speranza, F., Daneman, M., & Schneider, B. A. (2000). How aging affects the reading of words in noisy backgrounds. *Psychology and Aging, 15*, 253–258.

Spieler, D. H., & Balota, D. A. (2000). Factors influencing word naming in younger and older adults. *Psychology and Aging, 15*, 225–231.

Stine, E.A.L., & Wingfield, A. (1987). Process and strategy in memory for speech among younger and older adults. *Psychology and Aging, 2*, 272–279.

Stine-Morrow, E.A.L. (2007). The Dumbledore Hypothesis of cognitive aging. *Current Directions in Psychological Science, 16*, 289–293.

Stine-Morrow, E.A.L., Gagne, D. D., Morrow, D. G., & DeWall, B. H. (2004). Age differences in rereading. *Memory and Cognition, 32*, 696–710.

Stine-Morrow, E.A.L., Miller, L.M.S., Gagne, D. D., & Hertzog, C. (2008). Self-regulated reading in adulthood. *Psychology and Aging, 23*, 131–153.

Stine-Morrow, E.A.L., Miller, L.M.S., & Hertzog, C. (2006). Aging and self-regulated language processing. *Psychological Bulletin, 132*, 582–606.

Stine-Morrow, E.A.L., Miller, L.M.S., & Leno, R. (2001). Patterns of on-line resource allocation to narrative text by younger and older readers. *Aging, Neuropsychology, and Cognition, 8*, 36–53.

Stine-Morrow, E.A.L., Morrow, D. G., & Leno, R. (2002). Aging and the representation of spatial situations in narrative understanding. *Journal of Gerontology: Psychological Sciences, 57B*, P91–P97.

Stine-Morrow, E.A.L., Shake, M. C., Miles, J. R., & Noh, S. R. (2006). Adult age differences in the effects of goals on self-regulated sentence processing. *Psychology and Aging, 21*, 790–803.

Therriault, D. J., Rinck, M., & Zwaan, R. A. (2006). Assessing the influence of dimensional focus during situation model construction. *Memory & Cognition, 34*, 78–89.

Thompson, L. A. (1995). Encoding and memory for visible speech and gestures: A comparison between young and older adults. *Psychology and Aging, 10*, 215–228.

Thornton, R., & Light, L. L. (2006). Language comprehension and production in normal aging. In J. Birren & K. W. Schaie (Eds.), *Handbook of the Psychology of Aging* (6th ed., pp. 129–161). Burlington, MA: Elsevier Academic Press.

Verhaeghen, P. (2003). Aging and vocabulary score: A meta-analysis. *Psychology and Aging, 18*, 332–339.

Vitevitch, M. S., & Sommers, M. S. (2003). The facilitative influence of phonological similarity and neighborhood frequency in speech production in younger and older adults. *Memory and Cognition, 31*, 491–504.

Waters, G. S., & Caplan, D. (2005). The relationship between age, processing speed, working memory capacity, and language comprehension. Memory, 13, 403–413.

White, K. K., & Abrams, L. (2002). Does priming specific syllables during tip-of-the-tongue states facilitate word retrieval in older adults? *Psychology and Aging*, *17*, 226–235.

Whiting, W. L., Madden, D. J., Langley, L. K., Denny, L. L., Turkington, T. G., Provenzale, J. L., et al. (2003). Lexical and sublexical components of age-related change in neural activation during word identification. *Journal of Cognitive Neuroscience*, *15*, 475–487.

Wilson, R. S., Bennett, D. A., Gilley, D. W., Beckett, L. A., Barnes, L. L., & Evans, D. A. (2000). Premorbid reading activity and patterns of cognitive decline in Alzheimer Disease. *Archives of Neurology*, *57*, 1718–1723.

Wingfield, A., Alexander, A. H., & Cavigelli, S. (1994). Does memory constrain utilization of top-down information in spoken word recognition? Evidence from normal aging. *Language and Speech*, *37*, 221–235.

Wingfield, A., & Grossman, M. (2006). Language and the aging brain: Patterns of neural compensation revealed by functional brain imaging. *Journal of Neurophysiology*, *96*, 2830–2839.

Wingfield, A., Poon, L. W., Lombardi, L., & Lowe, D. (1985). Speed of processing in normal aging: Effects of prosody and linguistic structure. *Journal of Gerontology*, *40*, 579–585.

Wingfield, A., Stine, E.A.L., Lahar, C. J., & Aberdeen, J. S. (1988). Does the capacity of working memory change with age? *Experimental Aging Research*, *14*, 103–107.

Wingfield, A., Tun, P. A., Koh, C. K., & Rosen, M. J. (1999). Regaining lost time: Adult aging and the effect of time restoration on recall of time-compressed speech. *Psychology and Aging*, *14*, 380–389.

Wingfield, A., Tun, P. A., & McCoy, S. L. (2005). Hearing loss in older adults: What it is and how it interacts with cognitive performance. *Current Directions in Psychological Science*, *14*, 144–148.

Zwaan, R. A., Magliano, J. P., & Graesser, A. C. (1995). Dimensions of situation model construction in narrative comprehension. *Journal of Experimental Psychology: Learning, Memory, and Cognition*, *21*, 386–397.

Zwaan, R. A., & Rapp, D. N. (2006). Discourse comprehension. In M. J. Traxler & M. A. Gernsbacher (Eds.), *Handbook of Psycholinguistics* (2nd ed., pp. 725–764). New York: Academic Press.

Zwaan, R. A., Stanfield, R. A., & Yaxley, R. H. (2002). Language comprehenders mentally represent the shape of objects. *Psychological Science*, *13*, 168–171.

CHAPTER 4

EVERYDAY PROBLEM SOLVING

Jennifer A. Margrett, Jason C. Allaire,
Tara L. Johnson, Kate E. Daugherty,
and Sarah R. Weatherbee

Within the cognitive aging literature, everyday problem-solving research has gained momentum as proponents point to the value added by using such an approach (see Allaire & Marsiske, 2002). By focusing on what older adults actually do in their day-to-day lives, clinicians and researchers can improve ecological validity and reduce the artificiality of testing situations often employed in experimental research. Also, gerontological professionals may better approximate how older adults perform in their own real-life settings outside of a contrived laboratory setting. These efforts may lead to increased assessment efficiency as well as beneficial psychosocial consequences, such as increased research participation by older adults and greater self-efficacy when performing familiar and "real" tasks (Marsiske & Margrett, 2006). However, a central issue remains regarding everyday problem solving, namely its relation to daily functioning and, in part, the difficulty identifying an appropriate standard consistent with actual daily demands by which success can be determined (Marsiske & Margrett, 2006).

In the following sections, we examine several issues related to everyday problem solving in adulthood. First, we describe the construct of everyday problem solving and how it differs from the traditional psychometric approach used to assess cognitive ability. Second, several methodological considerations related to everyday problem-solving assessments are outlined, including the nature of the problem, scoring criteria, and content. Such issues are paramount as we consider aging and assessment of everyday abilities. Third, we examine the value added by adopting an everyday problem-solving approach, namely the relation to older adults' real-world outcomes, including functioning, cognitive status, and mortality.

DEFINING AND EXAMINING EVERYDAY PROBLEM-SOLVING ABILITY IN ADULTHOOD

Everyday problem solving is difficult to define, even among researchers in the field. As summarized by Marsiske and Margrett (2006), various classifications for this construct include everyday cognition, practical problem solving, and practical intelligence. Reasons for this diversity are likely due to the range of methods employed to assess variables of interest that result from varied theoretical traditions (Marsiske & Margrett, 2006). Everyday *problem solving*, rather than *cognition* or *intelligence*, is often used as a broad term for this approach (Marsiske & Margrett, 2006) because *problem solving* is easier to explain to research participants and lay persons compared to the latter terms (Willis & Schaie, 1993).

The everyday problem-solving approach can be differentiated from two other approaches common to cognitive aging that focus on the psychometric and clinical features of intellectual abilities (Margrett & Deshpande-Kamat, 2009). The traditional psychometric approach focuses on individual abilities (e.g., working memory, processing speed) and their assessment, particularly as related to age differences and changes. Key questions often focus on how abilities relate to one another, the development of performance norms, and the characterization of changes in abilities over the life course. Also of interest have been trends in these abilities among age cohorts or different generations. In contrast, the clinical approach centers on distinguishing normal from abnormal cognitive ability (e.g., presence of mild cognitive impairment or dementia) as well as understanding of the mechanisms underlying abnormal cognition. A key issue for clinicians is determination of mental status, which is often determined in a dichotomous manner (i.e., Is performance above or below a designated threshold?).

Everyday cognition could be viewed as a blend of the psychometric and clinical approaches. Everyday problem solving is concerned with adults' real-world functional abilities and capacities and, particularly in older adulthood, being able to care for one's self and to manage personal affairs (Willis, 1996). Compared to the other two approaches, the field of everyday problem solving faces unique methodological challenges. What the field lacks is a unified approach to skill and competency assessment. From the clinical perspective emerges commonly accepted multidimensional measures of general cognitive status (e.g., Mini-Mental Status Examination [MMSE]; Folstein, Folstein, & McHugh, 1975). Measures such as the MMSE are useful tools in distinguishing broad categories of cognitive functioning (i.e., normal performance from dementia-impaired performance). The problem for many clinicians and researchers is that measures such as the MMSE provide a relative lack of sensitivity and the ability to distinguish less disparate groups. A real contribution of the field of everyday problem solving could be the development of measures distinguishing degrees of competency on higher-level cognitive skills. Throughout this chapter we discuss why such a goal is difficult to attain.

The everyday approach to cognitive aging combines a focus on the context in which an individual performs needed tasks (i.e., contextualism), how higher-order cognitive functioning relates to individual skills identified via the psychometric approach (i.e., componentialism), the relation of experience and practice with performance, and understanding the nature of older adults' strategies and solutions (i.e., postformalism; Marsiske & Margrett, 2006). Figure 4.1 depicts the theoretical relation between psychometric cognitive abilities, everyday problem solving, and functioning as well as the factors influencing each of these constructs. Practically, utilizing such an "everyday" approach to the assessment of cognitive skill is beneficial in that researchers can gain a more accurate understanding of how well older adults accomplish the tasks they likely face in their daily lives. Being able to perform everyday tasks is essential for functional health maintenance and independence, therefore, the term *everyday cognitive competence* is often coined (Willis, 1996). *Competence* can be viewed as the evaluation of performance or functioning, which is influenced by several factors, including the nature of the task and assessment criteria.

As mentioned by Willis (1996), the majority of real-world problem solving should be similar to what older adults face in their daily lives. However, assessing task performance and "competence" is complicated by the need to consider both individual and environmental contexts. One argument is that performance of everyday problem-solving ability should be evaluated on an individual basis of personal achievement because an older adult's goals may vary depending on environmental, social, and cultural demands (Blanchard-Fields & Chen, 1996). Performance that is deemed adequate will likely vary based on perspective. For instance, does self judgment, proxy-rating, or comparison with an objective indicator provide the "best" benchmark for determining the minimal level of performance required? It is reasonable to assume that information will vary across data sources and that the factors influencing assessments may be weighed differentially across sources (MacDonald, Martin, Margrett, & Poon, in press). Determination of the veridicality of varying assessments may not be an important aim as varied assessments may provide unique and complimentary information that serves to complete more of the picture.

As implied by the functional/complex nature of these tasks, everyday problem-solving ability is considered to be a higher-order cognitive skill representative of executive functioning and dependent upon constituent intellectual abilities such as memory and reasoning (Marsiske & Willis, 1995). We

Figure 4.1   Relation of Cognition, Problem-Solving Ability, and Everyday Functioning and Competence.

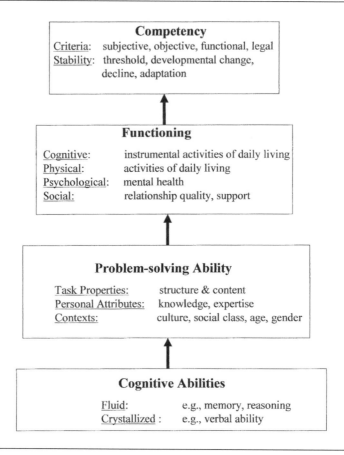

Sources: "Dimensionality of Everyday Problem Solving in Older Adults, by M. Marsiske and S. L. Willis, 1995. *Psychology and Aging, 10*, 269–283; "Cognition and everyday competence," by S. L. Willis, 1991. In K. W. Schaie (Ed.), *Annual Review of Gerontology and Geriatrics* (vol. 11, pp. 80–109). New York: Springer.

now turn to a brief discussion of the relation of everyday problem-solving ability to psychometric cognitive abilities and age-related differences.

EVERYDAY PROBLEM SOLVING: RELATION TO BASIC COGNITIVE ABILITIES AND AGE DIFFERENCES

Age group differences and intraindividual changes in performance of ability-specific assessments, such as memory, reasoning, verbal ability, and perceptual speed, are well documented (e.g., Schaie, 2005). Abilities relying on knowledge that becomes "crystallized," or strengthened by experience, tend to remain stable throughout middle adulthood and early later life (Schaie, 2005). Examples of such abilities are verbal comprehension and vocabulary. In comparison, "fluid" abilities, which are less dependent on experience, tend to peak in young adulthood (Schaie, 2005). These abilities are believed to be more innate and biologically driven and often center on the ability to deal with novel situations (e.g., reasoning). In comparison to the psychometric abilities, less is known about developmental changes in everyday cognition. Readers are referred to two recent reviews of the everyday problem-solving literature, which detail empirical studies in this area (see Marsiske & Margrett, 2006; Thornton & Dumke, 2005). We provide a brief summary here.

As noted by Marsiske and Margrett (2006), most research implementing the everyday problem-solving approach is of a cross-sectional nature. Problem-solving ability as measured by accuracy or efficiency tends to be negatively related to age (Marsiske & Margrett, 2006). In contrast, findings are more complex when considering problem-solving fluency, or the ability to generate multiple or more qualitative solutions. As discussed by Marsiske and Margrett, observed age-related differences on more ambiguous tasks may not represent later life "deficits," but rather meaningful differences in older adults' problem-solving goals and style. This harkens back to our discussion of the "best" or most useful assessment, which likely depends on the researcher's or clinician's aims and their understanding and appreciation of respondents' goals. A central issue remains regarding everyday problem solving, namely its relation to everyday functioning and, in part, the difficulty identifying an "appropriate validation criterion" (Marsiske & Margrett, 2006).

In addition to a lack of longitudinal data, there is little research examining everyday cognition in very late life. However, some findings suggest that these skills may be preserved well into late life. For example, within the Georgia Centenarian Study, oldest-old and centenarian participants' ability to solve everyday problems was quite robust (Poon, Clayton, et al., 1992; Poon, Messner, Martin, & Noble, 1992).

The relation between secondary cognitive abilities (i.e., crystallized and fluid skills) and everyday problem-solving ability has been examined. As noted by Marsiske and Margrett (2006), crystallized and fluid skills both tend to be moderately to strongly correlated with problem-solving ability; this relationship may be due to some degree of overlap in assessments, particularly for fluid skills and well-structured problem-solving tasks. Additional research is needed to understand how changes in basic cognitive abilities (i.e., dedifferentiation of abilities, terminal change and drop; e.g., Bosworth & Siegler, 2002; de Frias, Lövdén, Lindenberger, Nilsson, 2007) relate to changes in everyday problem-solving ability in later adulthood.

METHODOLOGICAL CONSIDERATIONS IN EVERYDAY PROBLEM-SOLVING RESEARCH

Generalizing from empirical studies employing diverse theoretical and methodological perspectives is a challenge to researchers. As detailed by Willis (1991), three commonalities underlying problem-solving ability include the nature of the task, characteristics of the problem solver, and context; all of which must be considered when interpreting study findings regarding age differences. As described by Willis and others, the structure (e.g., less structured tasks with multiple solutions vs. well structured tasks with one correct solution) as well as the content (e.g., interpersonal dilemma vs. instrumental problem) of the task can vary. Individual and group differences are also evident across problem solvers, who may vary in important ways such as degree of knowledge, expertise, and efficacy (Willis). For instance, important caveats to consider are the problem solver's educational attainment and the problem content (e.g., age relevancy) as they influence cognitive task performance. Third, the context in which older adults solve problems impacts the task process and outcome.

Given the nature of problem solving, its assessment is more complex compared to the psychometric approach to individual intellectual skills. The everyday problem-solving perspective has led researchers to consider a variety of methodological domains within the everyday cognition literature. The strength of this approach is that diverse tasks are considered. However, the difficulty lies in comparisons across tasks when interpreting age differences. This section highlights several methodological challenges apparent in the everyday cognition literature.

Nature of the Everyday Problem

The majority of knowledge obtained related to everyday cognitive abilities relies almost solely on laboratory assessments, which have been characterized as heterogeneous and diverse (Allaire & Marsiske, 1999; Marsiske & Willis, 1995), largely due to variations in task structure, instruction, scoring, and problem domain. As a result of these variations, which likely stem from mixed theoretical roots (Marsiske & Margrett, 2006), the construct validity of such everyday problem-solving assessments is questionable (D'Zurilla, Maydeu-Olivares, & Kant, 1998) as is the generalizability of research findings across laboratories (Neely, 2006). Additionally, investigation of age-related differences and changes may be artificially masked or exacerbated depending on the methodological approach. If these varied methodologies prove to be valid and reliable, the generalizability of results could be strengthened.

Ill-Structured and Well-Structured Tasks

One apparent methodological discrepancy in the everyday cognition literature involves the structure of the problem-solving task. Some problems are considered ill-structured, others are described as well-structured, and some fall in between. Ill-structured tasks are often open-ended and lack a clear definition of the problem, the means to solve it, and/or an ultimate goal or endpoint (Allaire & Marsiske, 2002; Thornton & Dumke, 2005). As a result of the ambiguous nature of the problem, suggested solutions provided by an individual depend on how that person interprets aspects of the scenario that are not explicitly stated (Blanchard-Fields, 2007). An example of such an item comes from the work of Denney and Pearce (1989) in which respondents were presented with the following scenario: "Suppose an elderly woman needs to go somewhere at night. She cannot see well enough to drive at night and it's too far to walk. What should she do?" This is an ill-structured item because the situation is ambiguous (e.g., degree of neighborhood safety, availability of alternative transportation) and the goal is unclear (e.g., Is the most important goal to obtain a needed item or to remain safe?).

These types of ill-structured tasks are often described as unpredictable and continually transforming (Blanchard-Fields, 2007); as such, researchers and clinicians may not adequately assess a true "everyday" problem in the life of a particular older adult individual. Also relevant to understanding age-related differences and changes is the role of prior experience. The majority of ill-structured everyday cognitive assessments typically include hypothetical situations in which individuals draw on accumulated knowledge to solve problems (Blanchard-Fields, 2007). Acquired knowledge due to past experiences with problems may allow older adults to perform quite well.

Compared to ill-structured tasks, well-structured tasks are at the other end of the "definedness continuum" (Allaire & Marsiske, 2002). Well-structured tasks, such as completing a tax form correctly, typically draw upon primary cognitive abilities that tend to decline with older age (Blanchard-Fields, 2007). When completing well-defined tasks, the problem solver is presented with a clearly defined problem, the means and information to solve it, and a desired end state (Allaire & Marsiske, 2002). An example of a well-structured everyday task is Willis and Marsiske's (1993) Everyday Problems Test (EPT). The EPT provides participants with stimuli (e.g., insurance matrix) and asks various questions regarding the information presented (e.g., How much would it cost if Mr. Jones had a 21-day inpatient stay?). This type of task targets an individual's ability to accurately solve a problem using existing printed information. Another example of a well-structured task is a performance-based task called Observed Tasks of Daily Living, which utilizes real-life props (e.g., a telephone, money; Diehl et al., 2005; Diehl, Willis, & Schaie, 1995). Participants are asked to perform a variety of tasks (e.g., look up a telephone number and dial it, produce change from a lunch bill), behaviors are observed, and proficiency is scored. The means to solve the problem are clearly defined in both examples, as is the desired endpoint of the problem.

TASK INSTRUCTIONS AND SCORING PROCEDURES

The level of structure, definition, and clarity of ill- and well-defined tasks influences other measurement strategies, such as the task instructions and scoring procedures. Methodological issues as they concern performance differences in adult age groups have not been largely emphasized in recent research, but there is some evidence to suggest that varied instructions and scoring procedures may impact the extent to which age differences in everyday cognition are apparent.

Due to the nature of ill-structured tasks, the instructions are often designed to urge participants to specify multiple ways of solving the problem. Common everyday problem-solving instructions state, "Tell me all the ways you can solve this problem" (e.g., Haught, Hill, Nardi, & Walls, 2000; Heidrich & Denney, 1994) or some similar form of those instructions (e.g., "Generate as many safe and effective solutions as possible"; Allaire & Marsiske, 2002; Margrett & Marsiske, 2002). These types of task instructions advise participants to use their repertoire of coping strategies when encountering everyday problems. Given varying researcher goals, multiple methods exist to "score" participant responses on ill-defined tasks.

The two primary methods cited in the literature to score ill-structured problem responses are fluency and strategy evaluation, which may mask or exacerbate performance differences between age groups. Fluency refers to the sum of unique solutions generated by respondents (e.g., Artistico, Cervone, & Pezzuti, 2003; Berg, Meegan, & Klaczynski, 1999; Heidrich & Denney, 1994; Margrett & Marsiske, 2002; Strough, McFall, Flinn, & Schuller, 2008). A greater number of strategies is believed to indicate superior problem-solving ability, as several responses signify creativity or flexibility in thinking and practically would also serve to increase the likelihood of finding an effective solution (Denney & Pearce, 1989; Sinnott, 1989; Spivack & Shure, 1982).

Older adults may be at a disadvantage when fluency is the scoring procedure used. Denney, Pearce, and Palmer (1982) found that older individuals generated fewer solutions than younger and middle-aged individuals, even when presented with problems considered to be personally relevant to older adults. Other research demonstrates a tendency for older individuals to produce fewer solutions compared to younger individuals on ill-defined tasks (e.g., Berg et al., 1999; Crawford & Channon, 2002). One explanation for older adults' disadvantage on such tasks is their decline in constituent mental abilities related to everyday cognitive abilities (e.g., Allaire & Marsiske, 1999; Diehl et al., 1995). An alternative explanation is that older adults, due to their past experiences with problems, intentionally limit their solutions (Berg et al., 1999; Blanchard-Fields, Mienaltowski, & Seay, 2007; Labouvie-Vief, Hakim-Larson, & Hobart, 1987). For instance, older adults may write down only the best solutions (e.g., what has worked in the past) and purposely exclude other potential solutions (e.g., ones they would not implement), even when instructed to generate as many strategies as possible. Younger adults, on the other hand, may write down all possible solutions they imagine, including solutions that are likely to be ineffective (e.g., "shoot the dog" as a solution to having a neighbor with a pet that makes noise; Neely, 2005). If multiple ineffective strategies are produced, it could be detrimental to everyday life (e.g., ignoring a potentially dangerous situation, getting arrested). As a result, some researchers who use ill-defined tasks prefer to examine performance based on strategy effectiveness or strategy type rather than only fluency (e.g., Blanchard-Fields et al., 2007; Strough et al., 2008; Strough, Patrick, & Swenson, 2003; Watson & Blanchard-Fields, 1998). Strough and colleagues (2008) specifically argue that relying on fluency takes away from an understanding of the effectiveness of the strategies implemented in a given situation. One way to assess strategy type is to dichotomize participant solutions into categories of solutions such as problem-focused and emotion-focused (e.g., Blanchard-Fields, Stein, & Watson, 2004; Strough et al., 2008). Similarly, Neely (2006) examined four categories of strategies, including avoidance-denial, passive dependence, planful problem solving, and cognitive analysis. When strategy type is examined, older adults typically perform similar to younger adults (e.g., Blanchard-Fields, Jahnke, & Camp, 1995; Neely, 2006). Thus, it appears that this scoring procedure negates the age differences suggested by fluency outcome when completing ill-structured tasks.

Well-structured problems, like their ill-structured counterparts, use instructions that coincide with the nature of the task. Well-structured task instructions often ask individuals to rate the likelihood that a behavior would be used (e.g., Blanchard-Fields et al., 2007; Cornelius & Caspi, 1987), generate one correct solution based on information provided (e.g., Willis & Marsiske, 1993), or perform a task given appropriate props (e.g., Diehl et al., 2005). These instructions influence the scoring procedures used, which are typically in line with the psychometric approach to intelligence (Blanchard-Fields, 2007).

One type of scoring involves mean likelihood ratings provided by judges (e.g., Blanchard-Fields et al., 1995, 2007; Cornelius & Caspi, 1987). With this type of scoring, independent judges who are considered experts in the field rate endorsed behaviors to determine which individuals would be the most effective problem solvers. For example, judges determine if "telling a friend about the gossip" is better or worse than "leaving the situation." After assessing participants' endorsements using this scoring procedure, Cornelius and Caspi (1987) found a positive relationship between problem-solving ability and age. Older adults endorsed more efficient responses compared to younger adults. The results of a study by Blanchard-Fields and colleagues (2007) also indicated that older adults were more effective problem solvers when judges rated endorsed strategies.

Another common scoring method for well-structured tasks emphasizes performance accuracy or correctness of the response (e.g., Burton, Strauss, Hultsch, & Hunter, 2006; Kimbler, 2006; Marsiske & Willis, 1995). Specifically, an individual receives a score for the total number of correct responses. Higher scores indicate better problem-solving ability. The existing research using accuracy or performance-based scoring procedures tends to focus solely on older adults. Future research needs to address whether or not there are age differences using these types of scoring procedures and how the findings compare to scoring procedures used for ill-structured tasks.

In daily life, the necessary skills to succeed are likely to encompass all aspects of the solutions discussed previously, including creativity and flexibility in thinking as well as problem-solving effectiveness and accuracy. For example, there are incidences when an individual has many options to consider before implementing a strategy, such as when a family member hurts one's feelings or when criticism is received from one's boss. On the other hand, there may also be situations in which adults must generate one correct response to function appropriately or healthfully in daily life, such as understanding the dosage of medication necessary to survive or to avoid foods that are high in cholesterol. Although the problem-solving outcomes that are assessed vary substantially in terms of ill- versus well-structured tasks (e.g., Allaire & Marsiske, 2002; Thornton & Dumke, 2005), both types of tasks are pertinent to fully understand everyday cognition and the capacity of older adults to complete meaningful activities of daily living.

Problem Domain and Content

In addition to instruction and scoring issues surrounding ill- and well-structured tasks, the content of the problem to be solved also varies both across laboratories and even within individual everyday cognitive assessments (Blanchard-Fields et al., 2007; Marsiske & Margrett, 2006; Strough et al., 2008; Thonrton & Dumke, 2005). Researchers have examined performance differences on instrumental or practical tasks as well as the emotionality of the problem. Whether or not the target of the problem is one's self or another person may also differentially influence problem-solving performance.

Instrumental and Interpersonal Domains

Some problems are classified as being more interpersonal in nature because the problem involves other people, whereas other problems are defined as instrumental because they primarily involve concerns regarding competence and individual functioning. Watson and Blanchard-Fields (1998), for example, used the following interpersonal problem in their study, "A person has a 16-year-old daughter who keeps taking the car several times a week. The family only has one car." Artistico and colleagues (2003) used the following instrumental item in their study, "A person finds himself/herself having difficulties getting to sleep at night. What should he/she do?" Some problem types possess both interpersonal and instrumental components, which makes dichotomizing tasks more difficult (Blanchard-Fields et al., 2007). Whether the problem is interpersonal, instrumental, or mixed, the issues to be solved are germane to adults' lives because they target a wide range of situations encountered during daily living. However, a limited number of studies have examined performance differences across age groups on these various problem types.

In a recent everyday problem-solving study, younger, middle-aged, and older adults were compared on fluency and strategy type when completing ill-structured interpersonal (dealing with friend conflicts) and instrumental (dealing with household tasks) issues (Neely, 2006). For the instrumental problems, middle-aged adults generated more solutions compared to older adults. However, when strategy type was assessed, all age groups were equally proactive in their strategy use. For interpersonal problems, Neely found that younger adults generated more solutions compared to older adults in the study; however, when strategy type was assessed, older adults were actually more proactive than younger adults in their reported strategy use. Blanchard-Fields and colleagues (2007) found that when completing instrumental problems, younger adults endorsed more avoidant-denial strategies than older adults, but older adults preferred more passive-dependent, planful problem solving and cognitive analysis strategies. For interpersonal problems, older adults endorsed more avoidant-denial and cognitive analysis strategies than younger adults. Perhaps the patterns of differences varied between these two recent studies because of the issues surrounding scoring, as discussed previously. Neely coded reported strategies on an open-ended task, whereas Blanchard-Fields and colleagues asked participants to endorsed strategies that were provided.

Emotionality of Content

A line of research by Blanchard-Fields and her colleagues has also examined the influence of emotional content on problem-solving strategies. For example, Blanchard-Fields, Jahnke, and Camp (1995) manipulated whether everyday problems were low in emotional involvement (e.g., returning defective merchandise, a tenant's problem), medium in emotional involvement (e.g., wife returning to workforce, moving to a new town), or high in emotional involvement (e.g., caring for an ill parent, dealing with an alcoholic spouse). They were interested in how the emotionality of problems influenced the types of strategies used to solve the problem (i.e., problem-focused, cognitive-analytical, passive-dependent, or avoidant-denial). Results revealed that highly emotional problems resulted in a greater variety of strategies used, especially for older adults. Overall, problem-focused strategies were used less often during highly emotional problem solving, whereas passive-dependent and cognitive-analytical problems were used more often as the degree of emotional involvement increased.

One criticism of this study was that the problems were hypothetical and may not have adequately addressed the true nature of real-life problem solving. Thus, Blanchard-Fields, Stein, and Watson (2004) instructed participants to describe a personal problem that was *not* emotional for them (e.g., disagreement with relatives, transferring to a new college) and to also report a problem that *was* highly emotional for them (e.g., death of a child, parent, or spouse; communication problems). After describing the problem, participants were asked to report the ways in which they handled the situations. The results indicated that highly emotional problems resulted in a higher degree of strategies used, whereas low emotionality of problems resulted in a lower degree of strategies used. Additionally, middle-aged adults were more likely to take action when confronting an emotional problem, whereas younger and older adults reported using more passive strategies.

While Blanchard-Fields and colleagues' research examined strategy type rather than strategy effectiveness, Weitzman and Weitzman (2001) qualitatively examined four levels of strategy use associated with various types of problems reported by middle-aged women. Their results indicated that lower levels of strategy effectiveness were implemented when a real-life problem involved a high degree of emotional distress. In contrast, higher levels of strategy effectiveness were reported when a personal problem was less emotionally charged. When the findings regarding emotional components of various problems are considered together, it can be concluded that the emotionality of a situation clearly influences one's way of responding to a problem. Thus, researchers who use and also create assessments to examine everyday problem-solving outcome should consider the emotional content of each item included in the task.

In addition to examining the actual emotional components of the task, some researchers have tried to alter the problem-solving setting to induce various emotions when completing a task. Kimbler (2006) manipulated verbal statements provided to middle-aged and older participants before completing a well-structured everyday problem-solving task. Participants received either standard instructions (the control group), practical support (availability of researcher to assist, if needed), or emotional support (appreciation for participation). Study findings indicated that participants who were made to feel appreciated (emotional component) performed better on the everyday task compared to those who were given practical support or standard instructions. Kimbler's results suggest that even subtle verbal manipulations made prior to completion of an everyday problem-solving task may influence performance.

Target of the Problem

Individuals are bound to encounter all sorts of problems during the course of living, and those problems will likely vary in terms of structure, content, and emotionality. Another aspect to consider regarding problem content is whether the individual is dealing with his or her own personal issue or whether the problem is that of others. In other words, the target of the problem may be different (self problem vs. another person's problem). As illustrated in some previous examples, researchers may ask individuals, "What do you do to solve the problem?" (e.g., Allaire & Marsiske, 2002), whereas other researchers may ask, "What should he/she do to solve the problem?" (e.g., Artistico et al., 2003). When presented with a dilemma, individuals may think differently about their own personal problems compared to consideration of another person's situation. One's own personal problems may elicit a greater emotional reaction than when considering a problem affecting someone else. For example, if you have an argument with a loved one and need to figure out what to do yourself, the situation is emotional. However, if your coworker has an argument with a loved one and asks you for help, the situation is much less emotional for you.

Neely (2006) examined whether manipulating the target of the problem affected fluency or strategy types used to solve hypothetical ill-structured tasks. Her findings revealed that younger adults generated more solutions compared to older adults when solving problems that asked, "What should *you* do to solve the problem?" Middle-aged adults generated more solutions compared to younger and older adults when solving problems that ask, "What should *the* person do to solve the problem?" However, when strategy types were analyzed, there were no age differences in proactive strategy use for "self" or "other" targets. This finding supports our previous point regarding age differences that may or may not emerge when considering varied methodologies.

Some of the methodological problems discussed previously arise when assessing other aspects of cognition, such as intelligence (e.g., primary abilities, secondary abilities). Perhaps the multiple methods used to examine everyday problem solving are currently essential in the field of everyday cognition to uncover the contextual elements underlying everyday cognitive performance. Various methodologies that use tighter controls may further reveal that everyday cognition is multidimensional, like intelligence, and one unifying aspect of everyday cognition likely does not exist. Using several assessments to examine the different components of everyday cognition may be essential to fully capture the true nature of it. Further research is needed in order to propose a concrete theoretical model of everyday cognition, and longitudinal work may help reveal what happens to various aspects of everyday cognition over time.

REAL-WORLD CORRELATES

As discussed earlier, the study of everyday cognition was predicated on the notion that traditional measures of cognition may fail to appropriately capture older adults' cognition in context and that more ecologically valid assessments are needed (e.g., Berg & Sternberg, 1985). Consequently, the literature is replete with varied assessments of everyday cognition and studies examining age differences in and predictors of performance on these measures (e.g., Marsiske & Margrett, 2006; Thornton & Dumke, 2005). Unfortunately, less attention has been paid to addressing the question of whether or not there is value added by assessing everyday cognition (Allaire & Marsiske, 2002; Berg, 2008; Weatherbee & Allaire, 2008). If everyday cognition captures cognition in the real world, then it stands to reason that performance on such measures should be strongly related to real-world outcomes. In fact, everyday cognition should be more related to these real-world outcomes than measures of cognition if the thesis that initiated the field is correct. Otherwise, studying everyday cognition does not "buy" us anything, other than what was afforded by traditional psychometric measures of cognitive functioning.

This section provides a review of the limited work examining the relationship between everyday cognition and important real-world outcomes. These outcomes may vary depending on whether the focus is on instrumental everyday cognition (Allaire & Marsiske, 1999), where the outcome might be daily functioning (e.g., ability to perform instrumental activities of daily living [IADL]), or socioemotional/interpersonal everyday cognition (e.g., Berg & Klaczynski, 2002; Blanchard-Fields & Chen, 1996; Blanchard-Fields et al., 2007), where emotional well-being might be of interest.

Instrumental Everyday Cognition and Outcomes

Most of the attempts to link everyday cognition with real-world outcomes come from the work focusing on instrumental domains. This focus is not surprising given that the ability to solve instrumental everyday problems regarding medication, nutrition, or financial management should have real-world implications (Willis, 1991; Willis & Schaie, 1986). Empirical studies link instrumental everyday cognitive abilities with important outcomes including day-to-day functioning, mortality, and cognitive impairment.

Everyday Functioning

Diehl and colleagues (1995) administered an objective measure of everyday cognition in which older adults use actual stimuli, such as a medication bottle or a page from the phone book, and are asked to solve everyday problems based on those stimuli. Performance on this measure predicted older adults' performance on an in-home behavioral observation of IADL performance. Allaire and Marsiske (2002) examined the relationship between older adults' self-ratings of competency performing instrumental tasks of daily living and performance on the Everyday Cognition Battery (ECB; Allaire, 1998; Allaire & Marsiske, 1999), which assesses older adults' memory, reasoning, and knowledge abilities within the instrumental domains of medication use, financial management, and food preparation/nutrition. Using an ethnically heterogeneous sample of 174 older adults ranging from 60 to 91 years, performance on the ECB was positively and significantly associated with older adults' everyday competency. More importantly, the ECB explained all of the variance associated with basic cognitive abilities as well as providing unique predictive salience in accounting for almost 50% of the variance in older adults' everyday competency.

Mortality

In addition to everyday functioning, previous cognitive aging research has examined mortality as an outcome of everyday cognitive functioning. This area is important for the validity of everyday cognitive assessments given that previous cross-sectional research has established a link between decline in basic cognitive functioning and an increased risk of mortality (Bosworth, Schaie, & Willis, 1999; Johansson et al., 2004; Maier & Smith, 1999; Small & Bäckman, 1997; Swan, Carmelli, & LaRue, 1995). Weatherbee and Allaire (2008) identified 56 participants from the original ECB data collection (Allaire & Marsiske, 1999, 2002) who were deceased and used performance on three of the ECB subtests (Reasoning, Memory, and Knowledge) in 1996 to predict time to death. Results indicated that better performance on two of the tests, the ECB Knowledge and ECB Reasoning tests, was significantly associated with a decrease in the risk of death. Moreover, the ECB Knowledge test, which captures domain-specific knowledge, remained significant even after controlling for performance on basic cognitive abilities as well as self-rated health. It is possible that limitations in everyday knowledge could actually be associated with real-world behaviors that potentially compromise competency and put older adults at risk for serious adverse outcomes such as death (i.e., Maier & Smith, 1999). This mechanism makes intuitive sense given that ECB taps adaptive knowledge regarding medication usage, nutrition, and financial management.

Similar results were reported by Allaire and Willis (2006), who used data from 773 rural older adults assessed at two time points separated by 2 years. After controlling for general cognitive status as assessed by the MMSE (Folstein et al., 1975), better performance on a measure of instrumental everyday cognition at Time 1 was associated with a decreased risk of mortality. In addition, decline in performance from Time 1 to Time 2 was significantly associated with an increased risk of mortality.

Mild Cognitive Impairment

Mild cognitive impairment (MCI) is hypothesized as the transitional period between normal aging and dementia, where conversion rates from MCI to dementia range from 6%–25% depending on the assessment method and study duration (Petersen et al., 2001). MCI is marked by reduced cognitive capacity defined by a number of different criteria (Jorm, Christensen, Korten, Jacob, & Henderson, 2001; Jorm et al., 2004; Petersen, 2000). The maintenance of activities of daily living is one of the factors differentiating mild cognitive impairment (MCI) from dementia (Petersen). However, there is growing evidence to suggest that difficulties performing more complex instrumental everyday tasks might be observed in older adults with MCI (e.g., Farias et al., 2006; Griffith et al., 2003; Okonkwo, Wadley, Griffith, Ball, & Marson, 2006; Perneczky et al., 2006; Wadley et al., 2007). Therefore, performance on real-world measures of everyday cognition may be useful in identifying older adults with or at risk for MCI.

In the longitudinal study of rural older adults by Allaire and Willis (2006), discussed earlier, older adults were assigned ratings using the Clinical Dementia Rating scale (CDR; Hughes, Berg, Danziger, Coben, & Martin, 1982). Participants that received a CDR of 0 (no impairment) were assigned to the *intact group*, older adults with ratings of possible/incipient impairment (CDR = .05) were assigned to the *possible impaired group*, and those participants with a CDR of 1 or greater were assigned to the *impaired group*. At both occasions of measurement (separated by 2 years), the nonimpaired participants performed significantly higher, on average, than the possible impaired and impaired groups. In addition, the impaired group performed significantly worse than the possible impaired group. Everyday Problems for the Cognitively Challenged Elderly (EPCCE) performance of the non-impaired group was approximately 1.68 and 1.76 SD units above that of the impaired group at Time 1 and Time 2, respectively. In addition, relative to the nonimpaired participants, decline in everyday problem-solving performance over the 2-year interval was significantly greater for impaired participants and those participants who transitioned from nonimpaired to impaired over the course of the study.

Conclusions and Future Directions

As discussed throughout this chapter, compared to a traditional, psychometric approach, adopting an everyday approach can afford clinicians and researchers an opportunity to assess skill and performance on tasks that older adults are more likely to encounter in their own daily lives. The everyday cognition field has propelled cognitive aging research forward beyond the laboratory. The fruits of this effort have been development of more naturalistic tasks and appreciation of task and problem-solver context. The next challenge appears to be careful consideration of how best to evaluate performance. Along with the flexibility and benefits related to adopting an "everyday" approach to the assessment and study of cognitive development, several areas need to be explored in order to advance this line of inquiry. This review of the everyday problem-solving literature suggests several avenues for future research with the underlying objective of developing assessments that are both sensitive to individual contexts and useful in detecting and predicting meaningful change.

First, we agree with Marsiske and Margrett (2006) that to advance the field it is critically important that researchers establish and validate everyday problem-solving performance against criteria meaningful within older adults' lives. It is clear that criteria are needed by which to assess performance and judge competency. This is not an easy or straightforward task because the nature of *everyday cognition* is quite complex and can vary from person to person; even for one person, ability can vary from task to task and certainly over time as ability and goals change. Adding to the complexity is the diversity of tasks discussed throughout this chapter and the degree of domain specificity, which has not been fully explicated. Several important outcomes related to everyday problem-solving ability are evident, such as IADL and functional ability, mental status, and mortality; however, it is less clear how to distinguish competency within the realm of everyday problems. Determining competency may be more concrete for instrumental tasks that are well structured and require a linear or rationale approach (e.g., completing an insurance form). The task is more daunting for ill-structured problems, including those of a socioemotional nature, which vary due to individual perceptions, expectations, and goals (e.g., resolving a disagreement with a family member).

A second issue central to this line of inquiry is the question, "What is an 'everyday' cognitive ability?" This question is increasingly complex as the nature of everyday life changes, seemingly at a faster and faster rate. The answer may lie in considering how skills vary by problem-solver characteristics and context as noted by Willis (1991). The cognitive skills needed to survive and excel throughout one's life certainly vary by cultural and age-cohort context. Within the psychometric approach to cognition, researchers have documented cohort or generational differences in cognitive development and ability. For example, mathematical ability decreased across successive generations—a change speculated to be the result of the handheld calculator, which freed individuals from regularly performing mathematical operations mentally or by hand (Schaie, 2005). Additional research is needed to investigate analogous cohort changes within everyday problem-solving ability. In contemporary societies, which skills are needed and thus further developed versus which skills are no longer an "everyday" necessity? Technology seems central to this question. For example, during the course of the 2008 U.S. presidential election, debate ignited following remarks by Senator John McCain alluding to the limited scope of his computer literacy and knowledge (Leibovich, 2008). Many Americans voiced the opinion that technological abilities are a necessary and crucial everyday skill in contemporary society. The debate likely symbolizes a "technological divide" across cohorts. With rapidly increasing technology use, it is not clear what impact technological skills will have on the field of everyday cognition and cognitive intervention. There is a rise in computer-assisted technologies to enhance the lives of older adults and persons with disabilities; however, it is not clear that the technological solutions posed will resonate with or be effectively used by these consumers.

In addition to technology and cohort-related differences in everyday skill perceptions and use, current demographics compel us to consider cultural context. Several pertinent research questions arise when we consider the aforementioned issues and investigations incorporating multiple cultures. Issues related to task, learner, and context should be in the forefront of cognitive research (e.g., Manly, Bryd, Touradji, & Stern, 2004; Prince, 2000; Willis, 1991). Several key issues emerge related to age and culture and their effects on clinical and research efforts. First, the question arises as to which cognitive skills are nurtured and required throughout an adults' life. Relevant to the current discussion is identification of skills that are expected, supported, and/or practiced in later life. Second, what is the degree of cultural specificity as related to needed everyday cognitive skills? How does cultural context and background impact the criterion by which we assess everyday competency in adulthood and older age? How do individuals from multicultural backgrounds fare in late life? Finally, we might inquire if the theoretical hierarchy relating cognitive abilities, problem solving, and functioning holds across cultural groups. These questions are reminiscent of prior theoretical and empirical work examining cognitive development in childhood as well as the work of individuals examining culturally relevant skills in early childhood and the equivalence of measures.

A final issue is sensitivity of assessment. As noted earlier, changes in the ability to perform needed daily activities are evident in dementia and may signal significant decline within the context of mild cognitive impairment. Measures that capture real-time change and can assist prevention and intervention efforts are warranted. Yet to be fully explored is the nature of change in everyday problem-solving ability (see Nesselroade, 2001, for a discussion). In addition to traditional longitudinal work, empirical studies of intraindividual variability in everyday problem solving are needed. Such an approach assumes that the everyday cognitive competency captured at one occasion of measurement might not represent performance the previous or following days. That is, older adults' abilities to solve cognitively complex tasks might fluctuate from one day to the next depending on factors such as stress, affect/mood, or alertness.

In summary, the everyday cognition perspective has helped to advance the ecological validity of cognitive aging research via development of more naturalistic assessments, consideration of individual contexts, and recognition of the diversity of problem outcomes, which may not fall neatly into a dichotomous division of correctness. However, much work lies ahead as researchers attempt to further bridge the psychometric and clinical approaches. Researchers must grapple with developing appropriate validation criteria, addressing issues of more macro-focused context, such as culture and technology, and improving methodological approaches that are sensitive to change.

REFERENCES

Allaire, J. C. (1998). *Investigating the Antecedents of Everyday Cognition: The Creation of a New Measure.* Unpublished master's thesis, Wayne State University, Michigan.

Allaire, J. C., & Marsiske, M. (1999). Everyday cognition: Age and intellectual ability correlates. *Psychology and Aging, 14*(4), 627–644.

Allaire, J. C., & Marsiske, M. (2002). Well- and ill-defined measures of everyday cognition: Relationship to older adults' intellectual ability and functional status. *Psychology and Aging, 17,* 101–115.

Allaire, J. C., & Willis, S. L. (2006). Competence in everyday activities as a predictor of cognitive risk and mortality. *Aging, Neuropsychology, and Cognition, 13*(2), 207–224.

Artistico, D., Cervone, D., & Pezzuti, L. (2003). Perceived self-efficacy and everyday problem-solving among young and older adults. *Psychology and Aging, 18,* 68–79.

Berg, C. A. (2008). Everyday problem solving in context. In S. Hofer & D. Alwin (Eds.), *Handbook of Cognitive Aging: Interdisciplinary Perspectives* (pp. 207–223). Thousand Oaks, CA: Sage.

Berg, C. A., & Klaczynski, P. A. (2002). Contextual variability in the expression and meaning of intelligence. In R. J. Sternberg & E. L. Grigorenko (Eds.), *The General Factor of Intelligence: How General Is It?* (pp. 381–412). Mahwah, NJ: Lawrence Erlbaum Associates.

Berg, C. A., Meegan, S. P., & Klaczynski, P. (1999). Age and experiential differences in strategy generation and information requests for solving everyday problems. *International Journal of Behavioral Development, 23*, 615–639.

Berg, C. A., & Sternberg R. J. (1985). A triarchic theory of intellectual development during adulthood. *Developmental Review, 5*(4), 334–370.

Blanchard-Fields, F. (2007). Everyday problem solving and emotion: An adult developmental perspective. *Current Directions in Psychological Science, 16*, 26–31.

Blanchard-Fields, F., & Chen, Y. (1996). Adaptive cognition and aging. *American Behavioral Scientist, 29*(3), 231–248.

Blanchard-Fields, F., Jahnke, H. C., & Camp, C. (1995). Age differences in problem-solving style: The role of emotional salience. *Psychology and Aging, 10*, 173–180.

Blanchard-Fields, F., Mienaltowski, A., & Seay, R. B. (2007). Age differences in everyday problem-solving effectiveness: Older adults select more effective strategies for interpersonal problems. *The Journals of Gerontology: Psychological Sciences, 62B*, P61–P64.

Blanchard-Fields, F., Stein, R., & Watson, T. L. (2004). Age differences in emotion-regulation strategies in handling everyday problems. *Journals of Gerontology: Psychological Sciences, 59*, 261–269.

Bosworth, H. B., Schaie, W. K., & Willis, S. L. (1999). Cognitive and sociodemographic risk factors for morality in the Seattle longitudinal study. *Journals of Gerontology: Psychological Sciences, 54B*(5), 273–282.

Bosworth, H. B., & Siegler, I. C. (2002). Terminal change in cognitive functioning: An updated review of longitudinal studies. *Experimental Aging Research, 28*(3), 299–315.

Burton, C. L., Strauss, E., Hultsch, D. F., & Hunter, M. A. (2006). Cognitive functioning and everyday problem solving in older adults. *Clinical Neuropsychologist, 20*, 432–452.

Cornelius, S. W., & Caspi, A. (1987). Everyday problem solving in adulthood and old age. *Psychology and Aging, 2*, 144–153.

Crawford, S., & Channon, S. (2002). Dissociation between performance on abstract tests of executive function and problem solving in real-life-type situations in normal aging. *Aging & Mental Health, 6*, 12–21.

D'Zurilla, T. J., Maydeu-Olivares, A., & Kant, G. L. (1998). Age and gender differences in social problem-solving ability. *Personality and Individual Differences, 25*, 241–252.

de Frias, C. M., Lövdén, M., Lindenberger, U., & Nilsson, L. G. (2007). Revisiting the dedifferentiation hypothesis with longitudinal multi-cohort data. *Intelligence, 35*, 381–392.

Denney, N. W., & Pearce, K. A. (1989). A developmental study of practical problem solving in adults. *Psychology and Aging, 4*, 438–442.

Denney, N. W., Pearce, K. A. & Palmer, A. M. (1982). A developmental study of adults' performance on traditional and practical problem-solving tasks. *Experimental Aging Research, 8*, 115–118.

Diehl, M., Willis, S., & Schaie, K. W. (1995). Everyday problem solving in older adults: Observational assessment and cognitive correlates. *Psychology and Aging, 10*(3), 478–491.

Diehl, M., Marsiske, M., Horgas, A. L., Rosenberg, A., Saczynski, J. S., & Willis, S. L. (2005). The Revised Observed Tasks of Daily Living: A performance-based assessment of everyday problem solving in older adults. *Journal of Applied Geron-tology, 24*, 211–230.

Farias, S. T., Mungas, D., Reed, B. R., Harvey, D, Cahn-Weiner, & DeCarli, C. (2006). MCI is associated with deficits in everyday functioning. *Alzheimer Disease and Associated Disorders, 20*(4), 217–223.

Folstein, M. F., Folstein, S. E., & McHugh, P. R. (1975). Mini-mental state: A practi-cal method for grading the cognitive state of patients for the clinician. *Journal of Psychiatric Research, 12*(3), 189–198.

Griffith, H. R., Belue, K., Sicola, A., Krzywanski, S., Zamrini, E., Harrell, L., et al. (2003). Impaired financial abilities in mild cognitive impairment: A direct assess-ment approach. *Neurology, 60*(3), 449–457.

Haught, P. A., Hill, L. A., Nardi, A. H., & Walls, R. T. (2000). Perceived ability and level of education as predictors of traditional and practical adult problem solving. *Experimental Aging Research, 26*, 89–101.

Heidrich, S. M., & Denney, N. W. (1994). Does social problem solving differ from other types of problem solving during the adult years? *Experimental Aging Research, 20*, 105–126.

Hughes, C., Berg, L., Danziger, W., Coben, L., & Martin, R. (1982). A new clinical scale for the staging of dementia. *The British Journal of Psychiatry, 140*, 566–572.

Johansson, B., Hofer, S. M., Allaire, J. C., Maldonado-Molina, M. M., Piccinin, A. M., Berg, S., et al. (2004). Change in cognitive capabilities in the oldest old: The ef-fects of proximity to death in genetically related individuals over a 6-year period. *Psychology and Aging, 19*(1), 145–156.

Jorm, A. F., Christensen, H., Korten, A. E., Jacob, P. A., & Henderson, A. S. (2001). Memory complaints as a precursor of memory impairment in older people: A lon-gitudinal analysis over 7–8 years. *Psychological Medicine, 31*, 441–449.

Jorm, A. F., Masaki, K. H., Davis, D. G., Hardman, J., Nelson, J., Markesbery, W. R., et al. (2004). Memory complaints in nondemented men predict pathologic diag-nosis of Alzheimer disease. *Neurology, 63*(2), 1960–1961.

Kimbler, K. J. (2006). *The Effect of Experimentally-provided Supportive Messages on Middle-age and Older Adults' Performance on Everyday Problems.* Unpublished doctoral disser-tation, West Virginia University.

Labouvie-Vief, G., Hakim-Larson, J., & Hobart, C. J. (1987). Age, ego-level, and the life-span development of coping and defense processes. *Psychology and Aging, 2*, 286–293.

Leibovich, M. (2008, August, 3). McCain, the analog candidate. *The New York Times.* Retrieved August 3, 2009, from: http://www.nytimes.com/2008/08/03/weekinreview/03leibovich.html?_r=1&ref=weekinreview&oref=slogin.

MacDonald, M., Martin, P., Margrett, J., & Poon, L. W. (in press). Correspondence of perceptions about centenarians' mental health. Manuscript submitted for publica-tion. *Journal of Aging and Mental Health.*

Maier, H., & Smith, J. (1999). Psychological predictors of mortality in old age. *Journals of Gerontology: Series B: Psychological Sciences and Social Sciences, 54B*(1), 44–54.

Manly, J. J., Bryd, D. A., Touradji, P., & Stern, Y. (2004). Acculturation, reading level, and neuropsychological test performance among African American elders. *Applied Neuropsychology, 11*(1), 37–46.

Margrett, J. A., & Deshpande-Kamat, N. (2009). Cognitive functioning and decline. In D. Carr (Ed.), *Encyclopedia of the Life Course and Human Development.* Farmington Hills, MI: Gale.

Margrett, J. A., & Marsiske, M. (2002). Gender differences in older adults' everyday cognitive collaboration. Collaboration in later life. *International Journal of Behavior Development, 26,* 45–59.

Marsiske, M., & Margrett, J. A. (2006). Everyday problem solving and decision making. In J. E. Birren & K. W. Schaie (Eds.), *Handbook of the Psychology of Aging* (6th ed., pp. 315–342). Boston, MA: Academic Press.

Marsiske, M., & Willis, S. L. (1995). Dimensionality of everyday problem solving in older adults. *Psychology and Aging, 10,* 269–283.

Neely, T. L. (2005). *The Effects of Contextual Factors on Dyadic Everyday Problem Solving in Adulthood.* Unpublished master's thesis, West Virginia University.

Neely, T. L. (2006). *The Effects of Age, Instructions, and Problem Content on Everyday Problem-solving Outcome Using Two Scoring Procedures.* Unpublished dissertation, West Virginia University.

Nesselroade, J. R. (2001). Intraindividual variability in development within and between individuals. *European Psychologist, 6*(3), 187–193.

Okonkwo, O. C., Wadley, V. G., Griffith, H. R., Ball, K., & Marson, D. C. (2006). Cognitive correlates of financial abilities in mild cognitive impairment. *Journal of the American Geriatrics Society, 54*(11), 1745–1750.

Perneczky, R., Pohl, C., Sorg, C., Hartmann, J., Tosic, N., Grimmer, T., et al. (2006). Impairment of activities of daily living requiring memory or complex reasoning as part of the MCI syndrome. *International Journal of Geriatric Psychiatry, 21*(2), 158–162.

Petersen, R. C. (2000). Aging, mild cognitive impairment, and Alzheimer's disease. *Neurologic Clinics, 18*(4), 789–805.

Petersen, R. C., Stevens, J. C., Ganguli, M., Tangalos, E. G., Cummings, J. L., & DeKosky, S. T. (2001). Early detection of dementia: Mild cognitive impairment (an evidence-based review): Report of the Quality Standards Subcommittee of the American Academy of Neurology. *Neurology, 56,* 1133–1142.

Poon, L. W., Clayton, G. M., Martin, P., Johnson, M. A., Courtenay, B. C., Sweaney, A. L., et al. (1992). The Georgia Centenarian Study. *International Journal of Aging and Human Development, 34,* 1–17.

Poon, L. W., Messner, S., Martin, P., & Noble, C. A. (1992). The influences of cognitive resources on adaptation and old age. *International Journal of Aging and Human Development, 34*(1), 381–390.

Prince, M. (2000). Methodological issues for population-based research into dementia in developing countries: A position paper from the 10/66 Dementia Research Group. *International Geriatric Psychiatry, 15*(1), 21–30.

Schaie, K. W. (2005). *Developmental Influences on Adult Intellectual Development: The Seattle Longitudinal Study.* New York: Oxford University Press.

Sinnott, J. D. (1989). *Everyday Problem Solving: Theory and Applications.* New York: Praeger.

Small, B. J., & Bäckman, L. (1997). Cognitive correlates of mortality: Evidence from a population-based sample of very old adults. *Psychology and Aging, 12*(2), 309–313.

Spivack, G., & Shure, M. B. (1982). The cognition of social adjustment. In B. B. Lahey & A. E. Kazdin (Eds.), *Advances in Clinical Child Psychology* (vol. 5, pp. 323–372). New York: Plenum.

Strough, J., McFall, J. P., Flinn, J. A., & Schuller, K. L. (2008). Collaborative everyday problem solving among same-gender friends in early and later adulthood. *Psychology and Aging, 23*, 517–530.

Strough, J., Patrick, J. H., & Swenson, L. M. (2003). Strategies for solving everyday problems faced by grandparents: The role of experience. In B. Hayslip, Jr., & J. H. Patrick (Eds.), *Working With Custodial Grandparents* (pp. 257–275). New York: Springer.

Swan, G., Carmelli, D., & LaRue, A. (1995). Performance on the digit symbol substitution test and 5-year mortality in the Western Collaborative Group Study. *American Journal of Epidemiology 141*, 32–40.

Thornton, W.J.L., & Dumke, H. A. (2005). Age differences in everyday problem-solving and decision-making effectiveness: A meta-analytic review. *Psychology and Aging, 20*, 85–99.

Wadley, V. G., Crowe, M., Marsiske M., Cook S. E., Unverzagt, F. W., Rosenberg, A. L., et al. (2007). Changes in everyday functioning in individuals with psychometrically defined mild cognitive impairment in the Advanced Cognitive Training for Independent and Vital Elderly Study. *Journal of the American Geriatrics Society, 55*(8), 1192–1198.

Watson, T. L., & Blanchard-Fields, F. (1998). Thinking with your head and your heart: Age differences in everyday problem-solving strategy preferences. *Aging, Neuropsychology, and Cognition, 5*, 225–240.

Weatherbee, S. R., & Allaire, J. C. (2008). Everyday cognition and mortality: Performance differences and predictive utility of the everyday cognition battery. *Psychology and Aging, 23*(1), 216–221.

Weitzman, P. F., & Weitzman, E. A. (2001). Everyday interpersonal conflicts of middle-aged women: An examination of strategies and their contextual correlates. *International Journal of Aging and Human Development, 52*, 281–295.

Willis, S. L. (1991). Cognition and everyday competence. In K. W. Schaie (Ed.), *Annual Review of Gerontology and Geriatrics* (vol. 11, pp. 80–109). New York: Springer.

Willis, S. (1996). Everyday cognitive competence in elderly persons: Conceptual issues and empirical findings. *The Gerontologist, 36*(5), 595–601.

Willis, S. L., & Schaie, W. K. (1986). Training the elderly on the ability factors of spatial orientation and inductive reasoning. *Psychology and Aging, 1*(3), 239–247.

Willis, S. L., & Schaie, K. W. (1993). Everyday cognition: Taxonomic and methodological considerations. In J. M. Puckett & H. W. Reese (Eds.), *Mechanisms of Everyday Cognition* (pp. 33–43). Hillsdale, NJ: Lawrence Erlbaum Associates.

Willis, S. L., & Marsiske, M. (1993). *Manual for the Everyday Problems Test.* University Park, PA: Department of Human Development and Family Studies, Pennsylvania State University.

CHAPTER 5

PERSONALITY AND EMOTION IN LATER LIFE

Karen Hooker, Soyoung Choun, and Brandi Hall

In this chapter, we aim to present current thinking on personality with an emphasis on how personality in later life may differ from earlier parts of the life span. Why is it that personality may be increasingly important for understanding healthy aging and how late life is experientially lived? Personality is related to well-being and other important life outcomes such as occupation, longevity, and marital status (e.g., Caspi, Roberts, & Shiner, 2005; Ozer & Benet-Martinez, 2006), and it is as important as socioeconomic status and IQ in predicting such outcomes (Roberts, Kuncel, Shiner, Caspi, & Goldberg, 2007).

Personality is sometimes thought of quite narrowly as only involving traits, such as how extraverted one is or how conscientious. While traits are an important part of personality, they are not all of personality; thus, one goal of this chapter is to introduce a more comprehensive, "six foci" model of personality that recognizes processes as well as personality structures such as traits.

We take an explicit life span approach that highlights processes that amplify initial differences over time (Light, Grigsby, & Bligh, 1996), acknowledges the importance of timing of events in the life course, recognizes that historical trends impact lives, and strives to understand how linked lives create change by examining the changing individual in changing social context (Settersten & Trauten, 2008).

"WE GROW NEITHER BETTER NOR WORSE, BUT MORE LIKE OURSELVES"

This statement, posted on the billboard outside of a community church, depicts the complex diversity of aging in an elegantly simple manner. As emphasized throughout this volume, there are both important changes, as well as continuity over the life span. Relatively early in adulthood people make decisions (e.g., what career to pursue, whether to get married, what kind of lifestyle to live, whether to become parents, and so on) that have an enormous impact on how later life is experienced. Because development in adulthood is to some extent personally guided, differences between individuals tend to grow wider so that, in late adulthood, there is more heterogeneity in personality, health, cognition, and abilities than at any other point in the life span. Personality is the guiding force that directs this orchestration of our life course. It is important to understand how it operates and continues to develop throughout life.

Personality is the domain that explains much of our behavior, and behaviors—especially those that become patterns—explain outcomes such as health and social support. Adults' thoughts about self, others, and characteristic ways of relating to the world are the focus of this chapter. Key questions researchers have addressed are: (1) Is personality in adulthood stable, or are changes likely to occur? (2) Can personality characteristics be protective factors or risk factors for mental and physical illness? and (3) How do older individuals maintain their identity, self-esteem, and psychological well-being in the face of losses so often associated with later life (e.g., widowhood, loss of friends, retirement, relocation) and inevitable physical declines that come with age?

PERSONALITY DEFINITION

A useful definition of personality was constructed by one of the founders of the field, Gordon Allport (1961): "Personality is the dynamic organization within the individual of those psychophysical systems that determine his [sic] characteristic behavior and thought" (p. 28). There are several important components to this definition: (1) personality is dynamic—that means it is changeable or at least has the potential to change; (2) personality is organized—it consists of patterns that can be recognized and associated with a person over time; (3) personality is a construct that is based within the individual—it is internal to a person and is, in some ways, the defining set of characteristics that make us who we are; (4) personality comprises psychophysical systems—this allows for consideration of mind–body interfaces and fits in well with the biopsychosocial framework we endorse; and finally, (5) personality is what determines one's characteristic behavior and thought—it is the internal compass that guides what we do and what we think.

Different theorists put different emphases on internal or external influences on personality. For example, those coming from a traditional psychodynamic framework view personality as an internal structure that is formed within the first few years of life, after which change is possible only in the context of years of intensive psychotherapy. On the other end of the theoretical spectrum are behavioral theorists who assume that changes occur in environments with different reinforcement characteristics. To a certain extent, this makes sense; people behave differently in different situations (Mischel, 1968). If you think of yourself as an example, chances are that you behave quite differently in a classroom than at a social gathering. To some extent, environments and the different sets of people in these different environments "pull" for different behaviors. However, if there were no underlying continuity or coherence to behavior, chaos would reign. There is a need to find a balance between views of personality as "set in stone" versus views of personality as "chameleon-like," or changing to match every situation. Most personality researchers today endorse an interactive view of personality that emphasizes the person-in-context, with the important recognition that individual characteristics guide the perception of situations and choice of contexts (including people with whom to interact).

OVERVIEW OF FRAMEWORKS FOR UNDERSTANDING PERSONALITY

As is clear from the previous definition of personality, there is an unchanging essence within individuals that allows us to operate in a social world that makes sense. Yet, if personality were rigidly stable, we would not be able to respond to constantly changing conditions throughout each day (e.g., partner's mood changes), much less to events that can change the context of one's life over a span of weeks, months, and years (e.g., becoming a parent, wartime experience, retirement, etc.). Thus, a model of personality must be able to address both stability and change. How personality may develop throughout adulthood and into old age has been an interesting question for which we are just beginning to have adequate data to examine. The broad sweep of the construct of personality and the methodological complexities of determining continuity, change, and development both within and between individuals have led to decades of reasonable disagreements among theoretical "camps." A full treatment of these differences is not possible here (see Heatherton & Weinberger, 1994), however, recent attempts at rapprochement (Hooker & McAdams, 2003; McAdams & Pals, 2006; Mischel, 2004) show promise that models that can handle the full complexity of personality can serve to guide empirical research (Mroczek, Spiro, & Griffin, 2006).

Traditionally, when psychologists discussed *personality*, they were referring to the internal organization of individual characteristics and qualities that make individuals distinct from one another. For example, when someone is described as "outgoing," then he or she is likely to behave in a gregarious and sociable manner, which distinguishes this person from an individual who might be described as "quiet," "shy," or "reserved." For several years, personality in adulthood has generally been understood in terms of these universal traits. Today, however, goals, motives, emotions, and self-concept are incorporated into conceptions of the personality system. *Personality*, broadly defined, represents both personal characteristics as well as how individuals behave, relate, feel, and experience their environment. Cantor (1990) identified this dichotomy as the difference between "having" and "doing" aspects of personality. More specifically, individuals may "have" certain personality characteristics, but what individuals try to "do" and how they go about accomplishing their goals are also defining characteristics of individuals. Understanding how these characteristics develop, as well as how they are changed or maintained across the life span, is also important.

Much of our early knowledge of the field of personality was derived from research conducted by child developmentalists who attempted to extend child behaviors and characteristics to early adulthood. Many scientists assumed that little development occurred after adulthood. In fact, James (1890) believed that "personality is set like plaster by age 30" (p. 126). It was not until the mid-20th century that theorists, such as Jung and Erikson, proposed personality development models that extended beyond childhood and adolescence to well into later adulthood. Personality is an area of particular interest for gerontologists because it may be one domain for which positive growth is possible throughout the life span.

Personality Stability: Structural Trait Perspective

In the gerontological literature, Costa and McCrae's (1980) Five-Factor Model (FFM) of personality has been well received because of its clarity and extensive research on the universality (McCrae & Terracciano, 2005) and stability of global traits across the adult life span. The "Big Five" traits include *o*penness to experience, *c*onscientiousness, *e*xtraversion, *a*greeableness, and *n*euroticism (the OCEAN acronym is sometimes used). According to McCrae and Costa (2003), a person with high scores of *openness* may be imaginative and exhibit nonconforming behavior, whereas someone with low scores in openness may have conservative values and be uncomfortable with life complexities. High levels of *conscientiousness* are represented in a person who is dependable and responsible, and low levels of conscientiousness are represented in a person who is self-indulgent and unable to delay gratification. An individual who is talkative and socially assertive likely has high levels of *extraversion*, but a person who is submissive and avoids close relationships may score low on this trait. High levels of *agreeableness* can be understood as warmth, compassion, and consideration for others, and low levels of agreeableness include critical, skeptical, or hostile behaviors toward others. Finally, an individual who is irritable and anxious may score high on the trait *neuroticism*, but a calm and relaxed person would likely score low on neuroticism.

Trait theorists generally believe that the FFM's biologically based traits are fixed and remain virtually unchanged well into later life. Furthermore, it has been argued that our genetically predisposed traits may predict our behavior and development. The stability of these factors is debatably an important element in one's sense of identity and at the heart of personality. Because traits can be perceived as the core of personality, trait theorists maintain that external factors (e.g., cultural environment, social roles, and relationships) may vary over time; however, personality traits should not be expected to exhibit much change. Numerous studies have been able to demonstrate moderate to high stability on the Big Five traits for periods of up to 30 years (e.g., McCrae & Costa, 2003). This evidence seemed to support the theoretical perspective that this aspect of personality will remain relatively stable across the life span.

Positive Changes with Age

More recently, however, there is evidence that personality traits continue to change during midlife and beyond, and the picture of change is a positive one for aging. Studies have identified a shift in certain personality traits in adulthood as a response to specific goal pursuits; for example, individuals engaged in work and stable marital relationships tend to express more conscientiousness (Roberts, Caspi, & Moffitt, 2003). Longitudinal studies have shown that measures of social assurance tended to peak in middle age, social vitality declined with age, and self-control increased with age (Helson, Jones, & Kwan, 2002). Trait theorists attribute changes in traits during adulthood to changing social contexts that demand different behaviors at different points in the life span.

Culture and Personality

Culture can be an important factor in shaping personality, yet individuals are so embedded in culture that its influence often goes unrecognized (Oishi, 2004). Examination of personality through a cultural lens leads to a more socially and contextually sensitive view of personality. By exploring cultural contexts, we can examine which aspects of personality are universal across culture and history.

Much of the research on culture and personality has examined the FFM across various cultures, although most of these studies have been conducted by Westerners (Heine & Buchtel, 2009). The majority of these studies have concluded that, with slight exceptions, the FFM can be generalized across cultures (see McCrae & Allik, 2002), although the validity of the FFM across cultures remains an area of investigation. Scores on the FFM cannot capture all aspects of a person within a specific culture. Furthermore, because the study of personality has tended to focus on unique differences between people, the search for individual differences in cross-cultural research can sometimes ignore intracultural variations (Oishi, 2004).

Markus (2004) expands beyond the use of personality traits in examination of the role of culture in influencing the self. She has argued that individuals in different cultures have strikingly different construals of self and others. Markus and Kitayama (1991) identified East Asians as having models of the self, based on interdependence. This means that self-constructs may be influenced by the degree that one is affiliated with the larger cultural group. European Americans, on the other hand, tend to have construals of the self that are rooted in independence, or being differentiated from the larger cultural group. These distinct models of self ultimately influence individual cultural beliefs, actions, and motivations (Markus, 2004). Furthermore, they represent assumptions about cultures that are often overlooked by researchers yet play an integral role in shaping society through policy, practice, and social institutions, which in turn affects individual personality development.

Personality Growth and Change: Social-Cognitive Processing Perspectives

Although traits are clearly important for understanding a person, and may even reflect some level of positive change or growth into adulthood, it should not be assumed that traits comprise all of personality. Trait models emphasize the individual and may underestimate the role of context in personality development, particularly the social connectedness individuals have across the life span (Labouvie-Vief & Diehl, 1999). Unlike trait theorists, life span developmental theorists would argue that the *self* is at the center of personality and also view self-constructs, such as motivation and goal pursuits, as central to one's personality. Additionally, developmental theorists emphasize the different historical, cultural, and environmental contexts that dynamically interact with individuals to produce growth or decline across the life span.

Traits are considered acontextual, and so they cannot reliably predict or lead to specific behavioral outcomes. For example, because an individual is extraverted at a family dinner, does not necessarily mean this person will be extraverted in other life situations. Therefore, although traits can be useful for understanding some human behaviors, they do not capture the full richness of individual lives. A fuller, more nuanced understanding of people should rely on a view of individuals to understand not simply who they are, but also what they are trying to accomplish (Cantor, 1990).

Motivational aspects of the self may play a key role in understanding how individuals adapt over the life span, particularly in later life. Some researchers have been able to demonstrate that increased flexibility across the life span is a key to successful adaptation in later adulthood. For example, older adults who are able to selectively optimize and compensate for normative age-related declines exhibit potential for growth in later life (Baltes & Baltes, 1990). According to Heckhausen and Schulz (1995), older adults who are able to shift their control beliefs from internal to external may be exhibiting a strategy related to optimal aging. Furthermore, the role of possible selves (i.e., an individual's ideas of what they would like to become or what they are afraid of becoming) can be a key motivational and protective factor in later life (Markus & Nurius, 1986). For example, older adults who reported more health-related, hoped-for possible selves and who also felt they had some control over their health perceived themselves as being healthier (Hooker, 1992).

The long-standing divide between personality structures and processes highlights a need for triangulation in understanding personality, and the field has moved toward an acceptance of co-occurring change and stability in individuals. A relatively new model of personality called *the six foci of personality* (Hooker & McAdams, 2003) integrates personality structures (i.e., traits, personal action constructs, and life stories) with personality processes (i.e., states, self-regulation, and self-narration) in order to provide a richer understanding of individuals. Each of the six focal areas of personality can be researched and linked, which will ultimately result in a more integrative, comprehensive understanding of personality and its importance over the life span. This theoretical model poses many exciting new challenges and empirical questions for future research in the field of personality and aging.

The three levels of personality were originally presented by McAdams (1995) and represented in a triarchic model of personality. He conceptualized three independent, "loosely related," levels of personality: traits, personal concerns, and life story (McAdams, 1995, p. 371). Hooker (2002) expanded on this model by identifying McAdams's levels of personality as all structural in nature and incorporating process constructs (states, self-regulation, and self-narration) to parallel each of the structures at three levels (see Figure 5.1).

The six foci model is not hierarchical in nature, but reflective of the integration of structures and processes associated with personality. This model also allows researchers to address patterns of diverse lives while seeing themes of uniformity across lives. For example, Murray and Kluckhohn (1953) stated that "Every man [*sic*] is in certain respects (a) like all other men, (b) like some other men, (c) like no other man" (p. 53). This often quoted adage parallels the levels identified in the six foci model of personality (e.g., Runyan, 1983). More specifically, all people fall on a continuum of a relatively universal set of traits (Level I); particular goals and developmental tasks are relevant to some, but not all people (Level II); and one's life story (Level III) is uniquely created (Hooker & McAdams, 2003).

Figure 5.1   The Six Foci Model of the Personality System.

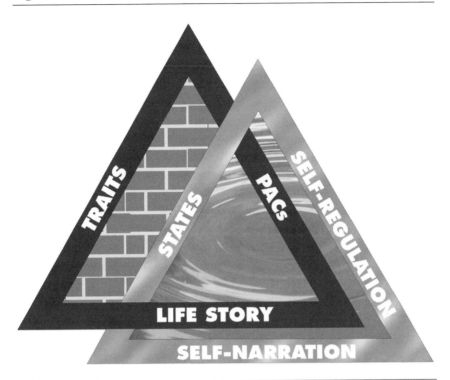

Source: Hooker, 2002.

The first level of the six foci model includes both *traits*, the broad and universal descriptions of a person that are relatively stable across time, and *states*, the moment-to-moment changes a person experiences. States can include emotions and moods such as joy and anxiety, or physiological states such as fatigue or hunger. Full understanding of how these two aspects of personality may interact is just beginning to receive attention (e.g., Fleeson, Malanos, & Achille, 2002; Shifren & Hooker, 1995). For example, how do variable states affect stable traits and vice versa?

The second level of the six foci model includes constructs known as *personal action constructs* (PACs; Little, 1983). These are much less broad than traits, represent the motivational aspects of human behavior, and emphasize the context of each individual's time, place, and social role. There are clear differences in individuals' PACs across the life span, and these include goals, developmental tasks, motivations, possible selves, and the "doing" side of personality (Cantor, 1990). Due to the emphasis on person–environment interactions, this level of personality demonstrates considerable change over the life span.

Self-regulatory processes, such as self-efficacy and outcome expectancy, are also included on the second level of the six foci model. These processes relate to the ability to feel in control and tend to be domain specific (Lachman, 1986). Psychological control has been an important area of research in both personality and gerontology. For example, a person with high self-efficacy may feel more successful in meeting goals and, thus, take on increasingly challenging roles. Consequently, self-regulatory processes can facilitate or inhibit motivation and goal setting, which elucidates the importance of these processes in conjunction with PACs.

The third level of the six foci model of personality includes the *life story*, the person's narrative understanding of the self, and processes of *self-narration*. Humans create internalized, evolving stories of their past in order to provide their lives with a sense of meaning, unity, and purpose. Life stories contain plots, themes, and characters that are central to a person's identity and can contribute to individuals' concepts of who they are and who they may become. The life story will continue to develop over the life course as relationships and situations change; it also gives us the richest and deepest sense of who an individual truly is.

Processes of self-narration include social cognitive activities such as remembering, reminiscing, and storytelling; these activities influence how and what we reveal in our life story. According to McAdams (1995), "when an interviewer asks a person to tell the story of his or her own life, the narrative account that is obtained is not synonymous with the internal life story" (p. 385). Thus, the processes of self-narration, as well as social context, can influence which aspects of the internal life story are shared with others.

A benefit of the six foci model of personality is the comprehensiveness of the conceptual framework. Clearly, a more inclusive and multilevel approach to studying personality will lead to increased knowledge about a person across the life span. In addition, it provides researchers of the 21st century with a common language to understand and unify the science of personality in adulthood, which has historically been divided by theoretical differences.

SIX FOCI MODEL OF THE PERSONALITY SYSTEM

Traits

As described in the previous section, personality traits can be thought of as general dispositions to think, feel, and behave in consistent ways. In our everyday language, literally thousands of trait-descriptive terms can be identified (e.g., Allport & Odbert, 1936). Examples might be "friendly," "generous," "hostile," and "loud," and these are the types of characteristics commonly referred to as "personality" among the general public. However, many of these terms can be subsumed under broader, higher-order traits. There is general consensus among personality researchers that an all-encompassing taxonomy of traits can be adequately described by a five-factor model, mentioned previously as "the Big Five" (e.g., Digman, 1990; Goldberg, 1993; John, 1990).

In longitudinal studies, these traits have shown high levels of normative stability (e.g., Fraley & Roberts, 2005; Roberts & DelVecchio, 2000) suggesting that, at least in terms of trait models of personality, there is empirical evidence of impressive stability in adulthood over several decades, but some changes do occur for some individuals. Rank-order stability continues to increase in adulthood to about age 50. Even then the test–retest correlation is well below unity, providing evidence that changes can and do occur. While it is often the case that the best predictor of personality traits in old age is personality traits earlier in the life span, this is an overgeneralization. With this caveat in mind, however, it is often true that, for example, an extraverted young adult is likely to be an extraverted older adult. The 20-year-old woman who is social chair of her sorority may be the leader of philanthropic causes in her community when she is 60. The 19-year-old male leading his buddies in cheers at soccer games may, at 70, be the outgoing greeter of new mosque members after services. Just keep in mind that despite stability in relative ranking of traits among groups of individuals, people can still move up or down on the trait continuum (Helson, Kwan, John, & Jones, 2002; Jones & Meredith, 1996).

Are There Discernible Patterns of Change in Personality Traits across the Life Span?

Interestingly, a review of longitudinal studies that included people ranging in age from 10 to 101 found several trends (Roberts, Robins, Trzesniewski, & Caspi, 2003). Traits associated with the Big Five factor of neuroticism tended to decrease, and most of the decline seemed to take place in young adulthood. A meta-analysis that synthesized results from many studies showed that, on average, there were increases in agreeableness, conscientiousness, emotional stability (reverse of neuroticism), and the part of extraversion related to social dominance (Roberts, Walton, & Viechtbauer, 2006; see also Roberts & Mroczek, 2008). Decreases were shown in the part of extraversion related to social vitality and in openness to experience, starting in the decade of the 50s. In fact, it appears that social maturity—becoming more confident, responsible, and calm—is characteristic of aging.

A More Nuanced Way of Looking at Change

Interestingly, Mroczek and Spiro (2007) found that *direction and rate* of change in neuroticism predicted probability of survival over 18 years. Those whose level of neuroticism was high and increased over the follow-up period were more likely to die than those who had low neuroticism as well as those who had high neuroticism that decreased over time. This suggests that it is not simply the level of a trait that is important for predicting outcomes, but the direction and rate of change therein.

Traits associated with extraversion showed a complex pattern: Traits associated with dominance showed increases from adolescence through middle age, while traits associated with sociability increased in adolescence and then decreased in adulthood. Traits associated with the Big Five factors of agreeableness and conscientiousness showed increases through middle age, and finally, traits associated with openness to experience showed increases through young adulthood, stability, then decreases in later life. Thus, a picture of changes in personality traits in adulthood emerges that has been described as depicting the maturity principle (Caspi et al., 2005). "Most people become more dominant, agreeable, conscientious, and emotionally stable over the course of their lives. These changes point to increasing psychological maturity over development, from adolescence to middle age" (Caspi et al., 2005, p. 468). The potential for change always exists; even among centenarians traits have been shown to be malleable (e.g., Adkins, Martin, & Poon, 1996).

States

States connote processes that can be transitory and rapidly changing, or more stable, depending on internal or environmental triggers. The key is that change, or the potential for change, is expected. Constructs such as mood, energy level, anxiety, stress, and efficacy are some of the areas studied within this domain. Given the inherent lability of states, research instruments must be sensitive enough to capture short-term changes, and assessments must be relatively frequent (Nesselroade, 1987; Nesselroade, 1991). This intensive measurement of individuals over time allows for the study of intraindividual variability, that is, change within the person. Given the proper research design (Nesselroade, 1990), short-term fluctuations should be viewed against a backdrop of more permanent longer term changes to understand how differences between individuals (interindividual differences) get created. The more challenging methodological issues may help to explain the relative dearth of studies in this area (Nesselroade & Ram, 2004), although a recent renaissance in these types of studies has been necessary (e.g., Molenaar, 2004; Nesselroade, 2001; Nesselroade & Ram, 2004). Researchers are beginning to examine individual variation within different temporal frames (daily, monthly, yearly) to understand how intraindividual variability and changes in this variability differ between persons (e.g., Sliwinski & Mogle, 2008; Sliwinski, Smyth, Stawski, & Almeida, under review).

Some argue that traits comprise density distributions of states (e.g., Fleeson, 2001). Despite wide differences between people, people do experience the full spectrum of behaviors for different traits when measured over a period of several weeks. Individual differences in levels of traits correlated with the frequencies of actions consistent with that trait (Fleeson et al., 2002). Some individuals felt extroverted one day, but less so the next. Those who consistently enacted extraverted behaviors were more likely to score highly on a trait measure of extraversion. These studies demonstrate that research on states hold promise for capturing intraindividual personality processes, but they also demonstrate the need for studies that track variability over long periods.

PERSONAL ACTION CONSTRUCTS

Personal action constructs (PACs; Little, 1983) are cognitive structures that emphasize *goal directedness* of behavior. They are shaped by life phases (e.g., retirees likely have different goals than new parents) and social context (roles, social class, gender). PACs are important for understanding development because change and malleability are key. Identity issues regarding how one gets from *who one is today* to *who one hopes to be in the future* are addressed in this part of the personality system. These types of questions fall under the rubric of intentional self-development (e.g., Diehl, 2006; Hooker, 1999; Lerner & Busch-Rossnagel, 1981). The current assemblage of PACs include constructs such as current concerns (Klinger, 1975), personal projects (Little, 1983), life tasks (Cantor & Kihlstrom, 1987), personal strivings (Emmons, 1986), identity goals (Gollwitzer & Wicklund, 1985), and possible selves (Markus & Nurius, 1986). All of these constructs are related to goals, with the differences between them being level of abstraction and temporal frame. For example, a personal project might be harvesting one's tomatoes (concrete goal with a short time frame); contrast this PAC with the hoped-for self of being a community leader, a goal that would entail considerable efforts sustained over time.

Possible selves are one of the most often-studied areas of inquiry in relation to PACs. They represent *hoped-for selves* (i.e., what people are trying to become) and *feared selves* (i.e., what people are afraid of becoming). These highly personalized images provide insight into the motivational underpinnings directing individuals toward goals they should pursue, avoid, or abandon. Possible selves can be measured with scales that are psychometrically sound (Hooker, 1999; Ryff, 1991) yet change in response to efforts at personal growth (Cross & Markus, 1991; Frazier, Hooker, Johnson, & Kaus, 2000). Younger adults, for example, often envision a greater number of possible selves related to career, whereas older adults tend to envision greater numbers related to health (Cross & Markus, 1991; Hooker, 1992). Cross-sectional studies suggest that possible selves may change in correspondence with normative developmental tasks (Hooker, 1999) and, therefore, may play a key role in successful adult development.

Aging brings with it the challenge of balancing potential resource gains (e.g., practical knowledge, material belongings) with those involving losses (e.g., physical decline). There is an extensive literature on control processes in later life (Lachman, 2006) and related constructs such as mastery and self-efficacy (Bandura, 1997). Overall, there is a fairly positive message: Older adults are masters at life management and allocate declining resources in ways that maximize well-being (Staudinger & Kunzmann, 2005). Compared to younger adults, older adults are more likely to: pursue goals that are self-concordant (Sheldon, 2008), have fewer competing goals (Riediger, Freund, & Baltes, 2005), have goals that are more elaborated (Hooker, 1999), and prioritize maintenance by striving to regulate loss rather than seeking new gains (e.g., Ebner, Freund, & Baltes, 2006). It is also clear that by midlife most adults have at least one self-relevant health goal (Frazier & Hooker, 2006; Hooker & Kaus, 1994), and health becomes increasingly incorporated into goal structures throughout later life (Frazier et al., 2000). Thus, it may be easier to build on the already existing goals in the area of health to bring about strategies for implementing changes. This is important because research has shown that health-engagement control strategies are effective at mitigating the negative effects of daily physical symptoms and common late-life stressors (e.g., Wrosch, Dunne, Scheier, & Schulz, 2006, Wrosch & Schulz, 2008).

Self-Regulatory Processes

Researchers in the field of adult development and aging have a long history of studying self-regulation and have been particularly interested in sense of control (Langer & Rodin, 1976; Schulz, 1976) in relation to specific developmental domains and outcomes (Lachman, 1986; Lachman & Weaver, 1998). This line of research has produced numerous studies demonstrating a link between rates of mortality in institutionalized older adults and sense of personal control (Langer & Rodin, 1976). Interestingly, Eizenman, Nesselroade, Featherman, and Rowe (1997) found that variability in perceived control over a period of 25 weeks—that is, lots of fluctuation—predicted mortality 5 years later, whereas average levels of control were not predictive. Feeling a sense of mastery has also been linked to the effectiveness of stress reduction strategies used by adults facing midlife challenges (Lachman & Bertrand, 2001).

Resilience is an area of self-regulation research that has been examined throughout the life span. Heckhausen's (2001) research, for example, draws attention to the way middle-aged adults use compensatory strategies and adaptive behaviors to maintain resilience in the face of age-related loss. Self-evaluation, emotion regulation, and goal setting are among the most potent of these self-regulatory processes (Staudinger & Kunzmann, 2005). These researchers found that despite the increased likelihood of encountered instead of elicited experiences in old age, most older-aged adults maintain their sense of control and personal agency. In fact, people maintain and regain levels of subjective well-being and adjust to life tasks *more effectively* as they age (Staudinger & Kunzmann, 2005).

The SOC model (Baltes & Baltes, 1990; Baltes & Carstensen, 1999; Freund & Baltes, 2000) explains the maintenance of self-regulation across the life span in terms of three processes—selection, optimization, and compensation—regarded by some life span researchers as the universal principles of developmental regulation. These universal adaptive processes include selecting goals or outcomes, optimizing the means to achieve these goals or outcomes, and compensating for loss so that successful outcomes can still be achieved (Baltes & Baltes, 1990). For example, a woman who used to be a schoolteacher before she retired may wish to enhance her sense of usefulness by *selectively* volunteering to read to young school children two times a week. However, her congestive heart failure may make this difficult, physically, to do. She might still choose to volunteer if she can *optimize* her sense of usefulness there by working with children who could benefit most from her extra time and by *compensating* for her heart condition by using oxygen to support her in this task. The SOC model provides a general framework for understanding adaptive processes across the life span as well as across multiple domains. Baltes and Carstensen (1999), for example, applied the SOC model to the goal processes older adults use in their social relationships. They found that many older adults select goals related to maintaining family relationships, optimize these goals by investing more time in family relationships (compared to other types of relationships), and compensate for the loss of friendships and other relationships by maximizing salience of family ties.

Aging brings with it the challenge of balancing potential resource gains (e.g., practical knowledge, material belongings) with those involving losses (i.e., physical decline). The strategic selection and pursuit of goals that maximize gains and minimize losses helps to enhance our ability to adapt as we age (Baltes & Baltes, 1990; Riediger et al., 2005). Research on personal action constructs and the processes of self-regulation not only provide insight into adult personality development, but also play a key role in optimal aging.

Life Story(ies)

The life-narrative approach is an emergent field of study in the science of personality development. Knowledge at this third level of personality provides deeply personal and wholly unique understanding of what is "core" in a person's life. Yet, the sociohistorial events of peoples lives (e.g., Hurricane Katrina, the election of America's first African American president), are necessarily grounded in their particular culture and ongoing stream of history. Thus, ironically, it is at the most unique level of personality that the link to society is most evident.

Late life is uniquely suited to understanding this level of personality because individually unique themes and patterns of life come into focus from this more molar perspective. We can learn much about personality by discovering how and why individuals select and reconstruct experiences to align with present goals and perceptions as viewed through the lens of an uncertain but anticipated future. Life stories are the internalized structures reflective of an individual's contextualized life. There is not a single life story. In each telling, it changes based on the audience, the reason for the story being elicited, and the context of the person's life at that moment in time. People create life stories by reconstructing the past and anticipating the future and, in so doing, engender a sense of meaning, unity, and purpose in their lives. True to narrative form, these internalized structures give license to plots, characters, images, themes, and scenes, with each act of revision a window into self-understanding. Narrating the life story to others through remembering, reminiscing, or storytelling induces social cognitive processes. The individual uniqueness of each person is most likely to be manifested in this third level of the six foci model.

Life stories continually evolve as new themes within relationships emerge and interweave with changing plots and life settings. Consequently, identity and creation of self elicit empirical attention throughout the adulthood years (e.g., Labouvie-Vief, Chiodo, Goguen, Diehl, & Orwoll, 1995; Whitbourne & Connolly, 1999). When woven together, these richly textured threads, what McAdams's (1995; McAdams & Pals, 2006) called the revitalizing life myths, create a unified and coherent structure.

The main characters in life stories represent idealizations of the self. Integrating these various aspects of self becomes a major challenge during middle and later adulthood when attention often turns toward creating a satisfying ending. When well crafted, endings provide the means through which self can leave a legacy and foster new beginnings. Life stories in middle and older adults have a clear quality of "giving birth to" a new generation, allowing for a sense of generativity (Erikson, 1959; McAdams, 1995, 1996).

Generativity, the Eriksonian challenge ascendant in midlife, refers to interest in establishing and guiding the next generation. It is a commitment to the larger society—beyond the self and nuclear family. If one is unable to do this in middle age, a sense of stagnation sets in. There are many different ways to be generative (Kotre, 1984), such as becoming a mentor for a junior person at work or parenting teenagers in such a way that they are prepared to lead productive lives in society.

People derive personal meaning from being generative by constructing a life story or narrative that helps them create a particular identity (Whitbourne, 1999). Life stories provide the means by which people prove to themselves and others that they have either changed or remained the same, identifying specific events to support their claims. Whitbourne's (1987) research on identity assimilation (i.e., using existing identity) and accommodation (i.e., adjusting existing identity) found that identity assimilation was used prominently among older adults but also that identity accommodation was more prominent among adults in their earlier years (Sneed & Whitbourne, 2003). Identity assimilation helped older adults maintain and enhance positive self-regard while identity accommodation was associated with poor psychological health. The ability to integrate age-related changes into one's identity and maintain a positive view of self is crucial to aging successfully (Holahan, 2003; Sneed & Whitbourne, 2003). This emergent field of identity development relies on life narratives, the internalized and evolving story that integrates past, present, and future into a coherent and vitalizing myth (McAdams, 1995, 2001). Self-narrative processes guide the telling of these stories.

Self-Narration

Remembering, reminiscing, and storytelling evolve within the social contexts of people's everyday lives. Dynamic transactions between the person telling the story and his or her audience influence the way the narrative evolves and how identities of both narrator and audience become coconstructed. Consequently, developmental level, audience, or social context may change the ways in which individuals tell their stories (Adams, Smith, Pasupathi, & Vitolo, 2002; Bartlett, 1932; Fiese, Hooker, Kotary, Schwagler, & Rimmer, 1995; Pasupathi, 2001). Older adults show discriminative facility in that they are even more adept than younger adults at pitching the narrative of their story to the audience's developmental level.

Current evidence suggests that differences exist between younger and older adults in relation to autobiographical memories. Older adults, for example, may be more likely to preserve self-relevant and emotionally intense memories than younger adults (Dijkstra & Kaup, 2005). Moreover, what a person remembers and tells about their personal history may change to align with current realities, such as audience or current situational environment (Wilson & Ross, 2003). Autobiographical memories promote self-continuity, which can be important to goal-striving, self-knowledge, and well-being.

According to Erikson, ego-integrity is coming to terms with one's "one and only lifecycle and of the people who have become significant to it as something that had to be and that, by necessity permitted of no substitutions . . . in such final consolidation, death loses its sting" (1959, p. 98). If one can look back on one's life and feel that it had meaning and that one made the best of one's circumstances, then ego-integrity has been achieved and one is satisfied in later adulthood. If one is not satisfied with one's life, then the realization that time is too short to change it leads to a sense of despair and fear of death.

We do not yet have data on the extent to which autobiographical storytelling is related to mental health. However, it seems likely that older adults who have interesting stories to tell and recount these stories when they sense they would be welcome could be a cherished resource families should call upon to improve eudonic well-being (meaningfulness) for multiple generations.

Advantages of the Six Foci Model of Personality

In summary, the *six foci model of personality* provides for integration of diverse areas in personality. Accumulation and progress in science are more likely in a unified discipline. This model also captures the simultaneous development of both stability and change in structures and processes as they operate in tandem to create a coherent personality, which includes the self. Additionally, in order to address all six foci, multiple methods are necessary (e.g., quantitative and qualitative approaches) that increase the chance that the field will benefit from interdisciplinary collaboration. Finally, this model provides a foundation for the development of a common language, which in turn will strengthen the science of adult personality (Bolkan, Meierdiercks, & Hooker, 2008; Hooker & McAdams, 2003).

EMOTIONS IN LATER LIFE

Overview of Emotions

Emotions are an essential part of our lives and involve both mind and body. Every day people experience feelings, good or bad, including happiness, joy, sadness, or anxiety. Emotions may account for momentary physical changes, such as the smiling associated with happiness, blushing of embarrassment, tearing of sadness, and the pounding heart of nervousness (Oatley, 2004). *Emotion* is defined as "a state of the organism that affects behavior or simply as a response" (Schulz, 1985, p. 531). For that reason, emotions are seen sometimes as psychological events and other times as behavioral events (Schulz, 1985).

In general, *emotion* and *affect* are used to represent "personal and subjective feelings that may vary in intensity" of arousal (Schulz, 1985, p. 531). As the family of emotional phenomena, *mood*, such as cheerfulness, irritability, or sadness, may persevere for hours or days (Oatley, 2004). Emotions are short-lived psychological phenomena, whereas "moods and affective states are more common and longer duration" (Schulz, 1985, p. 532). However, terms such as *emotion, affect, and mood* are often used interchangeably because the term *emotion* covers a broad rage of phenomena (Oatley, 2004; Schulz, 1985).

According to Levenson (1994), "emotions represent efficient modes of adaptation to changing environmental demands" (p. 123). Emotions are usually based on appraisals of events relating to goals, concerns, and aspirations (Oatley, 2004). Lazarus (1993) emphasizes appraisal as a universal process involving evaluation of the importance of what is happening to one's personal well-being. Therefore, to understand emotions, we consider how emotions reflect individual's intense reactions to the environment through components such as cognitive appraisal, subjective feeling, expression, and regulation (Juslin & Laukka, 2003). Emotions can be viewed as an adaptive function in times of stress (Folkman & Lazarus, 1985; Lazarus, 1993), yet emotion itself is rarely addressed from an adult developmental prospective (Schulz, 1985). There are relatively few studies of the role of positive emotions in the stress process in later adulthood (Ong, Bergeman, Bisconti, & Wallace, 2006).

PERSONALITY THEORY AND ITS LINK TO EMOTION

One of the most important functions of personality is to regulate well-being. The part of the personality system related to PACs and self-regulatory processes is most relevant to understanding how this is accomplished. The pursuit of personal goals has been linked to psychological well-being and life satisfaction in adults (McGregor & Little, 1998; Sheldon & Kasser, 1998). The extent to which people are meeting (or failing to meet) their goals is linked to affective consequences such as happiness or depression (Klinger, 1975). Contrary to views of aging that focus on cognitive decline and physical deterioration, research on emotional functioning has led to many new and optimistic discoveries regarding the aging process. We now know that older adults are very successful at regulating emotions and appear to experience a greater proportion of positive to negative emotions compared to younger adults (Carstensen, Pasupathi, Mayr, & Nesselroade, 2000; Gross et al., 1997; Mroczek, 2001).

While there has been an extensive history of theory and research studying the influence of age-related changes in cognition, the impact of emotion has only relatively recently gained similar interest (Blanchard-Fields & Kalinauskas, 2008). Historically, emotion was viewed as an irrational component of human life, separate from cognition (Labouvie-Vief, 1999). Within the past decade, a growing body of research has investigated the complex interaction among emotion and cognition (Blanchard-Fields & Kalinauskas, 2008). It has been of particular interest to better understand why individuals seem to get better at regulating their emotions with age. Well-being is at least as high, if not higher, among older adults compared to younger adults despite older adults' cognitive, physical, and health-related challenges. This contradiction is known in the field as "the paradox of aging."

What Do We Know about Aging and Emotion? The Emotion Salience Effect

Regardless of age, individuals seem to exhibit a bias to remember emotionally charged stimuli as opposed to neutral information, which is known as the emotion salience effect (Buchanan & Adolphs, 2002; Fung & Carstensen, 2003). Numerous studies have indicated that with age, individuals expend more of their cognitive resources on emotional information rather than neutral information (e.g., Carstensen & Turk-Charles, 1994; Comblain, D'Argembeau, Van der Linden, & Aldenhoff, 2004; Hashtroudi, Johnson, & Chrosniak, 1990). In one study, Comblain and colleagues (2004) found that older adults reported richer accounts of previously viewed pictures when recollection was based on emotional reactions. Similarly, in a study conducted by Carstensen and Turk-Charles (1994), after reading narratives older adults remembered more emotional information than younger adults. In another study, older adults tended to better remember events associated with thoughts and emotion, while younger adults recollected more contextual information (Hashtroudi et al., 1990). These early studies investigating the interplay between emotion and cognition, however, failed to differentiate positive from negative information.

The Positivity Effect

More recent studies have shown that older adults may show a bias toward positive emotional stimuli (Carstensen & Mikels, 2005). Some contemporary theories have explained this bias by proposing that older adults process more positive information than negative information. This is known in the literature as the positivity effect (Carstensen & Mikels, 2005). Many studies have reported that older adults tend to prefer positive information over negative information (Carstensen, Mikels, & Mather, 2006). For example, during autobiographical recall tasks, older adults remember more positive information (Kennedy, Mather, & Carstensen, 2004). Older adults look at more happy faces than sad faces (Mather & Carstensen, 2003) and remember more positive pictures than negative pictures (Charles, Mather, & Carstensen, 2003). As individuals age, they even tend to view their childhood in a more positive light (Field, 1981). The positivity effect has been reported in diverse realms of research (e.g., Isaacowitz, Wadlinger, Goren, & Wilson, 2006; Kennedy et al., 2004; Mather & Carstensen, 2003), but it is important to note that there have been mixed results (Wurm, Labouvie-Vief, Aycock, Rebucal, & Koch, 2004).

Socioemotional Selectivity Theory

Many studies, predominantly in the social cognitive and emotion-related literature, have found that older individuals tend to process positive information more than negative information (e.g., Carstensen & Mikels, 2005; Kennedy et al., 2004). One of the most prominent life span theories of adult development that has aimed to better understand the interplay between emotion and cognition, and in particular the positivity effect, is the socioemotional selectivity theory (SST; Carstensen, 1995; Carstensen, Isaacowitz, & Charles, 1999). SST suggests that motivational processes may be the key to better understanding the previously mentioned "paradox of aging." As people grow older and time is perceived as limited, motivations shift from future-oriented informational goals to more present-oriented emotional goals (Carstensen et al., 1999). Younger individuals who see time as open-ended seek experiences that will provide valuable information for their developing career and family domains—which typically translates into larger social networks. Social network size decreases with age, however, as time and energy are focused on emotionally meaningful relationships (Carstensen et al., 1999). The theory proposes that the shift of motivation accounts for the positivity effect, as older individuals tend to focus on positive information to enhance present moods (Carstensen & Mikels, 2005; Carstensen et al., 2006).

Originally, the socioemotional selectivity theory posited that older adults selectively process emotional rather than factual information (Carstensen & Mikels, 2005; Carstensen et al., 2006). With theoretical development, the positivity effect is now suggested to reflect older individuals' tendencies to enhance present moods and regulate emotions by focusing on positive information (Carstensen & Mikels, 2005; Carstensen et al., 2006).

Other life span theoretical perspectives also aim to better understand the positivity effect. The cognitive-affective theory of development suggests that individuals gain knowledge with age from their past experiences of regulating emotions (Labouvie-Vief, 2003). Thus, although emotions may become more complex, older individuals tend to seek simple strategies and regulate emotions to maximize their well-being (Labouvie-Vief, 2003). Other theoretical approaches have aimed to explain the positivity effect in terms of selective processing that posits a negativity suppression effect in which attention is thought to be diverted away from negative stimuli (Blanchard-Fields & Kalinauskas, 2008; Rozin & Royzman, 2001).

The Negativity Effect

Some researchers have suggested that this positivity effect may be misleading (Blanchard-Fields & Kalinauskas, 2008). Rather than selectively processing positive emotions, some theoretical approaches suggest that individuals may actually focus more on negative information (Rozin & Royzman, 2001). This is known as the negativity effect. The negativity effect appears consistently in the young adulthood literature (Murphy & Isaacowitz, 2008). For example, younger adults show a bias of experiencing stronger psychological reactions to negative stimuli rather than positive stimuli (David, Green, Martin, & Suls, 1997). Less is known regarding how older adults process negative information, but some suggest that previous research findings of the positivity effect may reflect a dampening of the negativity effect with age (Murphy & Isaacowitz, 2008). For example, a diminished negativity effect was found when older adults were asked to remember emotionally valenced words (Grühn, Smith, & Baltes, 2005). Similarly, utilizing the Iowa Gambling Task, Wood, Busemeyer, Koling, Cox, and Davis (2005) found that older adults exhibited less of a negativity bias than younger adults, while also focusing more on emotionally valent information. Other studies, however, have found negativity effects in older adults (Charles et al., 2003). Charles and colleagues (2003) reported that older individuals spent more time attending to negative information. The clear extent of the potential magnitude of the negativity effect remains uncertain (Murphy & Isaacowitz, 2008).

What is clear is that older adults are superior to younger adults at regulating their emotions. "Accentuate the positive, eliminate the negative" was the refrain of a popular song that does appear to have some basis in the psychological literature of later life. Age does appear to be linked with better emotional control (Gross et al., 1997; Lawton, Kleban, Rajagopal, & Dean, 1992; Phillips, Henry, Hosie, & Milne, 2008). Older adults also appear to be able to limit the cognitive resources taken up by management of negative emotions better than younger adults (Scheibe & Blanchard-Fields, 2009).

THE IMPORTANCE OF PERSONALITY TO SUCCESSFUL AGING

To date, personality has taken a back seat in our models of successful aging. The important contributions of Rowe and Kahn (1987, 1998), drawn from the MacArthur study of successful aging, emphasize: (1) avoidance of disease and disability, (2) high cognitive and physical functioning, and (3) engagement in life. Personality is arguably a major contributor to all of these factors. Perhaps because it has been construed somewhat narrowly in the recent past gerontological literature as pertaining only to stable traits, this left little room for people to develop and improve in this domain. Yet, as described previously, this is not the case given our recent knowledge of trait change, as well as the dynamic processes involved in the six foci model.

Even life span developmental models of Baltes and colleagues (e.g., Baltes & Baltes, 1990; Baltes, Lindenberger, & Staudinger, 2006), which include goals related to processes of selection, optimization, and compensation in the SOC model, do not use the term *personality* to describe these dynamic processes. Yet, personality is arguably the driving force behind many of the factors leading to optimal aging, such as health-related behaviors, social support, coping strategies, and how one plans for and meets goals. Even pursuing and succeeding in getting an education—the variable that has been shown to be related to outcomes as widely divergent as maintaining a healthy weight and avoiding dementia in later life—can be seen as influenced by personality. Limited conceptions of personality may be affecting the empirical and theoretical attention it deserves in our models of successful aging.

Personality and Physical Health

In any discussion of older adults, a particularly important aspect of personality is its association with health. Most older adults have at least one chronic health condition (Wolff, Starfield, & Anderson, 2002), and health has been shown to be the strongest predictor of emotional well-being in later life (e.g., Larson, 1978; Okun, Stock, Haring, & Witter, 1984). There are many studies that document an association of disease and personality characteristics (e.g., Booth-Kewley & Friedman, 1987; Contrada, Cather, & O'Leary, 1999; Danner, Snowdon, & Friesen, 2001; Friedman & Booth-Kewley, 1987; Smith & Spiro, 2002; Williams & Wiebe, 2000). Extraversion and conscientiousness have both been associated with longevity, and neuroticism and agreeableness (low) predict cardiovascular disease and early mortality.

There are several pathways by which personality and health could be related. First, there could be a direct causal relationship. This would be the case to the extent that traits shape experiences that trigger physiological reactions (e.g., such as cardiovascular reactivity or changes in immune system functioning) that over time are damaging to health. The links between hostility and cardiovascular reactivity are well-established (e.g., Siegler et al., 2003). Secondly, personality may act indirectly to influence health outcomes via behaviors that influence health. Extraversion, for example, has been linked to social support (e.g., Smith & Gallo, 2001), known to be related to health. Neuroticism and conscientiousness (low) are related to negative health behaviors such as smoking, lack of exercise, poor diet, and excessive alcohol consumption (Smith & Gallo, 2001), which are all linked to poorer health outcomes. A third causal pathway might be via processes that happen postdiagnosis. Neuroticism is related to poorer coping behaviors, and conscientiousness is linked with adherence to treatment regimens.

Personality and Cognitive Health

Cognitive abilities have not typically been studied as an "outcome" of personality, but it is plausible and likely that they are linked, both directly and indirectly. For example, a trait such as conscientiousness predicts stronger goal setting and self-efficacy (Judge & Ilies, 2002), which would lead to better performance on cognitive tasks. Similarly, to the extent that cognitive abilities are stimulated and maintained with social engagement, traits associated with social activities such as extraversion, agreeableness, and (low) neuroticism would be relevant.

To what extent might personality be predictive of disease outcomes, such as dementia? Certainly changes in personality are common among those with diagnosed dementia (e.g., Chatterjee, Strauss, Smyth, & Whitehouse, 1992) and have been recognized as indicators of early change among persons with Alzheimer's disease (AD; e.g., Jost & Grossberg, 1996; Petry, Cummings, Hill, & Shapira, 1988; Rubin, Morris, & Berg, 1987). Emerging literature shows that changes in personality traits could be noncognitive indicators of early-stage or preclinical AD. Balsis, Carpenter, and Storandt (2005) examined personality changes on the Blessed Dementia Scale and argued that personality changes *precede* cognitive changes that form the basis of AD diagnosis. Duchek, Balota, Storandt, and Larsen (2007) showed that on the basis of both self and informant reports of personality traits (NEO-FFI), those with early-stage AD scored higher on neuroticism and lower on conscientiousness than did healthy controls. Furthermore, Wilson, Schneider, Arnold, Bienias, and Bennett (2007), in the Religious Orders study, showed prospectively that those scoring in the 90th percentile on the neuroticism scale (as measured by NEO-FFI) were twice as likely to develop AD as those in the lowest (10th) percentile. In another study with the same sample and prospective design, Wilson and colleagues (2007) showed that those scoring in the 90th percentile on conscientiousness had an 89% reduction in risk of AD as well as a reduced risk of MCI. Interestingly, while conscientiousness was not related to level of global cognition or MCI at baseline, over a 12-year period the trajectories of declines in global cognition, visuospatial ability, and four different aspects of memory were steeper and more negative for those with low conscientiousness scores compared to those with high scores (Wilson et al., 2007). Finally, in a study utilizing the participants in the Swedish Twin Registry (Crowe, Andel, Pedersen, Fratiglioni, & Gatz, 2006), there was some evidence that high neuroticism and low extraversion (using the EPI-Q) was predictive of cognitive impairment 25 years later. Thus, personality does seem to be associated with cognitive outcomes in later life. Indeed, data support the idea that personality change may be linked with cognitive change and may, in fact, be a harbinger of AD.

SUMMARY

Personality research in adulthood and later life continues to be a flourishing field, and the advancement of integrative personality development models should foster increased collaboration and multidisciplinary research in the future. The domain of personality will continue to play a promising role in the study of aging because it may determine how some individuals achieve healthy, adaptive, and creative personal performance, particularly in the second half of life.

REFERENCES

Adams, C., Smith, M. C., Pasupathi, M., & Vitolo, L. (2002). Social context effects on story recall in older and younger women: Does the listener make a difference? *Journal of Gerontology: Psychological Sciences, 57B*, 28–40.

Adkins, G., Martin, P., & Poon, L. W. (1996). Personality traits and states as predictors of subjective well-being in centenarians, octogenarians, and sexagenarians. *Psychology and Aging, 11*, 408–416.

Allport, G. W. (1961). *Pattern and Growth in Personality.* New York: Holt, Rinehart and Winston.

Allport, G. W., & Odbert, H. S. (1936). Trait-names: A psycho-lexical study. *Psychological Monographs, 47*, 171–220.

Balsis, S., Carpenter, B. D., & Storandt, M. (2005). Personality change precedes diagnosis of dementia of the Alzheimer type. *Journal of Gerontology: Psychological Sciences, 60B*, P98–P101.

Baltes, M. M., & Carstensen, L. L. (1999). Social psychological theories and their applications to aging: From individual to collective social psychology. In V. L. Bengtson & K. W. Schaie (Eds.), *Handbook of Theories of Aging* (pp. 209–226). New York: Springer.

Baltes, P., & Baltes, M. (1990). Psychological perspectives on successful aging: The model of selective optimization with compensation. In P. Baltes & M. Baltes (Eds.), *Successful Aging: Perspectives From the Behavioral Sciences* (pp. 1–34). Cambridge, UK: Cambridge University Press.

Baltes, P. B., Lindenberger, U., & Staudinger, U. M. (2006). Life span theory in developmental psychology. In W. Damon (Series Ed.) & R. M. Lerner (Vol. Ed.), *Handbook of Child Psychology* (6th ed., vol. 1, pp. 569–664). New York: Wiley.

Bandura, A. (1997). *Self-efficacy: The Exercise of Control.* New York: Freeman.

Bartlett, F. (1932). *Remembering: A Study in Experimental and Social Psychology.* New York: Cambridge University Press.

Blanchard-Fields, F., & Kalinauskas, A. S. (2008). Theoretical perspectives on adult development and learning. In M. C. Smith & T. G. Reio, Jr. (Eds.), *Handbook of Research on Adult Development and Learning* (pp. 3–33). Mahwah, NJ: Lawrence Erlbaum Associates.

Bolkan, C. R., Meierdiercks, P., & Hooker, K. (2008). Stability and change in the six-foci model of personality: Personality development in midlife and beyond. In M. C. Smith & T. G. Reio, Jr. (Eds.), *Handbook of Research on Adult Development and Learning* (pp. 220–240). Mahwah, NJ: Lawrence Erlbaum Associates.

Booth-Kewley, S., & Friedman, H. S. (1987). Psychological predictors of heart disease: A quantitative review. *Psychological Bulletin, 101*, 343–362.

Buchanan, T. W., & Adolphs, R. (2002). The role of the human amygdala in emotional modulation of long-term declarative memory. In S. C. Moore & M. Oaksford (Eds.), *Emotional Cognition: From Brain to Behaviour* (pp. 9–34). Amsterdam: Benjamins.

Cantor, N. (1990). From thought to behavior: "Having" and "doing" in the study of personality and cognition. *American Psychologist, 45,* 735–750.

Cantor, N., & Kihlstrom, J. (1987). *Personality and Social Intelligence.* Englewood Cliffs, NJ: Prentice Hall.

Carstensen, L. L. (1995). Evidence for a life-span theory of social selectivity. *Current Directions in Psychological Science, 4,* 151–156.

Carstensen, L. L., Isaacowitz, D. M., & Charles, S. T. (1999). Taking time seriously: A theory of socioemotional selectivity. *American Psychologist, 54,* 165–181.

Carstensen, L. L., & Mikels, J. A. (2005). At the intersection of emotion and cognition: Aging and the positivity effect. *Current Directions in Psychological Science, 14,* 117–121.

Carstensen, L. L., Mikels, J. A., & Mather, M. (2006). Aging and the intersection of cognition, motivation and emotion. In J. Birren & K. W. Schaie (Eds.), *Handbook of the Psychology of Aging* (6th ed., pp. 343–362). San Diego, CA: Academic Press.

Carstensen, L. L., Pasupathi, M., Mayr, U., & Nesselroade, J. (2000). Emotion experience in the daily lives of older and younger adults. *Journal of Personality and Social Psychology, 79*(4), 1–12.

Carstensen, L. L., & Turk-Charles, S. (1994). The salience of emotion across the adult life course. *Psychology and Aging, 9,* 259–264.

Caspi, A., Roberts, B. W., & Shiner, R. (2005). Personality development. *Annual Review of Psychology, 56,* 453–484.

Charles, S., Mather, M., & Carstensen, L. L. (2003). Aging and emotional memory: The forgettable nature of negative images for older adults. *Journal of Experimental Psychology: General, 132,* 310–324.

Chatterjee, A., Strauss, M., Smyth, K., & Whitehouse, P. (1992). Personality changes in Alzheimer's disease. *Archives of Neurology, 49,* 486–491.

Comblain, C., D'Argembeau, A., Van der Linden, M., & Aldenhoff, L. (2004). The effect of ageing on the recollection of emotional and neutral pictures. *Memory, 12,* 673–684.

Contrada, R. J., Cather, C., & O'Leary, A. (1999). Personality and health: Dispositions and processes in disease susceptibility and adaptation to illness. In L. A. Pervin & O. P. John (Eds.), *Handbook of Personality* (2nd ed., pp. 576–604). New York: Guildford.

Costa, P. T., Jr., & McCrae, R. R. (1980). Still stable after all these years: Personality as a key to some issues in adulthood and old age. In P. Baltes & O. Brim, Jr. (Eds.), *Life-span Development and Behavior* (vol. 3, pp. 65–102). New York: Academic Press.

Cross, S., & Markus, H. (1991). Possible selves across the lifespan. *Human Development, 34,* 230–255.

Crowe, M., Andel, R., Pedersen, N. L., Fratiglioni, L., & Gatz, M. (2006). Personality and risk of cognitive impairment 25 years later. *Psychology and Aging, 21,* 573–580.

Danner D., Snowdon, D. A., & Friesen, W. V. (2001). Positive emotions in early life and longevity: Findings from the Nun Study. *Journal of Personality and Social Psychology, 80*(5), 804–813.

David, J., Green, P., Martin, R., & Suls, J. (1997). Differential roles of neuroticism, extraversion, and event desirability on mood in daily life: An integrative model of top-down and bottom-up influences. *Journal of Personality and Social Psychology*, 73, 149–159.

Diehl, M. (2006). Development of self-representations in adulthood. In D. K. Mroczek & T. D. Little (Eds.), *Handbook of Personality Development* (pp. 373–398). Mahwah, NJ: Lawrence Erlbaum Associates.

Digman, J. (1990). Personality structure: Emergence of the five-factor model. *Annual Review of Psychology*, 41, 417–440.

Dijkstra, K., & Kaup, B. (2005). Mechanisms of autobiographical memory retrieval in younger and older adults. *Memory & Cognition*, 33(5), 811–820.

Duchek, J. M., Balota, D. A., Storandt, M., & Larsen, R. (2007). The power of personality in discriminating between healthy aging and early-stage Alzheimer's disease. *Journal of Gerontology: Psychological Sciences*, 62B, P353–P361.

Ebner, N. C., Freund, A. M., & Baltes, P. (2006). Developmental changes in goal orientation from youth to late adulthood: From striving for gains to maintenance and prevention of losses. *Psychology and Aging*, 21, 664–678.

Eizenman, D., Nesselroade, J., Featherman, D., & Rowe, J. (1997). Intraindividual variability in perceived control in an older sample: The MacArthur Successful Aging Studies. *Psychology and Aging*, 12, 489–502.

Emmons, R. A. (1986). Personal strivings: An approach to personality and subjective well-being. *Journal of Personality and Social Psychology*, 51, 1058–1068.

Erikson, E. H. (1959). Identity and the life cycle. *Psychological Issues Monograph 1*. New York: International University Press.

Field, D. (1981). Retrospective reports by healthy intelligent elderly people of personal events of their adult lives. *International Journal of Behavioral Development*, 4, 77–97.

Fiese, B., Hooker, K., Kotary, L., Schwagler, J., & Rimmer, M. (1995). Family stories: Gender differences in the early stages of parenthood. *Journal of Marriage and the Family*, 57, 763–770.

Fleeson, W. (2001). Toward a structure- and process-integrated view of personality: traits as density distribution of states. *Journal of Personality & Social Psychology*, 80(6), 1011–1027.

Fleeson, W., Malanos, A. B., & Achille, N. M. (2002). An intraindividual process approach to the relationship between extraversion and positive affect: is acting extraverted as "good" as being extraverted? *Journal of Personality & Social Psychology*, 83(6), 1409–1422.

Folkman, S., & Lazarus, R. S. (1985). If it changes it must be a process: Study of emotion and coping during three stages of a college examination. *Journal of Personality & Social Psychology*, 48, 150–170.

Fraley, R. C., & Roberts, B. W. (2005). Patterns of continuity: A dynamic model for conceptualizing the stability of individual differences in psychological constructs across the life course. *Psychological Review*, 112, 60–74.

Frazier, L. D., & Hooker, K. (2006). Possible selves in adult development: Linking theory and research. In C. Dunkel & J. Kerpelman (Eds.), *Possible Selves: Theory, Research, and Application* (pp. 41–59). Huntington, NY: Nova Science.

Frazier, L. D., Hooker, K., Johnson, P. M., & Kaus, C. R. (2000). Continuity and change in possible selves in later life: A 5-year longitudinal study. *Basic and Applied Social Psychology*, 22(3), 237–243.

Freund, A. M., & Baltes, P. B. (2000). The orchestration of selection, optimization, and compensation: An action-theoretical conceptualization of a theory developmental regulation. In W. J. Perrig & A. Grob (Eds.), *Control of Human Behavior, Mental Processes and Consciousness* (pp. 35–58). Mahwah, NJ: Lawrence Erlbaum Associates.

Friedman, H. S., & Booth-Kewley, S. (1987). The "disease-prone personality": A meta-analytic view of the construct. *American Psychologist, 42*, 539–555.

Fung, H. H., & Carstensen, L. L. (2003). Sending memorable messages to the old: Age differences in preferences and memory for advertisements. *Journal of Personality and Social Psychology, 85*(1), 163–178.

Goldberg, L. (1993). The structure of phenotypic personality traits. *American Psychologist, 48*, 26–34.

Gollwitzer, P. M., & Wicklund, R. A. (1985). The pursuit of self-defining goals. In J. Kuhl & J. Beckmann (Eds.), *Action Control: From Cognition to Behaviour* (pp. 61–88). Berlin: Springer.

Gross, J. J., Carstensen, L. L., Pasupathi, M., Tsai, J., Skorpen, C. G., & Hsu, A. Y. C. (1997). Emotion and aging: Experience, expression, and control. *Psychology and Aging, 12*, 590–599.

Grühn, D., Smith, J., & Baltes, P. B. (2005). No aging bias favoring memory for positive material: Evidence from a heterogeneity-homogeneity list paradigm using emotionally toned words. *Psychology and Aging, 20*, 579–588.

Hashtroudi, S., Johnson, M. K., & Chrosniak, L. D. (1990). Aging and qualitative characteristics of memories for perceived and imagined complex events. *Psychology and Aging, 5*, 119–126.

Heatherton, T. F., & Weinberger, J. L. (Eds.). (1994). *Can Personality Change?* Washington, DC: American Psychological Association Press.

Heckhausen, J. (2001). Adaptation and resilience in midlife. In M. E. Lachman (Ed.), *Handbook of Midlife Development* (pp. 345–394). New York: Wiley.

Heckhausen J., & Schulz, R. (1995). A life-span theory of control. *Psychological Review, 102*, 284–304.

Heine, S. J., & Buchtel, E. E. (2009). Personality: The universal and the culturally specific. *Annual Review of Psychology, 60*, 369–394.

Helson, R., Jones, C. J., & Kwan, V.S.Y. (2002). Personality change over 40 years of adulthood: HLM analyses of two longitudinal samples. *Journal of Personality and Social Psychology, 83*, 752–766.

Helson, R., Kwan, V. S., John, O. P., & Jones, C. (2002). The growing evidence for personality change in adulthood: Findings from research with personality inventories. *Journal of Research in Personality, 36*, 287–306.

Holahan, C. K. (2003). Stability and change in positive self-appraisal from midlife to later aging. *International Journal of Aging and Human Development, 56*, 247–267.

Hooker, K. (1992). Possible selves and perceived health in older adults and college students. *Journal of Gerontology: Psychological Sciences, 47*(2), P85–P95.

Hooker, K. (1999). Possible selves in adulthood: Incorporating teleonomic relevance into studies of the self. In F. Blanchard-Fields & T. Hess (Eds.), *Social Cognition and Aging* (pp. 97–122). New York: Academic Press.

Hooker, K. (2002). New directions for research in personality and aging: A comprehensive model for linking levels, structures, and processes. *Journal of Research on Personality, 36*, 318–334.

Hooker, K., & Kaus, C. R. (1994). Health-related possible selves in young and middle adulthood. *Psychology and Aging, 9,* 126–133.

Hooker, K., & McAdams, D. P. (2003). Personality reconsidered: A new agenda for aging research. *Journal of Gerontology: Psychological Sciences, 58B,* P296–P304.

Isaacowitz, D. M., Wadlinger, H. A., Goren, D., & Wilson, H. R. (2006). Selective preference in visual fixation away from negative images in old age? An eye-tracking study. *Psychology and Aging, 21,* 40–48.

James, W. (1890). *Principles of Psychology.* New York: Holt.

John, O. P. (1990). The "big five" factor taxonomy: Dimensions of personality in the natural language and in questionnaires. In L. A. Pervin (Ed.), *Handbook of Personality: Theory and Research* (pp. 66–100). New York: Guilford Press.

Jones, C., & Meredith, W. (1996). Patterns of personality change across the life span. *Psychology and Aging, 11,* 57–65.

Jost, B., & Grossberg, G. (1996). The evolution of psychiatric symptoms in Alzheimer's disease: A natural history study. *Journal of the American Geriatrics Society, 44,* 1078–1081.

Judge, T. A., & Ilies, R. (2002). Relationship of personality to performance motivation: A meta-analytic review. *Journal of Applied Psychology, 87,* 797–807.

Juslin, P. N., & Laukka, P. (2003). Communication of emotion in vocal expression and music performance: Different Channels, same code? *Psychological Bulletin, 129,* 770–814.

Kennedy, Q., Mather, M., & Carstensen, L. L. (2004). The role of motivation in the age-related positivity effect in autobiographical memory. *Psychological Science, 15,* 208–214.

Klinger, E. (1975). Consequences of commitment to and disengagement from incentives. *Psychological Review, 82,* 1–25.

Kotre, J. (1984). *Outliving the Self: Generativity and the Interpretation of Lives.* Baltimore, MD: Johns Hopkins.

Labouvie-Vief, G. (1999). Emotions in adulthood. In V. L. Bengtson & K. W. Schaie (Eds.), *Handbook of Theories of Aging* (pp. 253–267). New York: Springer.

Labouvie-Vief, G. (2003). Dynamic integration: Affect, cognition, and the self in adulthood. *Current Directions in Psychological Science, 12*(6), 201–206.

Labouvie-Vief, G., Chiodo, L. M., Goguen, L. A., Diehl, M., & Orwoll, L. (1995). Representations of self across the life span. *Psychology & Aging, 10,* 404–415.

Labouvie-Vief, G., & Diehl, M. (1999). Self and personality development. In J. C. Cavanaugh & S. K. Whitbourne (Eds.), *Gerontology: An Interdisciplinary Perspective* (pp. 238–268). New York: Oxford University Press.

Lachman, M. E. (1986). Locus of control in aging research: A case for multidimensional and domain-specific assessment. *Psychology & Aging, 1*(1), 34–40.

Lachman, M. E. (2006). Perceived control over aging-related declines. *Current Directions in Psychological Science, 15,* 282–286.

Lachman M. E., & Bertrand, R. M. (2001). Personality and the self in midlife. In M. E. Lachman (Ed.), *Handbook of Midlife Development.* New York: Wiley.

Lachman, M., & Weaver, S. (1998). Sociodemographic variations in the sense of control by domain: Findings from the MacArthur Studies of Midlife. *Psychology and Aging, 13,* 553–562.

Langer, E., & Rodin, J. (1976). The effects of choice and enhanced personal responsibility for the aged: A field experiment in an institutional setting. *Journal of Personality and Social Psychology, 61,* 191–198.

Larson, R. (1978). Thirty years of research on the subjective well-being of older Americans. *Journal of Gerontology, 33,* 109–125.

Lawton, M. P., Kleban, M. H., Rajagopal, D., & Dean, J. (1992). Dimensions of affective experience in three age groups. *Psychology and Aging, 7,* 171–184.

Lazarus, R. S. (1993). From psychological stress to the emotions: A history of changing outlooks. *Annual Review Psychology, 44,* 1–21.

Lerner, R. M., & Busch-Rossnagel, N. A. (1981). Individuals as producers of their development: Conceptual and empirical bases. In R. M. Lerner & N. A. Busch-Rossnagel (Eds.), *Individuals as Producers of Their Development: A Life-span Perspective* (pp. 1–36). New York: Academic Press.

Levenson, R. W., (1994). Human emotion: A functional view. In P. Ekman & R. J. Davidson (Eds.), *The Nature of Emotion: Fundamental Questions* (pp. 123–126). New York: Oxford University Press.

Light, J. M., Grigsby, J. S., & Bligh, M. C. (1996). Aging and heterogeneity: Genetics, social structure, and personality. *The Gerontologist, 36*(2), 165–173.

Little, B. R. (1983). Personal projects: A rationale and method for investigation. *Environment and Behavior, 15,* 273–309.

Markus, H. R. (2004). Culture and personality: Brief for an arranged marriage. *Journal of Research in Personality, 38,* 75–83.

Markus, H. R., & Kitayama, S. (1991). Culture and the self: Implications for cognition, emotion, and motivation. *Psychological Review, 98,* 224–253.

Markus, H., & Nurius, P. (1986). Possible selves. *American Psychologist, 41,* 954–969.

Mather, M., & Carstensen, L. L. (2003). Aging and attentional biases for emotional faces. *Psychological Science, 14,* 409–415.

McAdams, D. P. (1995). What do we know when we know a person? *Journal of Personality, 63*(3), 365–396.

McAdams, D. (1996). Narrating the self in adulthood. In J. Birren, G. Kenyon, J. Ruth, J. Schroots, & T. Svensson (Eds.), *Aging and Biography: Exploration in Adult Development* (pp. 131–148). New York: Springer.

McAdams, D. P. (2001). The psychology of life stories. *Review of General Psychology, 5,* 100–122.

McAdams, D. P., & Pals, J. (2006). A new big five: Fundamental principles for an integrative science of personality. *American Psychologist, 61*(3), 204–217.

McCrae, R. R., & Allik, J. (Eds.). (2002). *The Five-factor Model of Personality Across Cultures.* New York: Kluwer Acad./Plenum.

McCrae, R. R., & Costa, P. T. (2003). *Personality in Adulthood: A Five-factor Theory Perspective* (2nd ed.). New York: Guilford Press.

McCrae, R. R., & Terracciano, A. (2005). Universal features of personality traits from the observer's perspective: Data from 50 cultures. *Journal of Personality & Social Psychology, 88*(3), 547–561.

McGregor, I., & Little, B. R. (1998). Personal projects, happiness and meaning: On doing well and being yourself. *Journal of Personality and Social Psychology, 74,* 494–512.

Mischel, W. (1968). *Personality and Assessment*. New York: Wiley.

Mischel, W. (2004). Toward an integrative science of the person. *Annual Review of Psychology, 55*, 1–22.

Molenaar, P.C.M. (2004). A manifesto on psychology as idiographic science: Bringing the person back into scientific psychology, this time forever. *Measurement, 2*, 201–218.

Mroczek, D. K. (2001). Age and emotion in adulthood. *Current Directions in Psychological Science, 10*, 87–90.

Mroczek, D. K., & Spiro, A. (2007). Personality change influences mortality in older men. *Psychological Science, 18*(5), 371–376.

Mroczek, D. K., Spiro, A., III, & Griffin, P. W. (2006). Personality and aging. In J. E. Birren & K. W. Schaie, (Eds.), *Handbook of the Psychology of Aging* (6th ed., pp. 363–377). Burlington, MA: Elsevier.

Murphy, N. A., & Isaacowitz, D. M. (2008). Preferences for emotional information in older and younger adults: A meta-analysis of memory and attention tasks. *Psychology and Aging, 23*, 263–286.

Murray, H. A., & Kluckhohn, C. (1953). Outline of a conception of personality. In C. Kluckhohn & H. A. Murray (Eds.), *Personality in Nature, Society, and Culture* (2nd ed., pp. 3–32). New York: Alfred A. Knopf.

Nesselroade, J. R. (1987). Some implications of the trait-state distinction for the study of development over the life span: The case of personality. In P. B. Baltes, D. L. Featherman, & R. M. Lerner (Eds.), *Life-span Development and Behavior* (vol. 8, pp. 163–189). Hillsdale, NJ: Lawrence Erlbaum Associates.

Nesselroade, J. R. (1990). Adult personality development: Issues in assessing constancy and change. In A. Rabin, R. A. Zucker, R. A. Emmons, & S. Frank (Eds.), *Studying Persons and Lives* (pp. 41–85). New York: Springer.

Nesselroade, J. R. (1991). The warp and woof of the developmental fabric. In R. Downs, L. Liben, & D. Palermo (Eds.), *Visions of the Development, the Environment, and Aesthetics: The Legacy of Joachim F. Wohlwill*. Hillsdale, NJ: Lawrence Erlbaum Associates.

Nesselroade, J. R. (2001). Intraindividual variability in development within and between individuals. *European Psychologist, 6*, 187–193.

Nesselroade, J. R., & Ram, N. (2004). Studying intraindividual variability: What we have learned that will help us understand lives in context. *Research in Human Development, 1*, 9–29.

Oatley, K. (2004). *Emotions: A Brief History*. Maden, MA: Blackwell Publishing.

Oishi, S. (2004). Personality in culture: A neo-Allportian view. *Journal of Research in Personality, 38*, 68–74.

Okun, M. A., & Stock, W. A., Haring, M. J., & Witter, R. A. (1984). Health and subjective well-being: A meta-analysis. *International Journal of Aging and Human Development, 19*, 111–132.

Ong, A. D., Bergeman, C. S., Bisconti, T. L., & Wallace, K. A. (2006). Psychological resilience, positive emotions, and successful adaptation to stress in later life. *Journal of Personality and Social Psychology, 91*, 730–749.

Ozer, D., & Benet-Martinez, V. (2006). Personality and the prediction of consequential outcomes. *Annual Review of Psychology, 57*, 401–421.

Pasupathi, M. (2001). The social construction of the personal past and its implications for adult development. *Psychological Bulletin, 127*(5), 651–672.

Petry, S., Cummings, J., Hill, M., & Shapira, J. (1988). Personality alterations in dementia of the Alzheimer type. *Archives of Neurology, 45,* 1187–1190.

Phillips, L. H., Henry, J. D., Hosie, J. A., & Milne, A. B. (2008). Effective regulation of the experience and expression of negative affect in old age. *Journals of Gerontology: Psychological and Social Sciences, 63,* P138–P145.

Riediger, M., Freund, A. M., & Baltes, P. B. (2005). Managing life through personal goals: Intergoal facilitation and intensity of goal pursuit in younger and older adulthood. *Journals of Gerontology: Psychological Sciences, 60B,* P84–P91.

Roberts, B. W., Caspi, A., & Moffitt, T. E. (2003). Work experiences and personality development in young adulthood. *Journal of Personality and Social Psychology, 84,* 582–593.

Roberts, B. W., & DelVecchio, W. F. (2000). The rank-order consistency of personality traits from childhood to old age: A quantitative review of longitudinal studies. *Psychological Bulletin, 126,* 3–25.

Roberts, B. W., Kuncel, N. R., Shiner, R., Caspi, A., & Goldberg, L. R. (2007). The power of personality: The comparative validity of personality traits, socioeconomic status, and cognitive ability for predicting important life outcomes. *Perspectives on Psychological Science, 2,* 313–345.

Roberts, B. W., & Mroczek, D. (2008). Personality trait change in adulthood. *Current Directions in Psychological Science, 17,* 31–35.

Roberts, B. W., Robins, R. W., Trzesniewski, K. H., & Caspi, A. (2003). Personality trait development in adulthood. In J. T. Mortimer & M. J. Shanahan (Eds.), *Handbook of the Life Course* (pp. 579–595). New York: Springer.

Roberts, B. W., Walton, K., & Viechtbauer, W. (2006). Patterns of mean-level change in Personality traits across the life course: A meta-analysis of longitudinal studies. *Psychological Bulletin, 132,* 1–25.

Rowe, J. W., & Kahn, R. L. (1987). Human aging: Usual and successful. *Science, 237,* 143–149.

Rowe, J. W., & Kahn, R. L. (1998). *Successful Aging.* New York: Pantheon Books.

Rozin, P., & Royzman, E. B. (2001). Negativity bias, negativity dominance, and contagion. *Personality and Social Psychology Review, 5,* 296–320.

Rubin, E., Morris, J., & Berg, L. (1987). The progression of personality changes in senile dementia of the Alzheimer's type. *Journal of the American Geriatrics Society, 35,* 721–725.

Runyan, W. M. (1983). Idiographic goals and methods in the study of lives. *Journal of Personality, 51*(3), 413–437.

Ryff, C. D. (1991). Possible selves in adulthood and old age: A tale of shifting horizons. *Psychology and Aging, 6,* 286–295.

Scheibe, S., & Blanchard-Fields, F. (2009). Effects of regulating emotions on cognitive performance: What is costly for young adults is not so costly for older adults. *Psychology and Aging, 24,* 217–223.

Schulz, R. (1976). Effects of control and predictability on the physical and psychological well-being of the institutionalized aged. *Journal of Personality and Social Psychology,* 563–573.

Schulz, R. (1985). Emotion and affect. In J. E. Birren & K. W. Schaie (Eds.), *Handbook of the Psychology of Aging* (2nd ed., pp. 531–543). New York: Van Nostrand Reihold Company.

Settersten, R. A., & Trauten, M. E. (2008). Theorizing the new terrain of old age: Hallmarks, freedoms, and risks. In V. Bengtson, M. Silverstein, D. Putney, & S. Gans (Eds.), *Handbook of Theories of Aging* (pp. 455–470). New York: Springer.

Sheldon, K. M. (2008). Changes in goal-striving across the life span: Do people learn to select more self-concordant goals as they age? In M. C. Smith & T. G. Reio, Jr. (Eds.), *Handbook of Adult Development and Learning* (pp. 551–567). Mahwah, NJ: Lawrence Erlbaum Associates.

Sheldon, K. M., & Kasser, T. (1998). Pursuing personal goals: Skills enable progress, but not all progress is beneficial. *Personality and Social Psychology Bulletin, 24*, 1319–1331.

Shifren, K., & Hooker, K. (1995). Daily measurements of anxiety and affect: A study among spouse caregivers. *International Journal of Behavioral Development, 18*(4), 595–607.

Siegler, I. C., Costa, P. T., Brummett, B. H., Helms, M. J., Barefoot, J. C., Williams, R. B., et al. (2003). Patterns of change in hostility from college to midlife in the UNC Alumni Heart Study predict high-risk status. *Psychosomatic Medicine, 65*, 738–745.

Sliwinski, M., & Mogle, J. (2008). Time-based and process-based approaches to analysis of longitudinal data. In S. M. Hofer & D. F. Alwin (Eds.), *Handbook of Cognitive Aging: Interdisciplinary Perspectives* (pp. 477–491). Thousand Oaks, CA: Sage.

Sliwinski, M. J., Smyth, J. Stawski, R. S., & Almeida, D. M. (under review). Short-term and long-term variability and change in emotional states and their association with health and social connections in older adults.

Smith, T. W., & Gallo, L. C. (2001). Personality traits as risk factors for physical illness. In A. Baum, T. Revenson, & J. Singer (Eds.), *Handbook of Health Psychology* (pp. 139–172). Hillsdale, NJ: Lawrence Erlbaum Associates.

Smith, T. W., & Spiro, III, A. (2002). Personality, health, and aging: Prolegomenon for the next generation. *Journal of Research in Personality, 36*, 363–394.

Sneed, J. R., & Whitbourne, S. K. (2003). Identity processing and self-consciousness in middle and later adulthood. *Journal of Gerontology: Psychological Sciences and Social Sciences, 58*, 313–319.

Staudinger, U., & Kunzmann, U. (2005). Positive adult personality development: Adjustment and/or growth? *European Psychologist, 10*(4), 320–329.

Wilson, R. S., Schneider, J. A., Arnold, S. E., Bienias, J. L., & Bennett, D. A. (2007). Conscientiousness and the incidence of Alzheimer's disease and mild cognitive impairment. *Archives of General Psychiatry, 64*, 1204–1212.

Whitbourne, S. K. (1987). Personality development in adulthood and old age: Relationships among identity style, health, and well-being. In K. W. Schaie (Ed.), *Annual Review of Gerontology and Geriatrics* (pp. 189–216). New York: Springer.

Whitbourne, S. K. (1999). Identity and adaptation to the aging process. In C. Ryff & V. Marshall (Eds.), *The Self and Society in Aging Processes* (pp. 122–149). New York: Springer.

Whitbourne, S. K., & Connolly, L. A. (1999). The developing self in midlife. In S. B. Willis & J. Reid (Eds.), *Life in the Middle: Psychological and Social Development in Middle Age* (pp. 25–45). San Diego: Academic Press.

Williams, P. G., & Wiebe, D. J. (2000). Individual differences in self-assessed health: Gender, neuroticism, and physical symptom reports. *Personality and Individual Differences, 28*, 823–835.

Wilson, A. E., & Ross, M. (2003). The identity function of autobiographical memory: Time is on our side. *Memory, 11*(2), 137–149.

Wilson, R. S., Schneider, J. A., Arnold, S. E., Bienias, J. L., & Bennett, D. A. (2007). Conscientiousness and the incidence of Alzheimer disease and mild cognitive impairment. *Archives of General Psychiatry, 64*, 1204–1212.

Wolff, J. L., Starfield, B., & Anderson, G. (2002). Prevalence, expenditures, and complications of multiple chronic conditions in the elderly. *Archives of Internal Medicine, 162*, 2269–2276.

Wood, S., Busemeyer, J., Koling, A., Cox, C. R., & Davis, H. (2005). Older adults as adaptive decision makers: Evidence from the Iowa Gambling Task. *Psychology and Aging, 20*, 220–225.

Wrosch, C., Dunne, E., Scheier, M. F., & Schulz, R. (2006). Self-regulation of common age-related challenges: Benefits for older adults' psychological and physical health. *Journal of Behavioral Medicine, 29*, 299–306.

Wrosch, C., & Schulz, R. (2008). Health-engagement control strategies and 2-year changes in older adults' physical health. *Psychological Science, 19*, 537–541.

Wurm, L. H., Labouvie-Vief, G., Aycock, J., Rebucal, K. A., & Koch, H. E. (2004). Performance in auditory and visual emotional Stroop tasks: A comparison of older and younger adults. *Psychology and Aging, 19*, 523–535.

Chapter 6

The Content and Consequences of Age Stereotypes

Carrie Andreoletti

Stereotypes of aging permeate our youth-centered culture. We are bombarded with advertisements for products that promise to ameliorate the negative effects of aging and keep us looking and feeling younger: creams to make wrinkles disappear, pills to increase virility, and video games to improve memory. Companies that market these products are acutely aware that people over the age of 65 are part of the fastest growing segment of our population, with this group projected to double in the next 20 years. By the year 2030, an estimated 21% of the U.S. population, approximately 66 million people, will be age 65 or over (U.S. Bureau of the Census, 2007). With the oldest of the baby boomers now entering their seventh decade, understanding the content and consequences of age stereotypes has never been more important.

Age stereotypes are unique because unlike stereotypes related to characteristics such as sex and race—qualities that are for the most part fixed at birth—age is dynamic. Because the majority of us will make it to old age, we will ultimately become members of this stereotyped out-group. Thus, early in life a person will identify with the in-group (young) and later in life with the out-group (old). For this reason, age stereotypes can be thought of as both social and self-related cognitions; thus, age stereotypes are developmentally dynamic and become charged with self-involvement as we age (Heckhausen &

I would like to thank Leonard J. Kent, Valerie Kent, Marianne Fallon, Carolyn R. Fallahi, and Robin L. West for their helpful comments on earlier drafts of this chapter.

Krueger, 1993). This dynamic quality makes the study of age stereotypes a rich and valuable resource for understanding adult development and aging.

One way researchers have examined age stereotypes is by focusing on their *content* (for a review see Kite, Stockdale, Whitley, & Johnson, 2005). What are stereotypes about aging? What attitudes and beliefs do people hold about aging and older adults? There is also a large body of research focused on the *process* of stereotyping (for reviews see Fiske, 1998; Hummert, 1999). Where do stereotypes about aging come from? How and why do we use stereotypes? Research on ageism examines how stereotypic beliefs about aging result in *prejudice* and *discrimination* against older adults (for a comprehensive volume see Nelson, 2002). How do beliefs about aging influence how we treat older adults? Finally, researchers have also begun to examine how age stereotypes might influence older adults' behavior in a number of domains, including cognitive and physical functioning (for reviews see Hess, 2006; Horton, Baker, Pearce, & Deakin, 2008). Can age stereotypes influence older adults' memory? What is the impact of age stereotypes on the health and well-being of older adults?

Although all of these questions are important, this chapter focuses primarily on the content of age stereotypes and concludes with a discussion of some of their potential consequences for the aging adult. The chapter begins with some basic definitions and theoretical frameworks for understanding stereotypes in general.

STEREOTYPES DEFINED

The study of stereotypes in general has been approached by social scientists from two different perspectives: the individual and the collective (Stangor & Schaller, 1996). The individual perspective assumes that people develop beliefs about important social groups in their environment based on interpersonal interactions with members of those groups. Over time, the beliefs become stereotypes and influence how a person responds to and perceives members of a stereotyped group. The study of stereotypes from an individual perspective is concerned with individual differences in the development and function of stereotypical beliefs. In contrast, the collective approach defines stereotypes as consensually held beliefs about a specific social group that are learned and maintained through language and communication in a given culture. According to the collective approach, direct contact with members of the stereotyped group is not essential for the development of stereotypes; rather, parents, peers, teachers, leaders, and the mass media transmit shared knowledge about stereotyped groups indirectly. Whereas research from the individual perspective tends to focus more on the process of stereotyping, research from the collective perspective tends to be more focused on the content of stereotypical beliefs (Stangor & Schaller, 1996).

Schneider (1996) has argued for the need to consider both the individual and collective approaches together. Despite differences, both approaches contribute important knowledge about stereotypes and are concerned with how stereotypes influence behavior. Knowing the content of consensually held stereotypes is important because these are the stereotypes most likely to have the greatest social impact in terms of how people in a stereotyped group are perceived and treated by society as a whole (Schneider, 1996). Knowledge about individual differences in the development and function of stereotypes is also important for learning how to change stereotypes and prevent prejudice and discrimination that can stem from stereotypical beliefs (Schneider, 1996). Finally, in considering the consequences of age stereotypes on the behavior of older adults themselves, both individual and collective stereotypes are likely to play a role.

Social psychologist Gordon Allport (1954) defined a stereotype as "an exaggerated belief associated with a category" (p. 191), a definition that allows us to consider the possibility that stereotypes may have some basis in accurate perceptions. Although some researchers have studied the accuracy of stereotypes (for a review see Lee, Jussim, & McCauley, 1995), the definition of a stereotype need not reflect their accuracy or inaccuracy. Allport also argued that stereotypes can be either favorable or unfavorable, but regardless, their purpose is to rationalize behavior toward the stereotyped group. As Cuddy and Fiske (2002) suggest, "accurate or not, stereotypes guide our social behavior and often govern what information we seek, heed, and remember" (p. 4). Simply stated, the most contemporary way to define stereotypes is as a collection of beliefs about a group of people (e.g., Schneider, 1996). This broad definition allows us to consider research on stereotypes from both the individual and collective perspectives as well as to include a wide array of positive and negative attributes (e.g., personality traits, demographic and role-related characteristics) under the term beliefs.

THEORETICAL UNDERPINNINGS

Much of the research on stereotypes has focused on the process of stereotyping as opposed to the content, which is assumed to be variable and somewhat elusive. Fiske and her colleagues (Cuddy & Fiske, 2002; Fiske, Cuddy, Glick, & Xu, 2002) have suggested that the study of stereotype process has been favored because it can be more easily grounded in theory, compared to stereotype content, which is tied to an ever-changing social context. Nevertheless, two theories have proved particularly useful for understanding stereotype content: the stereotype content model (Fiske et al., 2002) and social role theory (Eagly, 1987).

According to the stereotype content model (Fiske et al., 2002), two basic dimensions capture stereotypes of different social groups: competence (e.g., independent, skillful) and warmth (e.g., friendly, trustworthy). Stereotyped groups tend to be perceived high on one dimension and low on the other. Whether a particular out-group is perceived as competent or warm will depend on perceived power and status. High status groups (i.e., men) are more likely to be perceived as competent but "cold," whereas low status groups (i.e., elderly) are more likely to be perceived as warm but incompetent (Cuddy & Fiske, 2002).

Social role theory (Eagly, 1987) takes a somewhat different approach to understanding content. According to social role theory, stereotypes are the result of the social roles occupied by people belonging to the stereotyped social group. In the case of gender stereotypes, for example, men are perceived as having more *agentic* or *instrumental* traits (e.g., ambitious, dominant) because these traits are necessary for success in social roles typically occupied by men, such as working outside of the home and earning money to support a family. In contrast, women are perceived as having more *communal* or *expressive* traits (e.g., warm, nurturing) because these traits are necessary for success in social roles and occupations more commonly held by women, which tend to involve caretaking. Several studies have demonstrated that social roles can account for gender differences in perceived agency and communion (e.g., Eagly & Steffen, 1984; Jackson & Sullivan, 1990).

Social role theory and the stereotype content model are not mutually exclusive, and both approaches have been applied to understanding age stereotypes. According to the stereotype content model, social roles are important for determining a group's status. In addition, competence is considered a component of agency and warmth a component of communion. While agency is more commonly associated with youth, no age differences are typically found for communal traits (e.g., Kite, 1996; Knox & Gekoski, 1989; Kite, Deaux, & Miele, 1991), although older adults are perceived high on warmth (Cuddy & Fiske, 2002).

Examination of changes in social roles (and status according to the stereotype content model) can be used to predict changes in stereotype content. Diekman and Eagly (2000) found that stereotypes are dynamic to the extent that typical social roles are perceived to change over time. For example, they found that stereotypes of women are more dynamic than those of men because there have been greater changes in women's versus men's social roles within the last century. As women have entered the paid work force in greater numbers, they are perceived as having more agentic characteristics than older cohorts who were less likely to work outside of the home. In comparison, men have not taken on domestic responsibilities to the same extent that women have entered the workforce, and therefore, stereotypes of men have remained static over time. This has implications for understanding the content of age stereotypes. Given that social roles change over the life course, stereotypes of men and women are likely to change with age.

As older adults are living longer and remaining in the workforce longer, this will likely influence contemporary age stereotypes.

THE CONTENT OF AGE STEREOTYPES

Numerous methods have been developed for assessing beliefs about older adults. Although a comprehensive review is not provided here, there are several early researchers worth noting whose methods and instruments have made a lasting contribution. The methods developed in these early studies were frequently used and some continue to be in use today, although often with some modification.

Tuckman and Lorge (1952a, 1952b, 1953, 1958) are widely cited for their groundbreaking work on stereotypes of older adults. Their "Attitudes Toward Old People" scale was one of the first instruments developed to assess stereotypes of older adults. The scale consisted of 137 statements about older adults that tapped several different areas, including: activities and interests, family relations, physical problems, mental deterioration, and personality. People were asked to read each statement and circle "yes" if they were in general agreement or "no" if they were in general disagreement.

In the early 1960s, Kogan (1961a, 1961b; Kogan & Shelton, 1962) developed a different "Attitudes Toward Old People" scale, adapted from scales originally intended to assess attitudes toward ethnic minorities. His scale consisted of a matched set of 17 positive statements (i.e., "one of the more interesting qualities of most old people is their accounts of their past experiences") and 17 negative statements (i.e., "most old people get set in their ways and are unable to change") about older adults, which reflected such categories as the residential aspects of older adults' lives, the degree of tension and discomfort typically felt in the presence of older people, the homogeneity of older adults, intergenerational relations, dependency, cognitive style, personality, personal appearance, and power. People were asked to respond to each statement on a 7-point scale from 1 = *strongly disagree* to 7 = *strongly agree*, which allowed greater variability in the expression of attitudes about older adults than did Tuckman and Lorge's scale.

Another popular method for assessing stereotypes of older adults is Rosencranz and McNevin's (1969) Aging Semantic Differential (ASD). The ASD comprises 32 bipolar adjective pairs (e.g., productive–unproductive, independent–dependent, tolerant–intolerant), and people rate targets of different age groups (e.g., a male 70–85 years of age) on each adjective pair using 7-point scales. An advantage of this scale is that researchers can easily vary the characteristics (i.e., sex, age) of the target being rated, which allows for the comparison of stereotypes across different social groups.

Based on a review of the early research employing these measures, McTavish (1971) concluded that beliefs about older adults are generally negative. Specifically, he noted that older adults are stereotyped as "generally ill, tired, not sexually interested, mentally slower, forgetful and less able to learn new things, grouchy, withdrawn, feeling sorry for themselves, less likely to participate in activities (except perhaps religion), isolated, in the least happy or fortunate time of life, unproductive, and defensive in various combinations and with varying emphases" (p. 97). Few positive stereotypes emerged in his review, although older adults were perceived to be experienced, wise, and good to children (McTavish, 1971). Ten years later, Lutsky (1981) came to a somewhat different conclusion. He argued that attitudes toward older adults tend to be more positive or neutral rather than negative if you consider the conceptual meaning of the numbers used in the scales. For example, if you average the ratings made on a 7-point scale about a specific attribute of older adults, the mean rating would be in the middle of the scale (neutral) or more on the positive side. Although he noted that in comparison to stereotypes of younger age groups, stereotypes of older adults remained negative, he argued that the average of all of the studies he reviewed would most likely be neutral.

The study of stereotypes in general poses many methodological challenges, and research on age stereotypes is not exempt from these challenges. One major issue with research on stereotypes of older adults is the lack of consistent methodologies across studies, which makes it difficult to compare results from study to study (Kite & Johnson, 1988; Kogan, 1979; Lutsky, 1981). The content of age stereotypes generated in a given research program is directly related to the kinds of methods used as well as to the general design of the study. For example, when people are asked to rate both young and old targets they exhibit more extreme stereotypes than people who are asked to rate only young or only old targets (Kogan, 1979). Not only do stereotypes vary according to the types of instruments used to assess them (e.g., free-response, adjective checklist, rating scales), but also according to the characteristics of both the target and the perceiver. Despite these challenges, there is a large body of research from which we can still draw some general conclusions about age stereotypes.

Kite and Johnson (1988) systematically reviewed the research literature and statistically integrated the results of different studies on attitudes toward older and younger adults. Their analysis revealed that although results tended to depend on various methodological factors, stereotypes of older adults were more negative than those of younger adults, overall. Moreover, stereotypes of older adults were most negative on dimensions of general competence or physical attractiveness, while they were only slightly more negative than those of younger adults when ratings were of specific personality traits.

Reviews of the early literature led many to argue for the need to move beyond the basic question of whether the old are perceived more negatively than the young (e.g., Kite & Johnson, 1988; Kogan, 1979; McTavish, 1971). In the 20 years since Kite and Johnson published their seminal review, research in this area has grown considerably and has shifted toward understanding the multidimensional nature of age stereotypes. For example, Slotterback and Saarnio (1996) found that although negative stereotypes of older adults emerged in the physical domain (e.g., slow, weak), beliefs about older adults were more positive in the personal-expressive domain (e.g., responsible, kind) and equal to those about younger adults in the cognitive domain (e.g., wise, intelligent).

The increase in the number of studies examining age stereotypes across different domains allowed Kite and her colleagues to re-evaluate the general conclusions they had made about age stereotypes in their original review. Recently, Kite and her colleagues (2005) analyzed the results of 242 studies (compared to only 43 in 1988) and examined differences in attitudes toward young and older adults across several different domains and categories, including competence (e.g., intelligence, good memory), attractiveness (e.g., pretty, wrinkled), and stereotypic beliefs (e.g., old-fashioned, talks about the past). Although findings of individual studies varied, when considered together, older adults were viewed more negatively than younger adults in *all* domains. Consistent with past research, older adults were perceived as less competent and less attractive and were viewed more stereotypically than younger adults. However, further analyses revealed that these age differences were qualified by several factors. For example, although older adults generally were perceived more negatively than younger adults, these differences were smaller when detailed information (e.g., performance in a job interview) as opposed to vague information (e.g., target age only) was supplied about the target. This finding suggests that older adults are more at risk of being perceived in a negative light when little is known about them, which is most likely to happen when they are interacting with people they do not know.

THE IMPORTANCE OF TARGET CHARACTERISTICS

Despite the fact that previous research consistently reports that beliefs about older adults are more often negative than positive, one limitation of such research is that people are often asked to make judgments based on a label such as "elderly" or "older person" (Kite et al., 2005). The single category of "old people" is too general because different characteristics come to mind depending on whether we are thinking about a 65-year-old versus a 90-year-old, or an old man versus an old woman. People are likely to have distinct perceptions based on such subcategories of older people (e.g., Kogan, 1979). For example, Brewer, Dull, and Lui (1981) demonstrated that young adults do not consider older adults to be a single category of people. College students were asked to sort photographs of young and older adults into as many categories as they thought necessary. Photographs of the older adults had been previously judged based on their physical appearance as "Grandmotherly," "Elder Statesman," or "Senior Citizen." Although the students were unaware of these prior categorizations, they generally sorted the photographs of the older adults into the three categories. If young adults considered older adults to embody a single stereotype, they would have placed all of the pictures of older adults into one group. To determine whether young adults attribute different personality traits to the three different categories, Brewer and her colleagues asked another group of students to make trait ratings on photographs of older adults representing each of the categories. Photographs depicting "Senior Citizens" were associated with primarily negative traits, such as lonely or weak. By contrast, photographs depicting "Grandmotherly" and "Elder Statesman" types were associated with more positive traits, such as accepting and active. Thus, young adults hold multiple stereotypes of older adults that vary by subcategories of older people.

Other studies have demonstrated even more differentiated and complex categories of age stereotypes than the three suggested by Brewer et al. (1981). For example, Schmidt and Boland (1986) had college students list all of the traits that they considered to be associated with the typical old person. Students then sorted the traits into groups thought to be representative of different types of older people. Ultimately, 12 categories of older adults were created. Eight categories represented negative stereotypes (Despondent, Mildly Impaired, Vulnerable, Severely Impaired, Shrew/Curmudgeon, Recluse, Nosy Neighbor, and Bag Lady/Vagrant) and four categories represented positive stereotypes (John Wayne Conservative, Liberal Matriarch/Patriarch, Perfect Grandparent, and Sage). In a similar study, Hummert (1990) asked students to choose an age range that best represented each category of older adults. Negative stereotype categories (e.g., Shrew/Curmudgeon) were much more likely to be attributed to the older age ranges than were the positive stereotype categories (e.g., Perfect Grandparent). Taken together, these studies demonstrate the existence of multiple stereotypes of older adults that are more complex than what comes to mind when we simply consider the label "old person."

Although clearly important for demonstrating the complexity of age stereotypes, these early studies are limited in that they did not directly examine age stereotypes in relation to the gender of the target. For example, the characteristics that we associate with "Grandmother" are likely different from those we associate with "John Wayne Conservative." Moreover, there may be a double standard of aging, with men considered more attractive and women perceived as less attractive with age (e.g., Deutsch, Zalenski, & Clark, 1986). In their review of studies in which target gender was specified, Kite et al. (2005)

found that age stereotypes were more pronounced for female targets than for male targets. In particular, older women were perceived more negatively than their younger counterparts on ratings of behavior or behavioral intentions (e.g., willingness to help) and evaluative judgments (e.g., good/bad). These findings provide some support for the double standard of aging; however, male targets were not immune from age stereotyping. Indeed, older men were rated as significantly less competent than younger men, while differences in perceived competence between young and older women were much smaller. Although these conclusions are based on a limited number of studies, they suggest that target sex does indeed matter and should be taken into account when studying the content of age stereotypes.

While age stereotype research that considers target sex is scarce, even fewer studies have taken into account other variables that could impact perceptions, such as race or ethnicity. Although stereotypes about age, gender, and race have been studied independently, few studies have considered these variables together. Is a 75-year-old African American male stereotyped as a man, old, black, or some combination of the three? Is a 75-year-old white woman perceived the same way as a 75-year-old black woman or a 75-year-old white man? Because individuals always occupy multiple stereotyped categories, it is important to understand how these categories interact in order to understand peoples' behavior in the real world. To consider gender, race, and age irrespective of one another does little to capture the complexities inherent in real people and social groups. In an attempt to address this issue, Andreoletti and Leszczynski (2008) had college students rate 20 social groups (black/white, male/female, 5-, 15-, 25-, 45-, and 85-year-olds) on 10 characteristics, representative of either an agentic orientation (e.g., competitive, dominant) or a communal orientation (e.g., devoted to others, understanding). Although the results generally revealed traditional gender stereotypes with females perceived as more communal and males more agentic (e.g., Eagly, 1987), different patterns emerged when target age and race were taken into account. For example, while black and white older men were perceived as equally more dominant than women, black older women were perceived as significantly more dominant than white older women. That older adults are perceived differently depending on gender and race may have important implications for how they are treated in the real world.

PERCEIVER DIFFERENCES IN STEREOTYPES OF OLDER ADULTS

In addition to taking into account target variables such as sex and race when assessing age stereotypes, the possible influence of characteristics of the perceiver (i.e., those making the judgments) should also be considered. Most of the research on age stereotypes has been conducted with college student samples. Although perceiver characteristics such as age and sex are likely to be important, early research that considered such variables is sparse and inconclusive (Kite & Johnson, 1988; Lutsky, 1981; McTavish, 1971). Much of the research conducted over the past two decades has focused almost exclusively on college students' perceptions of older adults. However, there has been a considerable increase in the number of studies that have examined how other age groups (e.g., middle-aged and older adults) perceive older adults.

There are several reasons to expect that older adults might have different beliefs about aging than do young people. As perceivers, we generally see the in-group in a more favorable light (Tajfel, Billig, Bundy, & Flament, 1971) and also as more heterogeneous, or differentiated, than the out-group (Park & Rothbart, 1982). From a developmental perspective, beliefs about aging should get more complex with age because individuals have more life experience, which is likely reflected in their stereotypes and expectations about aging (Baltes, 1987). Thus, older adults should have more positive and complex views of aging than do younger adults. To test this notion, Hummert and her colleagues (Hummert, Gartska, Shaner, & Strahm, 1994) asked young, middle-aged, and older adults to generate traits they associated with the typical elderly adult. Although all age groups generated similar traits, when another group of adults was asked to sort the traits into subcategories, older adults created more subcategories than did the young and middle-aged adults, and middle-aged adults created more than the young adults. These findings demonstrate that although stereotypes of older adults are similar across perceiver age, older adults hold a wider range of stereotypes and thus have more differentiated or complex stereotypes than younger adults.

The degree of differentiation in stereotypes of older adults may depend on the degree to which the perceiver identifies with the target (Brewer & Lui, 1984). Consistent with Hummert's findings (Hummert et al., 1994), Brewer and Lui found that older adults sorted photographs of older adults into more categories than did younger adults. However, when young and older adults sorted behavior statements within subcategories of older adults (e.g., Senior Citizen, Grandmother), differentiation was greatest for only the specific subcategory with which the older adult most identified. For example, if an older person identified with the category of "Grandmother" then her representation of the category of grandmother was more complex than that of a younger person. However, a subcategory that she did not identify with, such as "Senior Citizen," was not anymore differentiated or complex than that of a younger person. This finding supports the notion that members of the in-group are perceived as more heterogeneous than those of the out-group.

Although it is clear from the research that older adults' age stereotypes are more complex than those held by younger adults, research supporting the notion that older adults have more positive views of aging than do younger adults is limited. Hummert and her colleagues (Hummert, 1993; Hummert, Garstka, Shaner, & Strahm, 1995) found that young and older adults agreed as to which stereotypes (both positive and negative) were most typical of the older population in general. Older adults, however, rated the stereotypes as much less typical of older adults than did younger adults. Thus, although older people were aware of prevalent stereotypes, they were less inclined to subscribe to them. Although younger people tended to assign only negative stereotypes to the age range of "75 and over," older people were much more likely to assign both positive and negative stereotypes to this age range. These findings suggest that older adults may have a some-what more positive view of aging than younger adults, but they also suggest that older adults may simply have a different idea of what constitutes "old" compared to younger adults. By contrast, a more recent study found evidence of a positive bias toward the old by both young and older people. Specifically, Chasteen, Schwarz, and Park (2002) found that not only did young and older people share similar old age stereotypes; both age groups accessed positive stereotypes faster than negative ones.

In a systematic review of research that considered age of the perceiver, Kite et al. (2005) found that older adults were somewhat less extreme in their age stereotypes, but results were modest. While older adults perceived fewer differences between young and older adults in the majority of domains (e.g., competence), older adults were perceived more negatively overall than younger adults, regardless of perceiver age. Taken together, these results do not provide much support for the in-group favorability bias. Kite et al. (2005) suggest that because older adults were once young, they have nothing to gain by devaluing younger adults. Older adults may seek to maintain a positive self-image through strategies other than favoring their in-group. Another explanation is that older adults may not perceive themselves to be in the same group as the older targets; thereby perceiving the older targets as the out-group, not the in-group. This fits with the finding that the discrepancy between one's actual and perceived age increases with age, with older adults tending to feel younger than they are (Montepare & Lachman, 1989).

In addition to perceiver age, Kite et al. (2005) also examined differences based on perceiver sex, although there is little reason to expect that one gender should hold more negative age stereotypes than the other. The findings for gender differences in age stereotypes were mixed and therefore difficult to interpret. The most interesting finding to emerge, however, was that men perceive greater age differences in competence than do women. Men may be more inclined to perceive age-related declines in competence because competence plays a central role in the male stereotype, but this finding is not strong enough to conclude that men hold more ageist attitudes than women (Kite et al. 2005). Although other perceiver characteristics such as race or ethnicity may influence beliefs about aging, too few studies have examined these variables to draw any meaningful conclusions.

Despite some of the limitations of the research on the content of age stereotypes, we can draw several general conclusions. First, stereotypes related to aging are alive and well in our culture. Second, stereotypes of older adults are more complex than was originally thought. Although early researchers operated under the assumption that stereotypes about older adults were primarily negative, there is now a large body of research demonstrating that the content of age stereotypes can be both positive and negative. Further, as demonstrated by research supporting the stereotype content model, people often hold both positive and negative stereotypes simultaneously (e.g., Fiske et al., 2002). One of the most important reasons for studying the content of stereotypes, an endeavor that may at times seem politically incorrect, is to understand how stereotypes can impact behavior (Schneider, 1996). Although much research has focused on people's use of age stereotypes to discriminate against older adults, a growing body of research focuses on how age stereotypes impact the behavior of older adults directly. This emerging research, which considers the impact of stereotypes from the target's perspective, will be the focus of the rest of the chapter.

THE CONSEQUENCES OF AGE STEREOTYPES

There are many theories regarding the possible consequences of age stereotypes on the behavior of the elderly (see Zebrowitz & Montepare, 2000). Over 25 years ago, Rodin and Langer (1980) suggested that stereotypes held by older adults themselves might result in a mindset that could create self-fulfilling prophecies. For example, a common stereotype is that memory declines with age (e.g., Hummert et al., 1994) and that there is little that can be done about it (Lachman, 1991). Thus, older adults experiencing memory difficulty may assume that such problems are beyond their control and may be less inclined to develop compensatory strategies (e.g., making lists). Failure to compensate may lead to greater memory limitations in the future, thus creating a self-fulfilling prophecy. In a similar vein, the stereotype of older adults as weak and frail might contribute to a fear of falling. A fear of falling can lead older adults to become less physically active, thereby actually increasing their risk of falling and becoming weak and frail. Langer (1989) remarked, "Much of what older people experience could be the result of negative stereotypes . . . we do not know how many of the infirmities are actually genetically programmed into our bodies, or how many may be due to premature cognitive commitments" (p. 92).

Research on "possible selves" offers one mechanism through which age stereotypes might influence the behavior of older people. Markus and Nurius (1986) conceptualized possible selves as personalized representations of what individuals could become, would like to become, and are afraid of becoming. The "hoped-for self" represents the person we hope to become, while the "feared self" represents the person we wish to avoid becoming. These future-oriented representations guide our behavior. Thus, it is possible that an older person could internalize negative stereotypes about aging, resulting in a negative or feared self, which could eventually impact his or her behavior (Cross & Markus, 1991). Though internalizing negative stereotypes of aging may have negative implications in some situations, research on possible selves in adulthood has shown that a feared self may actually benefit older adults. For example, older adults with a health-related feared self, which is more common as people age (Frazier, Hooker, Johnson, & Kaus, 2000; Hooker, 1992), are more likely to engage in healthy behaviors that will help them avoid becoming their feared self (Hooker & Kaus, 1992). Likewise, older adults who reported memory decline as part of their most feared self also reported that they were actively engaged in behaviors that would hopefully help them to avoid their feared self (Dark-Freudeman, West, & Viverito, 2006). Thus, negative stereotypes of aging may motivate people via possible selves to engage in behaviors that will help them defy such stereotypes.

Much attention has been given to two overlapping theories that also offer explanations for how age-related stereotypes can influence the behavior of older adults: stereotype threat (Steele, Spencer, & Aronson, 2002) and self-stereotyping (Levy, 1996). In contrast to research that has examined the relationship between stereotypes and behavior less directly, the experimental methods employed in the stereotype threat and self-stereotyping research allow us to infer a cause-and-effect relationship between age stereotypes and older adults' behavior.

Stereotype threat occurs when individuals are in a situation where they are at risk of confirming a negative stereotype about their group (Steele & Aronson, 1995). The experience of stereotype threat leads to lowered performance in the stereotype-relevant domain. For example, Steele and Aronson (1995) found that black students performed worse than white students on a standardized test they thought to be a measure of intellectual ability, thereby confirming the stereotype that blacks are less intellectually capable than whites, but when students were told that the exact same test did *not* assess intellectual ability, presumably removing stereotype threat, the black students performed as well as white students. An individual can be susceptible to a stereotype's influence, even without believing it; but those most likely to experience threat are those most invested in the stereotype-relevant domain (Steele et al., 2002). Stereotype threat has been documented in a variety of groups and domains, such as women and math performance (Spencer, Steele, & Quinn, 1999), white men and athletic ability (Stone, Lynch, Sjomeling, & Darley, 1999), and older adults and memory (e.g., Hess, Auman, Colcombe, & Rahhal, 2003; Rahhal, Hasher, & Colcombe, 2001).

Research on stereotype threat in older adults has been limited to the cognitive domain. Because declining memory is a common age-related stereotype held by young and older adults alike (e.g., Ryan, 1992; Ryan & Kwong See, 1993), older adults might be concerned about confirming this stereotype when they are in a situation where they know their memory is being evaluated. Indeed, Rahhal, Hasher, and Colcombe (2001) found that young adults outperformed older adults when instructions for a task emphasized memory, but there were no significant age differences when instructions emphasized learning. Similarly, Desrichard and Köpetz (2005) found that older adults performed worse when a task was presented as a memory versus a nonmemory task, whereas young adults' performance was not affected by how the task was presented. In another study, Hess et al. (2003) attempted to manipulate the degree to which older adults experienced stereotype threat by having them read brief reports that described either negative effects of aging on memory (maximizing stereotype threat) or positive effects of memory on aging (minimizing stereotype threat). Older adults who read about negative effects on memory performed more poorly on a subsequent memory task than those who experienced less threatening conditions. However, this was true only for older adults who placed greater value on their memory functioning, which is consistent with the idea that only those most invested in the stereotype-relevant domain (in this case memory) should be susceptible to stereotype threat.

While these studies demonstrate the power of the situation, researchers have been trying to determine the specific mechanisms that can explain how stereotype threat operates to influence memory performance in older adults. An early hypothesis was that stereotype threat leads to increased anxiety, which has a negative influence on performance. However, there has been little empirical support for this hypothesis (e.g., Chasteen, Bhattacharyya, Horhata, Tam, & Hasher, 2005; Hess & Hinson, 2006; Hess, Hinson, & Statham, 2004). Somewhat more promising has been the notion that stereotype threat may influence older adults' beliefs or performance expectations, which can then influence performance. For example, Desrichard and Köpetz (2005) found that older adults predicted that they would do worse when a task was described as a memory versus a nonmemory task, and these lowered expectations were indeed related to poorer performance. Hess, Hinson, and Hodges (in press) also found that stereotype threat negatively impacted performance expectations, but only for older adults with higher levels of education. Individual factors such as beliefs about one's memory ability (e.g., Desrichard & Köpetz, 2005), the belief that one belongs to a stigmatized group (e.g., Hess et al., in press), and age (e.g., Hess & Hinson, 2006; Hess et al., in press) have also been shown to be related to stereotype threat susceptibility. With regard to age, people in their 60s seem to be the most susceptible to stereotype threat, perhaps because they are now part of an age group that might be considered "old" in our society (Hess et al., in press).

Although these studies have provided evidence for the operation of stereotype threat in older adults in the cognitive domain, findings from other studies have been less consistent (e.g., Andreoletti & Lachman, 2004; Chasteen et al., 2005). As a result, some have questioned whether stereotype threat is the best framework for understanding how stereotypes impact the behavior of older adults (e.g., O'Brien & Hummert, 2006).

Stereotype threat is thought to occur at an explicit or conscious level. For example, older adults reading about negative effects of aging on memory would consciously activate the negative stereotype—perhaps even ruminate over it. However, implicit or unconscious processes can give rise to self-stereotypes, which can lead to stereotype-consistent behavior (see Bargh, 1994, for a review). For example, Levy (1996) asked older adults to perform a computer task during which words related to either positive (e.g., sage) or negative (e.g., decrepit) stereotypes of aging were flashed too quickly to allow conscious recognition. Viewing positive stereotypes, even when people had no explicit awareness that they had seen such primes, led to increased memory performance; negative stereotype activation led to decreased performance.

The consequences of exposing older adults to stereotypes of aging, even at an unconscious level, extend beyond the cognitive domain. Older adults increased their walking speed and improved their balance, for example, after implicit exposure to positive stereotypes, while those exposed to negative stereotypes showed no improvement (Hausdorff, Levy, & Wei, 1999). Similarly, implicit exposure to positive stereotypes resulted in improvements in older adults' handwriting—a reliable indicator of age—while exposure to negative stereotypes resulted in declines (Levy, Hausdorff, Hencke, & Wei, 2000). Stereotypes also influenced older adults' cardiovascular response to stress. Stress was induced in older adults by challenging them with several difficult mathematical and verbal tasks. Exposure to negative stereotypes before the tasks increased cardiovascular stress during the tasks (e.g., increased blood pressure and heart rate), whereas exposure to positive stereotypes decreased cardiovascular stress during the tasks (Levy et al., 2000). Although we often focus on describing the negative consequences of negative age stereotypes, these studies highlight the potential benefits of positive stereotypes for older adults.

In a systematic review of both the stereotype threat and self-stereotyping research related to aging, Horton and colleagues (2008) concluded that age stereotypes do indeed influence the behavior of older adults, particularly in the domain of memory. As researchers have begun to explore the relationship between stereotypes and health, there is some evidence that negative age stereotypes may impact older adults' willingness to engage in exercise and other healthy behaviors (for a review see Horton, Baker, & Deakin, 2007). More research is needed, however, to draw any firm conclusions about the influence of stereotypes in the physical domain (Horton et al., 2008).

Research on the consequences of stereotypes provides compelling evidence of the power of stereotypes for influencing older adults' behavior in a variety of situations, yet several questions remain. First, based on the available research, it is difficult to determine whether activating stereotypes implicitly versus explicitly has an impact on the degree to which stereotypes influence behavior. There is some evidence that behavioral consequences are most pronounced when age stereotypes are activated implicitly (e.g., Hess et al., 2004). This may be particularly true for positive stereotypes, given that explicitly activating positive stereotypes can lead to decreased performance or "choking" when expectations are high (e.g., Cheryan & Bodenhausen, 2000; Shih, Ambady, Richeson, Fujita, & Gray 2002). Second, questions remain about the mechanisms underlying the relationship between stereotypes and behavior. Research on possible selves and self-stereotypes suggests that stereotypes become internalized as part of the self-concept, thereby influencing behavior. Research documenting stereotype threat in older adults, however, has not been able to find a consistent explanation for how stereotype threat ultimately influences behavior. Finally, although studies in the laboratory show that the activation of stereotypes affects older adults' behavior in the short term; the long-term effects on behavior outside of the laboratory are unknown.

SUMMARY AND CONCLUSIONS

Research on the content of age stereotypes reveals that stereotypes of older adults are complex—the "typical" older adult does not exist. Age stereotypes can be both positive and negative and vary according to characteristics of both the target and the perceiver. Despite their complexity, negative stereotypes have been and continue to be a part of our culturally shared beliefs about aging. Nevertheless, baby boomers are more educated, wealthier, and better traveled than the older adults of previous generations. The way that today's older adults are choosing to spend their "third age," as it is now being called, is likely to have an influence, hopefully for the better, on how society views aging. Although one might hope that the prevalence of negative stereotypes about aging will decline as the population of active and healthy older adults continues to grow, that is probably too optimistic. A more likely scenario is that negative age stereotypes will remain, but over time, the age at which we consider someone "old" will increase. This notion is already reflected in the popular media—"60 is the new 40."

Even if 60 really is the new 40, research has shown that negative stereotypes can and do have negative consequences for older adults. The good news is that negative stereotypes can also motivate older adults to behave in ways to help them avoid realizing their greatest fears about aging. Moreover, activating positive stereotypes can lead to positive outcomes for older adults. Although someone might say, "those stereotypes don't apply to me," and the degree to which an individual buys into stereotypes about aging may very well influence their potential impact on the individual, research has shown that stereotypes can operate outside of conscious awareness. Greater awareness of stereotypes and their possible consequences is essential for older adults and may serve as a buffer against the most negative stereotypes (Horton et al., 2008). Without awareness, there is nothing one can do to avoid or compensate for the potential negative consequences of age stereotypes.

Despite the prevalence of negative stereotypes about aging and their potential consequences, most older people maintain a positive sense of well-being and report feeling happy and satisfied with their lives (Whitbourne & Sneed, 2002). A growing body of research has demonstrated that older adults have a variety of strategies for compensating for negative stereotypes and expectations. Indeed, people with more positive perceptions of aging outlive those with more negative perceptions (Levy, Slade, Kunkel, & Kasl, 2002). Thus, optimism may be the best defense.

REFERENCES

Allport, G. W. (1954). *The Nature of Prejudice.* Cambridge, MA: Addison Wesley.

Andreoletti, C., & Lachman, M. E. (2004). Susceptibility and resilience to memory aging stereotypes: Education matters more than age. *Experimental Aging Research, 30,* 129–148.

Andreoletti, C., & Leszczynski, J. P. (2008, May). *Gender, Race, and Age: Compound Stereotypes Across the Lifespan.* Poster presented at the annual meeting of the Association for Psychological Science, Chicago, IL.

Baltes, P. B. (1987). Theoretical propositions of life-span developmental psychology: On the dynamics between growth and decline. *Developmental Psychology, 23,* 611–626.

Bargh, J. A. (1994). The four horsemen of automaticity. In R.S.W.T.K. Srull (Ed.), *Handbook of Social Cognition* (pp. 1–40). Hillsdale, NJ: Lawrence Erlbaum Associates.

Brewer, M. B., Dull, V., & Lui, L. (1981). Perceptions of the elderly: Stereotypes as prototypes. *Journal of Personality and Social Psychology, 41,* 656–670.

Brewer, M. B., & Lui, L. (1984). Categorization of the elderly by the elderly. *Personality and Social Psychology Bulletin, 10,* 585–595.

Chasteen, A. L., Bhattacharyya, S., Horhata, M., Tam, R., & Hasher, L. (2005). How feelings of stereotype threat influence older adults' memory performance. *Experimental Aging Research, 31,* 235–260.

Chasteen, A. L., Schwarz, N., & Park, D. C. (2002). The activation of aging stereotypes in younger and older adults. *Journal of Gerontology: Psychological Sciences, 57B,* P540–P547.

Cheryan, S., & Bodenhausen, G. V. (2000). When positive stereotypes threaten intellectual performance: The psychological hazards of "model minority" status. *Psychological Science, 11*(5), 399–402.

Cross, S., & Markus, H. (1991). Possible selves across the life span. *Human Development, 34,* 230–255.

Cuddy, A.J.C., & Fiske, S. T. (2002). Doddering but dear: Process, content, and function in stereotyping of older persons. In T. D. Nelson (Ed.), *Ageism: Stereotyping and Prejudice Against Older Persons* (pp. 3–26). Cambridge, MA: MIT Press.

Dark-Freudeman, A., West, R. L., & Viverito, K. M. (2006). Future selves and aging: Older adults' memory fears. *Educational Gerontology, 32,* 85–109.

Desrichard, O., & Köpetz, C. (2005). A threat in the elder: The impact of task instructions, self-efficacy and performance expectations on memory performance. *European Journal of Social Psychology, 35,* 537–552.

Deutsch, F. M., Zalenski, C. M., & Clark, M. E. (1986). Is there a double standard of aging? *Journal of Applied Social Psychology, 16,* 771–785.

Diekman, A. B., & Eagly, A. H. (2000). Stereotypes as dynamic constructs: Women and men of the past, present, and future. *Personality and Social Psychology Bulletin, 26,* 1171–1188.

Eagly, A. H. (1987). *Sex Differences in Social Behavior: A Social-role Interpretation.* Hillsdale, NJ: Lawrence Erlbaum Associates.

Eagly, A. H., & Steffen, V. J. (1984). Gender stereotypes stem from the distribution of women and men into social roles. *Journal of Personality and Social Psychology, 46,* 735–754.

Fiske, S. T. (1998). Stereotyping, prejudice, and discrimination. In D. T. Gilbert, S. T. Fiske, and G. Lindsey (Eds.), *The Handbook of Social Psychology* (4th ed. pp. 357–411). New York: McGraw Hill.

Fiske, S. T., Cuddy, A.J.C., Glick, P., & Xu, J. (2002). A model of (often mixed) stereotype content: Competence and warmth respectively follow from perceived status and competition. *Journal of Personality and Social Psychology, 82,* 878–902.

Frazier, L. D., Hooker, K., Johnson, P. M., & Kaus, C. R. (2000). Continuity and change in possible selves in later life: A 5-year longitudinal study. *Basic and Applied Social Psychology, 2,* 237–243.

Hausdorff, J. M., Levy, B., & Wei, J. Y. (1999). The power of ageism on physical function of older persons: Reversibility of age-related gait changes. *Journal of the American Geriatrics Society, 47,* 1346–1349.

Heckhausen, J., & Kreuger, J. (1993). Developmental expectations for the self and most other people: Age grading in three functions of social comparison. *Developmental Psychology, 29,* 539–548.

Hess, T. H. (2006). Attitudes toward aging and their effects on behavior. In J. E. Birren & K. W. Schaie (Eds.), *Handbook of the Psychology of Aging* (pp. 379–406). Burlington, MA: Elsevier Academic.

Hess, T. M., Auman, C., Colcombe, S. J., & Rahhal, T. A. (2003). The impact of stereotype threat on age differences in memory performance. *Journal of Gerontology: Psychological Sciences, 58B*(1), P3–P11.

Hess, T. M., & Hinson, J. T. (2006). Age-related variation in the influences of aging stereotypes on memory in adulthood. *Psychology and Aging, 21,* 621–625.

Hess, T. M., Hinson, J. T., & Hodges, E. A. (in press). Moderators of and mechanisms underlying stereotype threat effects on older adults' memory performance. *Experimental Aging Research.*

Hess, T. M., Hinson, J. T., & Statham, J. A. (2004). Explicit and implicit stereotype activation effects on memory: Do age and awareness moderate the impact of priming? *Psychology and Aging, 19,* 495–505.

Hooker, K. (1992). Possible selves and perceived health in older adults and college students. *Journal of Gerontology, 47,* 85–95.

Hooker, K., & Kaus, C. R. (1992). Possible selves and health behaviors in later life. *Journal of Aging and Health, 4,* 390–411.

Horton, S., Baker, J., & Deakin, J. M. (2007). Stereotypes of aging: Their effects on the health of seniors in North American society. *Educational Gerontology, 33,* 1021–1035.

Horton, S., Baker, J., Pearce, G. W., & Deakin, J. M. (2008). On the malleability of performance: Implications for seniors. *Journal of Applied Gerontology, 27,* 446–465.

Hummert, M. (1990). Multiple stereotypes of elderly and young adults: A comparison of structure and evaluation. *Psychology and Aging, 5,* 182–193.

Hummert, M. L. (1993). Age and typicality judgments of stereotypes of the elderly: Perceptions of elderly vs. young adults. *International Journal of Aging and Human Development, 37,* 217–226.

Hummert, M. L. (1999). A social cognitive perspective on age stereotypes. In T. M. Hess & F. Blanchard-Fields (Eds.), *Social Cognition and Aging* (pp. 175–196). San Diego: Academic Press.

Hummert, M. L., Garstka, T. A., Shaner, J. L., & Strahm, S. (1994). Stereotypes of the elderly held by young, middle-aged, and elderly adults. *Journal of Gerontology, 49,* P240–P249.

Hummert, M. L., Garstka, T. A., Shaner, J. L., & Strahm, S. (1995). Judgments about stereotypes of the elderly: Attitudes, age associations, and typicality ratings of young, middle-aged, and elderly adults. *Research on Aging, 17,* 168–189.

Jackson, L. A., & Sullivan, L. A. (1990). Perceptions of multiple role participants. *Social Psychology Quarterly, 53,* 274–282.

Kite, M. E. (1996). Age, gender, and occupational label: A test of social role theory. *Psychology of Women Quarterly, 20,* 361–374.

Kite, M. E., Deaux, K., & Miele, M. (1991). Stereotypes of young and old: Does age outweigh gender? *Psychology and Aging, 6,* 19–27.

Kite, M. E., & Johnson, B. T., (1988). Attitudes toward older and younger adults: A meta-analysis. *Psychology and Aging, 3,* 233–244.

Kite, M. E., Stockdale, G. D., Whitley, B. E., Jr., & Johnson, B. T. (2005). Attitudes toward younger and older adults: An updated meta-analytic review. *Journal of Social Issues, 61,* 241–266.

Knox, V. J., & Gekoski, W. L. (1989). The effect of judgment context on assessments of age groups. *Canadian Journal of Aging, 8,* 244–254.

Kogan, N. A. (1961a). Attitudes toward old people in an older sample. *Journal of Abnormal and Social Psychology, 62,* 616–622.

Kogan, N. A. (1961b). Attitudes toward old people: The development of a scale and an examination of correlates. *Journal of Abnormal and Social Psychology, 62,* 44–54.

Kogan, N. (1979). Beliefs, attitudes and stereotypes about old people: A new look at some old issues. *Research on Aging, 1*, 11–36.

Kogan, N., & Shelton, F. C. (1962). Beliefs about "old people" and "people in general" in an older sample. *Journal of Genetic Psychology, 100*, 3–21.

Lachman, M. E. (1991). Perceived control over memory aging: Developmental and intervention perspectives. *Journal of Social Issues, 47*, 159–175.

Langer, E. J. (1989). *Mindfulness.* Reading, MA: Addison-Wesley.

Lee, Y.-T., Jussim, L. J., & McCauley, C. R. (Eds.). (1995). *Stereotype Accuracy: Toward Appreciating Group Differences.* Washington, DC: American Psychological Association.

Levy, B. (1996). Improving memory in old age through implicit self-stereotyping. *Journal of Personality and Social Psychology, 71*, 1092–1107.

Levy, B., Hausdorff, J. M., Hencke, R., & Wei, J. Y. (2000). Reducing cardiovascular stress with positive self-stereotypes of aging. *Journal of Gerontology: Psychological Sciences, 55B*, 1–9.

Levy, B., Slade, M. D., Kunkel, S. R., & Kasl, S. V. (2002). Longevity increased by positive self-perceptions of aging. *Journal of Personality and Social Psychology, 83*, 261–270.

Lutsky, N. (1981). Attitudes toward old age and elderly persons. In C. Eisdorfer (Ed.), *Annual Review of Gerontology and Geriatrics* (vol. 1, pp. 287–336). New York: Springer.

Markus, H., & Nurius, P. (1986). Possible selves. *American Psychologist, 41*, 954–969.

McTavish, D. G. (1971). Perceptions of old people: A review of research methodologies and findings. *The Gerontologist, 11*, 90–101.

Montepare, J. M., & Lachman, M. E. (1989). "You're only as old as you feel": Self-perceptions of age, fears of aging, and life satisfaction from adolescence to old age. *Psychology and Aging, 4*, 73–78.

Nelson, T. D. (Ed.). (2002). *Ageism: Stereotyping and Prejudice Against Older Persons.* Cambridge, MA: MIT Press.

O'Brien, L. T., & Hummert, M. L. (2006). Memory performance of late middle-aged adults: Contrasting self-stereotyping and stereotype threat accounts of assimilation to age stereotypes. *Social Cognition, 24*, 338–358.

Park, B., & Rothbart, M. (1982). Perception of out-group homogeneity and levels of social categorization: Memory for the subordinate attributes of in-group and out-group members. *Journal of Personality and Social Psychology, 42*, 1051–1068.

Rahhal, T. A., Hasher, L., & Colcombe, S. J. (2001). Instructional manipulations and age differences in memory: Now you see them, now you don't. *Psychology and Aging, 16*(4), 697–706.

Rodin, J., & Langer, E. (1980). Aging labels: the decline of control and the fall of self-esteem. *Journal of Social Issues, 36*, 12–29.

Rosencranz, J. A., & McNevin, T. E. (1969). A factor analysis of attitudes toward the aged. *The Gerontologist, 9*, 55–59.

Ryan, E. B. (1992). Beliefs about memory changes across the adult life span. *Journal of Gerontology, 47*, 41–46.

Ryan, E. B., & Kwong See, S. (1993). Age-based beliefs about memory changes for self and others across adulthood. *Journals of Gerontology, 48*, P199–P201.

Schmidt, D. F., & Boland, S. M. (1986). The structure of impressions of older adults: Evidence for multiple stereotypes. *Psychology and Aging, 1,* 255–260.

Schneider, D. J. (1996). Modern stereotype research: Unfinished business. In C. N. Macrae, C. Stangor, & M. Hewstone (Eds.), *Stereotypes and Stereotyping* (pp. 419–453). New York: Guilford Press.

Shih, M., Ambady, N., Richeson, J., Fujita, K., & Gray, H. (2002). Stereotype performance boosts: The impact of self-relevance and the manner of stereotype activation. *Journal of Personality and Social Psychology, 83,* 638–647.

Slotterback, C. S., & Saarnio, D. A. (1996). Attitudes toward older adults reported by young adults: Variation based on attitudinal task and attribute categories. *Psychology and Aging, 11,* 563–571.

Spencer, S. J., Steele, C. M., & Quinn, D. M. (1999). Stereotype threat and women's math performance. *Journal of Experimental Social Psychology, 35,* 4–28.

Stangor, C., & Schaller, M. (1996). Stereotypes as individual and collective representations. In C. N. Macrae, C. Stangor, & M. Hewstone (Eds.), *Stereotypes and Stereotyping* (pp. 3–40). New York: Guilford.

Steele, C. M., & Aronson, J. (1995). Stereotype threat and the intellectual test performance of African Americans. *Journal of Personality and Social Psychology, 69,* 797–811.

Steele, C. M., Spencer, S. J., & Aronson, J. (2002). Contending with group image: The psychology of stereotype and social identity threat. In M. P. Zanna (Ed.), *Advances in Experimental Social Psychology* (vol. 34, pp. 379–440). San Diego, CA: Academic Press.

Stone, J., Lynch, C., Sjomeling, M., & Darley, J. M. (1999). Stereotype threat effects on Black and White athletic performance. *Journal of Personality and Social Psychology, 77,* 1213–1227.

Tajfel, H., Billig, M., Bundy, R. P., & Flament, C. (1971). Social categorization and intergroup behavior. *European Journal of Social Psychology, 1,* 149–178.

Tuckman, J., & Lorge, I. (1952a). The effect of institutionalization on attitudes toward old people. *Journal of Abnormal and Social Psychology, 47,* 337–344.

Tuckman, J., & Lorge, I. (1952b). The influence of a course in the psychology of the adult on attitudes toward old people and older workers. *Journal of Educational Psychology, 42,* 400–407.

Tuckman, J., & Lorge, I. (1953). Attitudes toward old people. *Journal of Social Psychology, 37,* 249–260.

Tuckman, J., & Lorge, I. (1958). Attitudes toward aging of individuals with experiences with the aged. *Journal of Genetic Psychology, 92,* 199–204.

U.S. Bureau of the Census. (2007). *Statistical Abstract of the United States.* Washington, DC: Author.

Whitbourne, S. K., & Sneed, J. R. (2002). The paradox of well-being, identity, processes, and stereotype threat: Ageism and its potential relationships to the self in later life. In T. D. Nelson (Ed.), *Ageism: Stereotyping and Prejudice Against Older Persons* (pp. 247–273). Cambridge, MA: MIT Press.

Zebrowitz, L. A., & Montepare, J. M. (2000). Too young, too old: Stigmatizing adolescents and elders. In T. F. Heatherton, R. E. Kleck, M. R. Hebl, & J. G. Hull (Eds.), *The Social Psychology of Stigma* (pp. 334–373). New York: Guilford Press.

CHAPTER 7

ENVIRONMENTAL GERONTOLOGY: A SAMPLER OF ISSUES AND APPLICATIONS

Rick J. Scheidt and Benyamin Schwarz

Aging can be defined as a progressive deterioration of physiological function—an intrinsic age-related process of loss of viability and of increase in vulnerability. As time passes, the human organism changes as a result of biological, psychological, and social influences. From the biological perspective, aging is a progressive functional decline that weakens the ability of the organism to adjust to changing environmental conditions. Aging is a complex process composed of several features. With age a person experiences an exponential increase in risk of mortality, physiological changes that typically lead to a functional decline, and increased susceptibility to certain diseases. Aging is characterized by changes in appearance, such as a gradual reduction in height and weight loss due to loss of muscle and bone mass; a lower metabolic rate; slower reaction time; declines in short-term memory functions; declines in sexual activity; a functional decline in audition, olfaction, and vision; declines in kidney, pulmonary, and immune functions; declines in exercise performance; and multiple endocrine changes (Craik & Salthouse, 1992; Hayflick, 1994; Spence, 1995).

Biologists of aging seek ways to intervene in the human aging process, hoping to increase our years of active (versus dependent) life expectancy. Several difficulties, however, prevent us from intervening in this process directly. The first obstacle is our inability to distinguish the initial phenomena that *cause* the aging process (i.e., "primary" aging) from *age-associated* outcomes that are not directly age-determined (i.e., "secondary" aging). Primary aging refers to inevitable, normative, disease-free development during adulthood, while secondary aging refers to developmental changes related to disease, lifestyle, and other environmentally induced changes that are not universal or inevitable (Cavanaugh & Blanchard-Fields, 2006). All age-related chronic diseases are secondary, occurring in various bodily systems that suffer declines in functional integrity and immune capability. The incidence of many of these pathologies increases with age. These include diabetes, heart disease, cancer, arthritis, and kidney disease. However, it is important to stress that primary aging is not a disease process. The second obstacle has to do with the individuality of the aging process among different people. The pace and nature of aging vary considerably among individuals. As a result, biologists of aging distinguish between one's chronological age and one's biological age, or the physiological age of the organism. Two people of the same age may have very different physiological capacities. Furthermore, the disparity between the physiological functioning of each of the systems in these two people varies dramatically. The individuality of the aging process is perhaps more prevalent in reference to a person's psychological age. Lives tend to "fan out" with increasing age, and individual differences increase on many psychological dimensions. Thus, growing old is not an exclusive product of one single set of determinants. It is a product of our physiological integrity, our individual heredity, our behavioral and lifestyle choices, and our interactions with the physical and social environments that host our lives over time (Birren & Cunningham, 1985; Neugarten, 1968). This last domain—often referred to as environment-aging relations—is the raison d'être of this chapter.

AGING AND ENVIRONMENT

In a typical day, most of us conduct our lives in highly familiar environments. Routine activities are often performed automatically in places that function as mere backdrops, with an out-of-awareness quality. This habituated functioning has adaptive convenience as we deal with the tasks of everyday living. As we grow older, however, age-associated losses in physical, psychological, and social resources and competencies often bring a new appreciation of the challenges and behavioral demands posed by previously beneficial and innocuous settings. Normally supportive settings may become forbiddingly constrictive and, at times, pose risks to the health and well-being of older adults.

This problem scenario defines the heart of a relatively new and exciting multidisciplinary field known as *the ecology of aging* or environmental gerontology. The field seeks to understand the dynamic relationships between older adults and the environments they inhabit. It is mission-oriented, targeting practical problems in real-world settings (Scheidt & Windley, 1985, 2006). The ultimate goal is to use this knowledge to develop theory- and research-informed interventions that will produce, sustain, and improve healthy outcomes for elders who move about and reside within everyday environments.

A BRIEF GENEALOGY

Historically, environmental gerontology owes much to the influence of early psychologists who held that *environment*, previously treated as a background variable within many theories of human behavior, should be accorded front-and-center explanatory power. Two pioneers are especially noteworthy. Personality theorist Kurt Lewin viewed the individual *and* the environment as intrinsically interdependent. His field theory (1954) proposed that the subjective or experienced environment was more crucial for understanding human development than the strictly objective physical or social environment (Cairns, 1998). Due in part to his early lead, several prominent and current theories of life span human development accord significant status to environmental context (Thelen & Smith, 1998). During this same era, gerontologist Robert Kleemeier (1959) argued that a valid understanding of the aging process requires an ecological perspective that includes home and community. He was one of the first gerontologists to advocate for proper design of dwelling environments for elders.

Research on the theme of aging and environment evolved in earnest during the late 1960s, when the domain became a relevant issue in the field of gerontology (Carp, 1966; Lawton & Simon, 1967). Due to societal concerns with the problems of housing for elderly people and the need for improvement of institutional settings, the field proliferated during the 1970s (see e.g., Atchley & Byerts, 1975; Byerts, Howell, & Pastalan, 1979; Golant, 1979; Gubrium, 1973; Lawton & Nahemow , 1973; Pastalan & Carson, 1970; Tobin & Lieberman, 1976; Windley, Byerts, & Ernst, 1975). Rowles and Ohta (1983) noted that these societal concerns resulted in large-scale research funding during this era for specific design and evaluation projects. The Gerontological Society of America, through its Housing and Environment for Aging Project (1971–1975) and a subsequent Curriculum Development in Environment and Aging Program (1975–1978), played a major role not only in encouraging basic research but also in providing impetus to the translation of findings into design alternatives and policy strategies.

The field continued to flourish during the early 1980s (Altman, Lawton, & Wohlwill, 1984; Lawton, 1980; Lawton, Windley, & Byerts, 1982; Rowles & Ohta, 1983) and remains viable and active today on an international scale.

ILLUSTRATIVE THEORY AND RESEARCH

This chapter illustrates the value of thinking, research, and practice in the ecology of aging for improving the well-being and quality of life of elders. We offer three case study *samplers* that illustrate differences in theoretical perspectives, problem orientations, and levels of environment that typify research activity within this diverse field—a field that includes disciplines such as psychology, sociology, architecture and design, regional and community planning, geographical gerontology, occupational therapy, social policy, and health (Wahl & Oswald, in press). *Environment* is a complex higher-order concept that carries multiple meanings. We focus here on the spectrum of *residential* settings occupied by elders. Older adults (i.e., usually defined as 65 years and older) spend a great deal of time (an average of 80%) in the near environmental range of home, neighborhood, and community. This residency tends to be highly stable for most elders. Consequently, of the many environmental settings frequented by elderly Americans, the residential range tends to have more behavioral and psychological consequences and meanings for older adults (Baltes, Maas, Wilms, & Borchelt, 1999; Pinquart & Burmedi, 2004).

We begin with an introduction to an important ecological model that has influenced research and application in the ecology of aging for several years. We then offer a bit of information about competencies and contexts of elders that inform our research illustrations.

The General Ecological Model of Aging

Figure 7.1 displays the original "general ecological model of aging" (Lawton & Nahemow, 1973; Nahemow, 2000), arguably the most influential guiding framework for research and practice in the ecology of aging. We use it as a heuristic to illustrate briefly the central components of person–environment dynamics. The model has evolved over the past 25 years, reflecting the increasing complexity and sophistication occurring in the field. (A summary of its evolution and impact since its inception can be found in Scheidt and Norris-Baker, 2004.) Environmental "press" or demands (on the abscissa) can range from weak to strong.

The import of these demands on the individual depends partly on one's physical and psychological competencies (ordinate). Elders with better sensorimotor skills, biological health, self-esteem, and cognitive functioning respond more effectively to a greater range of environmental demands than those less capable in these domains (Lawton, 1999). The surface of the model reflects the behavioral and psychological outcomes that may be experienced as a result of these person–environment encounters. Several features are worth noting. First, the most pleasant psychological outcomes and adaptive behaviors occur when environmental demands are well within the competence levels of the individual to deal with them. However, for both weaker and stronger press levels, there is a zone of *marginal* comfort—or discomfort—experienced by those who respond to environmental challenges that slightly exceed their abilities to respond. Second, individuals who are more competent tend to deal more adaptively

Figure 7.1   The General Ecological Model.

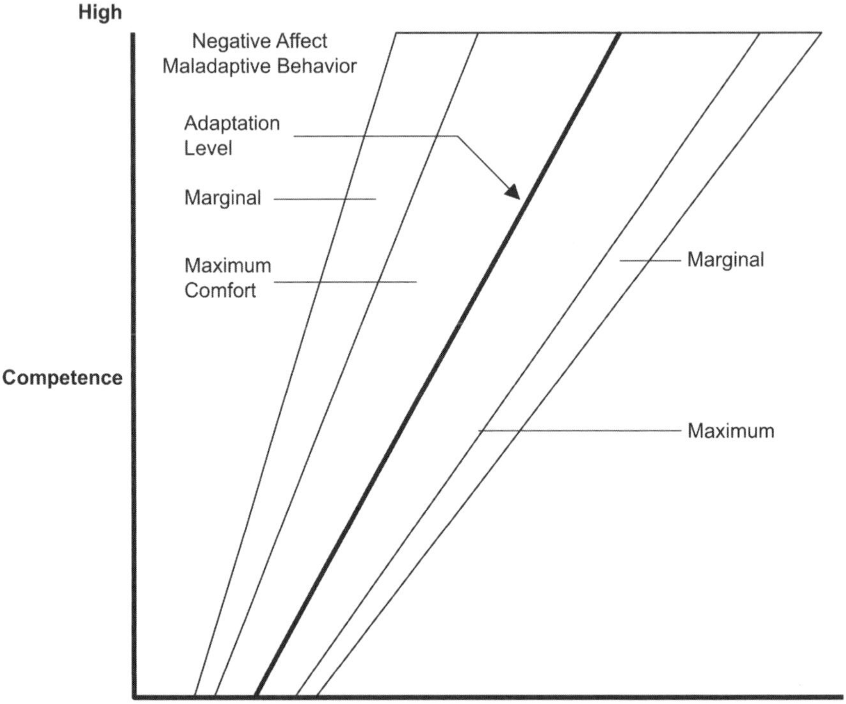

Source: "Ecology and the Aging Process," by M. P. Lawton & L. Nahemow, 1973. In C. Eisdorfer & M. P. Lawton (Eds.), *The Psychology of Adult Development and Aging* (pp. 619–674). Washington, DC: American Psychological Association.

and experience more positive emotions across a wider range of environmental challenges than do the less competent. Third, if environmental demands are too harsh, they can produce unpleasant emotions and maladaptive behavior for everyone. Fourth, more competent individuals experience a greater range of *weaker* press as aversive than do the less competent. They may, for example, become bored more easily with settings that have low stimulation value and suffer "excess disability" as a result. Fifth, by implication, for those who experience reductions in competence (e.g., resulting from progressive or more acute health-related decline), features of previously benign environments may be seen and experienced as stressful, with demands that exceed effective competency. It is important to note that physical or built environments may also deteriorate over time, producing new challenges for individuals with both stable and declining competence. It is not unusual, for example, for older adults to age-in-place in residential and community settings that may suffer rapid or chronic decline (Scheidt & Norris-Baker, 1999).

The model has proven useful for intervention efforts designed to improve adaptive functioning among elders who negotiate both familiar and new settings (Scheidt & Norris-Baker, 2004). Most immediate, it allows two targets for program efforts in this regard. Under some conditions, it may be possible to *increase* the functional competence levels of elders, affording adaptive responses to stronger environmental demands. This is particularly the case for those whose cognitive abilities and functional health may have declined due to harmful but potentially reversible effects of secondary aging. However, when competence levels are relatively "fixed" by irreversible declines in functioning due to aging or disease, options are open for *decreasing* environmental demands or stressors. These often include direct modifications of physical environments or front-loading the design of environments to accommodate populations of elders with more changing as well as rather fixed capacities. The facets and axiomatic assumptions of this general ecological model continue to provide the conceptual infrastructure for research and practice in the ecology of aging. They become apparent in each of the "sampler" issues we introduce in the second part of the chapter.

Residential Contexts of Older Adults: An Overview

Understanding the challenges and supports provided by "near" environments requires some knowledge of where older Americans reside as well as the living arrangements that provide the context for daily life in these settings. A few statistics are necessary.

There are slightly over 37 million people 65 years and older residing within the United States (U.S. Census Bureau, 2006). They account for over 12% of the total U.S. population. Residential options designed to address the diverse needs of elders have increased in recent years. The 2004 National Nursing Home Survey results showed approximately 1.3 million nursing home residents were 65 years and older (National Center for Health Statistics, 2008). Despite demographic trends showing actual and projected increases in the number of "oldest-old" (those 85 years and older) in the United States, the number of older adults who currently reside in nursing homes has actually dropped. Currently, 3.5% of older adults live in nursing homes, down from 5.4% in 1985 (Federal Interagency Forum on Aging-Related Statistics, 2008). To a significant degree, this reduction in long-term care residency is the result of care options designed to help older adults "age-in-place" in the community. Formal and informal environmental support systems, including home and community-based long-term services and supports (HCBS), assisted-living facilities, and ever-present family-based care, have made this possible in many cases. For most, this means an extended capability to remain living in their own homes. Nearly 80% of all older Americans own their own homes (U.S. Census Bureau, Housing and Household Economic Statistics Division, 2008). About 12% of older Americans live in rental housing, a portion of which is subsidized by the federal government. HCBS target individuals experiencing problems performing everyday activities (bathing, dressing, toileting) or other instrumental activities (including shopping or doing laundry). Not restricted to elders alone, services may be delivered to homes or apartments, adult foster homes, congregate care facilities, or assisted-living facilities. Assisted-living facilities and an explosion of recently available HCBS consumer-directed options have aided the creation of a *continuum of care*, filling the gap in care that formerly found elders limited to two housing choices—independent housing or long-term care.

Aging-in-Place and Places That Age

Consistent with the elements of the General Ecological Model, environmental gerontologists often consider more specific characteristics of older adults and of their home environments in order to understand and to enhance their contextual happiness. On the competence dimension, this is often accomplished by assessing *functional health*—the ability to perform activities of daily living (ADLs): bathing, dressing, eating, getting in/out of chairs, walking, or using the toilet (Katz, 1983). Wider *instrumental* activities of daily living (IADLs) are also assessed: using the telephone, light housework, heavy housework, meal preparation, shopping, or managing money. These practical competencies can be diminished by illness, chronic disease, and injuries that affect both mental and physical health. They have direct implications on a larger scale for health and social policies affecting work and retirement, but they also define a critical core of capabilities for dealing with the challenges of the near environment.

It is important to note that residential environments can change in ways that parallel those of their residents. Housing environments, like their inhabitants, exhibit increasing problems over time. The 2005 American Housing Survey shows that while most elderly Americans live in affordable and adequate housing, 38% reside in households that have one or more problems with housing costs, physical adequacy, or crowding. Most elders live in homes that are more than 20 years old. Maintenance requirements grow more difficult as residents grow older in declining environments (Administration on Aging, 2003). Changes in *both* person (P) and environment (E) factors can create a negative "multiplier effect," posing problems for everyday adaptation to environmental demands. These problems constitute the applied professional agenda of environmental gerontologists.

As older adults become aware of the restrictions in their own capacities, and the surrounding environmental influences become progressively more pervasive in limiting activity, they invariably resort to *selection* and *compensation*. Selection includes both environmental changes, such as relocation to a service-rich setting, and changes in active behavior, which can lead to passive adjustments or may be interpreted as a decrease in the number of commitments. When a sudden change, such as a stroke, severely impairs an elderly person, decisions must be made. Staying at home may not be possible, but the person can select an appropriate alternative setting, or the kind of care or rehabilitation he or she needs. Despite suffering reduced and lost capacities, individuals sometimes have *compensatory* mechanisms available to accomplish the same objectives in a specific domain. Similar to the concept of prosthetics, compensation deals with technical as well as human means that make up for impairments in order to support a person's autonomy. Relative independence can be accomplished through devices such as canes, handrails, and other home modifications, or through human assistance. This assistance may range from help with ADLs (e.g., housework, food preparation, and hygiene) to highly skilled nursing and medical care. Compensation might require the acquisition of new skills, new means, and new technology to enable older adults to pursue their lives as fully as possible (Schwarz & Brent, 1999). However, optimization of outcomes in situations of increasing loss is limited by what is possible, particularly with regard to frail elderly in need for long-term care, as Agich (1993) points out: "The reality of long-term care apparently forces even the staunchest proponents of autonomy as independence to deal with reality of an impaired decision-making capacity or incompetence that is an ineliminable feature of long-term care" (p. 10).

Three Applications of the Ecology of Aging

We offer here three illustrations of work in environmental gerontology that focus on various issues emerging from applied research on residential settings of elderly Americans: home modification, the subjective sense of place, and assisted-living settings. These three environmental scenarios illustrate differing orientations to the study of environment, including modification of the physical and social environmental settings of both home and assisted-living facilities, as well as the more subjective senses of place meaning and place identity. Though each scenario illustrates a different context-specific application or orientation, together they illustrate the normative or more usual objective circumstances and experiential issues faced by elders in the places where they live. The scenarios also illustrate the importance and varieties of research-informed interventions— and evaluations of their efficacy—targeting environments as well as older adults at varying levels of environmental scale and individual competence. Each illustration has strong and direct implications for environmental policy.

Research Sampler 1: Home Modification

When older individuals are seriously challenged or overwhelmed by tasks posed by the environment, the General Ecological Model suggests either enhancing their competencies (including adaptive capacities) or altering environments to reduce their "demand pressures." For elders with more intransigent functional health problems, the best alternative is to modify the environment—to change settings in order to improve the "fit" between personal needs and environmental demands. Environmental gerontologists have been very active at several levels to make home environments more accommodative to the changing needs of older residents. Strategies may include structural changes, special equipment, assistive devices, material adjustments, and behavioral changes (Pynoos, 2003, p. 107). Modifications can range "from something as simple as replacing cabinet doorknobs with pull handles to full-scale construction projects that require installing wheelchair ramps and widening doorways" (Administration on Aging, 2003, p. 1). They may involve widening doorways, lowering countertops of bathroom or kitchen cabinets, or enhancing adaptability in more immediate ways, such as installing grab bars in bathroom walls or movable cabinets to allow wheelchair space. Sometimes the intent of modification is to make a home more "visit-friendly." This might involve installing front porch ramps and making hallways accessible to disabled visitors. "Front-loading" efforts include designing home environments to accommodate varying needs of residents as they age (e.g., universal design), allowing them to live independently in their homes as long as possible (Administration on Aging, 2003). While problems currently exist in affordability and delivery of these services, the field boasts exemplary models of system integration involving both interagency cooperation and intra-agency coordination (Pynoos, 2003).

Elderly residents with more severe disabilities are more likely to adopt home modification strategies, as are those who live alone. However, we still lack adequate understanding of how income, gender, and ethnicity affect adoption of modification strategies. Also, there is little current understanding of psychological and social factors that affect the acceptance or rejection of modification strategies by elders (Gitlin, 1999). The level of need remains high, however. Wahl, Fänge, Oswald, Gitlin, and Iwarsson (2009) report that significant mismatches between older adults' functional capacities and housing characteristics are typical. As the General Ecological Model posits, this incongruity may result in greater negative effect and nonadaptive behavior for many elders.

Do home modifications have an impact on disability-related outcomes in later life? This is the paramount question for those who conduct research on environmental modifications for vulnerable populations. Gitlin (1999) examined 13 published studies conducted in the early 1990s that used randomized designs to assess the value of home modifications for physically frail elders living in North America, Europe, and Great Britain. Overall, results regarding the efficacy of these interventions on health status were inconclusive. It is difficult to compare outcomes *across studies* that differ greatly in "dose and intensity" of intervention, specific targets of intervention, population characteristics, compliance, and attrition rates. More descriptive studies using exploratory and case study designs indicate that elders show positive outcomes with respect to functional maintenance (Gitlin, 1999).

The most comprehensive review of the impact of home modifications to date has been conducted by Wahl and colleagues (2009). These researchers carefully examined 10 review papers and 29 original empirical studies to assess changes in ADLs and falls/accident–related outcomes in elders occurring between 1997 and 2006. The majority of the studies used a randomized control design. They concluded that home environment-based interventions did decrease disability-related outcomes, with the evidence on behalf of ADL-related changes "far more convincing" than studies examining falls/accident–related outcomes. The majority of the studies provided supportive or at least inconsistent evidence on behalf of the impact of home modifications on ADLs, while findings related to the positive impact on fall-prone elderly are currently inconsistent. As Gitlin (1999) noted almost a decade ago, although about one-third to one-half of all falls by adults 65 years and older are due to "extrinsic" factors, many different factors are associated with falls that occur inside the home, and few studies exhibit consistency in rooms or specific conditions associated with fall episodes (e.g., ill-fitting footwear, slippery or wet surfaces, sliding carpets, poor lighting, etc.). Wahl et al. (2009) and Gitlin (1999) urge researchers to consider falls within a fuller person–environment framework, taking into account how specific individual factors (e.g., age, functional competencies) may interact with highly specific environmental features. These considerations require a level of specificity beyond the heuristic uses of the General Ecological Model. Continued research on the efficacy of residential modifications will inform development of more specifically targeted interventions that will both support and optimize functioning of elders' aging-in-place in the United States.

Research Sampler 2: Home, House, and the Sense of Place

Although important, research that limits itself only to the creation of physically enabling environments neglects "equally important internal, psychologically-based ties between person and place that enhance quality of life" (Rowles, Oswald, & Hunter, 2004, p. 171). The importance of the perceived or subjective environment was noted by Lawton and Nahemow (1973) in the original statement of the General Ecological Model. In particular, "environmental press" do not reside intrinsically within the environment, but rather take on meaning when they evoke responses centered around the needs of individuals (Lawton & Nahemow, 1973, p. 659). Older adults who age-in-place form both cognitive and emotional relationships with their residential environments, converting a sense of "house" to the experience of "home," where "space" is transformed into "place" (Rowles & Watkins, 2003). Place meanings and place attachments may comprise important aspects of *self-identity* for many older adults. Though psychological stress may result from supportive press, it is more common that threats to residential environments may constitute threats to "self" and, directly as well as indirectly, to psychological and physical well-being (Rowles, 1990). The arena of "meaning of home" or environmental "belonging" (Wahl & Oswald, in press) is one of the most important aspects of the *subjective environment* investigated to date by environmental gerontologists. Geographical gerontologists and anthropologists have primarily employed qualitative methods to study the psychological representation of place, but more traditional measurement-oriented approaches have also been employed (Oswald et al., 2006).

Rowles and Watkins (2003) suggest that "being in place" is a critical part of the creation and maintenance of one's personal history. It is characterized by feeling comfortable, at home, and "at one with one's environment" (p. 78). Being in place involves physical, social, and autobiographical meanings. Physical intimacy with space grows as a result of habitual, long-term daily rhythms and routines. Those who age-in-place develop an inherent awareness of space that may be taken for granted. In terms of the General Ecological Model, this awareness occurs when one is psychologically located for a sustained period of time at the Adaptation Level, which is typified by relatively smooth and automatic relations with environmental demands. Space acquires social meaning over time through social interactions with others who may share the home environment. Awareness of the accumulated events and personal meanings of objects and items in the home lends increasing "autobiographical meaning" of the setting to the resident over time. Some researchers have noted the omission of this important dimension—chronicity or time—in the General Ecological Model (Nahemow, 2000; Scheidt & Norris-Baker, 2004).

The psychological conversion of "space to place" involves *history, habit, heart,* and *hearth* (Rowles & Watkins, 2003). Across the adult life course, one acquires a personal history of accommodating in life to new settings, while simultaneously sustaining and, if need be, severing, links to past settings. Elders who live for a long time in one place—in the same home—may have difficulty abandoning their home and relocating to another residence. Everyday interactions with places in the home become habitual; spaces are imbued with specific memories and meanings, reinforcing a sense of "autobiographical insidedness." Place attachment develops as residents use the home environment to express and affirm their personal histories (Rubinstein, 1989), and create "place as an emotional repository for all that [they] are" (Rowles & Watkins, 2003, p. 81). Finally, home becomes *hearth*—a place of ownership, possession, "a place of centering" that becomes the place "to which we often long to return" (p. 82).

Much of the research about home suggests that the need for a home is a fundamental human imperative, providing a locus of order and control in a world of chaos. Home imparts a sense of identity, security, and belonging. The phenomenon of home consists of tangible relationships between people and the places in which they dwell. It is noteworthy that the terms *house* and *home* seem to be used too often interchangeably by the public as well as in the literature. The fusion of house and home simply reinforce confusion and ambiguity in understanding the linkage between people and their place of residence. House and home are two concepts that have distinctly separate meanings. While a house is an object constructed of various building materials, a home is best conceived of as a relationship between people and their environment. A home is not a building but, rather, a complex condition that fulfills a hierarchy of human needs. Home has a psychological and metaphysical significance over and above being a shelter in which to conduct everyday life. Home is a set of rituals, personal rhythms, and routines of everyday life that need their temporal stability and continuum to develop (Schwarz, 1999). The passage of time appears to be central in the process of developing attachment to a place, and consequently, the home is a gradual product of the dweller's adaptation to her world. Pallasmaa (1995) raises the question of whether the home can become an architectural expression:

> Home is an individualized dwelling, and means of this subtle personalization seem to be outside of our concept of architecture. Dwelling, or the house, is the container, the shell for home. The substance of home is secreted, as it were, upon the framework of the dwelling by the dweller. Home is an expression of the dweller's personality and his unique patterns of life. Consequently, the essence of home is closer to life itself than an artifact. (p. 132)

Because the concept of home is a variable whose meaning cannot be easily measured or transferred, it is no wonder that there has been little measurement-oriented research in this area. Linking the concepts of place meaning and place attachment to psychological well-being is difficult. However, links between self, identity, and well-being have long existed in psychological theories of life span development (Wahl & Oswald, in press).

Nonetheless, outcome research on more broad-level effects of relocation as well as anecdotal case study research supports the importance of taking this domain of subjective experience into account in resident- and home-targeted interventions.

Rowles (2006) poses four provocative questions for future research in this domain: (1) How do people transform the *space* of residence into the locus of a sense of *home?* (2) How is the process of creating home affected by relocation? (3) How does the experience of being at home change with changing capability of the ageing individual? In what ways does home making and sustaining a sense of home evolve in association with age-related changes in the manner in which dwelling is inhabited? In other words, does the meaning and quest for home transform itself and become more intense toward the end of life? Finally, perhaps the most important question in the context of existential meaning of home in old age, (4) What is the relationship between being at home and belonging and the antithesis of this experience—being homeless and alienated? (pp. 28–29).

Along with these issues, Scheidt and Norris-Baker (1999) suggest a variety of "place therapy" strategies that target environments as well as their inhabitants. Individually targeted "reminiscence" therapy should include elements of remembered contexts, aware that relocation and aging-in-place are more than discrete events; they are processes that may carry different meanings in different phases of the adult life cycle. "Relocation preparation and adjustment" and "constructing familiarity" strategies target the transitions to new settings, while "ecoanalysis of the home" determines how resident images of "ideal" home may be affecting poor adjustment to the current home (Peled & Schwartz, 1999; Rowles & Watkins, 2003). The maintenance of links with prior environments has been the goal of "artifact transference," which attempts to "facilitate the transference and re-creation of a sense of place" (Rowles & Watkins, 2003, p. 93). Environmental targeting may include environmental designs that allow for space to be devoted to storage and display of valued objects and memorabilia. Scheidt and Norris-Baker (1999) advocate "behavior setting" therapy, focusing on strategies to defend threatened places and to create new places for critical activities and social interaction in tiny declining towns. At the most macro level, they recommend "community therapy" strategies, including ways of increasing social capital. They propose strategies for installing community rituals to enhance a sense of community identity and "place futurity," as well as strategies for igniting cooperation between elders who age-in-place and the often-younger newcomers who display very different experiences of "being in place" in the home and surrounding neighborhood (Scheidt & Norris-Baker, 1999).

We conclude this sampler with the words of Rowles, who noted that the concept of "home is integrally involved with ongoing quest to make sense of our lives and to centre ourselves in relation to our place in the universe and a higher spiritual sense of being and identity. As we approach the end of our life the quest for home on this level may become ever more insistent and compelling" (2006, p. 29).

Research Sampler 3: Assisted Living

Until the late 1980s, people with chronic diseases received long-term care either from their families in ordinary dwellings, or in nursing homes. Since the late part of the 20th century, a new long-term care setting—assisted living—has evolved as an alternative setting for long-term care. "Assisted living evolved, in large part, because older people wanted to avoid nursing homes and their families wished to spare them the regimented, abnormal life style associated with life in typical nursing home" (Kane & Brown-Wilson, 2001). The term *assisted living* stands for various kinds of entities. It represents an entire range of buildings and programs that serve older functionally impaired people who, on a continuing basis, need personal care to compensate for limitations in their activities of daily living (Kane & Wilson, 1993). Assisted living thus refers to purposively built group residential environments that offer protected living arrangements with around-the-clock delivery of professionally managed personal and health care services. It has the capacity to respond to scheduled and unscheduled needs for help in everyday activities, such as dressing, bathing, eating, grooming and mobility, medication management, and limited health services. In the language of the General Ecological Model, these environments serve older individuals who display middle- to lower-levels of competence and who require aid with ADLs and IADLs. Assisted-living environments are specifically engineered to reduce environmental press or demands in these spheres.

Ideal assisted-living arrangements are characterized by three essential attributes: first, a residential physical environment that takes its architectural character from single-family houses. The setting is expected to have a residential appearance, be small scale, and provide residential privacy that includes at a minimum a private room and a full bath that is not shared with other residents unless the resident explicitly wishes. The public spaces in the facility are designed to afford access to indoor and outdoor spaces in an effort to enhance resident autonomy and independence. Second, a philosophy of care that emphasizes consumer control, choice, dignity, and autonomy and promotes preferred lifestyle in what residents and their families consider a "normal," good quality of life. This philosophy is implemented through attempts to understand resident preferenced and priorities and efforts to allow residents control over their lives, their schedules, and their private dwellings. Third, an assisted-living arrangement should have a service capacity that can meet residents' routine services and special needs. "Essential elements in service capacity include offering or arranging: competent initial assessments of needs and preferences; individualized service planning; kind, capable, and responsive personal care 24 hours a day, 7 days a week; 3 meals a day; housekeeping; identification of changes in residents' physical functioning and condition; arrangements for specialized assessments and interventions; and responses to emergency situations. The provider must also offer or arrange routine nursing service, including mediations management, but 'nursing services' should not be construed as services that can only be performed by a registered or licensed nurse" (Kane & Brown-Wilson, 2001, p. 3).

Although assisted-living arrangements have existed for more than 20 years, there are still no national consensus or federal guidelines governing the characteristics of the population that can be served in these facilities, what services can be provided, what constitutes minimum staffing standards, or other aspects of assisted living. The different combinations of housing and service arrangements that today are considered as assisted living "make simple generalizations about either their physical settings or their care environments particularly challenging—and inevitably contribute to consumer confusion" (Golant, 2008, p. 7). Despite the ambiguity about the definition, the number of assisted-living arrangements continues to grow. Between 1998 and 2000, the number of licensed assisted-living residence units grew 33% "and then slowed to 13 percent between 2000 and 2002 and to 3 percent between 2002 and 2004; but between 2004 and 2007 the growth rate accelerated to 6 percent. By 2007 there were 947,585 units in 38,373 licensed facilities" (Mollica, 2008, p. vii).

We believe that the architectural setting of assisted living is more than just a background or stage on which older adults conduct their lives. The setting can provide or inhibit opportunities for privacy, independence, control, and choice. Thus, it is important to study environmental attributes of assisted living that aspire to translate program philosophy and therapeutic goals into a place that supports the personal autonomy of its inhabitants.

Over a period of 30 years, Regnier (2002) assembled 100 critical design considerations for the architectural design of assisted-living environments. These practical patterns focus primarily on environmental attributes that affect resident quality of life and make the building more attractive for family members and other visitors and more accommodating for staff members. Besides serving as excellent guidelines for potential architects and designers, these design recommendations can be taken as a list of hypotheses to be tested in post-occupancy evaluations of existing assisted living. Based on their conceptual model, which links the social context, the physical setting, and the organizational context, Cohen and Weisman (1991) identified nine therapeutic goals that establish the basis for caring for people with dementia in special care facilities. Although these goals were originally established for people with reduced mental capacities, they are equally suitable for people with physical disabilities. The goals include: ensure safety and security; support functional ability through meaningful activity; heighten awareness and orientation; provide appropriate environmental stimulation and challenge; develop a positive social milieu; maximize autonomy and control; adapt to changing needs; establish links to the healthy and the familiar; and protect the need for privacy. Zeisel (1999) and his colleagues (Zeisel, Hyde, & Levkoff, 1994) developed Environment-Behavior (E-B) criteria for design for people with dementia, which are suitable for assisted-living arrangements. His criteria include the following E-B concepts: exit control; walking paths; personal places, social spaces; healing gardens; residential features; independence; and sensory comprehensibility. These principles were put into practice in the design of several facilities around the country as well as in other parts of the world.

Ultimately, we are interested in buildings because of the people who occupy them and live around them. While a building needs to serve a social purpose, it is an instrumental good not an end in itself. Consequently, what we want to learn about assisted living as a place type are the same things we want to know about anything else people make: How does it serve the most important purpose, that of fulfilling the task that is unique to people? Namely, how does it perfect their nature and allow them to pursue the pleasures that are uniquely available to people as people? We suggest that the physical environment has a significant, perhaps central, role in therapeutic building type for frail elderly. It contributes to or directly enhances therapeutic processes. We recognize that no one aspect of the provision of therapeutic facilities, be it care providers, policies, or environmental attributes, can on its own produce a therapeutic environment. The environment does not control behavior—a hard architectural determinism—but rather, environment influences, limits, or affords opportunities. Thus, assisted-living setting design has focused on the provision of comprehensive care in the least restrictive therapeutic setting—an environment that promotes privacy, comfort, independence, and social interaction like that experienced at home.

Research on assisted living has grown as more assisted-living arrangements have developed. In spite of gaps in the knowledge, research findings demonstrate the importance of the central attributes of these combinations of housing and services for frail elderly (Polivka & Salmon, 2008; Zimmerman et al., 2005). Future assisted-living facilities will have to be able to respond to residents with more service needs as a result of their frailty. Assisted living will have to find ways to adapt and maximize their flexibility in order to serve older adults with low and high acuity care demands. One of the challenges to assisted living in the future includes the blurring of congregate (independent) living, assisted living, and nursing home into hybrids of these arrangements. The hope is that the more stringent regulations that will follow the amalgamations of these forms of housing and services will not devastate the special characteristics of assisted living. Another future challenge will be the occupancy price of assisted living, which could put it out of the reach of many American elderly. Finally, the future role of the government in providing funds for affordable shelter and care will continue to be limited. Therefore, experts predict that families will assume the largest financial burden of providing long-term care funds for their loved ones (Golant, 2008).

A CONCLUDING COMMENT

We believe that environmental gerontology will continue to play a lively and useful role in addressing needs of elderly Americans, particularly given the burgeoning population bubbles posed by the currently rapidly growing "old-old" (85 years and older) as well as the certain future arrival of the baby boom cohorts born between 1946–1964. It is likely that the field itself will expand to include new arenas of study and new sources of influence that will shape its future. This includes the increasingly powerful influence of environment-aging research in Europe on both topics and methods (Scheidt & Windley, 2006). For example, the study of expanded time frames for understanding person–environment relations has been suggested by some (Golant, 2008; Wahl & Oswald, in press). This might include historical transitions in the social environmental sphere (e.g., new contexts of care), the home environment (e.g., continuing care retirement communities; the culture change movement), the outdoor environment (e.g., new lifestyle and leisure activity patterns), technology domains (e.g., smart home technology and high-tech assistive devices), and in social and policy arenas (e.g., globalization and urbanization issues; Wahl & Oswald, in press). There is a continuing need for theories of "the middle range" that allow more specific environment-behavior targeting, beyond the useful, broad-level heuristic provided by the General Ecological Model (Scheidt & Windley, 1998). In addition, a number of existing populations remain understudied; these include special populations in special environmental circumstances (e.g., rural elders who age-in-place in declining and dying small towns; differing environmental needs and resources of ethnically and culturally diverse older in-migrants; older residents in long-term care facilities adopting the "culture change" paradigm; or aging in prisons). This applies to underutilized research paradigms as well. For example, an approach that treat researchers, elderly clients, and practitioners as partners in the problem-solving process—that is, action research—holds promise for affecting closer ties between our theories, our programmatic interventions, and the evaluation of their efficacy. This may allow us to fulfill the hope that our environments will be more happily congruent with our needs.

REFERENCES

Administration on Aging. (2003). *Fact Sheet: Home Modification.* Washington, DC: U.S. Dept. of Health and Human Services. Retrieved July 24, 2008, from: http://www. aoa.gov/AoAroot/Press_Room/Products_Materials/index.aspx.

Agich, G. (1993). *Autonomy and Long-term Care.* New York: Oxford University Press.

Altman, I., Lawton, M. P., & Wohlwill, J. F. (Eds.). (1984). *Elderly People and the Environment.* New York: Plenum Press.

Atchley, B. C., & Byerts, T. O. (Eds.). (1975). *Rural Environments and Aging.* Washington, DC: Gerontological Society of America.

Baltes, M. M., Maas, I., Wilms, H.-U., & Borchelt, M. (1999). Everyday competence in old and very old age: Theoretical considerations and empirical findings. In P. B. Baltes & K. U. Mayer (Eds.), *The Berlin Aging Study* (pp. 384–402). Cambridge, UK: Cambridge University Press.

Birren, J. E., & Cunningham, W. R. (1985). Research on the psychology of aging: Principles, concepts and theory. In J. E. Birren & K. W. Schaie (Eds.), *Handbook of the Psychology of Aging* (2nd ed., pp. 3–34) New York: Van Nostrand Reinhold Company.

Byerts, T. O., Howell, S. C., & Pastalan, L. A. (Eds.). (1979). *Environmental Context of Aging: Lifestyles, Environmental Quality and Living Arrangements.* New York: Garland STPM Press.

Cairns, R. B. (1998). The making of developmental psychology. In W. Damon (Series Ed.) & R. Lerner (Vol. Ed.), *Handbook of Child Psychology: Vol. 1. Theoretical Models of Human Development* (5th ed., pp. 25–106). New York: Wiley.

Carp, F. M. (1966). *A Future for the Aged.* Austin: University of Texas Press.

Cavanaugh, J., & Blanchard-Fields, F. (2006). *Adult Development and Aging* (5th ed.). Belmont, CA: Wadsworth/Thomson Learning.

Cohen, U., & Weisman, G. D. (1991). *Holding on to Home: Designing Environments for People With Dementia.* Baltimore, MD: The Johns Hopkins University Press.

Craik, F.I.M., & Salthouse, T. A. (Eds.). (1992). *Handbook of Aging and Cognition.* Hillsdale, NJ: Lawrence Erlbaum Associates.

Federal Interagency Forum on Aging-Related Statistics. (2008, March). *Older Americans 2008: Key Indicators of Well-being.* Federal Interagency Forum on Aging-Related Statistics. Washington, DC: Government Printing Office.

Gitlin, L. (1999). Testing home modification interventions: Issues of theory, measurement, design, and implementation. In. R. Schulz, G. Maddox, & M. P. Lawton (Eds.), *Focus on Interventions Research With Older Adults: Annual Review of Gerontology and Geriatrics* (vol. 18, pp. 190–246). New York: Springer.

Golant, S. M. (Ed.). (1979). *Location and Environment of Elderly Population.* Washington, DC: V. H. Winston & Sons.

Golant, S. M. (2008). The future of assisted living residences: A response to uncertainty. In S. M. Golant & J. Hyde (Eds.), *The Assisted Living Residence: A Vision for the Future* (pp. 3–45). Baltimore, MD: The Johns Hopkins University Press.

Gubrium, J. F. (1973). *The Myth of the Golden Years: A Socio-environmental Theory of Aging.* Springfield, IL: Charles C. Thomas.

Hayflick, L. (1994). *How and Why We Age.* New York: Ballantine Books.

Kane, R. A., & Brown-Wilson, K. (2001). *Assisted Living at the Crossroad: Principles for its Future*. Retrieved September 10, 2008, from: http://www.ilru.org/html/training/webcast/handouts/2002/10–09-JK/crossroads.html.

Kane, R. A., & Wilson, K. (1993). *Assisted Living in the United States: A New Paradigm for Residential Care for Frail Older Persons?* Washington, DC: American Association of Retired Persons.

Katz, S. (1983). Assessing self-maintenance: Activities of daily living, mobility, and instrumental activities of daily living. *Journal of the American Geriatrics Society, 31,* 721–727.

Kleemeier, R. W. (1959). Behavior and the organization of the bodily and the external environment. In J. Birren (Ed.), *Handbook of Aging and the Individual* (pp. 400–451). Oxford, UK: University of Chicago Press.

Lawton, M. P. (1980). *Environment and Aging*. Monterey, CA: Brooks/Cole.

Lawton, M. P. (1999). Environmental taxonomy: Generalizations from research with older adults. In S. Friedman & T. Wachs (Eds.), *Measuring Environment Across the Life Span* (pp. 91–124). Washington, DC: American Psychological Association.

Lawton, M. P., & Nahemow, L. (1973). Ecology and the aging process. In C. Eisdorfer & M. P. Lawton (Eds.), *The Psychology of Adult Development and Aging* (pp. 619–674). Washington, DC: American Psychological Association.

Lawton, M. P., & Simon, B. (1967). The ecology of social relationships in housing for the elderly. *The Gerontologist, 8,* 108–115.

Lawton, M. P., Windley, P. G., & Byerts, T. O. (Eds.). (1982). *Aging and the Environment: Theoretical Approaches*. New York: Springer.

Lewin, K. (1954). Behavior and development as a function of the total situation. In L. Carmichael (Ed.), *Manual of Child Psychology* (2nd ed.). New York: Wiley.

Mollica, R. (2008). Forward. In S. M. Golant & J. Hyde (Eds.), *The Assisted Living Residence: A Vision for the Future*. Baltimore, MD: The Johns Hopkins University Press.

Nahemow, L. (2000). The ecological theory of aging: Powell Lawton's legacy. In R. Rubinstein, M. Moss, & M. Kleban (Eds.), *The Many Dimensions of Aging* (pp. 22–40). New York: Springer.

National Center for Health Statistics. (2008). *National Nursing Home Survey Data Highlights: 2004 Current Resident Tables*. Retrieved July 17, 2008, from: http://www.cdc.gov/nchs/nnhs.htm.

Neugarten, B. (1968). *Middle Age and Aging*. Chicago: University of Chicago Press.

Oswald, F., Schilling, O., Wahl, H.-W., Fänge, A., Sixsmith, J., & Iwarsson, S. (2006). Homeward bound: Introducing a four domain model of perceived housing in very old age. *Journal of Environmental Psychology, 26,* 187–201.

Pallasmaa, J. (1995). Identity, intimacy, and domicile: Notes on the phenomenology of home. In D. Benjamin (Ed.), *The Home: Words, Interpretations, Meanings, and Environments* (pp. 131–147). Aldershot, UK: Avebury.

Pastalan, L. A., & Carson, D. H. (Eds.). (1970). *Spatial Behavior of Older People*. Ann Arbor, MI: University of Michigan—Wayne State University Institute of Gerontology.

Peled, A., & Schwartz, H. (1999). Exploring the ideal home in psychotherapy: Two case studies. *Journal of Environmental Psychology, 19,* 87–94.

Pinquart, M., & Burmedi, D. (2004). Correlates of residential satisfaction in adulthood and old age: A meta-analysis. In K. W. Schaie (Series Ed.), H. W. Wahl,

R. J. Scheidt, & P. G. Windley (Vol. Eds.), *Annual Review of Gerontology and Geriatrics: Vol. 23. Aging in Context: Socio-physical Environments* (pp. 195–222). New York: Springer.

Polivka, L., & Salmon, J. R. (2008). Assisted living: What it should be and why? In S. M. Golant & J. Hyde (Eds.), *The Assisted Living Residence: A Vision for the Future* (pp. 397–418). Baltimore, MD: The Johns Hopkins University Press.

Pynoos, J. (2003). Advancements in the home modification field: A tribute to M. Powell Lawton. In R. J. Scheidt & P. Windley (Eds.), *Physical Environments and Aging: Critical Contributions of M. Powell Lawton to Theory and Practice* (pp. 105–116). New York: Haworth Press.

Regnier, V. (2002). *Design for Assisted Living: Guidelines for Housing the Physically and Mentally Frail.* New York: Wiley.

Rowles, G. (1990). Place attachment among the small town elderly. *Journal of Rural Community Psychology, 11,* 103–120.

Rowles, G. D. (2006). Commentary: A house is not a home: But can it become one? In H.-W. Wahl, H. Brenner, H. Mollenkopf, D. Rothenbacher, & C. Rott (Eds.), *The Many Faces of Health, Competence and Well-being in Old Age* (pp. 25–32). The Netherlands: Springer.

Rowles, G. D., & Ohta, R. J. (Eds.). (1983). *Aging and Milieu: Environmental Perspectives on Growing Old.* New York: Academic Press.

Rowles, G., Oswald, F., & Hunter, E. (2004). Interior living environments in old age. In K. W. Schaie (Series Ed.), H. W. Wahl, R. J. Scheidt, & P. G. Windley (Vol. Eds.), *Annual Review of Gerontology and Geriatrics: Vol. 23. Aging in Context: Socio-physical Environments* (pp. 167–194). New York: Springer.

Rowles, G., & Watkins, J. (2003). History, habit, heart and hearth: On making spaces into places. In K. W. Schaie, H. W. Wahl, H. Mollenkopf, & F. Oswald (Eds.), *Aging Independently: Living Arrangements and Mobility* (pp. 77–96). New York: Springer.

Rubinstein, R. (1989). The home environments of older people: A description of the psychosocial processes linking person to place. *Journal of Gerontology: Social Sciences, 44,* S45–S53.

Scheidt, R., & Norris-Baker, C. (1999). Place therapies for older adults: Conceptual and interventive approaches. *International Journal of Aging and Human Development, 48,* 1–15.

Scheidt, R. J., & Norris-Baker, L. (2004). The General Ecological Model revisited: Evolution, current status, and continuing challenges. In K. W. Schaie (Series Ed.), H. W. Wahl, R. J. Scheidt, & P. G. Windley (Vol. Eds.), *Annual Review of Gerontology and Geriatrics: Vol. 23. Aging in Context: Socio-physical Environments* (pp. 34–58). New York: Springer.

Scheidt, R. J., & Windley, P. (1985). The ecology of aging. In J. Birren & K. W. Schaie (Eds.), *Handbook of the Psychology of Aging* (2nd ed., pp. 245–260). New York: Van Nostrand Reinhold.

Scheidt, R. J., & Windley, P. (1998). *Environment and Aging Theory: A Focus on Housing.* Westport, CT: Greenwood Press.

Scheidt, R. J., & Windley, P. (2006). Environmental gerontology: Progress in the post-Lawton era. In J. Birren & K. W. Schaie (Eds.), *Handbook of the Psychology of Aging* (6th ed., pp. 105–125). New York: Academic Press.

Schwarz, B. (1999). Assisted living: An evolving place type. In B. Schwarz & R. Brent (Eds.), *Aging Autonomy and Architecture: Advances in Assisted Living* (pp. 185–206). Baltimore, MD: The Johns Hopkins University Press.

Schwarz, B., & Brent, R. (1999). *Aging Autonomy and Architecture: Advances in Assisted Living.* Baltimore, MD: The Johns Hopkins University Press.

Spence, A. P. (1995). *Biology of Human Aging.* Englewood Cliffs, NJ: Prentice Hall.

Thelen, E., & Smith, L. (1998). Dynamic systems theories. In W. Damon (Series Ed.) & R. Lerner (Vol. Ed.), *Handbook of Child Psychology: Vol. 1. Theoretical Models of Human Development* (5th ed., pp. 563–634). New York: Wiley.

Tobin, S. S., & Lieberman, M. A. (1976). *Last Home for the Aged.* San Francisco: Jossey-Bass.

U.S. Census Bureau. (2006). *American Community Survey, 2006: S0103. Population 65 Years and Over in the United States.* Retrieved July 17, 2008, from: http://factfinder.census.gov/servlet/STTable?_bm=y&-geo_id=01000US&-qr_name=ACS_2007_3YR_G00_S0103&-ds_name=ACS_2007_3YR_G00_

U.S. Census Bureau, Housing and Household Economic Statistics Division. (2008). *Housing Vacancies and Homeownership* (CPS/HVS). Retrieved July 17, 2007, from: http://www.census.gov/hhes/www/housing/hvs/qtr108/q108ind.html

Wahl, H. W., Fänge, A., Oswald, F., Gitlin, L., & Iwarsson, S. (2009). The home environment and disability-related outcomes in aging individuals: What is the empirical evidence? *The Gerontologist, 49,* 355–367.

Wahl, H. W., & Oswald, F. (in press). Environmental perspectives on aging. In D. Dannefer & C. Phillipson (Eds.), *International Handbook of Social Gerontology.* New York: Sage.

Windley, P. G., Byerts, T. O., & Ernst, E. (Eds.). (1975). *Theory Development in Environment and Aging.* Washington, DC: Gerontological Society of America.

Zeisel, J. (1999). Life-quality Alzheimer care in assisted living. In B. Schwarz & R. Brent (Eds.), *Aging Autonomy and Architecture: Advances in Assisted Living* (pp. 110–129). Baltimore, MD: The Johns Hopkins University Press.

Zeisel, J., Hyde, J., & Levkoff, S. (1994). Best practices: An environment-behavior (E-B) model of physical design for special care units. *Journal of Alzheimer's Disease, 9,* 4–21.

Zimmerman, S., Sloane, P., Eckert, J., Gruber-Baldini, A., Morgan, L., Hebel, J., et al. (2005). How good is assisted living? Findings and implications from an outcome study. *Journal of Gerontology: Social Sciences 60B*(4), S195–S204.

CHAPTER 8

PERSONAL CONTROL AND AGING: HOW BELIEFS AND EXPECTATIONS MATTER

*Stefan Agrigoroaei
and Margie E. Lachman*

The best years of your life are the ones in which you decide your problems are your own. You do not blame them on your mother, the ecology, or the president. You realize that you control your own destiny.

—Albert Ellis

In this chapter, we define the concept of control, present a range of methods used to operationalize this construct, and summarize results about age-related changes in personal control in different domains. We also provide a conceptual model and empirical findings about the relationship between control beliefs and functioning in multiple aging-related domains and discuss intervention studies that have modified the sense of control.

The vast literature on control beliefs reflects the increasing interest in this concept and the large variety of labels, definitions, and operationalizations used by psychologists and other social and behavioral scientists (see Rodin, 1990; Skinner, 1996). Several trends emerge from this literature. First, much of the research is focused on perceived personal control (control beliefs) rather than on actual control over desired outcomes. Second, multidimensional theoretical and methodological approaches are usually used. Third, when studying personal control, it is important to take into account contextual factors, including the age of the participants. Finally, there is consistent evidence for the protective and adaptive value of sense of control across the life span (Lachman, 2006).

We acknowledge support from the National Institute on Aging (Grants P01 AG020166 and R01 AG17920).

Although many are interested in the general, broad trait-like aspects of control beliefs, there is evidence that control beliefs vary across domains such as health, cognitive functioning, finances, or personal relationships. In this chapter, we consider the overall sense of control and its components: perceived ability and contingency (Bandura, 1997; Lachman & Weaver, 1998a; Skinner, 1996). Both of these aspects of control can be examined in a general sense or with regard to specific domains.

We review the literature on general control and domain-specific control. For our discussion of the concept of self-efficacy, a component of control that is focused on perceived ability, we selected the domain of memory for illustrative purposes. In this context, self-appraisals of one's memory abilities or beliefs about memory capacity are referred to as memory self-efficacy (MSE). Given the salience of the memory domain for aging, the associated expectancies for decline, and the results generally showing the greatest benefits of high levels of memory beliefs in older people than in younger adults (Lachman & Andreoletti, 2006; West, Dark-Freudeman, & Bagwell, 2009), we use memory beliefs as an example to illustrate domain-specific control. We want to emphasize, as have Berry and West (1993, p. 373), that "the concept of relevance is not synonymous with expertise" and that "theoretically, a domain may be relevant to personal functioning or one's self-concept because it is problematic or because it is well-practiced and expert."

The overriding goal of this chapter is to consider what is known about the relevance of control beliefs to the aging process. Given the increased probability of uncontrollable losses and decreased likelihood of desired gains in later life, it is natural to expect that one's sense of control would diminish with aging. Yet, the evidence is that many adults believe there are things they can do to influence their health and other aspects of well-being as they age (Lachman, 2006). Moreover, there are individual differences in these beliefs, and these expectancies for control or lack thereof make a difference for aging-related outcomes.

DEFINITIONS AND MEASURES

One possible classification of the control concepts and their corresponding measures may be based on two dimensions: level of generality and number of facets or components of control. Personal sense of control broadly represents the perception that one can influence what happens in one's life. It includes beliefs or expectations about the extent to which one's actions can bring about desired outcomes. Depending on their research goals, researchers propose a wide diversity of outcomes. They vary from general (e.g., "What happens in my life is often beyond my control"), to domain specific (e.g., "How much control do you have over your health?"), and to task specific (e.g., "How much control did you have over your performance on the memory task?"). The domain-specific approach assumes that control beliefs may vary across different spheres of life (Lachman & Weaver, 1998a), for example, work, marriage, finances, cognition, and memory. Among the measures focused on the domains of cognition and memory, we mention the Personality in Intellectual Contexts Inventory (PIC; Lachman, 1986; Lachman, Baltes, Nesselroade, & Willis, 1982) and the Memory Controllability Inventory (MCI; Lachman, Bandura, Weaver, & Elliott, 1995). The PIC is a domain-specific measure of cognitive control beliefs that has been used in many studies examining the relationship between beliefs and performance (Cornelius & Caspi, 1986; Grover & Hertzog, 1991; Rebok, Rasmusson, & Brandt, 1995). This instrument includes three subscales related to control beliefs, namely, an Internal control scale and two External control scales (Chance control and Powerful Others control). The Internal scale is designed to measure the belief that improvements are possible through one's own effort and contains items such as, "I know if I keep using my memory I will never lose it." The chance scale includes items such as, "there's nothing I can do to preserve my mental clarity," which is designed to capture the belief that performance is controlled by unknown external factors. The Powerful Others scale refers to a reliance on other people for achieving outcomes and includes items such as, "I can only understand instructions after someone explains them to me."

The MCI contains 19 items grouped in 6 subscales. Two of them assess beliefs about memory ability: Present Memory Ability (e.g., "I can remember the things I need to") and Potential Memory Improvement (e.g., "I can find ways to improve my memory"). Beliefs about memory control are measured with the Memory Effort Utility (e.g., "If I use my memory often I won't lose it") and the Inevitable Memory Decrement (e.g., "When it comes to memory, there is no way I can make up for the losses that come with age") subscales. Two other supplementary subscales are used to evaluate the level of independence (e.g., "As I get older I won't have to rely on others to remember things for me") and the perceived likelihood of developing Alzheimer's (e.g., "I think there's a good chance I will get Alzheimer's disease").

We endorse a multidimensional theoretical and empirical approach (e.g., Bandura, 1997; Lachman & Weaver, 1998b) by examining beliefs about one's ability to bring about an outcome (e.g., "Is there anything I can do?") and the contingency between one's actions and outcomes (e.g., "If I do something will it make a difference?"). This approach is consistent with Skinner's (1996) twofold conceptualization of control in terms of competence and contingency. To summarize, two main sets of beliefs can be distinguished: one's own efficacy (internal control or personal mastery) and the responsiveness of the environment or other people (external control or perceived constraints).

Self-efficacy emphasizes the component of control that focuses on self-beliefs about one's capacity to accomplish a specific task. This concept, proposed by

Albert Bandura, describes "people's judgments of their capabilities to organize and execute courses of action required to attain designated types of performances" (1986, p. 391). In the domain of memory functioning, MSE is a construct that has its origins in Bandura's framework. It represents the evaluation people make of their ability to use their memories effectively in different situations. The increasing interest in the beliefs people have in their memory capacities is based on the evidence that these beliefs change with age, tend to explain the memory decline in older adults (e.g., Beaudoin, Agrigoroaei, Desrichard, Fournet, & Roulin, 2008; Desrichard & Köpetz, 2005; Suen, Morris, & McDougall, 2004; Valentijn et al., 2006; Zelinski & Gilewski, 2004), and are generally related to mental health variables (e.g., Fort, Adoul, Holl, Kaddour, & Gana, 2004; McDougall, 1995; Zelinski & Gilewski, 2004). MSE is measured with the Memory Self-Efficacy Questionnaire (MSEQ; Berry, West, & Dennehey, 1989), a task specific paper-and-pencil questionnaire that originally includes the descriptions of 10 memory exercises (classic laboratory tasks and everyday tasks) presenting 5 levels of difficulty. A shorter version, the MSEQ-4 (West, Bagwell, & Dark-Freudeman, 2005), also has been used recently. For each task, participants are required to decide whether or not they are capable of attaining each task and to state their level of confidence. Therefore, two different scores could be computed: MSE level (sum of positive responses provided with at least 20% confidence) and MSE strength (the average of confidence ratings for all memory situations). MSE can also be evaluated using particular subscales from instruments measuring domain-specific control beliefs (e.g., Present Memory Ability from the MCI) or from questionnaires designed to measure metamemory (e.g., Metamemory In Adulthood, MIA—Dixon & Hultsch, 1983; Memory Functioning Questionnaire, MFQ—Gilewski & Zelinski, 1988; or Multifactorial Memory Questionnaire, MMQ—Troyer & Rich, 2002). "Metamemory is an individual's knowledge, perceptions, and beliefs about the functioning, development, and capacities of her or his own memory and the human memory system" (McDougall, 1995, p. 358). We would like to highlight that not every self-assessment of memory abilities can qualify as a MSE measure. MSE is conceptually and methodologically different than memory complaints, single task-specific predictions of performance, or metamemory evaluations done after encoding or retrieval (Berry et al., 1989). Regarding the metamemory questionnaires, there is evidence (Hertzog, Dixon, & Hultsch, 1990; Hertzog, Hultsch, & Dixon, 1989; McDougall & Kang, 2003) that the scores obtained on the Capacity scale of the MIA and on the Frequency of Forgetting scale of the MFQ load on the same factor and that this factor is moderately correlated with the scores obtained on the MSEQ and with other measures of performance expectancy for memory tasks. Along the same lines, Troyer and Rich (2002) found that these specific scales from MIA and MFQ were highly correlated with the Ability scale of MMQ.

In addition to self-efficacy or personal mastery, the other main component of the two-process conception of control is perceived constraints. This indicates to what extent one believes there are obstacles or factors beyond one's control (e.g., other people or environmental contingencies) that interfere with reaching goals (Lachman & Firth, 2004; Miller & Lachman, 2000). Another concept similar to personal control is Locus of Control (LOC), a construct derived from Rotter's social learning theory (1966). This construct can vary in terms of dimensionality and domain specificity. For example, LOC was originally unidimensional and represented on a continuum having internal and external control as extremes. People with an internal LOC are more likely to believe that they themselves determine events. Those with an external LOC tend to believe that other factors, such as chance, circumstances, or powerful others, are controlling outcomes. It seems that this tendency corresponds to a high level of perceived constraints, which are typically seen as having external sources. In other studies, LOC is also conceptualized as having multiple dimensions and being domain specific (e.g., multidimensional health LOC; Wallston, 2005).

AGE DIFFERENCES IN PERSONAL CONTROL

Age differences in control beliefs seem to occur mainly because across the life span, adults experience fewer opportunities for control and more control-limiting situations. This is to say that, with aging, the loss of control is associated with an increasing acknowledgment of the constraints and limitations due to uncontrollable factors or due to reduced contingency between actions and outcomes (Lachman & Firth, 2004).

Although there is a widespread belief that we can control aspects of aging, there is also strong evidence from both cross-sectional and longitudinal studies that, on average, a sense of control decreases with age (Krause & Shaw, 2003; Lachman & Firth, 2004; Mirowsky, 1995). Nevertheless, a large majority of studies investigating control beliefs in adulthood have concentrated on comparing young and older adults, with little consideration of the middle years. For the most part, studies that have included middle-aged adults show inconsistent findings. Some studies reveal no differences in control beliefs between young adults and those in middle age (e.g., Brandtstädter & Rothermund, 1994), while another reports an increased sense of internal control as one moves from young adulthood to middle age (Staats, 1974), and sometimes elderly adults show more internal control compared to middle-aged adults (Lachman, 1985).

A national survey, Midlife in the United States (MIDUS), enabled us to examine perceived control among middle-aged adults in comparison with that of younger and older adults by use of a large representative sample from age 25 to 75 (Lachman & Firth, 2004; Lachman & Weaver, 1998a). Our findings revealed that although there were no age differences in a general sense of mastery, there were age-related increments in beliefs about external constraints; that is, older adults indicated facing more constraints than did members of the other age groups. Interestingly, however, older adults reported greater perceived control for life overall than did the younger and middle-aged adults, despite an awareness of increased perceived constraints (Lachman & Firth, 2004). Older adults seem to maintain their overall sense of mastery (beliefs about one's ability or self-efficacy), perhaps because they adjust the standards that they use to define their competence.

In the domain of memory functioning, research has consistently shown that age affects MSE, with older adults obtaining lower scores than younger adults. This pattern is obtained using different measures of MSE, from the Capacity scale of the MIA (Marquié & Huet, 2000; Wells & Esopenko, 2008), the Frequency of Forgetting scale of the MFQ (Zelinski & Gilewski, 2004), and the Ability scale of the MMQ (Fort et al., 2004), to the MSEQ (Beaudoin et al., 2008; Berry et al., 1989; Desrichard & Köpetz, 2005; Gardiner, Luszcz, & Bryan, 1997; McDougall, 1995; McDougall & Kang, 2003; West et al., 2009).

WHAT ARE THE BENEFITS OF FEELING IN CONTROL?

The role of control beliefs as a protective factor is often considered in the aging literature. Individual differences in perceptions of control are important because such expectations can influence behaviors and affect, whether or not they are veridical (Thompson, 1999). According to Bandura (1997), positive beliefs about efficacy and control can have far-reaching consequences, including less dependency on others, preference for cognitive challenges, less reliance on medication, less anxiety and stress, and increased motivation to use skills needed to be effective in the domains of work, family, and health.

There is a great deal of evidence that control beliefs are associated with successful aging (Baltes & Baltes, 1990; Rowe & Kahn, 1998). A high sense of control is typically associated with being happy, healthy, wealthy, and wise. In the MIDUS sample, those with a higher sense of control had a more optimistic view of adulthood. They reported that things were going well and expected them to either stay that way or even to get better in the future (see Lachman & Firth, 2004; Lachman, Röcke, Rosnick, & Ryff, 2008). We also have found that those with higher control are less depressed and have better self-rated health, fewer chronic conditions, and less-severe functional limitations. Sense of control also has been found to moderate the relationship between socioeconomic status (SES) and physical and mental health (Adler et al., 1994; Lachman & Weaver, 1998b). Among low SES adults, those who have a high sense of control are able to maintain levels of health and well-being comparable to those with higher SES.

In the domain of cognitive functioning, general sense of control, and especially beliefs specific to this domain, is tied to better memory and greater intellectual functioning (Berry & West, 1993; Grover & Hertzog, 1991; Hertzog et al., 1990; Lachman, 1986, 1991; Lachman & Jelalian, 1984; Stine, Lachman, & Wingfield, 1993; West & Yassuda, 2004). Although much of the work has been cross-sectional and correlational, there is longitudinal evidence that those who have higher control beliefs improve more on cognitive tests with practice and also are less likely to show aging-related declines in cognitive functioning over time (Caplan & Schooler, 2003). Moreover, recent work by Boron and Willis (2004) found that higher control beliefs on the PIC were associated with greater training gains in memory performance and reasoning. In another study, those with higher control beliefs benefited more from performance experience in that they were able to make effective adjustments in the selection of segment lengths in order to maximize recall during an online memory-processing task (Riggs, Lachman, & Wingfield, 1997). Complaints about memory are common throughout adulthood (Lachman, 2004), but those who have a higher sense of control are less likely to report memory problems (Lachman, Andreoletti, & Pearman, 2006).

In terms of benefits, general control beliefs and MSE seem to share the same nomological network. MSE is not only "an important mental health construct in aging" (Zelinski & Gilewski, 2004, p. 293), it is also a key predictor of cognitive change in later life. Several studies report a weak, but significant, relation between MSE and memory performance (e.g., Beaudoin et al., 2008; Berry et al., 1989; Cavanaugh & Poon, 1989; Desrichard & Köpetz, 2005; Gardiner et al., 1997; Hertzog et al., 1990; Lineweaver & Hertzog, 1998; Ponds & Jolles, 1996; Rebok & Balcerak, 1989; Suen et al., 2004; Valentijn et al., 2006; Zelinski & Gilewski, 2004).

Is a Sense of Control Always Adaptive?

Most of the work exploring a sense of control in relation to age-related well-being has focused on types of performance and situations that are to some extent controllable. There is some evidence that in uncontrollable situations, those with lower control beliefs do better, at least over the short run (Lachman, 2006). For example, Bisconti, Bergeman, and Boker (2006) found recent widows with greater levels of perceived control over their social support had poorer overall adjustment across the first 4 months of widowhood. In addition, despite the multiple positive consequences of internal control, external control beliefs appear to be more advantageous during serious illness periods in dealing with a chronic disease (Burish et al., 1984). Longitudinal studies over longer periods are needed to investigate whether a high sense of control may be more beneficial for resilience and coping over the long run. Those who have a strong sense of control would be expected to be better at finding ways to cope with uncontrollable events or unattainable goals or outcomes by using secondary (i.e., changing one's expectations or goals) rather than primary (i.e., persistence in goal attainment) control strategies (Wrosch, Heckhausen, & Lachman, 2006).

Although to some extent people may be able to prevent, postpone, or compensate for aging-related declines, it is rare to be able to influence diseases, illnesses, injuries, loss of loved ones, and, ultimately, when and how one's own aging process comes to an end (Lachman, 2006). Thus, to some extent a belief in control over aging has an illusory quality (Thompson, 1999). Nevertheless, for domains in which efforts do make a difference, there is consistent evidence that those who believe they can control aging-related outcomes fare better.

INTRAINDIVIDUAL VARIABILITY IN CONTROL

Considering variability as well as mean level and modeling intraindividual differences in change has recently received increased attention (Nesselroade & Salthouse, 2004; Robertson, Myerson, & Hale, 2006; Sliwinski & Buschke, 2004). A few studies have shown that LOC is not just a stable individual difference variable, but also has an important dynamic aspect (Eizenman, Nesselroade, Featherman, & Rowe, 1997). Moreover, compared to younger people, older adults show more short-term changes in LOC, in the sense that they seem to be more inconsistent regarding the LOC measures across 10 occasions (Bielak et al., 2007). The degree of consistency of control beliefs is as important, if not more so, than the exact nature of those beliefs (Eizenman et al., 1997), as variability in control beliefs was found to predict mortality to a greater degree than level of control. More specifically, people with more stable beliefs were found to live longer.

WHAT ARE THE MEDIATORS BETWEEN CONTROL BELIEFS AND COGNITIVE BENEFITS?

The relationships between control beliefs and memory or health are fairly well established (Lachman, 2006). Nevertheless, there is little work examining the processes linking control beliefs with outcomes in these domains. It is hypothesized that a lowered sense of control may have affective, behavioral, motivational, and physiological effects, for example, greater levels of stress and of anxiety, low level of effort, persistence and strategy use, as well as less frequent engagement in memory tasks or physical activities.

Miller and Lachman (1999) considered some of the possible mechanisms and proposed a conceptual model of the role of adaptive beliefs (e.g., control) and behaviors (e.g., strategy use, physical activity) in relation to aging-related changes derived from cognitive-behavioral theory (Bandura, 1997). In this conceptual framework the authors assume that the processes are reciprocal and cyclical in that outcomes and experiences (e.g., memory or health declines) can have an impact on control beliefs, which in turn can affect behavioral or physiological mediators as well as future outcomes (Bandura, 1997; Miller & Lachman, 1999). Thus, sense of control is considered to be an antecedent and consequence of age-related losses in memory (Lachman, Ziff, & Spiro, 1994; Miller & Lachman, 1999, 2000) and health (Skaff, 2007). In other words, this model (see Figure 8.1) shows a multidirectional process in which control beliefs are influenced by prior performance outcomes and beliefs about control also have an influence on subsequent performance and outcomes through their impact on behavior, motivation, and affect. For example, older adults who experience memory lapses or declines in physical strength may respond with a lowered sense of control in these domains, especially if these changes are attributed to uncontrollable factors. Such beliefs in low control can be detrimental if they are associated with distress, anxiety, inactivity, and giving up without expending the effort or using the strategies needed to support optimal outcomes.

In terms of empirical evidence, some research has already considered the possible mechanisms that link control beliefs and outcomes. In the health domain, for example, it was found that those who have a higher sense of control are more likely to exercise regularly and also to have better health (Lachman & Firth, 2004). In the memory domain, Lachman and Andreoletti (2006) investigated mechanisms linking control beliefs to memory in a study of 335 adults aged 21 to 83 by asking participants to recall a list of categorizable words such as types of fruits and flowers. They found that control beliefs were positively related to effective strategy use and to recall performance for middle-aged and older adults, but not for young adults. Moreover, the relationship between control beliefs and recall was mediated by strategy use for the middle aged and partially mediated for older adults. Those who had a higher sense of control were more likely to use an effective strategy, in this case categorizing the words, and they in turn had better recall. Although the directional relationship cannot be confirmed given the correlational design, they tested alternative directional models, and this mediational model provided the best fit. Other studies have also found that control beliefs are related to strategic behavior, including compensatory strategy use (Hertzog, McGuire, & Lineweaver, 1998; Riggs et al., 1997) and effective goal setting (West & Yassuda, 2004). Moreover, Amrhein, Bond, and Hamilton (1999) found that older adults with a lower sense of internal control had lower episodic memory recall and less categorical clustering, whereas the younger adults did not show any relations of control beliefs on either clustering or recall performance.

There are also empirical arguments supporting the role of stress level or stress reactivity as mediator between control beliefs and memory performance.

Figure 8.1   Conceptual Model of the Relationship between Control Beliefs and Aging-Related Performance Outcomes with Postulated Mediators.

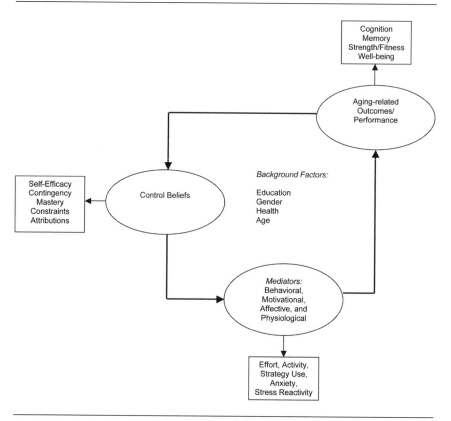

Source: "Perceived Control Over Aging-Related Declines: Adaptive Beliefs and Behaviors," by M. E. Lachman, 2006, *Current Directions in Psychological Science, 15,* 282–286; "The Sense of Control and Cognitive Aging: Toward a Model of Mediational Processes," by L.M.S. Miller and M. E. Lachman, 1999. In T. M. Hess & F. Blanchard-Fields (Eds.), *Social cognition and aging* (pp. 17–41). New York: Academic Press.

First, control beliefs play a key role in the stress response (Müller, Günther, Habel, & Rockstroh, 1998). Experiencing personal control in a challenging situation has been shown to reduce stress-related neuroendocrine response such as hypothalamic-pituitary-adrenal (HPA) axis response (Kirschbaum et al., 1995; Seeman & Robbins, 1994). Other results reveal that stressors can activate responses in the HPA and autonomic nervous system (e.g., slowing or increasing in heart rate), especially if the stimulus is appraised as out of personal control (Kemeny, 2003). Moreover, when stressors are seen as uncontrollable and the goal is important or desirable, the reactivity level is higher (Dickerson & Kemeny, 2004). Second, high levels of stress have been shown to affect memory performance among younger (Kirschbaum, Wolf, May, Wippich, & Hellhammer, 1996) and older adults (Lupien et al., 1997). The evidence suggests that acute stress affects memory performance by causing hippocampal damage (Kirschbaum et al., 1996; Lupien et al., 1997). Similarly, prolonged exposure to stress has also been associated with a loss of hippocampal neurons (McEwen & Sapolsky, 1995).

Self-reported anxiety is related to memory performance for older adults more so than for the young (Andreoletti, Veratti, & Lachman, 2006) and may be another mediator between control and memory performance. However, the relationships among control beliefs, anxiety, physiological stress, and cognitive performance, and their variability over the course of adulthood, remain virtually unexplored.

Concerning the MSE beliefs, a low level may result in a reduction in memory performance, for example, by increasing the level of anxiety and arousal (Bandura, Cioffi, Taylor, & Brouillard, 1988) or by creating an expectation of failure (Desrichard & Köpetz, 2005) that may lead individuals to put forth less effort and be less persistent (Berry & West, 1993; Cavanaugh & Green, 1990) in memory situations. In the literature, effort is usually operationalized as strategy use and persistence as allocated time or number of attempted items. Although Hertzog and his colleagues (1989) reported a consistent small negative correlation between an individual's MSE and that person's scores on the mnemonics usage scales, several studies have shown that MSE is not significantly linked to the tendency to use such strategies (Jonker, Smits, & Deeg, 1997; McDonald-Miszczak, Gould, & Tychynski, 1999; McDougall, 1995; Troyer & Rich, 2002; Wells & Esopenko, 2008). Furthermore, in a recent study, Wells and Esopenko did not find a relationship between MSE and the amount of time participants spent on a free-recall task. MSE, however, has been shown to impact the person's goal system and the choice of activities (Berry & West, 1993; West et al., 2009). For instance, Elliott and Lachman (1989) suggested that individuals with a lower MSE level tend to avoid challenging memory situations. According to the results obtained by Bagwell and West (2008), MSE also tends to predict individual investment in memory intervention programs.

WHAT ARE THE ANTECEDENTS OF CONTROL BELIEFS AND MEMORY SELF-EFFICACY?

Many sociodemographic, sociocognitive, affective, and behavioral factors are associated with perceived control. Some of these sources of variation can be theoretically and/or empirically conceived as determinants of control beliefs in general and MSE in particular. Nevertheless, previous research has looked primarily at the consequences of control beliefs, and relatively few studies have focused on their sources or have addressed issues of causal direction (Lachman, 2006).

In terms of control beliefs, according to the reciprocal model (see Figure 8.1), beliefs about control not only have an influence on subsequent performance. They are also influenced by prior performance; that is, the experience with success and failures or declines, although this varies by age (Bandura, 1997; Lachman et al., 2006). Good objective and subjective health also appear to be related to greater sense of control. For example, there is evidence (Cairney, Corna, Wade, & Streiner, 2007; Mirowsky, 1995) that physical health status has an impact on perceived control. Furthermore, Wolinsky, Wyrwich, Babu, Kroenke, and Tierney (2003) identified mental well-being as a stable factor associated longitudinally with the sense of control. Other factors positively associated with higher sense of control are greater subjective life expectancy and higher education (Mirowsky, 1995, 1997; Slagsvold & Sorensen, 2008).

The literature on the potential antecedents of MSE appears to be more extensive. As predicted by Bandura's self-efficacy theory (1989; Welch & West, 1995), self-efficacy beliefs not only influence future performance, but are mainly formed based on performance on similar tasks in the past. In other words, a low MSE level would reflect the person's actual abilities and extent of cognitive decline. However, the directionality between objective and subjective memory is not easily determined, as most published studies focused on the relationship between MSE and memory were cross-sectional or correlational. Furthermore, this association is not observed systematically (e.g., Dellefield & McDougall, 1996; Neupert & McDonald-Miszczak, 2004; Rebok & Balcerak, 1989).

Several possible explanations can be addressed regarding the variability found in the results. For example, older adults may answer MSE questionnaires by drawing from old self-schemas, which are not concordant with current memory performance, rather than reflecting on actual recent memory experiences (Cavanaugh, Feldman, & Hertzog, 1998). Similarly, people can base their MSE or their self-perceptions of everyday memory performance on age stereotypes, which make salient the idea of memory declines in the elderly. Also, Hertzog and his colleagues (1990) have suggested that the performance predictions required by the MSEQ are also based on a person's evaluation of the tasks. Therefore, the weak correlation (or lack thereof) between responses to the MSEQ and actual memory-task performances may be due to inaccurate evaluations of the tasks contained in the questionnaire. Supporting this hypothesis, when subjects are asked to carry out familiar tasks (e.g., phone numbers, grocery list) rather than classic laboratory tasks (e.g., digits, words), there is a greater or more consistent correlation between MSE and actual performance (Berry et al., 1989). Moreover, the relationship between MSE and performance seems to be moderated by several other factors. The association appears stronger for older people (e.g., Cavanaugh & Poon, 1989).

Another potential factor impacting the MSE–performance association is the fit between their corresponding levels of measurement. On a specific task, it would be more likely for levels of performance to be related to specific self-efficacy measures than to general memory self-assessments. Along the same lines, other authors (e.g., Hertzog, Park, Morrell, & Martin, 2000) found that the relationship between subjective and objective measures of memory varied as a function of specific task-related characteristics.

Nevertheless, MSE cannot be reduced to a simple self-perception of cognitive performance. There is theoretical and empirical evidence that other psychosocial and behavioral factors can account for MSE variability over time (Agrigoroaei, 2007). For instance, according to Bandura's framework, people form their self-efficacy judgments not only on the mastery experience, but also on other sources of information (e.g., arousal, vicarious observation, etc.). Moreover, MSE, assessed with a domain-specific memory measure (MFQ) seems to be more influenced by negative affect (e.g., depression; Zelinski & Gilewski, 2004) than by memory performance. McDougall (1995) also showed that depression is negatively related to the level of MSE, using a task-specific measure, the MSEQ. However, this result is not stable, as others using the MSEQ found no relation between MSE and depression (Beaudoin et al., 2008; McDougall & Kang, 2003). Deleterious effects on MSE were also shown for high levels of anxiety (e.g., McDougall, 1995; McDougall & Kang, 2003; Ponds & Jolles, 1996).

Expectations of poor memory performance appear to be associated not only with low mood, but also with personality-related negative affect. The role of personality traits for efficacy judgments (Cavanaugh & Green, 1990; Gold & Arbuckle, 1990) is supported by the empirical evidence. For example, Ponds and Jolles (1996) and Lane and Zelinski (2003) found a negative correlation between neuroticism and MSE. According to the results obtained by Pearman and Storandt (2005), the association between neuroticism and self-evaluations of memory seems to be explained by the self-consciousness facet of neuroticism, independent of the anxiety component, and more specifically, by the concept of negative self-image (e.g., low self-esteem, inferiority). Pearman and Storandt's study also showed that the self-discipline dimension is positively associated with perceived memory capacities. Another personality trait, conscientiousness, also affects MSE, while controlling for neuroticism (Zelinski & Gilewski, 2004), although the result is not stable (Lane & Zelinski, 2003).

MSE is also associated with perceived level of health. According to Stevens, Kaplan, Ponds, and Jolles (2001), people who make fewer complaints about their health evaluate their memory abilities more positively. Similarly, Fort et al. (2004) observed a positive correlation between self-reported health and the perceived memory capacity. Concerning the negative effect of more objective indicators of deteriorating health, decreased MSE was observed in patients who had sustained a brain injury (Kit, Mateer, & Graves, 2007), those suffering from fibromyalgia (Glass, Park, Minear, & Crofford, 2005), and in people with narcolepsy (Hood & Bruck, 1997).

Other studies have suggested a relation between MSE and an active lifestyle. Stevens et al. (2001) showed that people who have frequent social contacts, independent of the size of their social network, tend to evaluate their memory capacities more highly. In the same study, MSE was positively linked to perceived activity scores. Older adults who considered themselves to be physically active also estimate having a good memory capacity. However, more objective measures of activity (such as the number of hours allocated to sports activities) are not significantly linked to MSE.

In addition, results consistently point to a positive association between MSE and the perception of a greater or lesser stability in memory functioning during adult development (Beaudoin et al., 2008; Hertzog et al., 1989; Jonker et al., 1997; McDonald-Miszczak et al., 1999). Those who think memory remains stable have a higher MSE. Along the same lines, according to Cavanaugh et al. (1998), memory self-assessments may result from an online process of information treatment that is guided by the person's implicit theories. In terms of empirical evidence, Lineweaver and Hertzog (1998) showed that implicit theories about memory in the general population are significantly correlated with personal beliefs about one's own memory. Because there is a cultural assumption that memory declines with age, perceived change in one's own memory abilities can be seen as an indicator of the degree of interiorization of this age stereotype (see chapter 7). Therefore, MSE appears to be a concept more closely tied to social cognition than to metamemory (Berry, 1999; Cavanaugh, 2000). Low control beliefs likely have their origins in negative stereotypes about aging and are reinforced through experiences of decline. Nevertheless, the association between age stereotypes and MSE was rarely empirically studied. Cross-cultural studies (Levy & Langer, 1994) demonstrated that older adults perform better in societies sharing a positive image about elderly people. We may suppose that the positive view of aging could reinforce the MSE level, which could in turn account for performance differences. Clearer evidence was provided by Levy (1996), showing that subliminally activating positive age stereotypes tends to increase the MSE, and the inverse is true when negative age stereotypes are activated.

Another sociocognitive factor potentially associated with MSE is represented by causal explanations people give for memory failures (Cavanaugh et al., 1998). Older adults tend to attribute memory decline to uncontrollable factors such as chance, context of evaluation, age, or innate abilities (Cromwell, 1994; De Beni, Mazzoni, & Pagotto, 1996; Devolder & Pressley, 1992). De Beni et al. showed a negative correlation between the stability of attribution style for failures and the level of confidence in memory abilities.

In another study (Lachman, Steinberg, & Trotter, 1987), internal, stable, and global attributions for successful performance were related to greater increases in memory predictions over time. Because age is considered a salient dimension for self-evaluations (Bandura, 1997), and it is out of direct control, we assume that attributions of memory problems to this factor would have a greater effect on MSE decrease.

ARE THE CONTROL BELIEFS MODIFIABLE?

Given the apparent benefits of control beliefs and the likelihood of declines in sense of control in later life, there are a number of studies that examined whether it is possible to modify control beliefs among older adults and if this would affect outcomes in a given domain. Many older adults assume they are too old to improve performance or functioning or to make up for losses in areas such as memory or physical ability. Interventions with a joint focus on modifying control beliefs (e.g., memory control beliefs, fear of falling) and behaviors (e.g., strategy use, physical activity) may be most effective (Lachman et al., 1997). The assumption is that enduring behavior change is unlikely without first instilling confidence that aging-related declines can be controlled. For example, a fear of falling is relatively common among older adults. This is typically manifested as a low sense of efficacy for engaging in activities without falling and a sense that falling is uncontrollable (Tennstedt et al., 1998).

A multifaceted intervention targeted beliefs about control over falls with 434 older adults who reported fear of falling and were randomly assigned to an intervention or a contact control condition (Tennstedt et al., 1998). Cognitive-restructuring strategies were used to reframe control beliefs. This entailed analysis and challenge of maladaptive beliefs (e.g., "I can't do this"; "I am too old"; "it won't do any good"; "I will get hurt") and information that efforts (e.g., using fall-prevention strategies; engaging in strength and balance exercises, which were also taught to participants) can make a difference for outcomes. The contact control group was given information about risk factors for falls and saw a video about ways to minimize the risk of falls. Those who completed the treatment increased their falls self-efficacy, sense of control over falls, level of intended activity, and physical mobility functioning significantly more than the control group did. Although the fear-of-falling intervention did not target falls reduction directly, greater mobility and increased activity should lead to a decrease in falls due to better physical conditioning. However, if intervention participants increased their activity levels as indicated by their intentions, they might also have inadvertently increased their risk of falls due to greater exposure. There were no significant differences between intervention and control subjects in the number of falls for up to 12 months (Tennstedt et al., 1998), which suggests, at least, that the intervention did not have unintended side effects. Consistent with the cognitive-behavioral conceptual model (see Figure 8.1), the best predictor of self-efficacy and control with respect to falling was previous fall status, and low falls self-efficacy was subsequently associated with maladaptive behavioral changes such as activity restriction, which can lead to increased risk of falling through muscle atrophy and deconditioning (Lachman et al., 1998).

Another study administered a home-based resistance training program in conjunction with cognitive restructuring of beliefs about the ability to engage in exercise and whether doing exercise would make a difference for health and well-being (Jette et al., 1999). They found improvements in strength for older adults, and participation and adherence rates were higher than in previous studies, but control beliefs did not increase significantly more in the treatment group. Nevertheless, those who had higher exercise control beliefs during the intervention increased their resistance level significantly more than those with lower control beliefs and were more likely to be exercising 3 to 6 months after the intervention was completed (Neupert, Lachman, & Whitbourne, 2009).

Interventions designed to increase subjective memory functioning or to enhance MSE and control have met with variable success (e.g., Caprio-Prevette & Fry, 1996). Memory control beliefs seem to be difficult to change, and the average effect size for subjective change is much smaller than for objective change. Moreover, even when control beliefs or self-efficacy are changed, actual performance changes are often not related. In their meta-analysis examining the effects of memory training on the subjective memory function of older adults, Floyd and Scogin (1997) found that interventions that combined mnemonic training and expectancy modification showed greater gains than a control group, while no single treatment worked any better than practice for changing control beliefs. Lachman, Weaver, Bandura, Elliott, and Lewkowicz (1992) found that older adults who received both cognitive restructuring and memory skills training showed the greatest improvements in sense of control and beliefs about the potential for improving their memory performance. There was not, however, an associated differential improvement in memory performance (Lachman et al., 1992), given that all treatment groups and the practice control group improved equally.

Schmidt, Zwart, Berg, and Deelman (1999) conducted an intervention study designed to challenge stereotypes about aging and emphasized the actual cognitive competence in older adults. Although their intervention did improve MSE and subjective memory, it did not change memory performance. In addition, they found that participants experiencing memory complaints were most likely to improve on subjective memory evaluations. Boron and Willis (2004) also found that training in memory and reasoning led to increases in cognitive specific control beliefs following the intervention.

Past work shows also that performance changes resulting from practice or strategy instruction alone do not necessarily have an effect on efficacy beliefs for older adults (Dittmann-Kohli, Lachman, Kliegl, & Baltes, 1991; Lachman et al., 1992). Even when retest improvements on memory are found, these do not necessarily translate into higher control beliefs for older adults. Nevertheless, some theories suggest that using strategies gives one a sense of efficacy and control. In this sense, Lachman et al. (2006) found that for older adults, MSE, but not task-specific control beliefs, was boosted by strategy manipulation.

Long-held beliefs about self-efficacy and control manifested in later life may be resistant to change. Although performance experience is typically the strongest source of information promoting self-efficacy change, Bandura (1997) speculated that older adults may need additional sources of feedback such as persuasive messages to promote adjustments in self-efficacy and the sense of control in domains with prevalent beliefs about decline such as memory. The empirical results seem to support this idea. Several researchers (e.g., Dellefield & McDougall, 1996; McDougall, 2000, 2001; Valentijn et al., 2005) have tried to determine whether memory-training programs can increase the MSE of older adults. For example, Valentijn et al. (2005) used a program based on keeping diaries with memory failures and successes, on teaching memory strategies, and on the acquisition of theoretical knowledge about how the memory works in old age. Their training program had a positive effect on the participants' memory performance for certain tasks, but it did not increase the MSE factor. In contrast, McDougall (2000, 2001) found that teaching the cognitive-behavioral skills needed to optimize or maintain everyday memory increased older adults' memory performance and scores on the MSEQ. The intervention used, called the Cognitive Behavioral Model of Everyday Memory, has the particularity to be based on Bandura's self-efficacy theory and combines memorization exercises, vicarious experiences, and verbal persuasion. More recently, West, Bagwell, and Dark-Freudeman (2008) proposed a training program that includes sessions relevant to all sources of self-efficacy. This intervention showed concomitant improvements in both MSE and memory performance. Hence, memory-training programs based on Bandura's framework seem to be somewhat successful in increasing older adults' beliefs in their memory ability.

CONCLUSION

The purpose of this chapter was to review the literature related to antecedents, processes, and consequences of sense of control in relation to aging. There are multiple components to control beliefs, most notably self-efficacy or personal mastery and perceived constraints or expectancies for external contingencies. Control beliefs are an important ingredient and protective factor for successful aging. Sense of control varies across individuals, across domains, and within persons over time. Those with higher control typically do better in a wide range of circumstances. This relationship is multidirectional and reciprocal, and we are just beginning to understand the underlying processes. Control beliefs are related to behaviors and physiological responses that have short-term and long-term effects on aging outcomes. Moreover, control beliefs show changes in response to aging. In some cases, perceived control may be less adaptive if the circumstances are uncontrollable or if there is a mismatch between expectations and reality. Although the sense of control seems to decline with age, there is good news in that control beliefs may be modified and enhanced throughout life, as has been shown in several intervention studies. Future work is needed to find ideal ways to intervene so as to establish links between control beliefs and desirable outcomes and to find optimal ways to maintain such changes.

REFERENCES

Adler, N. E., Boyce, T., Chesney, M. A., Cohen, S., Folkman, S., Kahn, R., et al. (1994). Socioeconomic status and health: The challenge of the gradient. *American Psychologist*, *49*, 15–24.

Agrigoroaei, S. (2007). *Memory Self-efficacy Decrease in Elderly People: Theoretical Review and Study of its Relations With Cognitive, Affective, and Socio-cognitive Factors.* Unpublished doctoral dissertation, Savoie University, France.

Amrhein, P. C., Bond, J. K., & Hamilton, D. A. (1999). Locus of Control and the age difference in free recall from episodic memory. *Journal of General Psychology*, *126*, 149–164.

Andreoletti, C., Veratti, B., & Lachman, M. E. (2006). Age differences in the relationship between anxiety and recall. *Aging & Mental Health*, *10*, 265–271.

Bagwell, D. K., & West, R. L. (2008). Assessing compliance: Active versus inactive trainees in a memory intervention. *Clinical Interventions in Aging*, *3*, 371–382.

Baltes, P. B., & Baltes, M. M. (1990). Psychological perspectives on successful aging: The model of selective optimization with compensation. In P. B. Baltes & M. M. Baltes (Eds.), *Successful Aging: Perspectives from the Behavioral Sciences* (pp. 1–34). New York: Cambridge University Press.

Bandura, A. (1986). *Social Foundations of Thought and Action: A Social Cognitive Theory.* Englewood Cliffs, NJ: Prentice Hall.

Bandura, A. (1989). Regulation of cognitive processes through perceived self-efficacy. *Developmental Psychology*, *25*, 729–735.

Bandura, A. (1997). *Self-efficacy: The Exercise of Control.* New York: Freeman.

Bandura, A., Cioffi, D., Taylor, C. B., & Brouillard, M. E. (1988). Perceived self-efficacy in coping with cognitive stressors and opioid activation. *Journal of Personality and Social Psychology*, *55*, 479–488.

Beaudoin, M., Agrigoroaei, S., Desrichard, O., Fournet, N., & Roulin, J.-L. (2008). Validation of the French version of the Memory Self-Efficacy Questionnaire. *European Review of Applied Psychology*, *58*, 165–176.

Berry, J. M. (1999). Memory self-efficacy in its social cognitive context. In T. M. Hess & F. Blanchard-Fields (Eds.), *Social Cognition and Aging* (pp. 69–96). San Diego: Academic Press.

Berry, J. M., & West, R. L. (1993). Cognitive self-efficacy in relation to personal mastery and goal setting across the life span. *International Journal of Behavioral Development, 16,* 351–379.

Berry, J. M., West, R. L., & Dennehey, D. M. (1989). Reliability and validity of the Memory Self-Efficacy Questionnaire. *Developmental Psychology, 25,* 701–713.

Bielak, A.A.M., Hultsch, D. F., Levy-Ajzenkopf, J., MacDonald, S.W.S., Hunter, M. A., & Strauss, E. (2007). Short-term changes in general and memory-specific control beliefs and their relationship to cognition in younger and older adults. *International Journal of Aging and Human Development, 65,* 53–71.

Bisconti, T. L., Bergeman, C. S., & Boker, S. M. (2006). Social support as a predictor of variability: An examination of the adjustment trajectories of recent widows. *Psychology and Aging, 21,* 590–599.

Boron, J. B., & Willis, S. L. (2004, November). *Control Beliefs and Cognitive Training Gain in Older Adults: ACTIVE Clinical Trial.* Paper presented at the 57th Annual Meeting of the Gerontological Society of America, Washington, DC.

Brandtstädter, J., & Rothermund, K. (1994). Self-percepts of control in middle and later adulthood: Buffering losses by rescaling goals. *Psychology and Aging, 9,* 265–273.

Burish, T. G., Carey, M. P., Wallston, K. A., Stein, M. J., Jamison, R. N., & Lyles, J. N. (1984). Health Locus of Control and chronic disease: An external orientation may be advantageous. *Journal of Social and Clinical Psychology, 2,* 326–332.

Cairney, J., Corna, L. M., Wade, T., & Streiner, D. L. (2007). Does greater frequency of contact with general physicians reduce feelings of mastery in older adults? *Journals of Gerontology: Psychological Sciences, 62B,* P226–P229.

Caplan, L. J., & Schooler, C. (2003). The roles of fatalism, self-confidence, and intellectual resources in the disablement process in older adults. *Psychology and Aging, 18,* 551–561.

Caprio-Prevette, M. D., & Fry, P. S. (1996). Memory enhancement program for community-based older adults: Development and evaluation. *Experimental Aging Research, 22,* 281–303.

Cavanaugh, J. C. (2000). Metamemory from a social-cognitive perspective. In D. C. Park & N. Schwarz (Eds.), *Cognitive Aging: A Primer* (pp. 115–130). Philadelphia, PA: Psychology Press.

Cavanaugh, J. C., Feldman, J. M., & Hertzog, C. (1998). Memory beliefs as social cognition: A reconceptualization of what memory questionnaires assess. *Review of General Psychology, 2,* 48–65.

Cavanaugh, J. C., & Green, E. E. (1990). I believe, therefore I can: Self-efficacy beliefs in memory aging. In E. A. Lovelace (Ed.), *Aging and Cognition: Mental Processes, Self-awareness, and Interventions* (vol. 72, pp. 189–230). Amsterdam: Elsevier Science.

Cavanaugh, J. C., & Poon, L. W. (1989). Metamemorial predictors of memory performance in young and older adults. *Psychology and Aging, 4,* 365–368.

Cornelius, S. W., & Caspi, A. (1986). Self-perceptions of intellectual control and aging. *Educational Gerontology, 12,* 345–357.

Cromwell, S. L. (1994). The subjective experience of forgetfulness among elders. *Qualitative Health Research, 4,* 444–462.

De Beni, R., Mazzoni, G., & Pagotto, S. (1996). Memory self-efficacy and attributional style in elderly people. Comparison among different ages and different living places. *Ricerche di Psicologia, 20,* 63–93.

Dellefield, K. S., & McDougall, G. J. (1996). Increasing metamemory in older adults. *Nursing Research, 45,* 284–290.

Desrichard, O., & Köpetz, C. (2005). A threat in the elder: The impact of task-instructions, self-efficacy and performance expectations on memory performance in the elderly. *European Journal of Social Psychology, 35,* 537–552.

Devolder, P. A., & Pressley, M. (1992). Causal attributions and strategy use in relation to memory performance differences in younger and older adults. *Applied Cognitive Psychology, 6,* 629–642.

Dickerson, S. S., & Kemeny, M. E. (2004). Acute stressors and cortisol responses: A theoretical integration and synthesis of laboratory research. *Psychological Bulletin, 130,* 355–391.

Dittmann-Kohli, F., Lachman, M. E., Kliegl, R., & Baltes, P. B. (1991). Effects of cognitive training an testing on intellectual efficacy beliefs in elderly adults. *Journals of Gerontology: Psychological Sciences, 46B,* P162–P164.

Dixon, R. A., & Hultsch, D. F. (1983). Metamemory and memory for text relationships in adulthood: A cross-validation study. *Journals of Gerontology: Psychological Sciences, 38B,* P689–P694.

Eizenman, D. R., Nesselroade, J. R., Featherman, D. L., & Rowe, J. W. (1997). Intraindividual variability in perceived control in an older sample: The Mac-Arthur Successful Aging Studies. *Psychology and Aging, 12,* 489–502.

Elliott, E., & Lachman, M. E. (1989). Enhancing memory by modifying control beliefs, attributions and performance goals in the elderly. In P. S. Fry (Ed.), *Advances in Psychology: Psychological Perspectives of Helplessness and Control in the Elderly* (pp. 339–368). North Holland: Elsevier Science Publishers B.V.

Floyd, M., & Scogin, F. (1997). Effects of memory training on the subjective memory functioning and mental health of older adults: A meta-analysis. *Psychology and Aging, 12,* 150–161.

Fort, I., Adoul, L., Holl, D., Kaddour, J., & Gana, K. (2004). Psychometric properties of the French version of the Multifactorial Memory Questionnaire for adults and the elderly. *Canadian Journal on Aging, 23,* 347–357.

Gardiner, M., Luszcz, M. A., & Bryan, J. (1997). The manipulation and measurement of task-specific memory self-efficacy in younger and older adults. *International Journal of Behavioral Development, 21,* 209–227.

Gilewski, M. J., & Zelinski, E. M. (1988). Memory Functioning Questionnaire. *Psychopharmacology Bulletin, 24,* 665–670.

Glass, J. M., Park, D. C., Minear, M., & Crofford, L. J. (2005). Memory beliefs and function in fibromyalgia patients. *Journal of Psychosomatic Research, 58,* 263–269.

Gold, D. P., & Arbuckle, T. Y. (1990). Interactions between personality and cognition and their implications for theories of aging. In E. A. Lovelace (Ed.), *Aging and Cognition: Mental Processes, Self-awareness, and Interventions* (vol. 72, pp. 351–377). Amsterdam: Elsevier Science.

Grover, D. R., & Hertzog, C. (1991). Relationships between intellectual control beliefs and psychometric intelligence in adulthood. *Journals of Gerontology: Psychological Sciences, 46B,* P109–P115.

Hertzog, C., Dixon, R. A., & Hultsch, D. F. (1990). Relationships between metamemory, memory predictions, and memory task performance in adults. *Psychology and Aging*, *5*, 215–227.

Hertzog, C., Hultsch, D. F., & Dixon, R. A. (1989). Evidence for the convergent validity of two self-report metamemory questionnaires. *Developmental Psychology*, *25*, 687–700.

Hertzog, C., McGuire, C. L., & Lineweaver, T. T. (1998). Aging, attributions, perceived control, and strategy use in a free recall task. *Aging, Neuropsychology, and Cognition*, *5*, 85–106.

Hertzog, C., Park, D. C., Morrell, R. W., & Martin, M. (2000). Ask and ye shall receive: Behavioural specificity in the accuracy of subjective memory complaints. *Applied Cognitive Psychology*, *14*, 257–275.

Hood, B., & Bruck, D. (1997). Metamemory in narcolepsy. *Journal of Sleep Research*, *6*, 205–210.

Jette, A. M., Lachman, M. E., Giorgetti, M. M., Assmann, S. F., Harris, B. A., Levenson, C., et al. (1999). Exercise: It's never too late! *American Journal of Public Health*, *89*, 66–72.

Jonker, C., Smits, C.H.M., & Deeg, D.J.H. (1997). Affect-related metamemory and memory performance in a population-based sample of older adults. *Educational Gerontology*, *23*, 115–128.

Kemeny, M. E. (2003). The psychobiology of stress. *Current Directions in Psychological Science*, *12*, 124–129.

Kirschbaum, C., Prussner, J. C., Stone, A. A., Federenko, I., Gaab, J., Lintz, D., et al. (1995). Persistent high cortisol responses to repeated psychological stress in a subpopulation of healthy men. *Psychosomatic Medicine*, *57*, 468–474.

Kirschbaum, C., Wolf, O. T., May, M., Wippich, W., & Hellhammer, D. H. (1996). Stress- and treatment-induced elevations of cortisol levels associated with impaired declarative memory in healthy adults. *Life Sciences*, *58*, 1475–1483.

Kit, K. A., Mateer, C. A., & Graves, R. E. (2007). The influence of memory beliefs in individuals with traumatic brain injury. *Rehabilitation Psychology*, *52*, 25–32.

Krause, N., & Shaw, B. A. (2003). Role-specific control, personal meaning, and health in late life. *Research on Aging*, *25*, 559–586.

Lachman, M. E. (1985). Personal efficacy in middle and old age: Differential and normative patterns of change. In G. H. Elder, Jr. (Ed.), *Life-course Dynamics: Trajectories and Transitions, 1968–1980* (pp. 188–213). Ithaca, NY: Cornell University Press.

Lachman, M. E. (1986). Locus of Control in aging research: A case for multidimensional and domain-specific assessment. *Journal of Psychology and Aging*, *1*, 34–40.

Lachman, M. E. (1991). Perceived control over memory aging: Developmental and intervention perspectives. *Journal of Social Issues*, *47*, 159–175.

Lachman, M. E. (2004). Development in midlife. *Annual Review of Psychology*, *55*, 305–331.

Lachman, M. E. (2006). Perceived control over aging-related declines: Adaptive beliefs and behaviors. *Current Directions in Psychological Science*, *15*, 282–286.

Lachman, M. E., & Andreoletti, C. (2006). Strategy use mediates the relationship between control beliefs and memory performance for middle-aged and older adults. *Journals of Gerontology: Psychological Sciences*, *61B*, P88–P94.

Lachman, M. E., Andreoletti, C., & Pearman, A. (2006). Memory control beliefs: How are they related to age, strategy use and memory improvement? *Social Cognition, 24*, 359–385.

Lachman, M. E., Baltes, P. B., Nesselroade, J. R., & Willis, S. L. (1982). Examination of personality-ability relationships in the elderly: The role of the contextual (interface) assessment mode. *Journal of Research in Personality, 16*, 485–501.

Lachman, M. E., Bandura, M., Weaver, S. L., & Elliott, E. (1995). Assessing memory control beliefs: The Memory Controllability Inventory. *Aging and Cognition, 2*, 67–84.

Lachman, M. E., & Firth, K. M. (2004). The adaptive value of feeling in control during midlife. In O. G. Brim, C. D. Ryff, & R. Kessler (Eds.), *How Healthy Are We? A National Study of Well-being at Midlife* (pp. 320–349). Chicago: University of Chicago Press.

Lachman, M. E., Howland, J., Tennstedt, S., Jette, A., Assmann, S., & Peterson, E. W. (1998). Fear of falling and activity restriction: The survey of activities and fear of falling in the elderly (SAFE). *Journals of Gerontology: Psychological Sciences, 53B*, P43–P50.

Lachman, M. E., & Jelalian, E. (1984). Self-efficacy and attributions for intellectual performance in young and elderly adults. *Journal of Gerontology, 39*, 577–582.

Lachman, M. E., Jette, A., Tennstedt, S., Howland, J., Harris, B. A., & Peterson, E. (1997). A cognitive-behavioral model for promoting regular physical activity in older adults. *Psychology, Health, and Medicine, 2*, 251–261.

Lachman, M. E., Röcke, C., Rosnick, C., & Ryff, C. D. (2008). Realism and illusion in Americans' temporal views of their life satisfaction: Age differences in reconstructing the past and anticipating the future. *Psychological Science, 19*, 889–897.

Lachman, M. E., Steinberg, E. S., & Trotter, S. D. (1987). Effects of control beliefs and attributions on memory self-assessments and performance. *Psychology and Aging, 2*, 266–271.

Lachman, M. E., & Weaver, S. L. (1998a). Sociodemographic variations in the sense of control by domain: Findings from the MacArthur Studies of Midlife. *Psychology and Aging, 13*, 553–562.

Lachman, M. E., & Weaver, S. L. (1998b). The sense of control as a moderator of social class differences in health and well-being. *Journal of Personality and Social Psychology, 74*, 763–773.

Lachman, M. E., Weaver, S. L., Bandura, M., Elliott, E., & Lewkowicz, C. J. (1992). Improving memory and control beliefs through cognitive restructuring and self-generated strategies. *Journals of Gerontology: Psychological Sciences, 47B*, P293–P299.

Lachman, M. E., Ziff, M. A., & Spiro III, A. (1994). Maintaining a sense of control in later life. In R. P. Abeles, H. C. Gift, & M. G. Ory (Eds.), *Aging and Quality of Life* (pp. 216–232). New York: Springer.

Lane, C. J., & Zelinski, E. M. (2003). Longitudinal hierarchical linear models of the Memory Functioning Questionnaire. *Psychology and Aging, 18*, 38–53.

Levy, B. (1996). Improving memory in old age through implicit self-stereotyping. *Journal of Personality and Social Psychology, 71*, 1092–1107.

Levy, B., & Langer, E. (1994). Aging free from negative stereotypes: Successful memory in China and among the American deaf. *Journal of Personality and Social Psychology, 66*, 989–997.

Lineweaver, T. T., & Hertzog, C. (1998). Adult's efficacy and control beliefs regarding memory and aging: Separating general from personal beliefs. *Aging, Neuropsychology, and Cognition, 5,* 264–296.

Lupien, S. J., Gaudreau, S., Tchiteya, B. M., Maheu, F., Sharma, S., Nair, N.P.V., et al. (1997). Stress-induced declarative memory impairment in healthy elderly subjects: Relationship to cortisol reactivity. *Journal of Clinical Endocrinology and Metabolism, 82,* 2070–2075.

Marquié, J. C., & Huet, N. (2000). Age differences in Feeling-of-Knowing and confidence judgments as a function of knowledge domain. *Psychology and Aging, 15,* 451–461.

McDonald-Miszczak, L., Gould, O. N., & Tychynski, D. (1999). Metamemory predictors of prospective and retrospective memory performance. *The Journal of General Psychology, 126,* 37–52.

McDougall, G. J. (1995). Memory self-efficacy and strategy use in successful elders. *Educational Gerontology, 21,* 357–373.

McDougall, G. J. (2000). Memory improvement in assisted living elders. *Issues in Mental Health Nursing, 21,* 217–233.

McDougall, G. J. (2001). Rehabilitation of memory and memory self-efficacy in cognitively impaired nursing home residents. *Clinical Gerontologist, 23,* 127–139.

McDougall, G. J., & Kang, J. (2003). Memory self-efficacy and memory performance in older males. *International Journal of Men's Health, 2,* 131–147.

McEwen, B. S., & Sapolsky, R. M. (1995). Stress and cognitive function. *Current Opinion in Neurobiology, 5,* 205–216.

Miller, L.M.S., & Lachman, M. E. (1999). The sense of control and cognitive aging: Toward a model of mediational processes. In T. M. Hess & F. Blanchard-Fields (Eds.), *Social Cognition and Aging* (pp. 17–41). New York: Academic Press.

Miller, L.M.S., & Lachman, M. E. (2000). Cognitive performance and the role of control beliefs in midlife. *Aging, Neuropsychology, and Cognition, 7,* 69–85.

Mirowsky, J. (1995). Age and the sense of control. *Social Psychology Quarterly, 58,* 31–43.

Mirowsky, J. (1997). Age, subjective life expectancy, and the sense of control: The horizon hypothesis. *Journals of Gerontology: Social Sciences, 52B,* S125–S134.

Müller, M. M., Günther, A., Habel, I., & Rockstroh, B. (1998). Active coping and internal Locus of Control produces prolonged cardiovascular reactivity in young men. *Journal of Psychophysiology, 12,* 29–39.

Nesselroade, J. R., & Salthouse, T. A. (2004). Methodological and theoretical implications of intraindividual variability in perceptual-motor performance. *Journals of Gerontology: Psychological Sciences, 59B,* P49–P55.

Neupert, S. D., Lachman, M. E., & Whitbourne, S. B. (2009). Exercise self-efficacy and control beliefs: Effects on exercise behavior after an exercise intervention for older adults. *Journal of Aging and Physical Activity, 17,* 1–16.

Neupert, S. D., & McDonald-Miszczak, L. (2004). Younger and older adults' delayed recall of medication instructions: The role of cognitive and metacognitive predictors. *Aging, Neuropsychology, and Cognition, 11,* 428–442.

Pearman, A., & Storandt, M. (2005). Self-discipline and self-consciousness predict subjective memory in older adults. *Journals of Gerontology: Psychological Sciences, 60B,* P153–P157.

Ponds, R.W.H.M., & Jolles, J. (1996). Memory complaints in elderly people: The role of memory abilities, metamemory, depression, and personality. *Educational Gerontology*, *22*, 341–357.

Rebok, G. W., & Balcerak, L. J. (1989). Memory self-efficacy and performance differences in young and old adults: The effect of mnemonic training. *Developmental Psychology*, *25*, 714–721.

Rebok, G. W., Rasmusson, D. X., & Brandt, J. (1995). Prospects for computerized memory training in normal elderly: Effects of practice on explicit and implicit memory tasks. *Applied Cognitive Psychology*, *10*, 211–223.

Riggs, K. M., Lachman, M. E., & Wingfield, A. (1997). Taking charge of remembering: Locus of Control and older adults' memory for speech. *Experimental Aging Research*, *23*, 237–256.

Robertson, S., Myerson, J., & Hale, S. (2006). Are there age differences in intraindividual variability in working memory performance? *Journals of Gerontology: Psychological Sciences*, *61B*, P18–P24.

Rodin, J. (1990). Control by any other name: Definitions, concepts, and processes. In J. Rodin, C. Schooler & K. W. Schaie (Eds.), *Self-directedness: Cause and Effects Throughout the Life Course* (pp. 1–17). Hillsdale, NJ: Lawrence Erlbaum Associates.

Rotter, J. B. (1966). Generalized expectancies for internal versus external control of reinforcement. *Psychological Monographs*, *80*, 1–28.

Rowe, J. W., & Kahn, R. L. (1998). *Successful Aging*. New York: Pantheon Books.

Schmidt, I. W., Zwart, J. F., Berg, I. J., & Deelman, B. G. (1999). Evaluation of an intervention directed at the modification of memory beliefs in older adults. *Educational Gerontology*, *25*, 365–385.

Seeman, T. E., & Robbins, R. J. (1994). Aging and hypothalamic-pituitary-adrenal response to challenge in humans. *Endocrine Reviews*, *15*, 233–260.

Skaff, M. M. (2007). Sense of control and health: A dynamic duo in the aging process. In C. M. Aldwin, C. L. Park, & A. Spiro III (Eds.), *Handbook of Health Psychology and Aging* (pp. 186–209). New York: Guilford Press.

Skinner, E. A. (1996). A guide to constructs of control. *Journal of Personality and Social Psychology*, *71*, 549–570.

Slagsvold, B., & Sorensen, A. (2008). Age, education, and the gender gap in the sense of control. *International Journal of Aging and Human Development*, *67*, 25–42.

Sliwinski, M., & Buschke, H. (2004). Modeling intraindividual cognitive change in aging adults: Results from the Einstein Aging Studies. *Aging, Neuropsychology, and Cognition*, *11*, 196–211.

Staats, S. (1974). Internal versus external Locus of Control for three age groups. *International Journal of Aging and Human Development*, *5*, 7–10.

Stevens, F.C.J., Kaplan, C. D., Ponds, R.W.H.M., & Jolles, J. (2001). The importance of active lifestyles for memory performance and memory self-knowledge. *Basic and Applied Social Psychology*, *23*, 137–145.

Stine, E. L., Lachman, M. E., & Wingfield, A. (1993). The roles of perceived and actual control in memory for spoken language. *Educational Gerontology*, *19*, 331–349.

Suen, L. W., Morris, D. L., & McDougall, G. J. (2004). Memory functions of Taiwanese American older adults. *Western Journal of Nursing Research*, *26*, 222–241.

Tennstedt, S., Howland, J., Lachman, M. E., Peterson, E. W., Kasten, L., & Jette, A. (1998). A randomized, controlled trial of a group intervention to reduce fear of falling and associated activity restriction in older adults. *Journals of Gerontology: Psychological Sciences, 53B*, P384–P392.

Thompson, S. C. (1999). Illusions of control: How we overestimate our personal influence. *Current Directions in Psychological Science, 8*, 187–190.

Troyer, A. K., & Rich, J. B. (2002). Psychometric properties of a new metamemory questionnaire for older adults. *Journals of Gerontology: Psychological Sciences, 57B*, P19–P27.

Valentijn, S.A.M., Hill, R. D., Van Hooren, S.A.H., Bosma, H., Van Boxtel, M.P.J., Jolles, J., et al. (2006). Memory self-efficacy predicts memory performance: Results from a 6-year follow-up study. *Psychology and Aging, 21*, 165–172.

Valentijn, S.A.M., Van Hooren, S.A.H., Bosma, H., Touw, D. M., Jolles, J., Van Boxtel, M.P.J., et al. (2005). The effect of two types of memory training on subjective and objective memory performance in healthy individuals aged 55 years and older: A randomized controlled trial. *Patient Education and Counseling, 57*, 106–114.

Wallston, K. A. (2005). The validity of the Multidimensional Health Locus of Control Scales. *Journal of Health Psychology, 10*, 623–631.

Welch, D. C., & West, R. L. (1995). Self-efficacy and mastery: Its application to issues of environmental control, cognition, and aging. *Developmental Review, 15*, 150–171.

Wells, G. D., & Esopenko, C. (2008). Memory self-efficacy, aging, and memory performance: The roles of effort and persistence. *Educational Gerontology, 34*, 520–530.

West, R. L., Bagwell, D. K., & Dark-Freudeman, A. (2005). Memory and goal setting: The response of older and younger adults to positive and objective feedback. *Psychology and Aging, 20*, 195–201.

West, R. L., Bagwell, D. K., & Dark-Freudeman, A. (2008). Self-efficacy and memory aging: The impact of a memory intervention based on self-efficacy. *Aging, Neuropsychology, and Cognition, 15*, 302–329.

West, R. L., Dark-Freudeman, A., & Bagwell, D. K. (2009). Goals-feedback conditions and episodic memory: Mechanisms for memory gains in older and younger adults. *Memory, 17*, 233–244.

West, R. L., & Yassuda, M. S. (2004). Aging and memory control beliefs: Performance in relation to goal setting and memory self-evaluation. *Journals of Gerontology: Psychological Sciences, 59B*, P56–P65.

Wolinsky, F. D., Wyrwich, K. W., Babu, A. N., Kroenke, K., & Tierney, W. M. (2003). Age, aging, and the sense of control among older adults: A longitudinal reconsideration. *Journals of Gerontology: Social Sciences, 58B*, S212–S220.

Wrosch, C., Heckhausen, J., & Lachman, M. E. (2006). Goal management across adulthood and old age: The adaptive value of primary and secondary control. In D. K. Mroczek & T. D. Little (Eds.), *Handbook of Personality Development* (pp. 399–421). Mahwah, NJ: Lawrence Erlbaum Associates.

Zelinski, E. M., & Gilewski, M. J. (2004). A 10-item Rasch modeled memory self-efficacy scale. *Aging & Mental Health, 8*, 293–306.

CHAPTER 9

END-OF-LIFE ISSUES

Jessica Richmond Moeller, Mary M. Lewis,
and James L. Werth, Jr.

The 20th century, with its rapid progress in medical science, fundamentally changed the nature of the dying process in much of the Western world. Advances throughout the century in medicine and life-sustaining technology expanded the options one has near the end of life (i.e., "the time period when health care providers would not be surprised if death occurred within about 6 months"; American Psychological Association Ad Hoc Committee on End-of-Life Issues, 2002, p. 1) and resulted in a dramatic increase in life expectancy and quality of life.

There are many issues that may present themselves when a person is nearing the end of life. Although it is not possible to discuss every issue in this chapter, we address several general overarching areas that have emerged and risen to the forefront over the past several decades. Specifically, this chapter focuses on what dying in the United States is like for older adults in the 21st century, definitions of death and common end-of-life terminology, various treatment options near the end of life, and factors in end-of-life decision making in older adults.

It is important to note at the outset that the United States has become increasingly diverse over the years, with 35% of the population belonging to an ethnic minority group in 2000 (U.S. Census Bureau, 2001). Because issues associated with death and dying are very personal and sensitive, it is not surprising that an individual's culture may play a large role in the end-of-life choices people make. Although a thorough discussion of cross-cultural issues at the end of life is beyond the purview of this chapter, brief attention is given to these issues as we discuss the various areas of end-of-life issues and decision making (see Klessig, 1992; Kwak & Haley, 2005, for more comprehensive reviews and suggestions for addressing these differences). An important caveat to keep in mind when reading this chapter, specifically the parts on racial, ethnic, and cultural differences, is that culture is not monolithic. Often more differences exist within cultures than between cultures, especially as factors such as level of acculturation come into play, therefore, we caution that one cannot simply compile a list of what all Koreans, Muslims, or members of any particular cultural group believe. Rather, when working with individuals near the end of life, it is most important to treat the person first and foremost as a unique being.

DYING IN THE UNITED STATES IN THE 21ST CENTURY

The ways in which Americans experience death in the United States have changed dramatically in the last half-century. Americans are living longer, dying in different settings, utilizing more medical technology, and exerting more control over their deaths. In 2005, the average life expectancy, collapsed across race and gender, was 77.8 years (Kung, Hoyert, Xu, & Murphy, 2008), an increase of 10.6 years since 1950. In general, women have a longer life expectancy than men, 80.4 years compared to 75.2 years, respectively (Kung et al.). Differences in these numbers also emerge across race. For example, European American women are expected to live 80.8 years at birth compared to 76.5 years for African American women. Similar differences are seen in men: 75.7 years life expectancy for European American men compared to 69.5 years for African American men (Kung et al.).

Although individuals are living longer today compared to 50 years ago, the leading causes of death for older adults have not changed. The three leading causes of death in 2004, heart disease, cancer, and cerebrovascular disease (stroke), are the same as the top three leading causes of death in 1950 (Kochanek, Murphy, Anderson, & Scott, 2004). These three leading causes of death are observed for older adults across most races (European American, African American, American Indian, Asian or Pacific Islander), although sometimes in a slightly different order. A few exceptions include male and female Native American Indians aged 65–84 where diabetes surpasses stroke for the third leading cause of death, and European American men aged 65–85 and women aged 65–74 where chronic lower respiratory disease surpasses stroke (Centers for Disease Control and Prevention/National Center for Health Statistics, n.d.).

One might infer that if individuals are dying from the same illnesses today as they were 50 years ago, yet they are living longer before they die, advances in medical technology may be given credit. These developments not only prolong the life span, but also alter the location in which death occurs.

The location of one's death is important when discussing end-of-life care because different settings may follow different procedures when one nears the end of life. Typically, older adults in the United States die in one of three settings: their home, the hospital, or nursing homes or skilled nursing facilities (Gruneir et al., 2007). However, within the hospital category patients can die as inpatients, outpatients, on arrival, and so on. Therefore, just because a person dies at the hospital does not mean that was necessarily the place where he was receiving his end-of-life care.

Several researchers have reported that Americans currently report a primary preference for dying at home (Hays, Galanos, Palmer, McQuoid, & Flint, 2001; Tang, 2003). Despite this, the majority of people die in an institutional setting. Flory and colleagues (2004) analyzed death certificates from 1980–1998 in order to discuss the trends that exist regarding place of death and how these trends may have changed over time as the health system changed. Results showed that initially (1980–1983) the rates of in-hospital deaths remained stable. However, a significant decrease in in-hospital deaths was observed from 1983 (a high of 54%) to 1998 (a low of 41%). Consequently, this decrease in hospital deaths resulted in an increase of at-home and nursing home deaths. Specifically, home deaths rose from 17% to 22%, and nursing home deaths rose from 16% to 22% during the same time period. Flory's group also identified the top 10 causes of death for their sample and examined location of death for each cause. Although the percentages for each location were fairly consistent across 7 of the top 10 causes of death, differences occurred for diabetes, chronic obstructive pulmonary disease (COPD), and cancer. In-patient hospital deaths attributed to diabetes and COPD declined by more than 15%; however, the most striking difference was observed for individuals dying of cancer. From 1980 to 1998, the percentage of cancer patients dying while inpatients at a hospital dropped from 70% to 37%, and subsequently, the number of individuals dying from cancer at home rose from 15% to 38%. Finally, Flory's group examined racial differences in location of death; however, because of inconsistencies in death certificates over the years, the researchers were only able to compare European Americans (Hispanics were included with European Americans), African Americans, and "other." Data showed that, in 1980, the rates of death by location were similar across races; on the other hand, in 1998, fewer European Americans died as hospital in-patients (40%) compared to African Americans (48%). These differences were magnified even more when analyzed by gender as well as race. Specifically, African American women were more likely to die in the hospital (50%) than European American women (39%). Overall, the researchers reported that by 1998, individuals died outside of the hospital setting (e.g., at home or in nursing homes) more frequently (45%) than died as hospital inpatients (41%). Flory et al. suggested that this change demonstrated the evolution of medical care at the end of life. They stated that because the changes in location of death occurred gradually and consistently over their time period of 18 years, this change is evolutionary as opposed to revolutionary.

DEFINITIONS OF DEATH
AND END-OF-LIFE TERMINOLOGY

Having just described when, where, and from what Americans typically die, we next discuss how death is defined as well as how death occurs. *Death* is generally defined as the cessation of life. Specifically, the Uniform Determination of Death Act (1980) states "an individual who has sustained either (1) irreversible cessation of circulatory and respiratory functions, or (2) irreversible cessation of all functions of the entire brain, including the brain stem, is dead" (as cited in DuBois, 1999, p. 126). Although a specific definition of death exists, several ways in which the cessation of life may occur have been subject to much ethical and legal debate. In this section, we define and discuss three ways in which death may occur for older adults: (a) by withholding or withdrawing treatment, (b) by suicide, (c) and by physician-assisted suicide and euthanasia. Each of these manners in which death occurs involve varying levels of decision making and control by the dying individual. There are other ways of dying that we do not discuss in this chapter, such as death resulting from natural causes (e.g., a heart attack while someone is asleep) or from accidents or murder.

Withholding and Withdrawing Treatment

When an individual is terminally or chronically ill, there may come a point in her life where she makes the decision to stop receiving medical treatment. A decision to stop medical treatment can involve various types of treatment, including: artificial nutrition and hydration, a ventilator, dialysis, antibiotics, and chemotherapy, among others. There are three distinct forms of cessation of treatment that are sometimes blurred in the literature. When a decision to cease treatment is made by the competent patient or the patient's loved ones, it is usually referred to as either withholding or withdrawing life-sustaining treatment. These concepts differ in that the decision to *withhold* treatment refers to not starting a treatment, whereas the decision to *withdraw* treatment refers to stopping a treatment that has already been started. Competent individuals have had the right to refuse treatment since the early 1900s, and research has shown that the most common cause of death for ICU patients is death from their illness following the decision to withhold or withdraw life-sustaining medical treatment (accounting for anywhere from 65%–90% of ICU deaths; Keenan et al., 1997). Public opinion polls conducted from 1973–1991 indicated that 62%–85% of Americans (depending upon the year) believed that terminally ill patients should be able to instruct their physician to let them die if that is their wish (Allen et al., 2006).

There are significant cross-cultural differences that exist with regard to deciding to start or discontinue life-sustaining medical treatment. Caralis, Davis, Wright, and Marcial (1993) found that more African American and Hispanic participants indicated that they would want their medical doctor to keep them alive regardless of how ill they were, when compared with non-Hispanic European American participants. Moreover, non-Hispanic European Americans were more likely to agree to stop life-sustaining medical treatment in some situations (89%) compared to African Americans (63%) and Hispanics (59%) (Caralis et al.). Klessig (1992) examined the effect of values and culture on life-support decisions with 287 participants from 7 different cultural groups (African American, Chinese, Filipino, Iranian, Jewish, Korean, and Mexican American) and compared them to a reference group of European Americans ($n = 43$). She provided participants with eight different terminal or hopeless scenarios involving the decision to either start or stop life-sustaining medical treatment and asked them to indicate what their decision would be for each scenario. Her results showed that, as a group, Filipino, Iranian, Korean, and African Americans were more likely than the other groups to strongly agree (more than 80% of participants agreed) or agree (60%–80% agreed) with the decision to *start* life support, whereas Jewish participants and the reference group of European Americans were more likely to disagree (less than 20% agreed). Chinese and Mexican Americans were more equivocal in that 40% to 60% of the participants agreed with the decision to start treatment. Klessig also found differences between the groups in their decisions to *stop* life-sustaining medical treatment. Specifically, Jewish, Chinese, and the reference group were more likely to agree with the decision to withdraw treatment, while Filipino, Iranian, Korean, and African Americans were more likely to disagree with the decision to terminate treatment. Again, Mexican Americans were split in their responses. These studies provide examples of some of the cross-cultural differences that may exist when discussing treatment options.

The third end-of-life term used when making treatment decisions is *futility*. A situation is deemed futile when it is determined that additional treatment will only prolong the dying process without increasing the patient's quality of life (Burns & Truog, 2007). This is often the most difficult end-of-life decision for people to accept because the decision to stop a treatment that has been started or not to start any additional treatment is made by the medical team, over the objections of the patient or her loved ones. This type of situation is complicated by the ambiguity surrounding how to determine that the situation is futile. Issues of culture, ethnicity, spirituality, or other psychosocial factors may be especially intense in these instances. For example, cultures that hold a strong belief that enduring pain is a sign of strength and one's trust in God's plan, and only God can decide who should live or die (e.g., Iranians), may resent a physician's decision to stop treatment based on futility because it violates their religious beliefs (Klessig, 1992). Caralis and colleagues (1993) found that the majority of their sample (non-Hispanic European Americans, African Americans, and Hispanics) disagreed with physicians' making these treatment decisions "unilaterally," with only Hispanics being somewhat likely to defer to the medical doctor's best medical opinion. When physicians make these decisions, their intention is most likely in keeping with the ethical principles of beneficence and maleficence; however, members of various cultural groups may interpret these actions differently. If physicians are not sensitive to cultural differences, the result could be a lack of trust in medical professionals and future decisions not to seek medical treatment for other family members.

Suicide

Suicide is defined as a person actively causing his or her own death. Researchers have found that older adults (over 65) tend to report less suicidal ideation (i.e., thoughts of taking one's life) than do younger adults (Duberstein et al., 1999). Statistics also reveal a lower ratio of suicide attempts to suicide deaths for older (4:1) compared to younger (100–200:1) adults (Kung et al., 2008). Yet, despite this, the suicide death rate among older adults is higher than younger adults (Conwell, Duberstein, & Caine, 2002). Many risk factors that may contribute to the higher rate of suicides in later life have been identified. For example, Conwell and colleagues (1998) provided the following possible reasons why older adults are more likely to die from self-injurious behaviors than are younger adults: (a) living alone, which reduces older adults' chances of being rescued from a suicide attempt; (b) being in poorer physical health, which makes them less resilient to injury; and (c) being more meticulous in their ability to plan their actions (as opposed to impulsive) and more determined to carry out their plan, which leads to the use of more lethal means.

Suicide is currently the 13th ranked cause of death for older persons in the United States (Kung et al., 2008). In 2005, older adults made up only 12.4% of the U.S. population but represented 16.6% of the suicides. Because of these alarming statistics, many researchers and suicide prevention experts have examined possible risk factors for elderly suicide. Male gender, widowhood, and retirement are a few of the significant risk factors for suicide in the elderly (McIntosh, 1992; Richman, 1999). Having a chronic physical illness has also been identified as one of the most significant risk factors for suicide among older adults (McIntosh, 1992). Research has suggested that a medical illness may contribute to suicide in 35%–70% of older adults who died by suicide (Hughes & Kleepsies, 2001). Mental illness has also been documented consistently throughout the suicide literature as contributing significantly to an individual's risk for suicide; however, research also suggests that 5%–30% of suicides in older adults are not associated with psychiatric disorders (Hughes & Kleepsies). Waern and colleagues (2002) found that after controlling for mental illness, several physical illnesses, including visual impairments, neurological disorders, and malignant disease, were still associated with suicide in older adults. Recently efforts have been made to design effective prevention strategies based on these risk indicators to address the growing concern of suicide among older adults (U.S. Department of Health and Human Services [USDHHS], 2001).

Physician-Assisted Suicide and Euthanasia

A less common, although much more controversial, alternative at the end of life is assisted suicide. The American Association of Suicidology (AAS; 1996) defined *assisted suicide* as "the deliberate and knowing provision of information, the means, and/or help to another person for the act of suicide" (p. 6). When the person providing the information, means, or help is a physician (most commonly providing a prescription for a lethal dose of barbiturates), the qualifier "physician" is sometimes added, making the term *physician-assisted suicide.* There is some controversy over the use of this term because of the association of suicide with irrationality and impulsivity. Recently, several organizations have advocated for use of value-neutral terms instead of assisted suicide (e.g., American Medical Student Association, 2008; American Public Health Association, 2007), including the Oregon Department of Health Services (see O'Reilly, 2006), which regulates the Oregon Death with Dignity Act (to be described later). We use it in this chapter because it is still the most recognized phrase for this type of action.

Although the practice of assisted suicide has existed in the Netherlands since the 1970s (officially legalized in 2001), it was primarily the work of Dr. Jack Kevorkian and the passing of Oregon's Death with Dignity Act (DWDA) in 1997 that sparked the physician-assisted suicide debate in the United States.

In 1990, Dr. Kevorkian, a medical pathologist, made the startling announcement that he had aided in the death of a 54-year-old woman suffering from Alzheimer's disease (Webb, 1997). He had designed a suicide machine, termed the "mercitron," which would mix a lethal combination of medication and allow patients to administer it themselves by pulling a lever. Although highly controversial, Dr. Kevorkian assisted in the deaths of at least 93 patients without being convicted of assisted suicide or murder. He was acquitted of such crimes on three separate occasions by the Michigan courts (Webb). It was not until 1999 that Dr. Kevorkian was convicted of second-degree murder for performing euthanasia on a 53-year-old man with Lou Gehrig's disease. In this case, Dr. Kevorkian injected the medication that led to the man's death. The act of injecting changed his role from the "provider of the means" to the "administrator of the means" and moved the action from assisted suicide to euthanasia.

Although not legal in the United States, euthanasia warrants brief mention here as it is in practice in a few countries in Europe. Euthanasia refers to someone (usually a physician) intentionally taking an action that ends another person's life with the stated intent of alleviating or preventing perceived suffering (AAS, 1996). Its root is Latin and means good (*Eu*) death (*thanatos;* Materstvedt & Kaasa, 2002). What distinguishes euthanasia from physician-assisted suicide is the active administration of the lethal dose of medication by the person as opposed to simply providing the means and allowing the terminally ill patient to administer the means himself. Further complicating the distinction is the fact that there are several different "types" of euthanasia referenced in the literature. Distinctions have been made between voluntary, involuntary, and nonvoluntary euthanasia (Allen et al., 2006). (Distinctions have also been made between "active" and "passive" euthanasia.) Voluntary euthanasia refers to the deliberate termination of a patient's life at his explicit and direct request. Nonvoluntary euthanasia takes place when the patient is unconscious or incompetent and, thus, currently incapable of making an end-of-life decision. In this case, the physician or another person makes the decision for the patient based on what they believe is consistent with the patient's prior wishes. On the other hand, involuntary euthanasia occurs when the patient is competent and aware but his consent is not obtained. Involuntary euthanasia is not legal in any country and may be treated as a homicide.

In some cases, the language "active" and "passive" euthanasia is used (e.g., Hermsen & ten Have, 2002). *Active* euthanasia refers to someone taking an active role in causing an individual's death, such as a physician or family member who injects a lethal dose of medication into a person or the person's intravenous line. *Passive* euthanasia may be used to describe the process of allowing someone to die, such as by removing a ventilator. In the United States, the term *passive euthanasia* is not used because of the desire to distinguish between an ethically and legally acceptable action—withholding or withdrawing treatment—and an illegal and unethical action—euthanasia (i.e., deliberately causing someone's death).

Allen and colleagues (2006) examined data from several Gallup and Public Opinion polls to determine the trends in Americans' attitudes toward euthanasia and physician-assisted suicide and how those attitudes have changed over the last seven decades (specifically, 1936–2002). The researchers found that support for voluntary euthanasia as an option for a terminally ill patient increased from a low of approximately 40% during the time period

of 1936–1950, to a high of 72% in 2002. However, these numbers did fluctuate up and down from year to year. Racial differences have been observed
in Americans' attitudes toward voluntary euthanasia. For example, research
has shown that 20% fewer African Americans favor legalizing voluntary
euthanasia than European Americans (e.g., in 1994, 70% of European Americans supported legalization while only 50% of African Americans did; see
Figure 1 in MacDonald, 1998, p. 412, for a trend analysis). In addition, from
1990–1998, Americans were asked, "If a person has a disease that will
ultimately destroy their mind or body and they want to take their own life,
should a doctor be allowed to assist the person in taking their own life, or
not?" (Allen et al., p. 14). Again, the numbers fluctuated by year, but most
remained between 50% and 53% in favor of allowing medical doctors to perform physician-assisted suicide (with the exception of 58% in favor in 1993).
The percentages of those opposed to physician-assisted suicide showed more
variability (36%–47%) across the years (Allen et al.). The remaining respondents
did not offer opinions (3%–11%).

There have been many arguments provided for and against the practice
of physician-assisted suicide. Proponents advocate that legalizing physician-
assisted suicide is in line with individuals' rights for personal autonomy
and that it allows terminally ill patients to maintain their dignity and have
some control at the end of life (Rosenfeld, 2004). They further suggest
that palliative care and pain management can only go so far in ensuring
quality of life, and physician-assisted suicide provides an additional option
when these practices are no longer effective (Dieterle, 2007). Finally,
proponents advocate that providing measures that will alleviate a patient's
suffering while respecting her autonomy are consistent with the physician's
role and the current ethical and medical principles she follows. On the other
hand, opponents of legalizing physician-assisted suicide argue that providing assistance in a patient's suicide violates the Hippocratic Oath taken by
medical professionals. They further emphasize that suicide is morally unac-
ceptable and does not respect the sanctity of human life (Sears & Stanton,
2001). They also discuss the possibility of a "slippery slope" if physician-
assisted suicide is widely legalized—this choice will be extended beyond
persons who are terminally ill to individuals who are chronically ill, have
physical disabilities, or are mentally ill (Dieterle). Finally, they fear that the
option of physician-assisted suicide will pressure terminally ill people to
make this decision in order to avoid becoming a burden to their family and
loved ones.

Given the previous discussion of older adults' risk for taking their own
life, it is not surprising that opponents of physician-assisted suicide strongly
protested the passing of Oregon's Death with Dignity Act (DWDA). The
DWDA allows a terminally ill adult resident of Oregon to obtain and use
a prescription from her physician for a self-administered, lethal dose of

medication (Oregon Department of Human Services [ODHS], 2008). Many safeguards have been built into the law to prevent the abuse of this option, including: (a) the patient must make two verbal and one written request for assistance in dying separated by a period of at least 15 days; (b) the patient's terminal diagnosis must be confirmed by the attending physician as well as a consulting colleague; (c) the patient must be deemed capable of making such end-of-life decisions, and referral may be made to a psychiatrist or psychologist to rule out conditions that may impair decision making; and finally, (d) the patient must be informed of the alternatives she has (e.g., hospice) and strongly encouraged to discuss her decision with her loved ones (Ganzini et al., 2000; ODHS).

Despite these safeguards, many have voiced concerns that the legalization of physician-assisted suicide would hinder the hospice and palliative care movement that had recently begun to gain ground. Today, it would seem that these concerns are unfounded. The ODHS (2008) reports that, since its inception in 1997, 341 patients have died under the DWDA. The average age of those dying in 2007 was 65 (ODHS). In 2007, 85 prescriptions for lethal doses of medication were written, and 46 patients chose to use those medications to end their life. Of those patients who used the medication and completed physician-assisted suicide, 88% were under the care of hospice at the time they died, and 90% were able to die at home (ODHS). Of those choosing to end their lives, the most frequently reported end-of-life concerns were a loss of autonomy, decreased ability to participate in enjoyable activities, and a loss of dignity. The ODHS reported that more patients in 2007 reported a concern about adequate pain management compared with previous years.

When the DWDA was passed, there was significant concern regarding the impact it would have on the care of the terminally ill by Oregon physicians. Studies have examined Oregon physicians' perceptions of their ability to care for terminally ill patients (Ganzini et al., 2000, 2001). Ganzini's group (2001) examined physicians' efforts to improve their ability to care for people who are terminally ill for the time period of 1994–1998. Results showed that, since 1994, many physicians reported increased hospice referrals, reported increased knowledge in the prescribing of pain medication, and perceived greater access to hospice services for their patients. Goy and colleagues (2003) examined the perceptions of hospice nurses and social workers in Oregon on how Oregon physicians' care of terminally ill persons had changed since the passing of the DWDA. Their results are consistent with those of Ganzini et al. (2001) in that participants overall believed that physicians had made positive changes in their ability to care for hospice patients over the past 5 years. Specifically, improvements appeared to have been made in their willingness to prescribe sufficient pain medication, willingness to refer patients to hospice, knowledge about using pain medication with hospice patients, and competence for caring for hospice patients (Goy et al.).

END-OF-LIFE TREATMENT OPTIONS: PALLIATIVE CARE AND HOSPICE

The World Health Organization (n.d.) stated that good palliative care affirms life and views death as a normal process, does not hasten or post-pone death, provides relief from pain and other distressing symptoms, integrates the psychological and spiritual aspects of patient care, offers a support system to help patients live as actively as possible until death, and offers a support system to help family members cope with the patient's illness and their own bereavement. Palliative care, therefore, emphasizes comfort, (specifically, pain and symptom relief) and improving quality of life, regardless of a patient's prognosis and whether he is receiving curative treatment. It can be provided at any time in a patient's illness (i.e., not only at the end of life), for any number of illnesses and associated symptoms. It is important to note that palliative care and hospice care are not the same. Hospice refers to programs that focus on quality of life for *terminally ill* individuals (i.e., they must have a prognosis of 6 months or less). Further, hospice care is a narrower, more specific concept, referring to a program that provides comfort care at the home or other in-patient care facility near the end of life. Therefore, although hospice services provide palliative care, an individual does not need to be enrolled in hospice in order to receive palliative care.

Although the first hospice in the United States was established in 1974, it was not until Medicare began reimbursing patients for hospice care in 1983 that its utilization began to increase (Ogle, Mavis, & Wyatt, 2002). Despite the steady increase in hospice patients over the last 25 years, hospice is still an underutilized service. The National Hospice and Palliative Care Organization (NHPCO; 2007) estimated that 1.3 million people utilized hospice services in 2006, and 36% of U.S. deaths were individuals under hospice care. Although approximately 25% of deaths occur in nursing homes, only 5% of nursing home residents access hospice (Centers for Disease Control and Prevention, 2003; National Center for Health Statistics, 2004). Further, even though utilization of hospice by members of ethnic minority groups has grown in recent years (19.1% minority in 2006 vs. 17.8% minority in 2005), the majority of hospice patients are European American (80.9%) (NHPCO). Older adults (65 and older) make up 4/5 of all hospice patients, and adults 85 and older make up 1/3 of all hospice patients. Connor, Elwert, Spence, and Christakis (2007) examined the trends in hospice utilization for older adults aged 65 and older. Results indicated that in 2002, over 1/4 of older adults made use of hospice services (28.6%; Connor,

Elwert, et al.). Slight differences in race and gender were also observed in that women utilized hospice (30%) more frequently than men (27%), and European Americans (29%) more frequently than African Americans (22%; Connor, Elwert, et al.).

There are many potential benefits of hospice, and here we discuss those that pertain directly to the end-of-life issues discussed previously. One of the benefits of hospice is that the majority of patients will die in the place they call home, typically either a private residence or a nursing home. Specifically, in 2006, 74% of hospice patients died at "home," compared to 17% who died at a hospice inpatient facility, and approximately 9% who died at the hospital (NHPCO, 2007). Further, although when initially implemented the majority of patients receiving hospice care were those diagnosed with cancer, hospice care is available for a variety of illnesses. In 2006, cancer was still the single most common diagnosis for hospice patients (44.1%), but the combination of noncancer diagnoses (55.9%) outnumbered the cancer diagnoses (NHPCO). In fact, less than 25% of deaths in the United States are caused by cancer, with the majority of deaths resulting from chronic conditions. The NHPCO reported that in 2006, the top five chronic conditions of patients under the care of hospice included heart disease, debility unspecified, dementia, lung disease, and stroke or coma, although use of hospice by patients with dementia may be underreported (Munn, Hanson, Zimmerman, Sloane, & Mitchell, 2006).

There has been some concern in the literature that hospice may shorten the lives of patients as a result of the use of opioids and sedatives for pain and symptom management (Connor, Pyenson, Fitch, Spence, & Iwasaki, 2007), and some patients are concerned about addiction and tolerance (Lambert et al., 2007). Connor, Pyenson, et al. (2007) reported that rather than shortening life, hospice care may prolong the lives of some terminally ill patients. For four of the six illnesses (congestive heart failure [CHF] and five types of cancer) the researchers examined, they observed increases in survival rates for hospice patients compared to nonhospice patients with the same illnesses: (a) CHF patients under hospice care lived an average of 402 days compared to 321 days for those patients not receiving hospice care; (b) for the various types of cancer, increases in the average survival period for hospice patients with lung cancer (39 days longer), pancreatic cancer (21 days longer), and colon cancer (33 days longer) were significant compared to those patients not under hospice care. After controlling for possible differences in demographics and sample sizes, the researchers concluded that patients across all illnesses lived an average of 29 days longer when under the care of hospice than those individuals not receiving hospice care (Connor, Pyenson, et al., 2007). Therefore, another benefit is that hospice improves the patient's quality of life without necessarily shortening life or hastening death.

FACTORS IN END-OF-LIFE DECISION MAKING IN OLDER ADULTS

Much literature has examined the issues that may influence end-of-life decision making for older adults. In this section, we discuss two of the more common factors that affect a person's experience near the end of life, including the decision-making process for terminally ill individuals and their loved ones. We first explore the broad area of communication among medical professionals, patients, and caregivers. Specifically, we discuss what aspects of the patient's care should be discussed and with whom it should be communicated. We then focus on advanced directives and advanced care planning.

Communication Issues

Good communication among physicians, the patient, and the patient's caregivers regarding diagnosis, prognosis, treatment options, and end-of-life issues is critical when working with individuals near the end of life. Research has shown that factors such as age, educational level, and gender can be associated with differences in end-of-life care and decision-making (Morrison, 1998). Typically, individuals of younger age, with higher levels of education, and who are male wish to have the most information regarding their illness (Carr & Khodyakov, 2007; Morrison, 1998). The line of communication between physicians and the patient and/or patient's family has been the target of much research. Perceptions of the quality and utility of this communication vary across studies depending upon the participants (physicians versus patients and caregivers). Although in-depth coverage of this literature is beyond the scope of this chapter, the general themes in the literature are highlighted next (for more comprehensive reviews, see Hancock et al., 2007; Parker et al., 2007).

Hancock and colleagues (2007) conducted an extensive review of the literature to determine where the discrepancies in perceptions regarding communication near the end of life exist. Their review showed several general themes: (a) patients believe that physicians only offer information regarding prognosis and diagnosis when specifically requested by the patients; (b) physicians believe that if patients want information they will ask for it, and consequently, if the patient does not ask it means she does not want to know; (c) caregivers believe physicians press their personal treatment preference on the caregiver and sometimes even act as "gatekeepers" of information, only providing the information they think is necessary; and (d) physicians tend to perceive that they have provided all the information that is needed and that the patient and family have understood the information. Awareness of these misperceptions has led to suggestions regarding how these issues can be addressed in physician training.

Many cross-cultural differences exist in whether patients and their caregivers wish to be fully informed about the patient's diagnosis, prognosis, and treatment options. There are two medical models of care that may influence an individual's beliefs about appropriate communication near the end of life. In the United States, physicians follow the Western medical model, and prior to the 1970s, it was common for physicians not to inform the patient of a poor prognosis or diagnosis (Mitchell, 1998; Sagara & Pickett, 1998). However, the current practice among medical professionals in the United States emphasizes self-determination, patient autonomy, and full disclosure of the patient's diagnosis, prognosis, and the risks and benefits of various treatment options (Mitchell, 1998). Conversely, the medical model in place in many Eastern countries is considerably different because the emphasis is primarily on beneficence and maleficence, with little attention given to ensuring patient autonomy (Sagara & Pickett, 1998). Several studies have looked cross-culturally at the preferences for disclosure among patients in the United States and have discussed the possible outcomes one could expect. The following are three examples of such studies, one that examined multiple cultural groups and two that examined one specific cultural group.

Blackhall, Murphy, Frank, Michel, and Azen (1995) surveyed 200 elderly adults (age 65+) from each of four ethnic groups—African American, European American, Korean American, and Mexican American—regarding their attitudes about patient autonomy related to disclosing a diagnosis of metastatic cancer and a poor prognosis (patient will probably die). The researchers found that Korean Americans and Mexican Americans were significantly less likely than European Americans and African Americans to believe that the patient should be fully informed about their diagnosis and prognosis. Instead, these groups believed it was more important to inform the patient's family of the diagnosis and prognosis first and allow the family to decide whether to inform the patient. Blackhall and colleagues found Mexican Americans with higher levels of acculturation were more likely to hold views similar to those of the African American and European American participants regarding patient autonomy. Finally, although not all the differences were statistically significant, across all ethnic groups higher percentages were observed in favor of disclosing the *diagnosis* than were in favor of disclosing the poor *prognosis*. This finding suggests that disclosure for some things (i.e., diagnosis) may be more acceptable than others (i.e., prognosis).

One of the primary reasons cited by physicians for not disclosing a "poor" diagnosis/prognosis to the patient is that they do not want to cause the patient to lose hope, give up, or become psychologically burdened (Mitchell, 1998). This reasoning may be appropriate for some cultural groups. Carrese and Rhodes (1995) interviewed 34 Navajo individuals to discuss the participants' past experiences with Western medicine and their beliefs about disclosing "bad news" to patients. Traditional Navajo Indians practice Házhoojí Nitsihakees/Házhoojí (translated as "think and speak in a positive way") and Doo'ájíniidah (translated as "Don't talk that way!"). These general themes are applied to all aspects of life in that traditional Navajo believe thought and language have the ability to shape reality and control events. The researchers explored the specific application of these general beliefs to medical practices and found that when interacting with Western medical professionals these individuals prefer that all communication be positive, and they are not receptive to discussions about the potential risks of medical treatment, terminal diagnoses, or poor prognoses.

Beyene (1992) examined the issue of medical disclosure among Ethiopian refugees. Through case examples, Beyene pointed out some of the conflicts that may arise as a result of inconsistency between core Ethiopian values and Western medical practice. For example, in addition to the importance of informing the patient's family rather than the patient about a grim diagnosis, it is vital that bad news be shared with the family in the morning as opposed to in the evening, to avoid a sleepless night and additional burden on the family. Awareness of beliefs such as these can enhance the likelihood that quality care will be provided to both the patient and the patient's family.

Advanced Directives

As a result of several court cases (e.g., *In re Quinlan*, 1976; *Cruzan v. Director, Missouri Department of Health*, 1990) and legislation (e.g., the Patient Self-Determination Act [PSDA], 1990) in the latter half of the 20th century, people have more opportunities to be involved in end-of-life decision making and care. The desire of some people to have as much control over one's life as possible has led to the development of advanced directives and advanced care planning. Advanced directives are defined as written documents meant to make explicit the conditions under which individuals expect to receive certain treatment or to refuse or discontinue life-sustaining treatment, in the event they are no longer legally competent to make their own decisions (Cohen-Mansfield, 2007). These documents can aid in relieving some of the difficult decision making and burden that caregivers may experience when caring for a loved one near the end of life and attempting to decide what the person would want done.

There are two general types of advanced directives: living will and durable power of attorney. Although the specific format and specifications of these documents may vary by state, the general purpose is the same across jurisdictions. Living wills are documents written by the dying person that specify the kinds of treatment the individual wishes to have, as well as the types of treatment that may be discontinued or never started. A durable power of attorney form, sometimes called a health care proxy form, designates an individual who can make decisions for the dying person if the ill individual is no longer competent to make decisions.

The living will was the first type of advanced directive to be legalized with the passing of the Natural Death Act in California in 1977; in 1983, California enacted the Durable Power of Attorney for Health Care law, becoming the first state to legalize both types of directive (Webb, 1997). By 1992, all 50 states had legalized some type of directive; however, utilization of advanced directives was relatively low. It was hypothesized that low completion rates resulted from a lack of knowledge about what advanced directives were and how to complete them (Webb). Therefore, in 1991, the PSDA was implemented. The PSDA requires all hospitals, medical centers, and nursing homes that receive federal funds (most specifically from Medicare and Medicaid) to inform all patients at admission that they have a right to make their end-of-life wishes known in the form of an advanced directive. It is currently estimated that anywhere from 15%–25% of the general population have completed an advanced directive (Cohen-Mansfield, 2007). However, the completion rates tend to vary by race. Studies have found that African Americans (Degenholtz, Arnold, Meisel, & Lave, 2002; Hopp & Duffy, 2000) and Hispanics (Kiely, Mitchell, Marlow, Murphy, & Morris, 2001; Morrison, Zayas, Mulvihill, Baskin, & Meier, 1998) are less likely to have completed advanced directives than European Americans. Several reasons for these racial and ethnic differences have been offered in the literature. One possibility is that a lack of knowledge about advanced directives results in individuals being less likely to complete them (Kwak & Haley, 2005). Further, some studies have found differences in the attitudes that different racial groups hold about advanced directives (Kwak & Haley). Specifically, Waters (2001) reported that her interviews with African Americans showed a distrust in the health care system and fear that the wishes expressed in an advanced directive would not be carried out as reasons why her participants had not completed advanced directives. Negative past experiences with the health care system could further perpetuate these differences, particularly with individuals from lower socioeconomic status groups (Kwak & Haley).

In addition to living wills and durable powers of attorney, there are two directives that apply specifically to treatment interventions: Do Not Resuscitate (DNR) and Do Not Hospitalize (DNH) orders. The DNR order indicates that no resuscitation measures (typically cardiopulmonary resuscitation—CPR) should be undertaken if the patient goes into cardiac or respiratory arrest. The DNH order states that the patient or the patient's legal guardian does not want the patient to be hospitalized automatically. This does not mean that the patient should never be hospitalized; rather, a discussion needs to occur between the patient or patient's guardian and the treating physician to decide whether hospitalization is within the patient's best interest. DNH orders are typically issued when the patient's care is able to be managed primarily at the person's home or in a nursing home (Webb, 1997). Again, racial differences are observed. Kiely's group (2001) studied five different ethnic groups across four states and concluded that American Indians/ Alaskan native were significantly more likely to have a DNR than African Americans, Asians, and Hispanics, although less likely than European Americans. Degenholtz and colleagues (2002) found that Hispanic patients were three times less likely than European American patients to have a DNR order, whereas Kwak and Haley (2005) summarized the existing research literature and concluded that African Americans were less likely to have DNR orders than European Americans.

Despite the "good intentions" behind advanced directives, scholars have debated the utility of these documents. Although living wills can provide individuals with control and autonomy near the end of life because they specify which treatments should and should not be given/received (Cohen-Mansfield, 2007), in reality it is nearly impossible to predict the exact situation any person will face near the end of life, and thus, the preferences specified in a living will may not apply (Ditto, 2006). Therefore, some people state that durable powers of attorneys are superior to living wills because the designated proxy can make medical decisions based on the specific situation of the patient . On the other hand, the designated proxy may not know the person's wishes or may ignore them (Ditto). One final, more general, drawback to advanced directives is that many individuals do not thoroughly understand the implications of the treatment they are requesting. For example, research has shown that many people are unaware of the damage that CPR can do to the body (e.g., breaking ribs) and the fact that the actual survival rate after the procedure is less than 25% (Thorevska et al., 2005). Researchers have found that individuals often change their preferences regarding such interventions after receiving this additional information (Thorevska et al.).

Given the controversy surrounding the utility of advanced directives and the fact that only a relatively small proportion of the population actually have a completed advanced directive in place, end-of-life decision-making procedures for incompetent individuals who do not have advanced directives are important. Generally, when an individual is determined to be incompetent to make his own medical decisions there are three types of laws that may provide some direction for who can make decisions for the patient (Webb, 1997). The first two, those pertaining to living wills and durable power of attorney, already have been mentioned. Basically, these laws indicate which advanced directives are recognized, when they come into place (e.g., only when the patient has 6 months to live), who is eligible to be a decision maker for the patient, and so on. As mentioned earlier, one of the major criticisms of advanced directives is that they are often unclear and do not apply when the patient is in an end-of-life situation because they do not address the specifics of that situation. In this case, as well as when no written instructions exist, the third type of law—which has to do with family consent and is called either a surrogacy or succession law—may prove useful (Webb). States that have surrogacy or succession laws indicate a decision-making hierarchy that is implemented in such situations. These hierarchies differ by state, but one example for an older adult might be: spouse, adult children, next closest adult relative, friend of the family, and medical professional.

BIOPSYCHOSOCIOSPIRITUAL ISSUES IN END-OF-LIFE DECISION MAKING

In addition to the practical issues discussed previously, there are also numerous biological, psychological, social, and spiritual issues that impact decision making near the end of life. For example, illness trajectory could significantly impact how an older adult makes decisions about end-of-life care, and that disease trajectory could also impact psychological, spiritual, and social well-being (Lunney, Lynn, & Hogan, 2002; Murray et al., 2007). Numerous studies have explored the impact of the physical (pain, feeding tubes, body changes), psychological (depression, fear, existential anxiety, dignity, suffering), social (family impact, burden, relationships), and spiritual (meaning, hope, existence of an afterlife) issues near the end of life (Kaut, 2006). Prior research has indicated that sociodemographic factors such as age, gender, marital status, religious affiliation and culture also impact end-of-life decision making (Carr & Khodyakov, 2007; Kwak & Haley, 2005). Because a comprehensive summary of the various physical, psychological, social-familial, and spiritual concerns near the end of life is beyond the scope of this chapter, readers are pointed to other sources (e.g., Kaut, 2006; Werth, Gordon, & Johnson, 2002). This section addresses three main biopsycho-socialspiritual issues that have particular relevance to older adults: mental health and illness, grief and bereavement, and cognitive issues.

Mental Health/Mental Illness

Older adults may experience mental illness or emotional disturbance that may impact their decision making and end-of-life experience. The most common mental health issues seen in later life are depression, anxiety, and dementia, although adjustment disorders, bipolar disorder, schizophrenia, personality disorders, delirium, and substance abuse disorders are also seen in this population (USDHHS, 1999) and should be assessed in end-of-life decision making (Werth et al., 2002).

Depression

The statistics on rates of depression vary greatly, depending on the source and the diagnostic criteria. According to the U.S. Surgeon General's report released in 1999, 8%–20% of community-dwelling older adults suffer from depressive symptoms (Blazer, 1994; Zarit & Zarit, 1998). Depressive symptoms are also commonly found in older adults who are medically ill, with rates ranging from 17% to 37% (USDHHS, 1999; Zarit & Zarit). Older adults who are medically ill may demonstrate many of the vegetative symptoms of depression (e.g., changes in appetite, loss of energy, change in sleep), but may not have the cognitive or emotional symptoms that would indicate a depressive disorder; therefore, a thorough assessment is needed to clarify the diagnosis. Further, as we noted earlier, depression in late life can be associated with suicide, and death wishes may be related to suicidal ideation and depression, but little empirical literature exists (King, Heisel, & Lyness, 2005).

Anxiety

Anxiety disorders can actually be more common in late life than depression, with one study noting that 11.4% of adults over 55 met the criteria for an anxiety disorder (Flint, 1994; USDHHS, 1999). However, some studies indicate that those older adults reporting worry or nervousness can be as high as 17%–21% (Himmelfarb & Murrell, 1984; USDHHS, 1999). Further, anxiousness may be exacerbated at the end of life due to the link between anxiety and some physical illnesses (e.g., COPD; Mikkelsen, Middelboe, Pisinger, & Stage, 2004; Zarit & Zarit, 1998), as well as the emotional distress related to unresolved losses, fears about dying, or concerns about the future (Werth et al., 2002).

Other Psychosocial Issues

Even without the presence of a mental illness, there are psychological issues related to end-of-life decision making. Werth and colleagues (2002) categorized these into intrapersonal and interpersonal issues. Intrapersonally, the older adult may experience concerns with autonomy and sense of control, concern for dignity, beliefs about spirituality and existential meaning, fears for the future and losses, grief, and sense of hopelessness (Werth et al.). Interpersonal issues include feeling a burden to loved ones, issues related to culture, financial concerns, isolation and impact of loved ones, and coercion (Werth et al.). All of these factors may play a role in the older adult's decision making near the end of life.

Grief/Bereavement

Grief is a different process than depression and should be identified as such, although it may be difficult to differentiate the two (Werth et al., 2002). Older adults experience many losses in their lives, including loss of independence, health, mobility, relationships, finances, and their pending death. At times, older adults may be overwhelmed by these losses and unable to grieve properly because of the frequency of the losses (Corr, Nabe, & Corr, 2000). Multiple and frequent losses, combined with the need to make decisions, may result in stress and difficulty coping (Corr et al.).

For older adults, two aspects of grieving may be especially important—the ambiguous nature of some losses and the anticipation of grief. Many of the losses that older adults experience are ambiguous losses. This is a loss that is confusing or uncertain for the individual or family members, and can be frequently associated with chronic or dementing illnesses (Boss, 1999; Dupuis, 2002). For example, when a spouse has Alzheimer's disease, the married partner will grieve the fact that the loved one is not dead physically, but cognitively and emotionally the person is "gone." Ambiguous losses can be difficult because of the length of time associated with the loss and non-"fixable" aspect of the loss (e.g., death of a loved one, loss of health due to chronic illness). Anticipatory grief is the grief experienced prior to death or in response to a life-threatening illness (Rando, 2000) and can be quite stressful for the individual and loved ones. For example, one study demonstrated that anticipatory grief can be related to anger and loss of emotional control for the spouse of a terminally ill individual (Gilliland & Fleming, 1998). Further, anticipatory grief may be related to hopelessness near the end of life (Sullivan, 2003). In addition, some people may believe that death will relieve burden on the family (King, Kim, & Conwell, 2000) and, therefore, take this into consideration when making end-of-life decisions.

The past experience of grief also seems to make a difference in making end-of-life decisions for older adults. The experience of a loved one's painful death impacts decision making in the bereaved older adult, who is more likely to have a living will, durable health care power of attorney, or informal discussions with their health care provider about end-of-life decisions (Carr & Khodyakov, 2007).

Dementia and Other Cognitive Impairment

Dementia is the term given to any organic condition that results in a progressive cognitive decline; impacts cognitive functioning such as memory, language, and executive functioning; and consequently interferes with daily functioning (Kennedy, 2000; Lewis, 2007). The most common cause of dementia in the United States is Alzheimer's disease, impacting 8%–15% of older adults (Ritchie & Kildea, 1995). In many types of dementia, the cognition of the individual may fluctuate or may progressively decline, impacting ability to make decisions as well as legal capacity to make those decisions (Werth et al., 2002). Dementia is the condition that is most feared by older adults because of the type of disability it causes and the progressive mental deterioration associated with the disease process (Zarit & Zarit, 1998). Although dementia is not an inevitable part of the aging process, this continues to be a stereotype of aging. There is no single or simple way to diagnose dementia at this time, other than through autopsy (Zarit & Zarit). However, dementia is not the only disease process that can impact cognitive functioning in older adults. "Reversible" dementias, also called pseudodementias, are a result of medical illnesses or psychiatric disorders that can mimic the cognitive declines of dementia and are quite common in older adults, particularly those with medical conditions. Deliriums, which are triggered by underlying medical illnesses, medications, or environmental stressors, can be reversed when the underlying cause is identified and treated (Zarit & Zarit).

The challenges with cognitive impairment near the end of life are multifaceted. For example, initially older adults with delirium would not be able to make competent or informed decisions; however, once the delirium is treated and resolved, they may return to full competency and be able to make decisions. Thus, differentiating delirium from dementia is a crucial, yet sometimes difficult, determination. Older adults with dementia may still be able to make end-of-life decisions, particularly if they are in the early stages; however, as the disease progresses, the person may experience difficulty communicating wishes because of language impairment, or find that decision making becomes more difficult as their executive functioning declines (Lewis, 2007; Werth et al., 2002). Therefore, those older adults concerned about cognitive impairment may want to explore end-of-life decisions prior to any decline in functioning and enlist the help of family caregivers in the process (Caron, Griffith, & Arcand, 2005; Lewis; Werth et al.).

ISSUES UNIQUE TO OLDER ADULTS NEAR THE END OF LIFE

Older adults face some unique issues near the end of life that can be quite different from what younger adults or children face. Some of these include changes in decision making and competency resulting from normal changes in cognitive abilities, experience of chronic health issues, and differences between cohorts of younger and older adults.

Decision Making, Competency, and Capacity

In general, *competency* refers to a legal status and the mental ability to make decisions (Moye, 1999; Resnick & Sorrentino, 2005). Incompetence is determined by a court and is typically targeted toward a specific situation (Moye; Resnick & Sorrentino). *Capacity* typically refers to informed decision making and is rooted in informed consent (American Bar Association Commission on Law and Aging & American Psychological Association,

2005; Resnick & Sorrentino). In end-of-life decision making, capacity and competency may become important for individuals who are discussing initiating or ending treatments, particularly when family members or medical staff disagree with the decision. It should be noted that all individuals are inferred to be competent unless a court determines otherwise (Resnick & Sorrentino). In cases when an individual lacks capacity to make decisions, a health care proxy may be called in to make the decisions for that individual.

Older adults may face difficulty in making end-of-life decisions because of changes in normal cognition and physical status. Even without facing a terminal illness, an older adult's brain changes in later life, resulting in slowed processing speeds and declines in working memory (Zarit & Zarit, 1998). Further, older adults who rate their memory as poor may perform more poorly on memory tests (Johansson, Allen-Burge, & Zarit, 1997), similar to self-fulfilling prophecies. When an older adult has a terminal illness or chronic medical condition, this may further impact their cognition (Werth et al., 2002). One recent study demonstrated that decision-making capacity was lower in a terminally ill older adult sample than the healthy older adult sample, independent of age, race, education, or depression (Sorger, Rosenfeld, Pessin, Timm, & Cimino, 2007). Although numerous studies have explored cognition and decision making in older adults, little research exists on how these changes in cognition actually impact decision making near the end of life (Sorger et al.).

Impact of Chronic Health Issues on End-of-Life Decision Making

As people live to older ages, they experience more chronic health problems that lead to disability and sometimes death (Albert, 2004). Approximately 80% of older adults have at least one health condition that is chronic, and 50% report having two chronic health conditions (Wan, Sengupta, Velkoff, & DeBarros, 2005). These chronic conditions include nonfatal diagnoses such as arthritis, hearing impairment, and visual impairment, as well as potentially fatal conditions such as heart disease, diabetes, and malignant neoplasms (Albert). Clinicians working with older adults with chronic illnesses should be aware of the impact of pain, treatment adherence, rehabilitation potential, and the psychological impact of the illness on the individual (Knight & McCallum, 1998). It is also important to understand the course of the chronic illness and the potential impact on the individual's decision making. Many of these chronic conditions do not lead to sudden death, but rather a slow decline in capabilities over time. In a study of Medicare decedents, Lunney et al. (2002) found that almost half (47%) of deaths followed a frailty trajectory, with terminal illness and organ failure being the next most common trajectories (22% and 16%, respectively). Only 7% of deaths fit into the "sudden death" trajectory (Lunney et al.). Therefore, it appears that many older adults experiencing chronic health conditions will make end-of-life decisions in the context of slow, gradual decline rather than good health followed by a sudden death.

Older adults with chronic physical conditions will typically maintain the cognitive capacity to make decisions and discuss their end-of-life wishes with loved ones. However, when the chronic health condition is dementia, the older adult may have limited time to discuss end-of-life decisions before the cognitive decline progresses to the point where they cannot make decisions. In fact, family caregivers often are asked to make decisions about end-of-life care and treatment for their loved one, particularly as the disease progresses (Caron et al., 2005). Unfortunately, research indicates that even though family members may be aware of their loved one's end-of-life wishes, there are a number of family concerns and emotions that may influence the actions of the proxy, and decision making may change throughout the different end-of-life phases (e.g., curative phase, palliative phase; Caron et al.). Further complicating the end-of-life decision-making process, some research seems to indicate that cognitive impairment is correlated with an increased desire for assisted suicide (Pessin, Rosenfeld, Burton, & Breitbart, 2003). Although this study was conducted on middle-aged adults with AIDS-related dementia, other studies have shown increased desire for assisted suicide in older adult samples (Pearlman et al., 2005). Therefore, understanding the nature of the chronic conditions with which the older adult is contending may assist in understanding her end-of-life decision-making process.

Cohort Issues

Although no studies have been conducted on the differences between cohorts on end-of-life decision making, there are a number of differences between the current cohort of older adults and the upcoming cohort of older adults (e.g., baby boomers) that may make a significant impact on end-of-life decision making. For example, the current cohort of older adults are not as highly educated as the upcoming cohort (Knight, 2006; Knight & McCallum, 1998). Further, women in the baby boom cohort are more likely to have pursued careers outside of the home than those women in the World War II generation (Knight, 2006). One study on end-of-life planning in older adults reported that men were more likely than women to formally plan for the end of their lives and that education impacted end-of-life planning (Carr & Khodyakov, 2007).

Another difference between cohorts is that the current cohort of older adults identifies themselves as more religious and attends church services more frequently than younger cohorts (Kosmin, Mayar, & Keysar, 2001). Religiosity is frequently tied to end-of-life decisions, with highly religious individuals making end-of-life decisions consistent with sustaining life, rather than withholding or withdrawing treatment (Cicirelli, 1997). Also, religiosity may be tied with purpose and meaning in life, which can reduce death anxiety and death avoidance (Ardelt, 2008).

Further, younger cohorts have been raised in an era where they have actively participated in their health care decision making, rather than passively accepting what their physician recommended. Older adults who believe their physician should make decisions about health care are less likely to participate in end-of-life planning than those older adults who do not (Carr & Khodyakov, 2007). Research also indicates that the current cohort of older adults are more likely to want other people such as family or physicians to make end-of-life decisions for them rather than make that decision themselves (Cicirelli, 1997). Therefore, although the current trend in health care is for individuals to be autonomous and practice self-determination, many current cohorts of older adults may be reluctant or unwilling to adapt to this practice.

CONCLUSION

Older adults have a number of issues to consider near the end of life. From the practical matters of advanced directives, living wills, financial choices, and decision making; to the psychological, cognitive, social, spiritual, and emotional aspects of mental illness, culture, and grief; to the physical issues regarding disability, pain, and frailty, the variety and number of issues can be overwhelming. Various professionals can be allies to older adults and their loved ones during the end-of-life process as advocates, counselors, educators, evaluators, team members, and researchers (Werth et al., 2002). Providers who are involved in end-of-life care with older adults are cautioned to ensure that they are competent to provide end-of-life care with this population, as well as work through their own personal issues associated with dying and death that may impact their ability to provide appropriate care (Werth et al.). Although end-of-life care with older adults can be challenging, this work can provide significant rewards and can be a meaningful experience for the providers, the dying person, and the loved ones.

REFERENCES

Albert, S. M. (2004). *Public Health and Aging: An Introduction to Maximizing Function and Well-being.* New York: Springer.

Allen, J., Chavez, S., DeSimone, S., Howard, D., Johnson, K., LaPierre, L., et al. (2006). Americans' attitudes toward euthanasia and physician-assisted suicide, 1936–2002. *Journal of Sociology and Social Welfare, 33*, 2–23.

American Association of Suicidology. (1996). Report of the committee on physician-assisted suicide and euthanasia. *Suicide & Life-Threatening Behavior, 26*(Suppl.), 1–19.

American Bar Association Commission on Law and Aging & American Psychological Association. (2005). *Assessment of Older Adults With Diminished Capacity: A Handbook for Lawyers.* Washington, DC: American Bar Association and American Psychological Association.

American Medical Student Association. (2008). *Principles Regarding Physician Aid in Dying.* Retrieved June 20, 2008, from: http://www.amsa.org/about/ppp/pas.cfm.

American Psychological Association Ad Hoc Committee on End-of-Life Issues. (2002). *Fact Sheet on End-of-life Care.* Retrieved August 5, 2007, from: http://www.apa.org/pi/eol/factsheet1.pdf.

American Public Health Association. (2007). *Supporting Appropriate Language Used to Discuss End of Life Choices (Policy #LB-06–02).* Retrieved June 30, 2008, from: http://www.compassionandchoices.org/pdfs/APHA_Policy.pdf.

Ardelt, M. (2008). Wisdom, religiosity, purpose in life and death attitudes of aging adults. In A. Tomer, G. T. Eliason, & P. T. Wong (Eds.), *Existential and Spiritual Issues in Death Attitudes* (pp. 139–158). Mahwah, NJ: Lawrence Erlbaum Associates.

Beyene, Y. (1992). Medical disclosure and refugees: Telling bad news to Ethiopian patients. *The Western Journal of Medicine, 157*, 328–332.

Blackhall, L. J., Murphy, S. T., Frank, G., Michel, V., & Azen, S. (1995). Ethnicity and attitudes toward patient autonomy. *Journal of the American Medical Association, 274*, 820–825.

Blazer, D. (1994). Epidemiology of late-life depression. In L. S. Schneider, C. F. Reynolds, B. D. Lebowitz, & A. J. Friedhoff (Eds.), *Diagnosis and Treatment of Depression in Late Life* (pp. 9–20). Washington, DC: American Psychiatric Press.

Boss, P. (1999). *Ambiguous Loss: Learning to Live With Unresolved Grief.* Cambridge, MA: Harvard University Press.

Burns, J. P., & Truog, R. D. (2007). Futility: A concept in evolution. *Chest, 132*, 1987–1993.

Caralis, P. V., Davis, B., Wright, K., & Marcial, E. (1993). The influence of ethnicity and race on attitudes toward advance directives, life-prolonging treatments, and euthanasia. *The Journal of Clinical Ethics, 4*, 155–165.

Caron, C. D., Griffith, J., & Arcand, M. (2005). End-of-life decision making in dementia: The perspective of family caregivers. *Dementia, 4*, 113–136.

Carr, D., & Khodyakov, D. (2007). End-of-life health care planning among young-old adults: An assessment of psychosocial influences. *Journal of Gerontology: Social Sciences, 62B*, S135–S141.

Carrese, J. A., & Rhodes, L. A. (1995). Western bioethics on the Navajo Reservation: Benefit or harm? *Journal of the American Medical Association, 274*, 826–829.

Centers for Disease Control and Prevention. (2003). *Characteristics of Hospice Care Discharges and Their Length of Service, United States, 2003.* Retrieved June 9, 2008, from: http://www.cdc.gov/nchs/pressroom/03facts/hospicecare.htm.

Centers for Disease Control/National Center for Health Statistics. (n.d.) *Leading Causes of Death, 1900–1998.* Retrieved June 2, 2008, from: http://www.cdc.gov/nchs/data/dvs/lead1900_98.pdf.

Cicirelli, V. G. (1997). Relationship of psychosocial and background variables to older adults' end-of-life decisions. *Psychology and Aging, 12*, 72–83.

Cohen-Mansfield, J. (2007). Advance directives. In S. Carmel, C. A. Morse, and F. M. Torres-Gil (Eds.), *Lessons in Aging from Three Nations, Volume II: The Art of Caring for Older Adults* (pp. 161–177). Amityville, NY: Baywood.

Connor, S. R., Elwert, F., Spence, C., & Christakis, N. A. (2007). Geographic variation in hospice use in the United States in 2002. *Journal of Pain and Symptom Management, 34*, 277–285.

Connor, S. R., Pyenson, B., Fitch, K., Spence, C., & Iwasaki, K. (2007). Comparing hospice and nonhospice patient survival among patients who die within a three-year window. *Journal of Pain and Symptom Management, 33*, 238–246.

Conwell, Y., Duberstein, P. R., & Caine, E. D. (2002). Risk factors for suicide in later life. *Biological Society, 52*, 193–204.

Conwell, Y., Duberstein, P. R., Cox, C., Herrmann, J., Forbes, N., & Caine, E. (1998). Age difference in behaviors leading to completed suicide. *American Journal of Geriatric Psychiatry, 6*, 122–126.

Corr, C. A., Nabe, C. M., & Corr, D. M. (2000). *Death and Dying, Life and Living* (3rd ed.). Boston, MA: Wadsworth.

Cruzan v. Director, Missouri Department of Health, 497 U.S. 261 (1990).

Degenholtz, H. B., Arnold, R. A., Meisel, A., & Lave, J. R. (2002). Persistence of racial/ethnic disparities in advance care plan documents among nursing home resident. *Journal of the American Geriatrics Society, 50*, 378–381.

Dieterle, J. M. (2007). Physician assisted suicide: A new look at the arguments. *Bioethics, 21*(3), 127–139.

Ditto, P. H. (2006). Self-determination, substituted judgment, and the psychology of advance decision making. In J. L. Werth, Jr., & D. Blevins (Eds.), *Psychosocial Issues Near the End of Life: A Resource for Professional Care Providers* (pp. 89–109). Washington, DC: American Psychological Association.

Duberstein, P. R., Conwell, Y., Seidlitz, L., Lyness, J. M., Cox, C., & Caine, E. D. (1999). Age and suicidal ideation in older depressed inpatients. *American Journal of Geriatric Psychiatry, 7*, 289–296.

DuBois, J. M. (1999). Non-heart-beating organ donation: A defense of the required determination of death. *Journal of Law, Medicine & Ethics, 27*, 126–136.

Dupuis, S. L. (2002). Understanding ambiguous loss in the context of dementia care: Adult children's perspectives. *Journal of Gerontological Social Work, 37*, 93–115.

Flory, J., Young-Xu, Y., Gurol, I., Levinsky, N., Ash, A., & Emanuel, E. (2004). Place of death: U.S. trends since 1980. *Health Affairs, 23*, 634–641.

Flint, A. J. (1994). Epidemiology and comorbidity of anxiety disorders in the elderly. *American Journal of Psychiatry, 151*, 640–649.

Ganzini, L., Nelson, H. D., Lee, M. A., Kraemer, D. F., Schmidt, T. A., & Delorit, M. A. (2001). Oregon physicians' attitudes about and experiences with end-of-life care since passage of the Oregon Death with Dignity Act. *Journal of the American Medical Association, 285*, 2363–2369.

Ganzini, L., Nelson, H. D., Schmidt, T. A., Kraemer, D. F., Delorit, M. A., & Lee, M. A. (2000). Physicians' experience with the Oregon Death with Dignity Act. *New England Journal of Medicine, 342*, 557–563.

Gilliland, G., & Fleming, S. (1998). A comparison of spousal anticipatory grief and conventional grief. *Death Studies, 22,* 541–569.

Goy, E. R., Jackson, A., Harvath, T. A., Miller, L. L., Delroit, M. A., & Ganzini, L. (2003). Oregon hospice nurses and social workers' assessment of physician progress in palliative care over the past 5 years. *Palliative and Supportive Care, 1,* 215–219.

Gruneir, A., Mor, V., Weitzen, S., Truchil, R., Teno, J., & Roy, J. (2007). Where people die: A multilevel approach to understanding influences on site of death in America. *Medical Care Research and Review, 64,* 351–378.

Hancock, K., Clayton, J. M., Parker, S. M., Walder, S., Butow, P. N., Carrick, S., et al. (2007). Discrepant perceptions about end-of-life communication: A systematic review. *Journal of Pain and Symptom Management, 34,* 190–200.

Hays, J. C., Galanos, A. N., Palmer, T. A., McQuoid, D. R., & Flint, E. P. (2001). Preference for place of death in a continuing care retirement community. *Gerontologist, 41,* 123–128.

Hermsen, M. A., & ten Have, H.A.M.J. (2002). Euthanasia in palliative care journals. *Journal of Pain and Symptom Management, 23,* 517–525.

Himmelfarb, S., & Murrell, S. A. (1984). The prevalence and correlates of anxiety symptoms in older adults. *Journal of Psychology, 116,* 159–167.

Hopp, F. P., & Duffy, S. A. (2000). Racial variations in end-of-life care. *Journal of the American Geriatrics Society, 48,* 658–663.

Hughes, D., & Kleepsies, P. (2001). Suicide in the medically ill. *Suicide and Life-Threatening Behavior, 31*(Spring Suppl.), 48–59.

In re Quinlan, 355 A.2d 647 (N.J., 1976).

Johansson, B., Allen-Burge, R., & Zarit, S. H. (1997). Self-reports on memory functioning in a longitudinal study of the oldest old: Relation to current, prospective, and retrospective performance. *Journal of Gerontology: Psychological Sciences, 52B,* P139–P146.

Kaut, K. P. (2006). End-of-life assessment within a holistic bio-psycho-social-spiritual framework. In J. L. Werth, Jr., & D. Blevins (Eds.), *Psychosocial Issues Near the End of Life: A Resource for Professional Care Providers* (pp. 111–135). Washington, DC: American Psychological Association.

Keenan, S. P., Busche, K. D., Chen, L. M., McCarthy, L., Inman, K. J., & Sibbald, W. J. (1997). A retrospective review of a large cohort of patients undergoing the process of withholding or withdrawal of life support. *Critical Care Medicine, 25*(8), 1324–1331.

Kennedy, G. J. (2000). *Geriatric Mental Health Care: A Treatment Guide for Health Professionals.* New York: The Guilford Press.

Kiely, D. K., Mitchell, S. L., Marlow, A., Murphy, K. M., & Morris, J. N. (2001). Racial and state differences in the designation of advance directives in nursing home residents. *Journal of the American Geriatrics Society, 49,* 1346–1352.

King, D. A., Heisel, M. J., & Lyness, J. M. (2005). Assessment and psychological treatment of depression in older adults with terminal or life-threatening illness. *Clinical Psychology: Science and Practice, 12,* 339–353.

King, D. A., Kim, S.Y.H., & Conwell, Y. (2000). Family matters: A social systems perspective on physician-assisted suicide and the older adult. *Psychology, Public Policy, and Law, 6,* 434–451.

Klessig, J. (1992). The effect of values and culture on life-support decisions. *The Western Journal of Medicine, 157*(3), 316–322.

Knight, B. G. (2006). Unique aspects of psychotherapy with older adults. In S. H. Qualls & B. G. Knight (2006). *Psychotherapy for Depression in Older Adults* (pp. 3–28). Hoboken, NJ: Wiley.

Knight, B. G., & McCallum, T. J. (1998). Adapting psychotherapeutic practice for older adults: Implications of the contextual, cohort-based, maturity, specific challenge model. *Professional Psychology: Research and Practice, 29,* 15–22.

Kochanek, K. D., Murphy, S. L., Anderson, R. N., & Scott, C. (2004). Deaths: Final data for 2002. *National Vital Statistics Reports, 53*(5). Hyattsville, MD: National Center for Health Statistics.

Kosmin, B. A., Mayer, E., & Keysar, A. (2001). *American Religious Identification Study.* New York: The Graduate Center of the City University of New York. Retrieved August 3, 2009, from: http://www.gc.cuny.edu/faculty/research_briefs/aris.pdf.

Kung, H. S., Hoyert, D. L., Xu, J., & Murphy, S. L. (2008). Deaths: Final data for 2005. *National Vital Statistics Report, 56*(10), 1–121.

Kwak, J., & Haley, W. E. (2005). Current research findings on end-of-life decision making among racially/ethnically diverse groups. *The Gerontologist, 45,* 634–641.

Lambert, K., Oxberry, S., Hulme, C. W., Saharia, K., Rigby, A. S., & Johnson, M. J. (2007). Knowledge and attitudes to opioids in palliative care patients. *Palliative Medicine, 21,* 721–722.

Lewis, M. M. (2007) End-of-life decisions for people with dementia: Issues in care and policy. In T. H. Lillie & J. L. Werth, Jr. (Eds.), *End-of-life Issues and Persons With Disabilities* (pp. 124–134). Austin, TX: PRO-ED, Inc.

Lunney, J. R., Lynn, J., & Hogan, C. (2002). Profiles of elderly Medicare decedents. *Journal of the American Geriatrics Society, 50,* 1108–1112.

MacDonald, W. L. (1998). The difference between Blacks' and Whites' attitudes toward voluntary euthanasia. *Journal for the Scientific Study of Religion, 37,* 411–426.

Materstvedt, L., & Kaasa, S. (2002). Euthanasia and physician-assisted suicide in Scandinavia—with a conceptual suggestion regarding international research in relation to the phenomena. *Palliative Medicine, 16,* 17–32.

McIntosh, J. L. (1992). Epidemiology of suicide in the elderly. In A. A. Leenaars, R. W. Maris, J. L. McIntosh, & J. Richman (Eds.), *Suicide and the Older Adult* (pp. 15–35). New York: Basic Books.

Mikkelsen, R. L., Middelboe, T., Pisinger, C., & Stage, K. B. (2004). Anxiety and depression in patients with chronic obstructive pulmonary disease (COPD). A review. *Nordic Journal of Psychiatry, 58,* 65–70.

Mitchell, J. L. (1998). Cross-cultural issues in the disclosure of cancer. *Cancer Practice, 6,* 153–159.

Morrison, M. F. (1998). Obstacles to doctor-patient communication at the end of life. In M. D. Steinberg & S. J. Younger (Eds.), *End-of-life Decisions: A Psychosocial Perspective* (pp. 109–136). Washington, DC: American Psychiatric Press.

Morrison, R. S., Zayas, L. H., Mulvihill, M., Baskin, S. A., & Meier, D. E. (1998). Barriers to completion of health care proxies: An examination of racial/ethnic differences. *Archives of Internal Medicine, 158,* 2493–2497.

Moye, J. (1999). Assessment of competency and decision making capacity. In P.A. Lichtenberg (Ed.), *Handbook of Assessment in Clinical Gerontology* (pp. 488–528). New York: Wiley.

Munn, J. C., Hanson, L. C., Zimmerman, S., Sloane, P. D., Mitchell, C. M. (2006). Is hospice associated with improved end-of-life care in nursing homes and assisted living facilities? *Journal of the American Geriatrics Society, 54,* 490–495.

Murray, S. A., Kendall, M., Grant, E., Boyd, K., Barclay, S., & Sheikh, A. (2007). Patterns of social, psychological, and spiritual decline toward the end of life in lung cancer and heart failure. *Journal of Pain and Symptom Management, 34,* 393–402.

National Center for Health Statistics. (2004). *Hospice Care Discharges.* Retrieved June 9, 2008, from: http://www.cdc.gov/nchs/data/nhhcsd/hospicecaredischarges00.pdf.

National Hospice and Palliative Care Organization (NHPCO). (2007). *NHPCO Facts and Figures: Hospice Care in America.* Retrieved June 1, 2008, from: http://www.nhpco.org/files/public/Statistics_Research/NHPCO_facts-and-figures_Nov2007.pdf.

Ogle, K. S., Mavis, B., & Wyatt, G. K. (2002). Physicians and hospice care: Attitudes, knowledge, and referrals. *Journal of Palliative Medicine, 5,* 85–92.

Oregon Department of Human Services. (2008). Summary of Oregon's Death with Dignity Act—2007. Retrieved June 9, 2008, from: http://oregon.gov/DHS/ph/pas/docs/year10.pdf.

O'Reilly, K. B. (2006, Nov. 6). Oregon nixes use of term "physician-assisted suicide." *AMNews.* Retrieved June 30, 2008, from: http://www.ama-assn.org/amednews/2006/11/06/prsc1106.htm.

Parker, S. M., Clayton, J. M., Hancock, K., Walder, S., Butow, P. N., Carrick, S., et al. (2007) A systematic review of prognostic/end-of-life communication with adults in the advanced stages of a life-limiting illness: Patient/caregiver preferences for the content, style, and timing of information. *Journal of Pain and Symptom Management, 34,* 81–93.

Patient Self-Determination Act of 1990, Publ. L. No. 101–508, 4306, 4751 of the Omnibus Reconciliation Act of 1990.

Pearlman, R. A., Hsu, C., Starks, H., Back, A. L., Gordon, J. R., Bharucha, A. J., et al. (2005). Motivations for physician-assisted suicide: Patient and family voices. *Journal of General Internal Medicine, 20,* 234–239.

Pessin, H., Rosenfeld, B., Burton, L., & Breitbart, W. (2003). The role of cognitive impairment in desire for hastened death: A study of patients with advanced AIDS. *General Hospital Psychiatry, 25,* 194–199.

Rando, T. A. (2000). *Clinical Dimensions of Anticipatory Mourning: Theory and Practice in Working With the Dying, Their Loved Ones and Their Caregivers.* Champaign, IL: Research Press.

Resnick, P. J., & Sorrentino, R. (2005). Forensic issues in consultation-liaison psychiatry. *Psychiatric Times, 23,* 1–2.

Richman, J. (1999). Psychotherapy with the suicidal elderly: A family-oriented approach. In M. Duffy (Ed.), *Handbook of Counseling and Psychotherapy With Older Adults* (pp. 650–661). New York: Wiley.

Ritchie, K., & Kildea, D. (1995). Is senile dementia "age-related" or "ageing-related"? Evidence from meta-analysis of dementia prevalence in the oldest old. *Lancet, 346,* 931–934.

Rosenfeld, B. (2004). *Assisted Suicide and the Right to Die: The Interface of Social Science, Public Policy, and Medical Ethics.* Washington, DC: American Psychological Association.

Sagara, M., & Pickett, M. (1998). Sociocultural influences and care of dying children in Japan and the United States. *Cancer Nursing, 21*, 274–281.

Sears, S. R., & Stanton, A. L. (2001). Physician-assisted dying: Review of issues for health psychologists. *Health Psychology, 20*(4), 302–310.

Sorger, B. M., Rosenfeld, B., Pessin, H., Timm, A. K., & Cimino, J. (2007). Decision-making capacity in elderly, terminally ill patients with cancer. *Behavioral Sciences and the Law, 25*, 393–404.

Sullivan, M. D. (2003). Hope and hopelessness at the end of life. *American Journal of Geriatric Psychiatry, 11*, 393–405.

Tang, S. T. (2003). When death is imminent: Where terminally ill patients with cancer prefer to die and why. *Cancer Nursing, 26*(3), 245–251.

Thorevska, N., Tilluckdharry, L., Tickoo, S., Havasi, A., Amoateng-Adjepong, Y., & Manthous, C. A. (2005). Patients' understanding of advance directives and cardiopulmonary resuscitation. *Journal of Critical Care, 20*, 26–34.

U.S. Census Bureau. (2001). *U.S. Census, 2000.* Washington, DC: Author.

U.S. Department of Health and Human Services. (1999). *Mental Health: A Report of the Surgeon General—Executive Summary.* Rockville, MD: U.S. Department of Health and Human Services, Substance Abuse and Mental Health Services Administration, Center for Mental Health Services, National Institutes of Health, National Institute of Mental Health.

U.S. Department of Health and Human Services. (2001). *National Strategy for Suicide Prevention: Goals and Objectives for Action.* Rockville, MD: Author.

Waern, M., Rubenowitz, E., Runeson, B., Skoog, I., Wilhelmson, K., & Allebeck, P. (2002). Burden of illness and suicide in elderly people: Case controlled study. *British Medical Journal, 321*, 1355–1358.

Wan, H., Sengupta, M., Velkoff, V. A., & DeBarros, K. A. (2005). 65+ in the United States: 2005. *U.S. Census Bureau, Current Population Reports.* Washington, DC: U.S. Government Printing Office.

Waters, C. M. (2001). Understanding and supporting African Americans' perspectives on end-of-life care planning and decision making. *Qualitative Health Research, 11*, 385–398.

Webb, M. (1997). *The Good Death: The New American Search to Reshape the End of Life.* New York: Bantam Books.

Werth, J. L., Jr., Gordon, J. R., & Johnson, R. R., Jr. (2002). Psychosocial issues near the end of life. *Aging and Mental Health, 6*, 402–412.

World Health Organization. (n.d.). *WHO Definition of Palliative Care.* Retrieved June 24, 2008, from: http://www.who.int/cancer/palliative/definition/en/.

Zarit, S. H., & Zarit, J. M. (1998). *Mental Disorders in Older Adults: Fundamentals of Assessment and Treatment.* New York: The Guilford Press.

CHAPTER 10

SUCCESSFUL AGING

Alissa Dark-Freudeman

As health care improves and life expectancy increases, people are living longer and extending their quality of life. With an increasing population of older adults, greater attention is being paid to the later half of life. Research focused on older adults examines a wide range of topics including physical and cognitive function, the importance of social relationships and roles, and the types of goals older adults are working toward achieving. Declines in cognitive and physical ability (Seeman et al., 1994) occur. Social relationships are trimmed (Carstensen, 1992) and goals are narrowed (Cross & Markus, 1991; Hooker, 1992). In the face of physical and cognitive decline, loss of friends and loved ones, and a narrowing of goals and interests, what does it mean to age successfully?

There are several answers to that question. This chapter reviews medical models, psychological models, and lay views of successful aging. Medical models focus on physical and mental functioning, promoting healthy lifestyles, and delaying the onset of disease or disability. Psychological models focus on how an older individual continues to achieve important goals, feel in control over life circumstances, and maintain a sense of self despite age-related changes in function. Lay views incorporate both medical and psychological aspects of successful aging but also emphasize the importance of contextual factors. Although these models each provide different answers regarding what it means to age successfully, by coming from different perspectives and focusing on different outcomes, scholarly approaches are not mutually exclusive but can be integrated to create a more complete, albeit complex picture of what it means to age successfully.

MEDICAL MODELS OF SUCCESSFUL AGING

As markers of success, medical models of successful aging have primarily focused on longevity and the absence of disease and disability. Success is viewed as a positive outcome that one can achieve through appropriate choices to manage both physical and mental health. The primary goal is to postpone or lessen the degree of age-related loss experienced in the later half of life. The minimum morbidity model (Fries, 1990) and the model of successful aging proposed by Rowe and Kahn (1987, 1998) represent examples of medical models of successful aging.

Minimum Morbidity Model

Fries (1990) defines successful aging as the compression of morbidity (time between the onset of disease and death). Although life expectancy has been increasing for both men and women, these increases are not infinite. According to Fries (1990), the peak of life expectancy is being reached. As increases in life expectancy slow, the goal is to remain healthy as long as possible by delaying the onset of chronic disease. Chronic diseases are in large part a result of life style. Individuals who are physically active and seek proper nutrition and regular preventative medical care generally fare better than those who do not. The result of postponing the onset of chronic disease is that older adults will spend as little time as possible disabled or diseased before death. This compression of morbidity increases quality of life for the individual and also lightens the burden on family, friends, and society (Fries, 1980).

For example, Hubert, Bloch, Oehlert, and Fries (2002) followed a group of older adults between 1986 and 1999. The authors found that older adults reporting two or more risk factors such as smoking, being overweight, or being sedentary were more likely to become disabled earlier in life. In contrast, those older adults with fewer risk factors experienced less overall disability. In addition, Wang, Ramey, Schettler, Hubert, and Fries (2002) examined a group of elderly runners over a 13-year period. The results indicate that runners had significantly lower levels of disability and mortality over the 13-year period compared to a control group of inactive or less active older adults. These results support the compression of morbidity hypothesis by showing that a healthy lifestyle can postpone the onset of disease and disability in the later half of life.

Certainly most older adults would prefer to minimize the time spent diseased or disabled, but for many this simply may not be possible. A large number of older adults deal with increasing losses in mobility or mental capacity. The time coping with such decline, however gradual, can span years, if not decades. Viewed in this light, medical advances have actually assisted in the expansion of morbidity to a certain degree, allowing older adults with multiple chronic diseases, ranging from arthritis, neuropathy, diabetes, and heart disease, to carry on with varying degrees of disease and disability. These individuals adapt to their conditions with the assistance of medications, walkers, nurses, insulin therapy, pace makers and the like. Should we view such older adults as aging unsuccessfully?

Rowe and Kahn

Rowe and Kahn (1987, 1998) define both usual and successful aging largely from a biomedical perspective. An individual is considered to undergo *usual aging* when he or she is functioning well, is at risk for disease or disability, and is experiencing a combination of both inevitable and modifiable losses. In contrast, Rowe and Kahn define *successful aging* as maintaining a low risk of disease and disability, maintaining high physical and mental functioning, and actively engaging with life by maintaining autonomy and adequate social support systems. The focus of this definition of successful aging is primarily on avoiding disease and decline by living a healthy life. Psychosocial factors are considered important mainly in relation to how they positively impact physical functioning. The authors point out that much of what is considered age-related loss of function is not actually related to advancing chronological age, but is related to problematic lifestyle habits such as poor nutrition and lack of physical activity. The major point is that the majority of adults can experience better aging if they make the correct lifestyle choices and take good care of themselves. Although such a definition is encouraging, the reality is that many adults fail to make such positive lifestyle choices.

Rowe and Kahn have received quite a bit of criticism over the years. Many researchers believe this definition of successful aging excludes the majority of seniors, many of whom may be facing and managing chronic health conditions such as arthritis, hypertension, or diabetes. Instead critics argue that success is granted only to a few exceptional seniors while the rest are, by default, considered failures. Kahn (2003) has acknowledged this "unintended consequence" and points out that we should not view aging as a dichotomous variable in which an individual either succeeds or fails, but rather look at successful aging as a process made up of multiple domains each on its own continuum. Some individuals will fare better or worse than others within each domain. Further, the authors have repeatedly acknowledged that many people do quite well adapting to life with disability or disease (Kahn, 2003; Rowe & Kahn, 1998).

The recommendations that Rowe and Kahn (1998) make regarding the components of successful aging are derived from the MacArthur Study of Successful Aging. The MacArthur Study of Successful Aging set out to examine how physical, cognitive, psychological, and social factors contribute to successful aging within a group of older adults over time. The study examined a sample of high functioning older adults, who began the study when they were between the ages of 70 to 79, and followed these individuals for approximately 7 years. Results from several different aspects of the study are described here.

With regard to physical function, Reuben, Judd-Hamilton, Harris, and Seeman (2003) examined the relationship between inflammatory markers and activity level. Chronic inflammation is believed to be related to disease, functional decline, and mortality. Efforts to reduce inflammation would potentially improve health and satisfaction with life. Results indicated that high levels of recreational activity, including house and yard work, were significantly associated with lower levels of inflammatory markers. In addition to these results, Seeman et al. (1994) found that declines in physical performance over time were predicted by several variables, including age, education, and health. Health included several factors such as the presence or absence of diabetes, weight, blood pressure, and peak expiratory flow. These results highlight the importance of physical activity in maintaining health throughout later life. Individuals who are more physically active report lower levels of inflammation, are less likely to suffer from diabetes, are less likely to be overweight, and have lower blood pressure and higher peak expiratory flow, indicating better lung function. It is clear that lifestyle choices impact physical health and ultimately the degree to which one ages successfully by objective measures of physical functioning.

Like physical functioning, cognitive functioning has also been extensively investigated by MacArthur researchers. For example, Chodosh, Kado, Seeman, and Karlamangla (2007) examined the relationship between cognitive performance and depression. Results indicated that a majority of the participants in the MacArthur Study of Successful Aging experienced cognitive decline over the 7-year period. Further, higher levels of depression were associated with greater decline in cognitive performance and greater likelihood of cognitive impairment over time. In addition to this, several factors have been found that predict cognitive decline. Albert and colleagues (1995) examined cognitive performance in older adults over a 2-year period. Education, strenuous activity, and pulmonary peak expiratory flow were all direct predictors of cognitive change over this period. These results highlight the interdependence of physical, cognitive, and psychological domains. Individuals who were less depressed and more physically active experienced less cognitive decline over time than those who were not. Physical activity not only influences physical health but also impacts cognitive functioning.

In addition to physical and cognitive ability, the MacArthur study also examined the impact of social and personality factors on successful aging. Gruenewald, Karlamangla, Greendale, Singer, and Seeman (2007) examined the relationship between feelings of usefulness to others, psychological well-being, and health behaviors. The authors found that older adults who felt less useful to others also reported lower levels of psychological well-being and lower levels of social integration and social activity. These individuals also engaged in fewer positive health behaviors, such as physical activity, and more negative health behaviors, such as smoking. In addition, individuals who reported that they never or rarely felt useful to others were more likely to experience increases in disability or to die during the 7-year follow-up, compared to individuals who reported that they frequently felt useful. Along these lines, Eizenman, Nesselroade, Featherman, and Rowe (1997) followed a group of older adults over 27 weeks to examine weekly variations in perceived control. Individuals who reported less variability in perceived control were significantly more likely to be living years later. Thus, perceiving oneself as in control is important for healthy living, as is stability of perceived control over time. The results indicate that both social and psychological factors directly impact cognitive and physical functioning in later life. Individuals who are less depressed experience lower levels of decline in cognitive ability over time. Individuals who are more engaged socially and feel useful to others are not only less likely to experience declines in physical function but also to engage in more positive health behaviors. Further, individuals who report stable levels of perceived control are more likely to be alive than those who report greater variability in perceived control over time.

The results from the MacArthur Study of Successful Aging, and the model of successful aging that was developed from it, provided researchers, health care professionals, and the community with a new understanding of the relationship between aging and health. Maintaining active engagement physically, cognitively, and socially can protect older adults from decline and disease that were once believed to be inevitable parts of the aging process. Although such a model has many positive implications, medical definitions of successful aging may be missing part of the picture. Certainly health is important to the individual and society. It is also important to understand how physical and mental health change with age and how negative changes can be avoided or reduced. However, for the majority of seniors, declines will occur, and adaptations to changes in ability and health have to be made. Although psychosocial factors such as control have been considered in the literature cited previously, medical models have typically not addressed how and why such adaptations are made and how such adaptations impact the psychological health of seniors.

Rapprochement Among Successful Aging Theories

Baltes and Carstensen (1996, 2003) have criticized outcome-oriented definitions of successful aging, such as those typically emphasized in medical models. First, such definitions of successful aging are considered to be too narrow, focusing on only one domain, such as health or well-being.

Instead, definitions of successful aging should be broader, more inclusive, and include many domains and many criteria for success. Next, these definitions define success as an outcome with rigid standards that one either succeeds or fails in attaining. For example, a certain level of health should not be a requirement or prerequisite for successful aging. Many older adults suffer from chronic diseases or varying levels of disability yet feel good about themselves and their lives. To consider these individuals as aging unsuccessfully would be inaccurate. Last, and most importantly, these definitions completely ignore the process of how an individual achieves success during a time of life when losses in ability or function become more frequent. As a consequence, they fail to explain why many older adults who are facing disease or disability still consider themselves to be aging successfully or why others, who by objective standards appear to be aging successfully, do not consider themselves to be.

In contrast to more outcome-oriented definitions of successful aging, Baltes and Carstensen (1996, 2003) define successful aging as a journey rather than a destination. The authors suggest a process-oriented approach in which attention is focused not on some objective standard but on how an individual adapts to the challenges of aging and actively pursues his or her goals. Under such a definition, older adults who achieve their goals are successful, no matter what those goals may be. Such an approach avoids the need to develop some standard set of criteria upon which all individuals should be measured. This approach allows the meaning of successful aging to become personalized so that success can include more than just physical health or independence. A process-oriented approach also recognizes that aging involves an increasingly complex relationship between gains and losses, with losses becoming more prevalent toward the later half of life. Recognizing that losses occur and that these losses impact the goals that older adults set for themselves and how they approach attaining these goals is an important part of understanding the aging process.

Several models have attempted to address these issues. We review these models in the following sections.

PSYCHOLOGICAL MODELS OF SUCCESSFUL AGING

Several models have been proposed to describe the psychological aspects of aging successfully. Psychological models emphasize the process of achieving success, what success means at more individualized levels, and how declines and failures must be managed. Three key theories discuss the adaptation process: the model of selective optimization with compensation proposed by Baltes and Baltes (1990), the life span theory of control proposed by Schulz and Heckhausen (1996), and the dual-process model of goal pursuit and goal adjustment proposed by Brandtstädter and Greve (1994). Each of these models are reviewed in detail here, and current research supporting these models is discussed.

Selective Optimization with Compensation

Baltes and Baltes (1990) propose a model of successful aging that recognizes what the authors consider fundamental aspects of aging. Seven propositions are outlined to describe these fundamental aspects. First, one must distinguish between normal, successful, and pathological aging processes. Second, substantial variability exists in how individuals age, such that no two individuals will age alike. Third, latent physical and cognitive reserves exist within each individual. These reserves can be activated to mitigate age-related declines in cognitive and physical ability. Fourth, there are limits to these reserves, although we may not yet know what those limits are. Fifth, age-related declines in ability can be ameliorated by experience, accumulated knowledge, and technology. Sixth, as we age, the balance between gains and losses shifts as losses begin to outnumber gains. Seventh, our self or identity is resilient throughout the life span, although some individuals are more resilient than others. Based on these propositions, a model of successful aging was developed.

Successful aging is defined as maintaining the ability to achieve goals despite age-related losses in physical and mental ability. The model of successful aging proposed to assist older adults with adapting to these age-related losses is called *selective optimization with compensation* (SOC). *Selection* is the process of reducing the number of domains an individual engages in. By focusing resources on fewer domains and adjusting expectations of what it means to be successful in those domains older adults can maintain feelings of efficacy and satisfaction. Goals can still be achieved within domains of personal importance. *Optimization* is the process of focusing more energy and time on selected domains so that performance can be the best it can possibly be given current constraints. *Compensation* refers to using external aids to make up for losses in ability. Such aids can be simple strategies such as making lists to assist a memory that is not as sharp as it once was, or technological devices such as using a pacemaker or scooter.

This model is considered a meta-model (Marsiske, Lang, Baltes, & Baltes, 1995). The three processes occur throughout the life span as individuals select important goals or activities, work hard to achieve them, and compensate for mismatches between abilities and demands. This model also accounts for differences among individuals and explains how people in very different circumstances can each consider themselves to be aging well. By focusing on what is important to one person and what goals he or she is trying to achieve, this model allows for individual definitions of successful aging.

Research on SOC has started to uncover how older adults manage age-related declines in meaningful domains and how SOC strategies relate to psychological well-being. For example, Freund and Baltes (1998) examined older adults between the ages of 72 and 102 who had participated in a previous longitudinal study. Increased age was associated with less SOC strategy use. However, greater use of SOC strategies was associated with greater satisfaction with age, higher levels of positive emotion, lower levels of agitation, and lower levels of loneliness. Optimization and compensation were strongly related to aging well, however, selection was not. This indicates that SOC does play a role protecting or enhancing psychological well-being in adulthood; however, as we reach the end of life, declines in physical and cognitive resources may limit the degree to which SOC strategies can effectively be put to use.

In addition to these results, Jopp and Smith (2006) examined the use of SOC strategies in older adults between the ages of 71 and 91. No differences were found between the young-old and old-old in reported use of SOC strategies or satisfaction with aging. Both groups of older adults used loss-based selection more then elective selection, indicating that selection occurs most often when it is perceived as necessary. Overall, SOC strategy use was significantly related to both available resources (including health and cognitive status, social support, and socioeconomic status) and to satisfaction with aging. The young-old were more satisfied with aging when more resources were available and when more SOC strategies were used. The old-old were also more satisfied with aging when more resources were available; however, the old-old with fewer resources benefited most from SOC strategy use.

The research on SOC has shown that SOC strategy use is important for older adults. Higher levels of SOC strategy use are associated with higher levels of positive psychological outcomes. Older adults may use SOC strategies differently depending on the perceived availability of resources; however, the use of SOC strategies is beneficial regardless of resource availability.

Life Span Theory of Control

Schulz and Heckhausen (1996) define successful aging in terms of acquiring and maintaining control throughout the life span. The life span theory of control posits that throughout life we are continually striking a balance between two types of control: primary control and secondary control. Primary control increases from birth through middle age, then decreases as individuals move into the later half of life. Primary control is externally oriented and involves action. Secondary control is internally oriented and involves cognitive and psychological processes. Secondary control assists individuals in their efforts to maintain primary control. To develop successfully at any age requires that both forms of control be utilized, however, preference is given to primary control in which the individual acts as an agent, directly working toward achieving goals. Secondary control is activated when abilities do not match demands or expectations. For example, a professional golfer who has started to experience pain and stiffness associated with arthritis may exert primary control by practicing more, taking joint supplements, and stretching. However, when he can no longer overcome the effects of arthritis, he can reframe what it means to be a golfer and continue playing in local senior tournaments or perhaps begin mentoring younger golfers. Once secondary control has been used to reframe a goal in this manner, primary control can be effectively engaged once again in pursuit of the revised goal.

The authors also distinguish between different types of primary and secondary control. Selective primary control involves the intentional investment of personal resources on a goal. For instance in the previous example, the golfer spends more time practicing in preparation for a tournament. Compensatory primary control involves using external resources to supplement ability. In this case, the golfer may begin to have difficulty walking the course so he starts to rely on a golf cart. Selective secondary control involves focusing internal resources toward a goal. This results in the value of a chosen goal being weighted more than the alternative goals that were not chosen, for example, mentoring a winner becomes more important than winning oneself. Compensatory secondary control involves the use of internal strategies such as comparing oneself to others who are performing worse or redefining what success means within a personally meaningful domain when facing declines in ability. For example, the golfer may compare his or her performance to other senior golfers who are performing worse, or he may decide that the goal of competing in tournaments is no longer as important as it once was and give up competing in tournaments altogether. Within this framework, successful aging involves developing and maintaining primary control over important life events despite declines in physical and cognitive ability.

Research by Brandtstädter (1989) has found that among middle-aged and older adults, personal development is seen as increasingly impacted by external factors that are beyond one's control (Brandtstädter, 1989; Brandtstädter & Baltes-Gotz, 1990). Although external factors are perceived to have a greater impact on development in later life, perceptions of personal control also increase (Brandtstädter & Baltes-Gotz, 1990) as both primary and secondary control increase over time. Further, lower levels of personal control over development are associated with greater levels of depression (Brandtstädter, 1989). In contrast, individuals reporting high levels of personal control also report greater satisfaction with life and are more optimistic (Brandtstädter & Baltes-Gotz, 1990; Lang & Heckhausen, 2001).

Age differences have also been found in the degree to which individuals report engaging in primary or secondary control (Wrosch, Heckhausen, & Lachman,

2000). Wrosch et al. found that older adults report using a greater degree of secondary control strategies, such as positive reappraisals and lowering aspirations, compared to younger adults. Older adults also report using the primary control strategy—persistence—more often than younger adults. In general, greater primary control is related to higher levels of subjective well-being for both younger and middle-aged adults but not for older adults. In contrast, greater secondary control (in the form of positive reappraisals) is related to higher subjective well-being for middle-aged and older adults. Lowering aspirations was related to lower levels of subjective well-being across all age groups (Wrosch et al., 2000). Thus, it appears that older adults implement a combination of control strategies to maintain well-being. Primary control in the form of persistence indicates that older adults continue to invest time and effort into the goals that are important to them. However, primary control is supplemented by recruiting secondary control strategies such as positive reappraisals that can be implemented when primary control is not working as well as it once was to achieve goals in meaningful domains.

Lang and Heckhausen (2001) examined the relationship between perceived control and well-being among individuals between the ages of 20 to 90 over time. For younger, middle-aged, and older adults, higher levels of perceived control over development were associated with higher levels of life satisfaction. Perceived control was also associated with less frequent negative affect for younger and middle-aged adults but not for older adults. Next, the authors conducted a follow-up interview with older adults from the first interview. The results indicated that higher levels of perceived control during the first interview were associated with higher levels of life satisfaction 6 months later. Further, a strong sense of control positively impacted well-being only when individuals reported that positive events had occurred in their lives and that these events were personally caused. Higher levels of perceived control are not only related to higher levels of life satisfaction but also predict higher levels of life satisfaction over time. In addition, higher levels of perceived control can have positive influences on well-being when an individual feels like he or she is actively creating positive outcomes in his or her own life.

Overall, research has shown that there are age-related differences in primary and secondary control. Older adults acknowledge that external factors begin to exert greater influence on their lives. As a consequence, older adults report that they implement secondary control strategies more frequently than younger and middle-age adults. Certain secondary control strategies were associated with greater well-being, while certain secondary control strategies were not. Although the importance of secondary control increases, maintaining primary control is also important as individuals move through life. Specifically maintaining perceived control is related to greater satisfaction with life and higher levels of psychological well-being among older adults.

Dual-Process Model of Goal Pursuit and Goal Adjustment

Brandtstädter and Greve (1994) define successful aging as maintaining a positive and continuous sense of self throughout life. This becomes increasingly more difficult during the later half of life when valued personal traits may be on the decline and personally meaningful goals become more difficult to attain. Thus, a positive and continuous sense of self is maintained via the dual-process model of goal pursuit and goal adjustment. Goal pursuit and goal adjustment involve two main processes: assimilation and accommodation.

Assimilation requires external actions that assist individuals in pursuing personally meaningful goals. Assimilation includes several processes. First, assimilation includes the various activities an individual directly undertakes to achieve personally meaningful goals. Next, assimilation involves taking corrective action when an individual perceives that he or she is no longer on track to achieve a goal. Third, assimilation includes compensatory activities used to overcome declines in ability or gaps between ability and task demands. Last, assimilation includes actively participating in activities that confirm an individual's sense of self. For example, if an individual views herself as politically active, she will most likely vote regularly in local and national elections and volunteer for political campaigns or organizations to reinforce this part of her identity.

In contrast to assimilation, *accommodation* requires internal action and involves individual letting go of goals that are no longer within reach. Accommodation becomes necessary when assimilation is no longer working or when assimilation requires too much time or energy to be efficient. Accommodation includes several processes. First, an individual may devalue and disengage from goals that are no longer attainable. Simply put, an individual decides that a goal is no longer important and stops actively pursuing it. Next, an individual might reappraise what it means to meet a specific goal by adjusting standards of success within a personally meaningful domain. This flexibility allows for continued success in a domain of personal importance. Last, individuals may engage in self-enhancing comparisons. For example, an aging tennis player who notices a decline in his speed and reaction time may compare his ability to that of a friend who is performing more poorly than he is. This helps him to maintain positive feelings about his own ability even in the face of noticeable decline.

A great deal of research has examined how assimilative and accommodative coping strategies impact psychological well-being and how individuals of different ages implement these strategies to different degrees. For example,

Brandtstädter and Baltes-Gotz (1990) observed an age-related shift from assimilative to accommodative coping mechanisms indicating that older individuals engage in less tenacious goal pursuit (TGP) and instead engage in greater flexible goal adjustment (FGA) than middle-aged and younger adults. Further, both TGP and FGA predicted the absence of depression. A study by Brandtstädter and Rothermund (1994) examined the protective effects of accommodative coping strategies on feelings of control. They found support for the protective effect of accommodative processes. Specifically, losses of perceived control within a specific domain have less impact on one's general sense of control if the loss is accompanied by a reduction of the personal importance given to the goal. Brandtstädter and Renner (1990) also found that individuals engage in less TGP and greater FGA with increasing age. Higher levels of TGP and FGA were associated with lower levels of depression and greater life satisfaction. In addition, individuals high on both TGP and FGA reported experiencing fewer developmental deficits and greater developmental gains.

To examine changes in assimilation and accommodation over time, Rothermund and Brandtstädter (2003) followed a group of middle-aged and older adults over a 4-year period. The authors found that compensatory efforts increased up through age 70 and then abruptly decreased. The youngest cohort reported an increase in compensatory efforts over time; however, the older cohorts showed a decrease in compensatory efforts and an increase in perceived deficits and losses. Contentment did not show a significant change among any of the cohorts. The authors also examined how the impact of deficits and losses differed for individuals who maintained, increased, or decreased personal standards. Increases in deficits and losses were associated with greater declines in contentment among adults who increased or maintained personal standards than those who decreased them. Thus, it appears that perceived deficits in ability are associated with declines in assimilative processes. At some point compensation may no longer be efficient or even possible. Accommodative processes, on the other hand, act as a buffer. Individuals who did not engage in accommodation but instead maintained or increased their standards were less content over time. In contrast, the individuals who decreased their standards to be more in line with their current abilities were more content over time. This highlights the importance of accommodative coping mechanisms for maintaining both psychological well-being and contentment in later life.

Assimilative and accommodative coping strategies have also been examined in middle-aged and older adults seeking vision rehabilitation services (Boerner, 2004). Higher levels of assimilative and accommodative coping were associated with lower levels of depression and social dysfunction. The more participants reported using either coping mode, the less mental health problems they reported. The impact of accommodative coping on mental health was related to both age and level of disability. Accommodative coping was most effective for middle-aged adults who reported high levels of disability; however, for older adults, accommodative coping was beneficial no matter the level of disability (Boerner, 2004). Making adjustments directly in the form of assimilation and indirectly in the form of accommodation are important components of maintaining well-being when faced with loss in ability. In this case, individuals with vision impairments benefited from using both assimilation and accommodation. However, individuals facing greater impairment benefit most from accommodation strategies.

The psychological models of successful aging attempt to fill a gap left by the medical models of successful aging. Psychological models focus on how individuals continue to be agents of their own development often in spite of declines in physical, cognitive, and social resources. The model of selection with optimization and compensation (Baltes & Baltes, 1990) focuses on how individuals continue to meet their goals throughout the life span in the face of mismatches or declines in abilities or resources. The life span theory of control (Schulz & Heckhausen, 1996) focuses on how individuals maintain control over their life and their development in the face of increased mismatches or declines in abilities or resources. The dual-process model of goal pursuit and goal adjustment (Brandtstädter & Greve, 1994) focuses on how individuals maintain a sense of self and sense of purpose by continually renegotiating abilities and demands in the face of mismatches or declines in abilities or resources. All of these models seek to answer the following questions: How do older adults cope with loss of ability or loss of function? How do older adults redefine their goals to maintain a sense of purpose and agency? To answer these questions, these models look at the ways in which older adults compensate both directly and indirectly for loss and what types of goals older adults are trying to achieve. Further, all three models reach similar conclusions. Compensating for loss of ability and loss of function protects mental health. Older adults who work harder to achieve the goals that matter most to them are more satisfied with life. Older adults who adjust their goals or reframe what it means to be successful within important domains report higher levels of well-being and contentment. Learning to adapt to loss and continuing to use the skills and resources one has is beneficial.

The Limits of Compensation

Aging involves adaptation to loss. Older adults cope with the loss of friends and family and with the loss of physical and mental capacity. Adapting to loss is challenging. The psychosocial models presented previously emphasize the benefits of compensation; however, the presence of compensatory activities can often be the result of an underlying disease that has slowly started to impact physical or mental ability. Thus, compensatory actions are often a double-edged sword. On the one hand, compensation allows a goal to be achieved. On the other hand, compensation inevitably means that systems are not functioning as well as they used to.

Research in several areas, most notably the fields of neuroscience and physical rehabilitation underscore the fact that compensation is often a sign of impending decline, disease, or disability. Compensation occurs when systems are no longer functioning efficiently. For example, Verbrugge and Jette (1994) outline a comprehensive model of the disablement process. Pathology creates impairment, which in turn creates functional limitations, which may eventually lead to disability. When functional limitations occur, extraindividual and intraindividual processes are recruited to compensate for changes in ability. Extraindividual processes include seeking physical therapy, using equipment such as walkers or wheelchairs, and asking for personal assistance; intraindividual processes include things such as cognitive adaptation and changing the types, frequency, and duration of the activities engaged in. Greater attention is being paid to functional limitations and the intra- and extraindividual processes used to manage losses. Such compensatory activities provide insight into how declines in ability impact everyday life and lead to greater impairment. Some researchers refer to this intermediate stage as preclinical disability (Fried et al., 1996).

Preclinical disability occurs when individuals report that they do not have any difficulty completing a task but that they have changed the way in which they perform the task. These performance modifications occur to compensate for decreases in physical ability (Fried et al., 1996; Fried, Young, Rubin, & Bandeen-Roche, 2001). For example, an individual is able to walk up a flight of stairs, reports having no difficulty doing so, but uses the hand rail when he or she did not used to do so. These modifications or compensatory strategies are generally recognized "as something healthy people do not normally do" (Weiss, Hoenig, & Fried, 2007, p. 1218). Self-reported preclinical disability has been shown to predict disability independently of other risk factors and also predicts future disability as well as actual tests of physical performance (Fried et al., 1996; Fried et al., 2001; Manini, Cook, VanArnam, Marko, & Ploutz-Snyder, 2006; Wolinsky, Miller, Andresen, Malmstrom, & Miller, 2005). For example, research has shown that self-reported modification of walking a half mile and climbing a flight of stairs was associated with actual declines in walking speed, strength, and balance. Further, individuals reporting preclinical declines were at higher risk for becoming disabled over an 18-month period (Fried et al., 2001).

Research on older drivers is another area in which modifications occur to compensate for age-related losses in vision, hearing, and reaction time. Ruechel and Mann (2005) examined driving behavior of older adults. Most common adjustments included avoiding driving at night, avoiding specific areas because of traffic, avoiding interstates, and avoiding driving in the rain.

Half of the participants reported driving less than they did 5 years ago, and half anticipated making additional changes to their driving habits within the next 5 years. This reduction of driving is consistent with a study showing a reduction in community mobility with increased age as older adults leave home less frequently (Hendrickson & Mann, 2005). Although driving less is a way to manage age-related declines in abilities that impact driving ability, the majority of older adults reported that such changes impact their lives negatively. In these instances, leaving home less frequently and feeling less independent are negative consequences of compensatory behavior.

Compensation is an important strategy that allows older adults to cope with declines in both physical and cognitive abilities. Although compensation has many positive psychological benefits, compensation can also be indicative of disease processes that are slowly unfolding over the later half of life. Still the point remains that successful aging involves learning to cope with changes as they come along. With advancing age, we are more likely to experience changes in ability. Whether such changes require compensation in the form of using a hand rail or walker, if a person still gets from one place to the next, they are meeting their goals. Finding new ways to achieve personally meaningful goals despite these changes is successful aging at the most fundamental level.

SUCCESSFUL AGING ACCORDING TO OLDER ADULTS

In addition to the medical and psychological theories discussed previously, researchers have started to look beyond what physicians and psychologists define as successful aging and have turned their attention toward what older adults themselves define as success. Several approaches have been utilized to examine lay attitudes about successful aging, including: open-ended questionnaires, older adult rankings of the relative importance of the components of successful aging that have been identified in the successful aging literature, and focus groups in which older adults talk freely about what it means to age successfully. The following section reviews current research examining lay attitudes about successful aging using each of these methods. Not surprisingly, there is some overlap between what older adults and researchers define as successful aging. For example, physical and cognitive functions rank highly on both lists. Even so, some interesting differences are apparent.

Some researchers have examined how health status relates to successful aging by comparing the degree to which older adults feel they are aging successfully with current self-reported health. For example, Strawbridge and Wallhagen (2003) examined a group of older adults with three goals in mind. First, they examined the proportion of individuals considering themselves to be aging successfully; next, they examined the characteristics of these individuals; and last, they examined how the presence or absence of chronic conditions impacted self-ratings of successful aging. In general, about half of the participants considered themselves to be aging successfully. Participants who were younger, reported fewer chronic conditions, and had higher self-rated health were more likely to rate themselves as aging successfully. In contrast, only 17% of the participants with mobility impairments described themselves as successfully aging. The results support the importance of not only physical health, but mobility as an indicator of successful aging among older adults. These results indicate that as the incidence of chronic conditions increases, the likelihood of considering oneself successfully aging decreases. However, the presence or absence of chronic conditions is not the only determinant of whether an older adult rates himself as successful. Interestingly, a third of the participants with chronic health conditions rated themselves as successfully aging, while a third of participants without any chronic conditions rated themselves as unsuccessful. The authors point out that these individuals may hold the key to understanding how older adults view the aging process and why some individuals who, by objective standards, appear to be aging well do not consider themselves to be aging successfully.

Similarly, Bowling (2006) examined definitions of successful aging among a group of British seniors. Participants were first asked to define successful aging using an open-ended format. Participants were also asked to rate their own aging as successful or not. The majority of participants (76%) rated themselves as aging well. Two-thirds of the participants defined successful aging in terms of health and mobility. Half defined it in terms of mental or psychological health. Other aspects of successful aging frequently mentioned included an active social life, adequate finances, positive social relationships, and a safe neighborhood. Although the majority of participants included health and mobility as important components of successful aging, defining successful aging in terms of health was not related to health status. These results are consistent with results from Strawbridge and Wallhagen (2003), which showed that the presence or absence of chronic health conditions does not necessarily predict whether an older adult considered himself to be aging successfully or not. Clearly, good health is only part of the picture.

Other researchers have examined how older adults rate traditional definitions or components of successful aging. For example, in another study, Strawbridge, Wallhagen, and Cohen (2002) compared two definitions of successful aging: a subjective definition and the definition proposed by Rowe and Kahn (1998). First, participants were asked to rate how strongly they agreed with the following statement: "I am aging successfully (or aging well)." Next, using the Rowe and Kahn model of successful aging (1998), the authors defined successful aging using three criteria: absence of disease, disability, and risk factors such as smoking or obesity; maintaining physical and mental functions; and active engagement with life (including productivity

and social contact). Half of the participants rated themselves as aging successfully. However, when using the Rowe and Kahn criteria, only 18.8% of
these individuals were considered to be aging successfully. Comparing the
self-ratings to the Rowe and Kahn ratings, almost 37% of the people aging
successfully, according to the Rowe and Kahn criteria, did not consider
themselves to be aging well. Further, 47% of those not aging successfully,
according to these criteria, actually considered themselves to be aging
well. These results highlight the importance of subjective definitions of
successful aging and how there may be more to how success is defined at
an individual level.

Phelan, Anderson, LaCroix, and Larson (2004) also examined personal
views about successful aging in comparison to standard definitions of successful aging among two groups of older adults: Japanese Americans and
white Americans both residing in Washington. Overall, 90% of the participants reported thinking about aging successfully some time in their past.
Further, 60% of participants said that their thoughts about aging successfully had changed over time. Both groups rated the importance of 20 items
that were taken from the successful aging literature. Overall, both groups
rated the same 13 items as highly important. Items related to physical health
and function, mental health, and social health were viewed as important by
over 75% of both groups of participants. The only difference between the
groups was that over 75% of the white American participants also included
"Continuing to learn new things" as an important part of successful aging.
Items that were not highly important included longevity, influencing others,
and working.

Knight and Ricciardelli (2003) interviewed a group of older adults living
in Melbourne, Australia, to examine both personal definitions of successful
aging, as well as ratings of traditional definitions of successful aging. Older
adults were asked open-ended questions such as, "What do you think successful aging is?" or "What do you think it means to age successfully?" Major
themes were identified via content analysis. Eight themes emerged as important: health, activity, personal growth, happiness/contentment, relationships,
independence, appreciation/value of life, and longevity. Approximately 50%
of participants mentioned health and activity as aspects of successful aging.
Next, they presented older adults with definitions of successful aging pulled
from successful aging literature. Participants were asked to rate 10 components on a scale from 0 (not important) to 10 (most important). Participants
rated the following items: health, happiness, mental capacity, adjustment, life
satisfaction, physical activity, close personal relationships, social activity, sense
of purpose, and withdrawal. Although 9 of the 10 items received mean ratings
of 7 or higher, the most highly rated items were health, happiness, and mental
capacity. The least important items were social activity, sense of purpose, and
withdrawal. Withdrawal was the least important with a mean rating of 4.80.

Last, but certainly not least, researchers have also examined how older adults define successful aging by conducting in-depth interviews or focus groups in an effort to fully capture their thoughts and experiences. Such approaches provide insight into how older adults view the aging process, what domains are most important to older adults, and how adaptations to decline occur. For example, Bryant, Corbett, and Kutner (2001) interviewed a group of older adults in an effort to identify the main components of healthy aging. A model of healthy aging was developed based on interview responses. According to the authors, the main component of healthy aging was having something meaningful to *go and do*. Thus, health is not defined as the absence or presence of disease or disability but rather as the ability to find meaning in life by actively participating in it. This definition of health was supported by several other factors, including ability, attitude, and social resources. Ability included physical health, mobility, vision, mental function, and independence. Resources included adequate social support from friends and family and health care providers. Attitude was one of the most important components of healthy aging and included feelings of control, efficacy and esteem, a focus on others rather than oneself, keeping problems in perspective, personality, and for some, faith. These results highlight the importance of actively engaging in life and maintaining a positive attitude.

In a similar approach, Reichstadt, Depp, Palinkas, Folsom, and Jeste (2007) also utilized focus groups to ask older adults how they define successful aging and what they believe the necessary components of successful aging are. The authors identified 33 categories that resulted in 4 main themes: attitude/adaptation, security/stability, health/wellness, and engagement/stimulation. A positive attitude was seen as key to aging well; a positive attitude included the ability to recognize limitations and adapt to change. Participants also mentioned financial resources, knowing that they would be taken care of, and having adequate social support available. Health and wellness were mentioned frequently, but not everyone felt that good health was a prerequisite for successful aging. Last, participants mentioned that keeping active was essential to aging well. Activity included physical, mental, and social activities. The participants also noted that many of these themes support or compensate for one another. For example, a positive attitude was believed to compensate for failing health. Thus, the relationships between components of successful aging are not static and should not be considered in isolation. Rather, the complex relationships between domains should be examined as a whole to fully understand how an individual moves through the later half of life successfully and how losses in one domain may negatively or positively impact other domains of importance to the individual.

The results of research examining older adults' perceptions of successful aging show that the views older adults have are in line with both medical and psychological models of successful aging. Older adults view physical and mental health as important components of success. However, older adults report that remaining active or engaged is also important, along with maintaining a positive attitude. Interestingly, a positive attitude includes feelings of control and efficacy as well as being able to recognize limitations and adapt to change. Examining how older adults define success is an important part of developing a comprehensive model of successful aging. Current research on the opinions of older adults suggests that combining medical and psychological models of successful aging may be worthwhile. Such an approach will allow the complexities associated with aging and adaptation to age-related losses to be fully captured.

GENERAL CONCLUSIONS

Medical models focus on how mental and physical health can be maintained throughout life. Such models focus on more objective indicators of success. Through these models, society defines what successful aging should look like and prescribes ways in which we can all hope to age as successfully as possible by making sound lifestyle choices. From this perspective, losses in ability and function can be mitigated or avoided altogether if we stay physically and mentally active, seek proper nutrition, and receive regular preventative medical care.

Psychological models of successful aging attempt to define the process of successful aging. Such models focus on how we maintain a sense of control and a sense of self throughout the life span and how personal goals change over time as older adults are confronted with changes in physical, cognitive, and social resources. Psychological models allow success to be defined at the individual level. From this perspective, successful aging is the ability to maintain goals, personal control, and a sense of self by continually finding meaning and purpose in life despite an increase in loss of function.

In contrast, lay views of successful aging indicate that older adults define successful aging as a multifaceted process that includes elements from both psychological and medical models. For example, older adults value physical health and mobility, although these are not prerequisites for successful aging. Older adults often focus more generally on being active, which may or may not require high physical capability; this depends on the type of activities one emphasizes. Older adults also understand the critical importance of compensating for losses that occur and maintaining a positive attitude. Further, some older adults who are objectively healthy report that they are not aging well, whereas others who are facing chronic disease or disability feel like they are aging successfully. Such examples illustrate that aging well is a subjective experience that researchers do not fully understand.

Tapping into that more subjective experience represents a challenge. Variations in individual understandings of success could be due to variations in social comparison processes, for example, whether the individual evaluates himself in relation to age peers or his younger self. Or perhaps these variations are due to individual differences in life goals, for example, our understanding of successful aging for Janet, who most values her physical skills, may be different than our understanding of successful aging for Anne, whose intellectual acumen is central to how she perceives herself. Thus, we may need to first identify the key life goals of the individual before we can determine whether that individual is coping well. A modification of empirical approach might have heuristic value, that is, less emphasis on specific medical conditions, or specific compensatory mechanisms per se, and more emphasis on individual domains of value. From this perspective, the person who is aging successfully is the person whose medical status and psychological coping skills allow for that individual to effectively pursue a set of daily activities that have personal importance. Older adults are experiencing what it means to age, to lose ability, to compensate for loss, and to keep moving on. Incorporating the experiences and opinions of older adults into current definitions of successful aging may help provide a richer and more meaningful understanding of the aging process and what it means to age gracefully.

REFERENCES

Albert, M. S., Jones, K., Savage, C. R., Berkman, L., Seeman, T., Blazer, D., et al. (1995). Predictors of cognitive change in older persons: MacArthur studies of successful aging. *Psychology and Aging, 10*, 578–589.

Baltes, P. B., & Baltes, M. M. (1990). Psychological perspectives on successful aging: The model of selective optimization with compensation. In P. B. Baltes & M. M. Baltes (Eds.) *Successful Aging: Perspectives from the Behavioral Sciences* (pp. 1–34). New York: Cambridge University Press.

Baltes, M. M., & Carstensen, L. L. (1996). The process of successful ageing. *Ageing and Society, 16*, 397–422.

Baltes, M. M., & Carstensen, L. L. (2003). The process of successful aging: Selection, optimization, and compensation. In U. M. Staudinger & U. Lindenberger (Eds.), *Understanding Human Development: Dialogues With Lifespan Psychology* (pp. 81–104). Norwell, MA: Kluwer Academic Publishers.

Boerner, K. (2004). Adaptation to disability among middle-aged and older adults: The role of assimilative and accommodative coping. *Journal of Gerontology, 59B*, P35–P42.

Bowling, A. (2006). Lay perceptions of successful aging: Findings from a national survey of middle aged and older adults in Britain. *European Journal of Ageing, 3*, 123–136.

Brandtstädter, J. (1989). Personal self-regulation of development: Cross-sequential analyses of development-related control beliefs and emotions. *Developmental Psychology, 25*, 96–108.

Brandtstädter, J., & Baltes-Gotz, B. (1990). Personal control over development and quality of life perspectives in adulthood. In P. B. Baltes & M. M. Baltes (Eds.),

Successful Aging: Perspectives from the Behavioral Sciences. Cambridge, UK: Cambridge University Press.

Brandtstädter, J., & Greve, W. (1994). The aging self: Stabilizing and protective processes. *Developmental Review, 14,* 52–80.

Brandtstädter, J., & Renner, G. (1990). Tenacious goal pursuit and flexible goal adjustment: Explication and age-related analysis of assimilative and accommodative strategies of coping. *Psychology and Aging, 5,* 58–67.

Brandtstädter, J., & Rothermund, K. (1994). Self-percepts of control in middle and later adulthood: Buffering losses by rescaling goals. *Psychology and Aging, 9,* 265–273.

Bryant, L. L., Corbett, K. K., & Kutner, J. S. (2001). In their own words: A model of healthy aging. *Social Science and Medicine, 53,* 927–941.

Carstensen, L. L. (1992). Social and emotional patterns in adulthood: Support for the socioemotional selectivity theory. *Psychology and Aging, 7,* 331–338.

Chodosh, J., Kado, D. M., Seeman, T. E., & Karlamangla, A. S. (2007). Depressive symptoms as a predictor of cognitive decline: The MacArthur studies of successful aging. *American Journal of Geriatric Psychiatry, 15,* 406–415.

Cross, S., & Markus, H. (1991). Possible selves across the life span. *Human Development, 34,* 230–255.

Eizenman, D. R., Nesselroade, J. R., Featherman, D. L., & Rowe, J. W. (1997). Intraindividual variability in perceived control in an older sample: The MacArthur successful aging studies. *Psychology and Aging, 12,* 489–502.

Freund, A. M., & Baltes, P. B. (1998). Selection, optimization, and compensation as strategies of life management: Correlations with subjective indicators of successful aging. *Psychology and Aging, 13,* 531–543.

Fried, L. P., Bandeen-Roche, K., Williamson, J. D., Prasada-Rao, P., Chee, E., Tepper, S., et al. (1996). Functional decline in older adults: Expanding methods of ascertainment. *Journals of Gerontology, 51A,* M206–M214.

Fried, L. P., Young, Y., Rubin, G., & Bandeen-Roche, K. (2001). Self-reported preclinical disability identifies older women with early declines in performance and early disease. *Journal of Clinical Epidemiology, 54,* 889–901.

Fries, J. F. (1980). Aging, natural death, and the compression of morbidity. *New England Journal of Medicine, 303,* 130–135.

Fries, J. F. (1990). Medical perspectives upon successful aging. In P. B. Baltes & M. M. Baltes (Eds.), *Successful Aging: Perspectives from the Behavioral Sciences* (pp. 35–49). New York: Cambridge University Press.

Gruenewald, T. L., Karlamangla, A. S., Greendale, G. A., Singer, B. H., & Seeman, T. E. (2007). Feelings of usefulness to others, disability, and mortality in older adults: The MacArthur study of successful aging. *Journal of Gerontology, 62B,* P28–P37.

Hendrickson, C. C., & Mann, W. C. (2005). Changes over time in community mobility of elders with disabilities. *Physical and Occupational Therapy in Geriatrics, 23,* 75–89.

Hooker, K. (1992). Possible selves and perceived health in older adults and college students. *Journal of Gerontology, 47,* P85–P95.

Hubert, H. B., Bloch, D. A., Oehlert, J. W., & Fries, J. F. (2002). Lifestyle habits and compression of morbidity. *Journal of Gerontology, 57A,* M347–M351.

Jopp, D., & Smith, J. (2006). Resources and life-management strategies as determinants of successful aging: On the protective effect of selection, optimization and compensation. *Psychology and Aging, 21,* 253–265.

Kahn, R. L. (2003) Successful aging: Intended and unintended consequences of a concept. In L. W. Poon, S. H. Gueldner, & B. M. Sprouse (Eds.), *Successful Aging and Adaptation With Chronic Diseases* (pp. 55–69). New York: Springer.

Knight, T., & Ricciardelli, L. A. (2003). Successful aging: Perceptions of adults between 70 and 101 years. *International Journal of Aging and Human Development, 56,* 223–245.

Lang, F. R., & Heckhausen, J. (2001). Perceived control over development and subjective well-being: Differential benefits across adulthood. *Journal of Personality and Social Psychology, 81,* 509–523.

Manini, T. M., Cook, S. B., VanArnam, T., Marko, M., & Ploutz-Snyder, L. (2006). Evaluating task modification as an objective measure of functional limitation: Repeatability and comparability. *Journal of Gerontology, 61A,* 718–725.

Marsiske, M., Lang, F. R., Baltes, P. B., & Baltes, M. M. (1995). Selective optimization with compensation: Life-span perspectives on successful human development. In R. A. Dixon & L. Backman (Eds.), *Compensating for Psychological Deficits and Declines: Managing Losses and Promoting Gains* (pp. 35–79). Mahwah, NJ: Lawrence Erlbaum Associates.

Phelan, E. A., Anderson, L. A., LaCroix, A. Z., & Larson, E. B. (2004). Older adults' views of "successful aging"—How do they compare with researchers' definitions? *Journal of American Geriatrics Society, 52,* 211–216.

Reichstadt, J., Depp, C. A., Palinkas, L. A., Folsom, D. P., & Jeste, D. V. (2007). Building blocks of successful aging: A focus group study of older adults' perceived contributions to successful aging. *American Journal of Geriatric Psychiatry, 15,* 194–201.

Reuben, D. B., Judd-Hamilton, L., Harris, T. B., & Seeman, T. E. (2003). The associations between physical activity and inflammatory markers in high-functioning older persons: MacArthur studies of successful aging. *Journal of the American Geriatrics Society, 51,* 1125–1130.

Rothermund, K., & Brandtstädter, J. (2003). Coping with deficits and losses in later life: From compensatory action to accommodation. *Psychology and Aging, 18,* 896–905.

Rowe, J. W., & Kahn, R. L. (1987). Human aging: Usual and successful. *Science, 237,* 143–149.

Rowe, J. W., & Kahn, R. L. (1998). *Successful Aging: The MacArthur Foundation Study.* New York: Pantheon Books.

Ruechel, S., & Mann, W. C. (2005). Self-regulation of driving by older persons. *Physical and Occupational Therapy in Geriatrics, 23,* 91–101.

Schulz, R., & Heckhausen, J. (1996). A life span model of successful aging. *American Psychologist, 51,* 702–714.

Seeman, T. E., Charpentier, P. A., Berkman, L. F., Tinetti, M. E., Guralnik, J. M., Albert. M., et al. (1994). Predicting changes in physical performance in a high-functioning elderly cohort: MacArthur studies of successful aging. *Journal of Gerontology, 49,* 97–108.

Strawbridge, W. J., & Wallhagen, M. I. (2003). Self-rated successful aging: Correlates and predictors. In L. W. Poon, S. H. Gueldner, & B. M. Sprouse (Eds.), *Successful Aging and Adaptation With Chronic Diseases* (pp. 1–24). New York: Springer.

Strawbridge, W. J., Wallhagen, M. I., & Cohen, R. D. (2002). Successful aging and well-being: Self-rated compared with Rowe and Kahn. *The Gerontologist, 42,* 727–733.

Verbrugge, L. M., & Jette, A. M. (1994). The disablement process. *Social Science and Medicine, 38*, 1–14.

Wang, B.W.E., Ramey, D. R., Schettler, J. D., Hubert, H. B., & Fries, J. F. (2002). Postponed development of disability in elderly runners: A 13-year longitudinal study. *Archives of Internal Medicine, 162*, 2285–2294.

Weiss, C. O., Hoenig, H. M., & Fried, L. P. (2007). Compensatory strategies used by older adults facing mobility disability. *Archives of Physical Medicine and Rehabilitation, 88*, 1217–1220.

Wolinsky, F. D., Miller, D. K., Andresen, E. M., Malmstrom, T. K., & Miller, J. P. (2005). Further evidence for the importance of subclinical functional limitation and subclinical disability assessment in gerontology and geriatrics. *Journal of Gerontology, 60B*, S146–S151.

Wrosch, C., Heckhausen, J., & Lachman, M. E. (2000). Primary and secondary control strategies for managing health and financial stress across adulthood. *Psychology and Aging, 15*, 387–399.

CHAPTER 11

MEMORY AGING: DEFICITS, BELIEFS, AND INTERVENTIONS

*Jane Berry, Erin Hastings, Robin West,
Courtney Lee, and John C. Cavanaugh*

If any one faculty of our nature may be called more wonderful than
the rest, I do think it is memory. There seems something more speak-
ingly incomprehensible in the powers, the failures, the inequalities of
memory, than in any other of our intelligences.

Jane Austen, Mansfield Park

Of all mental faculties, memory is unique. It defines who we are and places our
lives on a narrative continuum from birth to death. It helps to structure our
days, it guides our daily tasks and goals, and it provides pleasurable interludes
as we anticipate the future and recall the past. As a core, defining feature of
the self (Birren & Schroots, 2006), memory takes on heightened meaning
as we age. In the face of other losses that accumulate with age, memory can
serve to preserve our sense of self and place in time. In normal aging, memory
loss is minor and relatively inconsequential to functional well-being, other
than passing annoyance at not being able to retrieve a name or a location
from time to time. In non-normal or pathological aging, as characterized by
Alzheimer's disease (AD), the loss of memory is severe and debilitating. In
addition to functional disability, people with AD ultimately lose their sense
of self. Connections to the past, to current events and relationships, and to
what the future holds fade and ultimately disappear. Such a bleak fate for "the
self" continues to spur researchers to look for causes and cures for normal
and pathological memory failure. Current cutting-edge research examines
the transition from normal to pathological memory aging, with particular
emphasis on mild cognitive impairment (MCI) as a transitional phase and as

an independent risk factor for AD. Concurrent efforts have focused on developing effective intervention and treatment programs aimed at biological, psychosocial, and cognitive levels. This chapter highlights current research on normative memory change with age, with a focus on self-regulation, self-efficacy, and memory maintenance and maximization. We also look at the special contexts of mild cognitive impairment and Alzheimer's disease, and close with an eye toward future directions in theory, research, and intervention.

Just when thought we couldn't bear another review of memory and aging, we find in fact that it's an exciting time for the field. New techniques in cognitive neuroscience (neuroimaging, diffusion tensor imaging; see chapter 1, this volume; Cabeza, 2001); sophisticated explanatory models (computational modeling, Buchler & Reder, 2007; self-regulated language processing, Stine-Morrow, Miller, & Hertzog, 2006), and compelling translational and training approaches (Camp, 2006; Skrajner & Camp, 2007; West, Bagwell, & Dark-Freudemann, 2008) are yielding new insights into memory aging. Renewed interest in lessons from life span research and the parallels between cognitive development and demise has emerged (Brehmer et al., 2008; Craik & Bialystok, 2006; Shing, Werkle-Bergner, Li, & Lindenberger, 2008). Research on emotion and its regulatory role in episodic and other forms of memory is yielding fascinating new data at both neurological and behavioral levels (Allen et al., 2005; Fernandes, Ross, Wiegand, & Schryer, 2008; St. Jacques, Dolcos, & Cabeza, 2009). Theory building and refinement continue apace (e.g., Allen et al.; Buchler & Reder), and the empirical corpus is expanding at exponential rates. There is keen interest in MCI and its boundaries at the normal and pathological edges of memory functioning, forcing a reexamination of whether normal and abnormal memory aging lie on a continuum or represent qualitatively distinct states (Bröder, Herwig, Teipel, & Fast, 2008; Craik, 2008; Lott, 1982; Morris & Cummings, 2005; Peng, 2003; Petersen & Bennett, 2005; Small, 2001).

In one empirical study of the continuum hypothesis, Bröder et al. (2008) found "globally decelerated learning" and "additional retrieval deficits" on free recall tests in people with MCI compared to healthy younger and older control participants on clustered word recall and recognition tasks across multiple trials. Older (OCG) and younger (YCG) control groups had comparable rates of learning (and that were positive trajectories) compared to the MCI group, who had a relatively flat curve. Examination of task components revealed similar processing by OCG and MCI groups at encoding and by OCG and YCG groups at retrieval. Despite comparable and suboptimal initial clustering ability at task onset in MCI and OCG participants, the OCG adults improved over trials and at rates comparable to YCG adults. MCIs did not improve over trials, thus exhibiting a serious learning deficit over trials.

Results such as these suggest that MCI is both similar to and distinct from normal aging.

ORIGINS OF MEMORY AGING RESEARCH: A RETURN TO ROOTS

Just over a century ago, G. Stanley Hall laid out the characteristics of adolescence (1904) and senescence (1922) in his seminal works on development and aging. Since then, youth has been considered the pinnacle of cognitive development—a point to which children rise and from which adults fall. Empirical work provides support for the idea of the young adult mind as a cognitive powerhouse, especially in terms of speed of processing (Kail, 1986, 1991a, 1991b; Kail & Park, 1994; Park et al., 2002; Salthouse, 1991). The young mind as standard or point of reference is also evident in work done in the 1930s and 1940s when the scientific study of children held sway over the field of psychology (Hirshbein, 2002). In the 1950s, research on aging in its own right began to systematically document changes—but only negative changes—associated with senescence, especially studies of reaction time and sensory abilities (Birren & Botwinick, 1955). These studies foreshadowed current speed of processing theories of cognitive and memory aging. The 1960s and 1970s witnessed the emergence of extended theoretical debates on cognitive ability in adulthood with corresponding empirical evidence to support both decline (Horn & Donaldson, 1976, 1977) and growth (Baltes & Schaie, 1974, 1976; Labouvie-Vief, 1976, 1977) perspectives. Youth remained the standard of intellectual functioning, however, and much of the field was characterized by documenting differences between extreme age groups (people in their 20s versus people in their 60s and 70s) with little attention to midlife and childhood as important markers of development. The 1980s and 1990s witnessed the emergence of competing and complementary models for studying aging, replete with evidence for various mediators (e.g., speed of processing, working memory) and moderators (e.g., strategy use) of age-related memory deficits.

Now, at the threshold of the 21st century, neuroimaging studies, computational and mathematical modeling, and refined methods and measures are producing new information on memory and aging at dizzying rates. And, ironically enough, researchers and theoreticians are casting an eye back to the origins of memory, in childhood, and taking a more expansive view than before. Once again, clues from infancy and childhood are informing the search for mechanisms of memory aging. Perlmutter (1978), for example, conducted a now classic application of metamemory in children to older adults, creating a taxonomy of metamemorial knowledge that laid the groundwork for subsequent studies of metamemory and aging (e.g., Dixon & Hultsch, 1983; but see Cavanaugh & Perlmutter, 1982, for a critique of nondevelopmental approaches to methodological extrapolations across the life span). Currently, Craik and Bialystock (2006) argue eloquently for an inverted-U shaped function to describe memory across the life span but with the caveat that aging memory is not simply a reversal or loss of capacity and skills learned in childhood but a reorganization of relevant representational and control components (see also Shing et al., 2008; Wingard, 1980). Gaultney, Kipp, and Kirk (2005) argue for maturational differences in the organization of memory processes and demonstrate that individual differences in working memory span predict memory recall but not strategy use in college students. Wingard (1980) reported developmental trends in strategy use among 4-year-old, 6-year-old, and 10-year-old children; college students; and older adults that indicate a life span increase in the use of semantically-based organizational strategies on free recall tasks. The youngest children (preschoolers) were more likely than older groups to use perceptual rather than semantic grouping strategies, and age differences in strategy use were not affected by age differences in capacity as measured by a digit-span task. These results are consistent with Gaultney et al. and Shing et al. who found age differences spanning childhood through adulthood in associative binding and effective use of memorization strategies. Furthermore, it is well known that increased speed of processing is related to cognitive development in childhood (Kail, 1986, 1991a, 1991b; Kail & Park, 1994), and decreased speed of processing is related to cognitive decline in adulthood (Salthouse, 1991). Zimmermann and Meier (2006) found that memory for prospective event-based tasks was worse in young children and older adults compared to adolescents and young adults. Thus, abundant data are emerging that support a more integrative life span developmental approach to studying and understanding memory functioning in the elderly.

MEMORY AGING: WHAT ARE THE PROBLEMS? WHAT IS PRESERVED?

Memory is multidimensional (Nilsson, 2003; Tulving, 2004), so it is unsurprising that some dimensions change more than others over the life span. This section reviews dimensions of memory that are relatively impaired and relatively spared.

Episodic and Semantic Memory

Working and episodic memory abilities are especially likely to decline in older adulthood (Verhaeghen, Marcoen, & Goossens, 1993), whereas semantic (Ronnlund, Nyberg, Bäckman, & Nilsson, 2005), text memory (Stine-Morrow, Soederberg Miller, Gagne, & Hertzog , 2008), and procedural memory abilities (Nilsson, 2003) are relatively preserved. Older adults have difficulty efficiently manipulating information in the active, "on-line" store (working memory) and are less skilled at remembering associations between items (episodic memory). Even some item-level information is particularly difficult for older adults, such as remembering names. Most adults experience these changes, and many don't like it. Complaints about forgetting and "having a bad memory" are common, even normative, in midlife. Proper names are especially vulnerable to retrieval difficulties, and the well-known experience of "almost knowing," the so-called tip-of-the-tongue (TOT) phenomenon, is practically universal by midlife (James, 2004; James, Fogler, & Tauber, 2008; Rendell, Castel, & Craik, 2005).

Our focus in this chapter is primarily on episodic memory problems in older adults because they are the most commonly experienced and are the most common target of training, intervention, and remediation efforts. Many older adults are interested in opportunities to improve and optimize memory functioning; thus, basic research aimed at understanding the causes of episodic memory failures and applied research designed to enhance memory functioning is important.

Episodic memory, which falls under the more general domain of declarative memory, is unique because when compared with all types of memory, it shows the most consistent decline in adulthood, relative to semantic and procedural memory (Nilsson, 2003). Working memory also declines and is important because higher order cognitive abilities, including episodic memory, depend upon it. Semantic memory is important because impairments in semantic memory point to the type of serious memory disorders that characterize Alzheimer's disease; an intact semantic memory system also provides crucial support for episodic memory tasks. Yet, episodic memory is unique because it requires recollection of the rich array of details and context surrounding new learning. Whereas semantic memory is concerned with factual information, it is context-free: In most situations of recalling factual knowledge (e.g., even-numbered interstate highways run east and west and odd-numbered ones run north and south), it isn't important when, how, and from whom one learned that information. This kind of information is well-learned and relatively fail-proof with age. Likewise, procedural memory—skill-based memory, how to do things—is even more robust in old age, relative to episodic memory. According to Nilsson, scant attention has been paid to procedural memory in older adulthood, which is a bit surprising, given how important procedural memory is to well-being. It is often implicit in its execution and is what allows us to drive, cook, garden, fish, bicycle, play tennis, golf, play music, and so on. Beyond the daily and life-long pleasure that habitual, motoric procedural memory ability provides to individuals, skill-based memory is proving to be a valuable resource in interventions with AD patients (Zanetti et al., 2001).

Memory Complaints

Research on memory complaints initially attempted to map these complaints onto actual experiences of forgetting with mixed success, due to lack of control for relevant covariates (e.g., ability, depression), disparate measurement instruments, and samples of participants of divergent age ranges. Current work has moved beyond the question of veridicality to a different kind of prediction, focusing instead on the question of whether complaints are a risk factor for serious memory disorders. A review of clinical and population-based studies found that age (older), sex (female), education (fewer years), and cognitive status (poor) are related to increased complaints about memory, even when depression is controlled (Jonker, Geerlings, & Schmand, 2000). Cook and Marsiske (2006) reported confirmatory results, showing that subjective complaints of memory are correlated with MCI when controlling for differences in depression. Both studies employed more precise methods than past research on complaints. Cook and Marsiske argued that subjective complaints coexisting with depression may reflect increased awareness and concern over memory failures among individuals presenting with complaints. This argument is consistent with earlier work that memory complaints are related to trait neuroticism and to the memory self-efficacy subscales (Capacity, Change, Anxiety) of the Metamemory in Adulthood (MIA) questionnaire (Ponds & Jolles, 1996). Higher frequency of daily stressors is also related to self-reported memory failures in older adults (Neupert, Almeida, Mroczek, & Spiro, 2006) and particularly so when experienced by individuals high in trait neuroticism (Neupert, Mroczek, & Spiro, 2008).

Beliefs about memory, and lifestyle choices, such as engaging in mental and physical activities, may provide a buffer against cognitive decline in adulthood (Jopp & Hertzog, 2007). Some authors have argued for the protective effect of an active lifestyle on AD (Fratiglioni & Wang, 2007). Others have shown that strategic, positive coping and perceived complaints of memory are related to well-being in old age (Verhaeghen, Geraerts, & Marcoen, 2000). Memory training and intervention studies aimed at optimizing memory functioning in older adults are yielding promising outcomes that may translate to work with MCI and even AD patients, particularly those interventions aimed at boosting morale and optimizing well-being, even when actual memory gains are inconsequential. Those studies are reviewed later in the chapter. Next, we turn to the more serious memory problems associated with MCI and AD.

SERIOUS PROBLEMS: DEMENTIA AND MILD COGNITIVE IMPAIRMENT

Advances in technology and medicine since the early 20th century heralded increases in life expectancy and longevity, but ironically, brought about an increase in age-related problems. Currently, there are approximately 2 million people aged 90 or older in the United States (Kawas & Corrada, 2006); the numbers of those estimated to have dementia are expected to rise from 8.1 million to 24.3 million by 2040 (Ferri et al., 2005). Not surprisingly, Americans aged 55 and older have cited Alzheimer's disease as the most feared disease, followed by cancer and stroke (Gatz, 2007).

Dementia refers to a cluster of diseases that typically have their onset in late-middle to older adulthood and in which there is progressive cognitive and behavioral deterioration. Specifically, dementia patients have both episodic and major semantic memory dysfunctions, showing greater deterioration in tests requiring abstract reasoning and analytical problem solving than in tests of crystallized intelligence (Brayne, 2007; Spaan, Raaijmakers, & Jonker, 2005).

Alzheimer's Disease

Alzheimer's disease (AD) is the most common cause of dementia, affecting at least 15 million people globally, and is the fifth leading cause of death among older Americans (Alzheimer's Association, 2008; Matsuda, 2007). It gradually erodes one's memory, personality, and physical abilities. It is characterized by anterograde amnesia, retrograde amnesia, relative preservation of remote rather than recent events, decline in general intellectual function, wandering, depressive mood, physical aggression, as well as serious deficits in memory and self-orientation in both time and place (Hamuro et al., 2006; Westmacott, Freedman, Black, Stokes, & Moscovitch, 2004). Memory loss typically commences between 5 to 7 years prior to clinical diagnosis of dementia. Although the presence of amyloid plaques and neurofibrillary tangles is normative in older brains, excessive amounts of each are present in the brains of individuals with AD (Yamaguchi, 2007). Patients tend to exhibit relatively stable performance until a few years prior to diagnosis, at which point rapid cognitive decline begins. They are expected to exhibit approximately twice the cumulative decline expected in their age-peers without dementia during the 10 years preceding clinical diagnosis (Sliwinski, Hofer, Hall, Buschke, & Lipton, 2003).

Measures of cognition, mood, and neuropathology can be used in tandem to make probable diagnoses of AD, but a definitive diagnosis can only be made at autopsy. Because one of the initial symptoms of both dementia and normal aging is mild memory loss, detection is often difficult as many dementia patients are either unaware of or in denial regarding the severity of their forgetfulness (Urakami, 2007). While there are a variety of tests of cognition that can be used to detect dementia, the most successful are those that are sensitive to explicit memory tests requiring semantic processing and implicit memory tests from which repetition priming effects can be derived (Spaan et al., 2005).

Recently, the importance of subjective memory complaints has emerged as a preclinical symptom in dementia. Patients may begin noticing changes so subtle that they do not even merit medical attention. To date, the precise relationship between memory complaints and dementia is inconclusive, but memory complaints, even with the absence of objective memory deficits, may be indicative of the very earliest signs of dementia (Busse, Bischkopf, Riedel-Heller, & Angermeyer, 2003; Godbolt et al., 2005). Early and differential diagnosis is critical because although most dementias are irreversible, some can be reversed (e.g., hydrocephalus, thyroid dysfunction, vitamin B_{12} deficiency) or at least slowed with proper diagnosis and treatment. Chopard and colleagues (2007) present a promising new diagnostic approach based on empirical analyses of two screening measures administered to individuals with mild to moderate dementia and nondemented age-matched controls (age range 60 to 96 years). Current trends in dementia research include better assessment and understanding of "at-risk" states and are especially focused on mild cognitive impairment.

Mild Cognitive Impairment (MCI)

Though diagnostic criteria for MCI vary in details, it is generally characterized by the presence of five criteria: (1) subjective memory complaint, (2) preserved general intellectual function, (3) memory impairment assessed by cognitive testing, (4) normal daily life activity, and (5) no dementia (Instrumental Activities of Daily Living [IADL]; Bröder et al., 2008; Meguro, 2007; Petersen et al., 1997; Royall, 2005; Touchon & Portet, 2004). There are two distinct types of MCI, amnestic MCI (aMCI) and nonamnestic MCI (naMCI), which are further divided into subtypes based on the type of cognitive deficits present: *aMCI, single domain* pertains to isolated memory deficits, *aMCI, multiple domain* refers to impairment of other cognitive domains such as language and attention, and *naMCI, single domain* and *naMCI, multiple domain* involve impairment in noncognitive domains depending on the number of impaired domains (Burns & Zaudig, 2002; Davis & Rockwood, 2004; Morris & Cummings, 2005).

MCI is considered an unstable and heterogeneous condition in that some MCI patients revert back to "normal" and others progress into dementia (Davis & Rockwood, 2004). Some studies report conversion rates for MCI to AD ranging from 41% in 1 year to 26.6%–30.3% in 3 years (Amieva et al., 2004; Devanand et al., 2007). Others report that 35% of MCI cases revert back to normal (Apostolova et al., 2006). The heterogeneity of MCI may be attributable to interactions between individual genetic, physiological, and pathological differences (Mattson & Magnus, 2006; Richie, Artero & Touchon, 2001). Such differences may account for variability in MCI diagnosis as well as the delineation and definition of degrees of severity (Burns & Zaudig, 2002).

The instability of MCI has led to several theories concerning the possible conversion of MCI to more serious problems (Mariani, Monastero, & Mecocci, 2007). One view argues that there is no disease entity of MCI that would necessarily progress to cognitive deficit but rather, certain dementia diseases may have MCI characteristics or "MCI status" (Meguro, 2007). Others believe MCI is an intermediate stage between the normal cognitive aging and the very earliest manifestations of AD (Morris & Cummings, 2005). Indeed, the current MCI literature has primarily shown four main outcomes of MCI: (1) cognitive decline and/or progression to dementia, (2) death, (3) improvement in cognitive functioning, and (4) stability (Palmer, Fratiglioni, & Winblad, 2003).

It is generally assumed, however, that many MCI patients will convert to a form of dementia, particularly Alzheimer's disease. Although more highly developed memory ability and a higher level of education provide some protection against cognitive decline (Chodosh, Reuben, Albert, & Seeman, 2002), it has been shown that individuals with any cognitive impairment exhibit an accelerated progression to AD and other forms of dementia (Petersen & Bennett, 2005). Those who, in fact, progress to AD are characterized by poor performance on language-related intellectual functions, verbal memory deficits, depression, and poor global cognitive performance at baseline. The likelihood of conversion has also been predicted by a loss of functional ability that is secondary to the worsening of executive function (Gabryelewicz et al., 2007; Guarch, Marcos, Salamero, Gastó, & Blesa, 2008; Rozzini et al., 2007). Further, the neurobiology of MCI closely resembles that of clinically diagnosed AD: Both MCI and AD patients have an over-representation of the apolipoprotein E (ApoE) allele, volumetric loss in the entorhinal cortex and hippocampus, neural loss, increased brain markers of oxidative stress, cell cycle changes, and abnormalities of the cholinergic system, all of which support the theory that MCI is the prodromal stage of AD (Morris & Cummings, 2005).

The transition from MCI to dementia is difficult to reliably detect, and thus, biomarkers and risk factors are important to identify. It has been shown that presence of ApoE, deposits of amyloid beta protein (Aβ42), increased levels of the protein tau, hypometabolism in the right temporo-parietal cortex, and white matter lesions are all predictive of the conversion from MCI to dementia (Arai, 2005; Burns & Zaudig, 2002; Petersen & Bennett, 2005; Sepe-Monti et al., 2007). Detection of these biomarkers paired with consistent, impaired cognitive performance, documentation of rate and nature of change in cognition, and neuroimaging results are more reliable than static measurement of these features in diagnosing MCI (Godbolt et al., 2005; Salmon & Hodges, 2005).

A diagnosis of MCI is central in identifying groups of at-risk individuals for further cognitive decline (Bischkopf, Busse, & Angermeyer, 2002; Burns & Zaudig, 2002; Ishikawa & Ikeda, 2007). Future research must focus on developing standardized, reliable, and valid diagnostic criteria in order to more fully understand the course of MCI and its outcomes, prevalence, and predictors. By fully understanding MCI pathology and epidemiology, steps toward effective treatments can be implemented. There is a progressive reduction of neurogenesis (growth of new neurons) and a significant degree of cortical atrophy over a life span (Klempin & Kempermann, 2007). Neurodegeneration has been attributed to the degradation of myelin integrity beginning with white matter in youth and gray matter in middle age (Elderkin-Thompson, Ballmaier, Hellemann, Pham, & Kumar, 2008; Kramer et al., 2007). Age-related atrophy is most prominent in the hippocampus and frontal lobes (particularly the prefrontal cortex), primarily responsible for memory and coordination of executive control functions, respectively (Cabeza, 2002; Elderkin-Thompson et al., 2008; Gluck, Myers, Nicolle, & Johnson, 2006; Head, Rodrigue, Kennedy, & Raz, 2008). These frontal-striatal and medial-temporal circuits are especially important for encoding and retrieval of information and are thus vital to memory formation (Gabrieli, 1998; Head et al., 2008; Stebbins et al., 2002). Activation of such circuits, however, weakens with age due to volumetric loss, hypometabolism, and decreases in blood flow (Kensinger, Brierley, Medford, Growdon, & Corkin, 2002).

Older brains appear to compensate for losses and reductions in neuronal matter and integrity. Cabeza (2002) reported age-related decreases in prefrontal activity and increases in left prefrontal cortical activity during cognitive tasks. Age-related differences in memory ability are associated with significant shrinkage in brain areas (e.g., prefrontal cortex, hippocampus, caudate nucleus) that are associated with higher level functioning and memory (Head et al., 2008; Stebbins et al., 2002). Recent research shows that hippocampal atrophy in normal adults is correlated with future development of AD (Gluck et al., 2006). Focus on the hippocampus as a source of normative and non-normative age-related memory deficits has intensified in recent years, due in part to complementary work at both theoretical (Naveh-Benjamin, 2000) and methodological (Cabeza, 2001; Raz, 2006) levels. We turn now to normative memory loss.

NORMATIVE AGE-RELATED MEMORY LOSS: THEORIES, MEDIATORS, AND MODERATORS

This section presents a select overview of explanations for memory deficits associated with aging, including models and hypotheses that test those variables that seem particularly compelling to us for understanding how memory works in adulthood.

The Associative-Binding Hypothesis

One of the more compelling current theories of episodic memory deficits in older adults is the associative-binding hypothesis (Naveh-Benjamin,

2000), which states that memory for the contextual information associated with item information is compromised in older adults. In a recent
meta-analysis of episodic memory impairments in older adults, Old and
Naveh-Benjamin (2008a) reported that older adults demonstrate poorer
memory for associative information than item information and that this effect
is more pronounced in intentional, explicit memory instructions versus incidental, implicit instructions. Others have also reported that older adults
are better at remembering content than context and single units of information versus associations among those units (Chalfonte & Johnson, 1996;
Spencer & Raz, 1995). In both recall and recognition memory tests for
person–action pairs, Old and Naveh-Benjamin (2008b) showed that older
adults had better recall for persons and actions alone versus retrieving
them together and had higher false alarm rates for the associative material
than for the action and person information alone. James and colleagues
(2008) replicated this effect with face–name and face–occupation stimulus pairs. Younger adults retrieved more faces, names, occupations, and
combination associations than older adults. Older adults were particularly
poor at retrieving face–name associations. These studies demonstrate the
difficulty older adults have in making new connections between units of
information.

Additional support for the associative-binding deficit is provided by
research on age differences on the *concreteness effect*. The concreteness effect refers to the relatively greater recall of concrete words over abstract
words. Peters and Daum (2008) showed that the effect is smaller for older
adults compared to younger and middle-aged adults, and they argued that it
was due to the inability of older adults to form connecting images between
two words and to capitalize upon vivid associations using imagery and other
semantic-based encoding support. This explanation is consistent with the
associative-binding hypothesis. Peters and Daum's use of a "know" (inciden-
tial, implicit processes) versus "remember" (intentional, explicit processes)
recollection paradigm yielded support for the associative-binding hypothesis
as an explanation for the diminished concreteness effect in older adults as
well as more general age-related episodic memory loss.

Thus, to summarize, older adults are better at remembering separate
units of information (pigeon, tree) but have difficulty integrating material
that connects or binds units (The pigeon flew from the tree.). Moreover,
research suggests that the neural basis for this deficit resides in the hippocampus and its related structures. Even when units are especially rich in
associative content, as in the case of concrete words, older adults are more
challenged than younger adults at making connections. The associative-
binding hypothesis has received extensive empirical support and is thus
considered one of the dominant current explanations for age-related episodic
memory deficits.

The Processing Resources Hypothesis

Several other paradigms offer plausible explanations for age-related memory deficits. One dominant theory is that depleted processing resources such as speed, attention, and inhibitory control are at the root of higher-order deficits in working memory and episodic memory (Craik & Byrd, 1982; Salthouse, 1991). Empirical work on the processing resources model of memory aging is vast and includes support for attentional control (Lindenberger, Marsiske, & Baltes, 2000; McDowd, 1997; McDowd & Craik, 1988; Schaefer, Krampe, Lindenberger, & Baltes, 2008), speed (Salthouse, 1993; Verhaeghen, 1999; Verhaeghen, Vandenbroucke, & Dierckx, 1998), and inhibitory control (Hasher, Chung, May, & Foong, 2002; Hasher & Zacks, 1988; Lustig, Hasher, & Zacks, 2007; but see Aslan, Bauml, & Pastotter, 2007). One study found that speed but not working memory mediated age differences in verbal recognition memory (Verhaeghen, 1999). In contrast, Hertzog, Dixon, Hultsch, and MacDonald (2003) found that negative change in episodic memory ability over a 6-year span was a function of both working memory and speed. Perceptual speed mediates age differences on paired-associates and free recall tasks of common nouns (Salthouse, 1993), and age differences in working memory are mediated primarily by processing speed (Salthouse & Babcock, 1991). Recent research confirms Salthouse's claim that processing speed is foundational to higher levels of cognitive functioning, even at the primary level of working memory. Specifically, Bailey, Dunlosky, and Hertzog (2009) found that age differences in processing speed explain age differences in working memory as measured by an operations-span task and a reading-span task.

Thus, to summarize, older adults process incoming information more slowly than younger adults. Older adults are also slower to integrate new information with existing information in the long-term, semantic store, as well as with other new information held briefly and concurrently in the working memory space. Episodic tasks that rely on making connections between related (or unrelated) items (the associative-binding hypothesis) are dependent upon these lower levels of processing and manipulation. The limited processing resources hypothesis is firmly established as a significant mediator of age-related memory deficits.

The Temporal Coding Hypothesis

A view consistent with both the associative-binding hypothesis and the processing resources hypothesis emphasizes impairment at the retrieval phase of recently learned information as the source of episodic memory impairment in older adults (Wingfield & Kahana, 2002). Both speed and association processes are implicated in this view. In their study, Wingfield and Kahana brought older and younger adults to a learning criterion of

100% in a category–exemplar recall task (e.g., furniture category with sofa, chair, table exemplars; animal category with goat, dog, bird exemplars). Younger and older adults had comparable rates of retrieval within categories, but older adults exhibited slowed responses when moving to the next or a new category to retrieve items from it. This suggests that older adults take longer to assess whether retrieval within a category is complete, and to remember or retrieve the next category itself to then commence retrieval of its items. When the categories are provided at retrieval, age differences in retrieval rates disappear. Taken together, these results suggest that retrieving newly learned categories and connecting them in a temporal order is a memory-demanding task with associative-binding components. Older adults' diminished ability to move efficiently between categories of items-to-be-retrieved is consistent with the associative-binding hypothesis.

In summary, one class of explanations for memory-related deficits in adulthood focuses on cognitive mechanisms such as speed, working memory, and encoding and retrieval processes. This class of mediator or explanatory variables is supported by empirical and theoretical work and, increasingly, neuroimaging data. At a different level of analysis, researchers have considered the impact of self-regulation and monitoring on memory functioning in adulthood. This domain of explanatory mechanisms includes strategy use, self-evaluative judgments about competencies (memory self-efficacy), and stereotypical beliefs about memory and aging. We turn to this research in the next sections.

Strategy Use

It is well known that being strategic when learning new information will aid subsequent recall. For example, grouping similar items together (e.g., cottage, condo, apartment; motorcycle, bicycle, scooter) at study helps to encode and retrieve those items. Children who are taught to use organizational strategies to remember lists of words recall more words on a subsequent memory test (and have higher self-efficacy for future memory tasks) than their untrained counterparts (Gaskill & Murphy, 2008). In a life span study of strategy use, Shing et al. (2008) showed that both children and older adults were deficient in strategy use on a word-pair recall task. Even with practice on the use of an elaborative visual imagery technique, older adults' performance did not improve (children's did). The failure of older adults to benefit from elaborative encoding processes is consistent with an associative-binding deficit (Naveh-Benjamin, 2000). Not all research supports the claim that strategy use is a viable explanation for age-related memory deficits. For example, Bailey and colleagues (2009) found no differences between younger and older adults' use of normatively effective strategies (e.g., imagery, rote repetition) and that processing speed but not strategy differences between age groups explained age deficits in working memory span. Although effective strategy use is related to working memory span performance (Bailey et al.), the evidence regarding strategy use as a causal mechanism for age-related learning deficits is mixed. Dunlosky, Hertzog, and Powell-Moman (2005) found that the quality of mediators does not vary by age group, but recall of mediators is poorer among older adults. It appears that younger adults (Verhaeghen & Marcoen, 1996) and children (Shing et al.) benefit more from instruction in the use of strategies to guide memory than do older adults, possibly due in part to an associative-binding deficit. We have argued elsewhere that older adults may be less likely to use strategies when memorizing because of low expectations for performance success and low self-confidence for the memory task (Berry, 1999; Berry & West, 1993; Cavanaugh, Feldman, & Hertzog, 1998; Cavanaugh & Green, 1990; West & Berry, 1994). Relevant work from this perspective is reviewed next.

Memory Beliefs and Self-Efficacy

Older adults are relatively less certain and more negative in their self-judgments of memory ability than younger adults, as indicated on several different measures of memory self-efficacy (Berry, West, & Dennehey, 1989; Desrichard & Kopetz, 2005; Gardiner, Luszcz, & Bryan, 1997; Hertzog, Dixon, & Hultsch, 1990; Rebok & Balcerak, 1989; West, Dennehy-Basile, & Norris, 1996). These data mirror the memory complaints that typify older adults' self-reports of everyday memory functioning reviewed earlier in this chapter. Higher levels of memory self-efficacy are related to better performance on memory tasks (Lachman, Andreoletti, & Pearman, 2006; McDonald-Miszczak, Gould, & Tychynski, 1999; Valentijn et al., 2006), but whether memory self-efficacy is a mediator of age-related deficits on memory tasks remains to be demonstrated. Among older adults, however, low memory self-efficacy is especially likely to hurt memory performance when the task is explicitly a memory task (Desrichard & Kopetz, 2005). Researchers are testing increasingly sophisticated models of the relation of self-efficacy to memory and other cognitive tasks (see Cervone, Artistico, & Berry, 2006, for a review). For example, Stine-Morrow, Shake, Miles, and Noh (2006) found that self-efficacy predicts accuracy on a reading test and that working memory and self-efficacy were related to task goals. An intriguing conclusion from this study is that memory monitoring may be resource-depleting for older adults. As such, it will be important to determine which components of successful memory outcomes are least depleting and most advantageous for older adults. A recent study on age differences in memory monitoring (Chua, Schacter, & Sperling, 2009) indicates that older adults' false sense of confidence (high confidence for misremembered information) demonstrates that older adults are less accurate in knowing what they know and don't know than are younger adults. These data suggest that, indeed, memory monitoring processes may be as problematic for older adults as memory recall itself (Stine-Morrow, Shake, et al., 2006; Stine-Morrow et al., 2008).

Research on beliefs about aging and their relevance to memory functioning is yielding intriguing new insights. Lineweaver, Bergner, and Hertzog (2009) have shown that memory beliefs are differentially attached to positive and negative "target" people in a person–perception paradigm. Young, middle-aged, and older adults believed memory decline was more likely among older (target) adults who exhibit negative personality characteristics (e.g., a grumpy, cautious) versus positive characteristics (e.g., an upbeat, engaged old woman). Thus, beliefs about memory decline in elderly adults may be more specific than universal.

Fine-grained analyses of the role of self-stereotyping and stereotype threat point to subtle influences of stereotypical beliefs on memory performance in older adults. Hess and colleagues (e.g., Hess & Hinson, 2006) and Hummert and colleagues (e.g., O'Brien & Hummert, 2006) have shown that adults at midlife are particularly susceptible to stereotypical information about memory aging, which interacts with self-identification processes (i.e., the extent to which one identifies with old age as a self-referent status). In the study by Hess and Hinson, midlife adults performed better on a memory task following exposure to negative stereotypes of aging. In stark contrast, O'Brien and Hummert found that midlife adults appeared to be more threatened by a comparison to older adults and performed worse on a memory recall task. Follow-up analyses indicated that this effect held only for those midlife adults who scored in the direction of "old" on an age identification measure. Thus, when stereotypes seem self-referent, they appear to be more likely to affect behavior, including memory.

In a related vein, older adults appear to be more sensitive to tasks that are framed as memory tasks versus nonmemory tasks. Desrichard and Kopetz (2005) found that "explicity" of an episodic memory task at instruction time moderated memory performance. Their participants performed a "running an errand" spatial memory task and were told either that their performance was an indicator of good memory abilities or good orientation abilities. Older adults with lower memory self-efficacy (MSE) were more affected by explicit memory instructions than those with higher MSE. MSE was correlated with memory performance in the former but not the latter group; it was not predictive when the task is nonexplicit. The memory nature of the task appeared to have activated self-evaluative processes in older adults, resulting in MSE ratings that were correlated with performance. Younger adults performed no differently under the two types of task instructions. Thus, when MSE is low and the memory component of a task is emphasized, memory performance is compromised in older adults.

In conclusion, memory self-efficacy, strategy use, and beliefs about memory are three components of a more comprehensive framework by which to study memory and aging that focuses on self-regulation, reviewed next.

Self-Regulation

Our beliefs about cognition, on-task behaviors (e.g., strategy use, monitoring, resource allocation), and affective responses are self-regulatory factors that can influence cognition (Stine-Morrow, Miller, & Hertzog, 2006). Seen as the exercise of agency on the part of the individual, self-regulation is a general phenomenon that has been extensively studied in many domains of function (Bandura, 1997; Carver & Scheier, 2001). There are theoretical models of the life span that primarily emphasize self-regulatory processes, although the authors do not identify these as self-regulatory models, for instance, the Selective, Optimization, and Compensation model (Baltes, Freund, & Li, 2005) or Craik's model of self-initiated processing (1994). Work focusing specifically on memory and aging in the context of self-regulation is relatively new and falls into two primary categories: (1) work showing that pre-existing self-evaluative beliefs (such as views of one's own self-efficacy or control) influence memory and responses to task goals and (2) work showing that manipulations of goals can improve performance outcomes. Although few scholars of strategies have couched their work in self-regulatory terms, we would also argue that intervention work with specific memory strategies is essentially teaching older adults to regulate their own cognitive outcomes.

To our knowledge, there is only one well-developed theoretical model of self-regulation of cognition in aging. Although that model focuses on discourse processing (Stine-Morrow, Miller, et al., 2006), the authors emphasize the extent to which older adults can modify their own performance outcomes. Such modification involves choices to allocate particular resources that will advance performance. These choices are constrained by ability, knowledge, motivation, specific interests, affect, feedback, and the particular demands of the task. Clearly, this kind of model may be applied broadly to many domains of cognitive function. Older adults may perform better on cognitively demanding memory tasks by maintaining positive affect and a more positive set of beliefs about their potential, by monitoring their own item-specific success, by allocating attentional or strategic resources to meet specific goals, and by responding appropriately to performance feedback derived from external or internal sources. Theoretically, a person's initial performance levels on a task may lead to generally positive or negative self-perceptions that will influence subsequent performance levels (Bandura, 1997). If unable to meet a goal, the individual might reduce effort or could allocate additional effort to the zone of proximal learning (those items she is most likely to learn, or those items that are nearly learned). Alternatively, poor performance on a first memory trial could lead to negative affect (e.g., self-doubt and anxiety), withdrawal from strong investment in the task (e.g., failure to employ memory strategies that are known and easily utilized), and poorer performance on all subsequent trials. In daily life, a withdrawal from memory challenge can result in forgetting how to use strategies and the loss of information-processing skills that are not regularly practiced. Subsequently, when a memory challenge cannot be avoided, the individual has lost both skill and self-confidence to tackle the task. This example clearly demonstrates that self-regulatory processes can be specific to the task context and involve beliefs about performance, affective reactions, and information-processing strategies (Stine-Morrow, Miller, et al., 2006). In this way, self-regulatory processes may be highly influential in determining how and when older adults can overcome memory deficits and perform well.

Beliefs are a central piece of the self-regulatory process. Beliefs about ability, such as self-efficacy or attributions, can serve to impair or enhance memory performance, depending on the context of testing; for example, age-stereotype activation can bring down the performance levels of older adults (Chasteen, Bhattacharyya, Horhota, Tam, & Hasher, 2005; Hess, Auman, Colcombe, & Rahhal, 2003). Active engagement in cognitive processing and allocation of resources to task goals may be controlled, in part, by beliefs (Miller & West, in press; Stine-Morrow, Shake, et al., 2006; West & Yassuda, 2004). Aging research on cognitive beliefs has emphasized the overall relationship between beliefs, metamemory, and performance (for reviews, see Berry, 1999; Cavanaugh & Green, 1990; Hertzog & Hultsch, 2000; Soederberg Miller & Lachman, 1999) as well as experimental paradigms, involving goal setting, stereotype activation, or other manipulations of beliefs (cf. Desrichard & Kopetz, 2005; Gardiner et al., 1997; Lachman, Weaver, Bandura, Elliott, & Lewkowicz, 1992; Levy, 1996; Miller & West, in press; Rahhal, Hasher, & Colcombe, 2001; Stein, Blanchard-Fields, & Hertzog, 2002; West, Thorn, & Bagwell, 2003). Beliefs about control, that is, feeling that one's performance is modifiable through one's own effort, or believing that individual "internal" effort is more important than external factors, are key to self-regulatory success (see chapter 8, this volume). Similarly, stereotypes about aging can also be influential in self-regulation (see chapter 6, this volume).

MAINTAINING AND MAXIMIZING FUNCTION

Many scholars have examined the conditions and circumstances that might help older adults to maintain rather than lose memory skills. A variety of paradigms have been employed to find ways to yield memory improvements for older adults. Early work addressed the basic question of whether older adults were able to improve memory at all (Poon, Walsh-Sweeney, & Fozard, 1980). More recent work has examined what kind of conditions lead to lasting improvement in daily memory (Rebok, Carlson, & Langbaum, 2007) and what particular individual differences might predict better outcomes (Bagwell & West, 2008). The extant scholarly research ranges from experimental studies examining the impact of different learning contexts—for example, intentional versus incidental learning (Kausler & Puckett, 1980) or everyday memory versus laboratory memory (West, 1986)—to highly complex multifactorial memory interventions designed to improve performance as well as self-perceptions of memory skill (Lachman et al., 1992; Valentijn et al., 2005; West et al., 2008).

There is no question that cognitive ability in general, and memory in particular, is relatively plastic in late life (Verhaeghen, 2000). Research has supported the value of cognitive engagement (Rebok et al., 2007; Schooler & Mulatu, 2001; Stine-Morrow, Parisi, Morrow, Greene, & Park, 2007) as well as the value of cognitive training for older adults (Ball et al., 2002; Camp, 1998; McDaniel, Einstein, & Jacoby, 2008). At the same time, there is very little evidence that any particular type of training or experimental manipulation can eliminate age differences, although age differences can certainly be reduced under encoding and retrieval conditions that provide supportive cuing (Kausler, 1994), such as recognition testing. One excellent portrayal of the nature of the age gap in potential for maximizing memory is work on testing-the-limits (Kliegl, Smith, & Baltes, 1989). This program of research showed that, while considerable plasticity exists in older adult memory skills, this plasticity is not as great as it is for younger individuals. Persons varying in age were provided with a sophisticated imagery mnemonic to assist in the learning of numbers and showed dramatic increases in the length of the digit series that they could memorize. Nevertheless, even with close to 40 hours of training, older adults remained significantly behind young adults in scores, supporting the notion that age-related information-processing changes set limits to the benefits of intervention (Kliegl et al., 1989).

Recognizing that older adults have processing limitations and are unlikely to avoid some degree of memory decline, we nevertheless maintain that understanding the factors that enhance memory performance for older adults and applying them in memory intervention programs may improve quality of life and increase self-esteem. Beyond these applied benefits, the scientific knowledge base will be strengthened by such research. Next, we review the memory training and goal regulation literature, as these topics are most likely to remain important in future work.

Goals Research

Goal setting has been investigated in relation to the self-regulatory models of memory processing introduced earlier. In the typical paradigm, an individual is given a specific performance goal, and score outcomes or on-task behaviors (e.g., strategy usage) are compared to that of a control group with no goal. Participants with a goal, whether self-set or established by an experimenter, may also be given feedback concerning their progress toward meeting the goal. It is clear that goals can change one's on-task behavior (Stine-Morrow, Shake, et al., 2006) and that having a goal leads to higher memory performance than studying without an explicit goal in mind (West, Bagwell, & Dark-Freudeman, 2005). These effects are not always the same in younger and older adults. At the same time, the benefit of goal setting is such that older adults with goals sometimes outperform younger adults in a control condition without goals or feedback (Stadtlander & Coyne, 1990).

Research on goal setting demonstrates that younger adults show a stronger response to having a goal than older adults. Across all types of goal-setting conditions, younger adults show significant memory gains, but older adult gains in response to goals are more limited in nature (West & Thorn, 2001; West, Welch, & Thorn, 2001). Looking across a series of list-learning studies conducted by West and colleagues, it appears that older adults require some indication of successful task progress in order to make goal-related gains (i.e., to realize memory test score improvements when given a memory goal). Signs of progress might include encouraging, positive feedback from the experimenter (West et al., 2005), or objective feedback showing that scores have exceeded goals (West et al., 2001), or a means by which the participant can easily observe increased scores on their own (West et al., 2003). Given that older adults tend to be less confident in their memory abilities, it is not surprising that willingness to invest effort to meet a performance goal might be affected by the outcome of such effort. When older adults are given objective feedback that shows a lack of success, then task engagement is reduced, resulting in poor performance (West et al., 2001). Not surprisingly, paradigms that tailor task difficulty to individual ability levels (using a baseline test) result in more consistent goal-related gains for older adults (e.g., West et al., 2003) than those that set the same standard goals for all participants (West & Thorn, 2001).

Self-regulatory beliefs such as self-efficacy, motivation, and control have been investigated in the goal-setting literature, with recent work expanding into the arena of memory and aging. Typically in this literature, individuals with goals remain more motivated (i.e., show higher effort, higher test scores, and willingness to work more) after extensive testing than those without goals, and this is true for both older and younger adults (e.g., West et al., 2001). Moreover, level of effort predicts goal-related gains (West, Dark-Freudeman, & Bagwell, 2009). Self-efficacy may also be an important factor in predicting responses to goals. Stine-Morrow, Shake, and colleagues (2006), for instance, demonstrated that self-efficacy scores derived from the capacity and change subscales of the Metamemory in Adulthood questionnaire (MIA; Dixon, Hultsch, & Hertzog, 1988) predicted "flexible processing in text memory" where individuals either focused on accuracy or efficiency, depending on the goal emphasized by task conditions. It is interesting to note that self-efficacy predicted processing even with working memory included in the predictive model as well. Further, the impact of self-efficacy was stronger for the older learners (Stine-Morrow, Shake, et al., 2006). Similarly, West and colleagues (2009) showed that the interaction of self-efficacy and goal condition, along with strategy usage, effort, and baseline recall scores, predicted gains across list-learning trials for older adults. Locus of control has also been examined, predicting goal-related gains for younger adults (West et al., 2009; West & Yassuda, 2004) and older adults (West & Yassuda, 2004). In general, self-regulatory factors of control beliefs, self-efficacy, and goal condition have consistently shown powerful impact on gains across trials.

The majority of goal-setting studies have looked at simple list-learning paradigms, although some have examined digit recall (Stadtlander & Coyne, 1990) or text recall (Stine-Morrow, Shake, et al., 2006). In the case of list learning, it appears that strategy usage is the primary mechanism for goal success. That is, both older and younger adults who are given a goal increase their usage of memory strategies (e.g., using categories) in order to achieve gains under goal conditions (West et al., 2009). In the shopping lists used thus far in this research, simple categories, such as fruits, meats, and beverages, can easily be identified and employed during encoding and retrieval by older adults. It is not clear whether older adults would accomplish as much under goal-setting conditions with tasks that required more sophisticated strategies, such as those requiring several steps in sequence (e.g., image–name match method for name recall). In the case of text recall, the data reveal that shifts in allocation of effort and attentional resources play a large role in goal-directed learning (Stine-Morrow, Shake, et al., 2006).

With text and list learning, younger adults consistently show score gains with goals, whereas older adults show such gains only under supportive conditions as noted previously, that is, with individualized task difficulty and conditions that provide "signs of progress" (West et al., 2009). Future research in this area would benefit from expansion of the types of cognitive skills investigated, including examination of goal effects on improvements in mental speed, reasoning, and a wider variety of memory tasks. Further, it is not yet clear whether older adults can successfully set their own memory goals for laboratory tasks with brief levels of experience or training (West et al., 2001), or how memory goals operate in daily life. If older adults could effectively set their own goals, this might be an invaluable skill for helping individuals to maintain training effects in the home, through regular practice of learned skills.

Memory Training

Moving beyond the simple provision of a goal, decades of research has examined the potential for memory intervention programs for older adults. This section examines the impact of training on performance and beliefs, durability of training effects, factors that influence the effectiveness of training, and how training may be applied to older adults with mild to severe cognitive impairment.

Comprehensive Group Memory Interventions

Early work in memory training often brought individual seniors into the laboratory for brief strategy instruction (e.g., Hultsch, 1969). In the 1980s, investigators chose a more comprehensive approach to intervention, providing up to 20 hours of training in group settings (e.g., Yesavage, Lapp, & Sheikh, 1989). Group training is more effective than individual training, and the inclusion of pretraining provides added benefits (Verhaeghen, Marcoen,& Goossens, 1992). Group intervention work has fallen into three categories: (1) focused on a single mnemonic technique, such as interactive imagery (Hill, Sheikh, & Yesavage, 1987; West & Crook, 1992) or targeting a specific memory task, such as name recall (see Yesavage et al., 1989) or number recall (e.g., Derwinger, Stigsdotter Neely, Persson, Hill, & Backman, 2003); (2) broad-based, offering a range of memory strategies, with the goal of improving memory performance on a variety of everyday memory materials, such as shopping lists, names, and stories (Ball et al., 2002; West et al., 2008); or (3) multifactorial in approach.

Multifactorial interventions include strategy training as well as other key elements that may bolster training impact, such as focusing on beliefs (Lachman et al., 1992; Valentijn et al., 2005; West et al., 2008), increasing everyday engagement (Rebok et al., 2007), training attentional strategies (Stigsdotter & Backman, 1989a; West et al., 2008; Yesavage & Rose, 1983), encouraging relaxation (Stigsdotter Neely & Backman, 1993a, 1993b; Yesavage, Shiekh, Tanke, & Hill, 1988), or educating trainees about memory aging (West et al., 2008). Briefer, problem-targeted versions of training do not yield the same benefits (Woolverton, Scogin, Shackelford, Black, & Duke, 2001). Stigsdotter and Backman (1989a) found that training on memory strategies alone (unifactorial training) improved the memory performance of older adults, but adding material on attention and relaxation produced pronounced improvements. Comprehensive multifactorial interventions have resulted in successful change on most memory measures (Flynn & Storandt, 1990; Scogin, Storandt, & Lott, 1985; Stigsdotter & Backman, 1989b; Stigsdotter Neely & Backman, 1993a, 1993b; Zarit, Cole, & Guider, 1981; Zarit, Gallagher, & Kramer, 1981). The most recent multifactorial program taught five strategies, didactically, over 6 weeks (West et al., 2008). In addition, trainees did extensive reading on memory and aging and all elements of the training program were designed to encourage positive beliefs about memory potential and increase memory activity levels in the home. Relative to a control group, the trainees improved on name and story recall at two levels of difficulty, used more memory strategies, and showed improvements in memory self-efficacy and control beliefs (West et al., 2008).

Maintenance and Transfer of Training Effects

One way to show the real-world impact of training is to show that gains are maintained over time. Memory improvement lasting only a few days or weeks is of limited value to older adults seeking to achieve real change in cognitive performance or stave off dementia. If trainees return to an unstimulating environment and do not practice trained strategies, it is unlikely their training experience will result in long-term gains (Rebok et al., 2007). Therefore, improvements made in training may not make a sustained difference in their everyday lives. Work with training of reasoning skills has demonstrated very good maintenance of training effects, up to 7 years (Willis et al., 2006), but for memory training, per se, the data are less optimistic.

One-month maintenance of training effects has been documented following self-paced video training of imagery techniques (West & Crook, 1992), self-taught memory skills training (Flynn & Storandt, 1990; Scogin et al., 1985), and multifactorial group training (Stigsdotter & Backman, 1989b; West et al., 2008). Results are more mixed regarding maintenance beyond 1 year following training. Many have failed to find long-term maintenance of training gains (Anschutz, Camp, Markley, & Kramer, 1987; Scogin & Bienias, 1988). However, there is some research suggesting that such long-term maintenance is possible. Stigsdotter and colleagues reported 6-month maintenance effects with a multifactorial memory training program and subsequently found that trainees maintained their improvements over 3 years later (Stigsdotter Neely & Backman, 1993a, 1993b). Additionally, results of the large-scale ACTIVE study also support the potential for long-term maintenance of training gains, showing 2-year maintenance of training gains (Ball et al., 2002) and, more recently, improvements maintained up to 5 years post-training (Willis et al., 2006).

The inability to transfer skills learned during training to tasks in other domains is a frequently reported limitation associated with training interventions (Derwinger et al., 2003; Rebok et al., 2007). The largest documented study of transfer to date has been the ACTIVE intervention (Ball et al., 2002). Participants were trained for memory, speed of processing, or inductive reasoning, or served in a wait-list control condition. All trainees improved in their specifically trained domain, but training effects did not transfer across domains in the initial investigation (Ball et al., 2002), for example, individuals trained in memory improved only on memory measures and not in speed or reasoning.

More recent evidence has shown that training gains may transfer from one laboratory task to a similar type of task (e.g., from visual to auditory discrimination), or from a laboratory task to general assessments of everyday cognitive functioning (Bherer et al., 2006; Bottirolli, Cavallini, & Vecchi, 2008; Erickson et al., 2007; Mahncke et al., 2006; Willis et al., 2006; Wolinsky, Unverzagt, Smith, Jones, & Wright, 2006). Given the hundreds of interventions that have examined transfer, and the relatively few that have achieved it, transfer is not easy to achieve. Nevertheless, demonstrations of transfer are important because they suggest that the impact of training is broader than once believed and that training may have real-world consequences for older adults.

Individual Differences

An important question regarding training is "who benefits most?" (McKitrick et al., 1999; West & Tomer, 1989). Although a few studies have examined this issue, there is much yet to be discovered. Interindividual variability may obscure training effects (Schaffer & Poon, 1982). There is evidence suggesting that increased age may yield fewer training gains, although more studies of middle-aged participants would be needed to confirm this finding (Bissig & Lustig, 2007; Brooks, Friedman, Pearman, Gray, & Yesavage, 1999; Schaffer & Poon, 1982; Verhaeghen et al., 1992). Depression or anxiety is negatively related to the level of performance gains experienced by individual trainees, although anxiety reduction can benefit more anxious trainees (Schaffer & Poon, 1982; Yesavage et al., 1989). Lower cognitive status appears to be associated with reduced training impact (Yesavage, Sheikh, Friedman, & Tanke, 1990), and the benefits of higher education on training-related gains show mixed effects (Bagwell & West, 2008; Verhaeghen et al., 1992). Interestingly, certain personality traits may influence who benefits most from training, with evidence for the benefits of openness to experience (Gratzinger, Sheikh, Friedman, & Yesavage, 1990) and intuitiveness (Yesavage et al., 1989). Motivational factors may also be influential, in that self-generation of strategies works better than didactic training (Derwinger, Stigsdotter Neely, & Backman, 2005), and greater gains occur for those individuals who are more compliant with the training regimens (Bagwell & West, 2008). Similarly, a low sense of control over memory or a weaker perceived potential to change may reduce immediate and long-term gains (Elliott & Lachman, 1989; Erber, Abello, & Moninger, 1988; Valentijn et al., 2006; West, Welch, & Yassuda, 2000).

A number of scholars have recognized the importance of such individual differences in beliefs and have targeted their interventions to change both beliefs and memory. There is meta-analytic evidence that group-based training can improve self-evaluations of memory (Floyd & Scogin, 1997), however, many of the articles included in that review were studies that had no control group. Without a control group, changes in self-evaluative beliefs may be due to factors that were not part of the strategy training program, such as the social stimulation provided by attending a group workshop (Lachman et al., 1992; West et al., 2008). In studies using a control group, these training-related improvements in self-evaluation of memory have been reported: decreased memory concerns (Mohs et al., 1998; Zarit, Cole, et al., 1981; Zarit, Gallagher, et al., 1981), increased feelings of control over memory (Lachman et al., 1992; Turner & Pinkston, 1993), and improved memory self-efficacy (West et al., 2008). When they do occur, changes in beliefs are not always accompanied by performance change. Simply raising trainees' confidence in their memory ability is not sufficient to produce change in objective performance (Lachman et al., 1992). Likewise, learning a set of strategies to improve objective memory performance does not guarantee that participants will feel capable enough to apply these strategies in their daily lives or beyond the training period.

For instance, Best, Hamlett, and Davis (1992) compared a traditional strategic training approach with an "expectancy change" intervention intended only to change beliefs. The training group improved performance only, and the expectancy group showed only altered beliefs. In addition, the relationship between measures of memory complaints and actual performance was weak, suggesting that improved performance did not necessarily lead to changes in self-evaluative beliefs and vice versa. More recently, Valentijn and colleagues (2005) compared self-taught participants who used a training manual with collective training (small group meetings), where both groups received information on memory, aging, strategies, and self-efficacy. Their training showed improvement over controls only on a few of their performance measures, but participants did report less stress and anxiety related to memory following training. Other training studies have also shown partial success, reporting improvement on either beliefs or performance (e.g., Rebok & Balcerak, 1989; Zarit, Cole, et al., 1981). The most successful program to date, enhancing both beliefs and performance, integrated traditional skills training with elements designed to change beliefs. The program "emphasized potential at any age" and encouraged participants to set personal goals and "not to be concerned with achieving a high score" (West et al., 2008, p. 311). By focusing trainees on their potential for improvement, allowing them to set their own pace, and emphasizing the learning process, the researchers were able to increase participants' memory self-efficacy and sense of control while significantly improving memory strategies and test scores (West et al., 2008).

Self-Help Approaches to Memory Intervention

Advances in technology have added new promise to the development and dissemination of self-help training programs, potentially making memory performance available to a broader range of older adults who may have difficulty attending or financially affording a lengthy workshop (Rebok et al., 2007). Further, self-help training may encourage better practice of learned strategies because they are practiced in the home rather than in a class setting (Baldi, Plude, & Schwartz, 1996). Some researchers have even suggested that any mentally stimulating activity may benefit cognitive performance, including memory (Park, Gutchess, Meade, & Stine-Morrow, 2007; Rasmusson, Rebok, Bylsma, & Brandt, 1999; but cf. Salthouse, 2006). However, research on self-guided training has shown mixed results.

Several researchers have had success with improving memory scores via self-guided training presented in a manual or handbook (Andrewes, Kinsella, & Murphy, 1996; Hastings & West, in press; Scogin et al., 1985; Woolverton et al., 2001), on video (e.g., West & Crook, 1992) or on CD-ROM (e.g., Baldi et al., 1996). Rasmusson and colleagues (1999) showed that no single training mode surpassed others; participants in group-based, self-paced, and computer-based training all improved on a behavioral memory test. Although the results of self-guided training are encouraging, some interventions have not yielded significant memory gains following self-guided training (Flynn & Storandt, 1990; Rebok, Rasmusson, Bylsma, & Brandt, 1997), and few researchers have examined maintenance of self-help training effects over time (e.g., Baldi et al., 1996; West & Crook, 1992; Woolverton et al., 2001).

With respect to beliefs, few studies have addressed the potential for self-help training to impact beliefs (Rebok et al., 1997; Valentijn et al., 2005). Scogin, Prohaska, and Weeks (1998) found that both group- and self-guided training improved memory performance and subjective memory assessment (although there was no control group). In a self-guided study using two different audiotape programs, participants did not significantly improve memory, but there was a significant change in the belief that memory loss can be prevented through effort (Rebok et al., 1997). Other investigators were unable to significantly change memory beliefs via a self-help training approach (Scogin, Storandt, & Lott, 1985 Valentijn et al., 2005; Woolverton et al., 2001). In a recent study, a self-help version of a training program led to just as much memory test gain as a group-based intervention, however, results for beliefs were mixed, with a self-help manual leading to significant changes in locus of control, but not self-efficacy (Hastings & West, in press).

Therefore, past research on self-help training has shown mixed results both with respect to memory change and change in self-evaluative beliefs. It could be the case then that elements of the group environment, aside from strategy training, may be responsible for some of the improvements in memory beliefs associated with group-based programs. Nevertheless, investigators should continue to test self-help approaches. An effective self-help program could have important cognitive health consequences for many older adults who are immobile and/or cannot afford to attend group training sessions away from home. Further research should explore what aspects of group-based training are critical to performance and beliefs improvement, and how to successfully apply these aspects to self-help programs. It is likely that the Internet will prove useful in this area, as it will allow for virtual interaction with others and instructors, potentially providing a social environment that resembles an actual classroom.

Traditional memory training has provided clear benefits to cognitively healthy older adults in terms of changes in both beliefs and performance. General recognition of the established benefits of comprehensive group training and self-help training and increases in the older population have led to an explosion of new methods for memory intervention in the last few years. For example, scholars are combining memory training with exercise training, or providing increased engagement through life experiences, such as being a volunteer teacher (Park et al., 2007; Rebok et al., 2007). Such creative new approaches may yet yield the "gold standard" outcome that scholars have been seeking—gains in memory skill that transfer to daily life and are maintained over years.

At-Risk and Impaired Individuals

Just as perfecting self-help approaches to training may be key for bringing memory gains to large populations of older adults, targeting seniors who are at risk for dementia also represents an important arena for future training advances. Individuals with mild cognitive impairment (MCI) represent one such high-risk group. Mild cognitive impairment, or MCI, has been defined as a transitional condition between normal aging and dementia (Bruscoli & Lovestone, 2004; Petersen et al., 1999). Once diagnosed with MCI, these individuals progress to Alzheimer's disease at a rate of about 10% each year, roughly five times the expected incidence of dementia in their healthy peers (Bruscoli & Lovestone, 2004). Because this population is likely to progress to dementia, and because the number of individuals with MCI will likely grow as the population ages (Petersen et al., 2008), it is important to assist these individuals to preserve independent functioning for as long as possible.

There is some controversy as to whether the memory ability of individuals with MCI is amenable to traditional intervention approaches. Yesavage and colleagues (1990) found that lower cognitive status was related to fewer treatment gains, and in one of the largest intervention studies to date, the AC-TIVE intervention, MCI participants improved similarly to their normally functioning peers in the reasoning and speed training groups, but not in the memory training group (Unverzagt et al., 2007). As a result, the ACTIVE investigators suggested that older adults with MCI may have a neuropathological deficit that limits memory training impact. However, the ACTIVE study offered a fairly complex and intensive training program that was not designed specifically for more impaired seniors. Given that memory training has resulted in some success in mild dementia (Sitzer, Twamley, & Jeste, 2006), training modifications should be possible that will make interventions accessible for MCI.

There are promising data. McCoy (2004) found that participants with MCI were able to achieve 30-day performance gains similar to that of their cognitively healthy peers from practice alone. In addition, a handful of training interventions have suggested that older adults experiencing MCI can show performance-related gains (e.g., Cipriani, Bianchetti, & Trabucchi, 2006; Talassi et al., 2007; Werner, 2000). One such intervention by Belleville and colleagues (2006) offered training with organization, Method of Loci, imagery, and PQRST, which stands for Preview-Question-Read-Summarize-Test. The researchers reported significant improvement in delayed list recall and face–name recall for older adults with MCI, but no change in text recall.

One potential limitation in the MCI training literature to date is that only two programs to our knowledge have simultaneously aimed to improve both performance and beliefs (Rapp, Brenes, & Marsh, 2002; Troyer, Murphy, Anderson, Moscovitch, & Craik, 2008). Individuals with MCI not only have lower objective memory, but they also show lower subjective memory than their cognitively healthy peers (Cook & Marsiske, 2006; Jonker et al., 2000), so training programs aimed at improving both beliefs and performance may be needed for this population. A 6-week intervention by Rapp and colleagues (2002) found no change in laboratory tests of memory or self-reported use of memory strategies following training. However, trained participants did report more perceived control over memory following the intervention, suggesting that it may be possible to modify beliefs in individuals with MCI. A more recent 7-week intervention by Troyer and colleagues (2008) increased participants' knowledge and use of memory strategies, and these gains were maintained at 3-month follow-up, but the program did not successfully modify beliefs or performance. However, the Troyer intervention emphasized MCI and the risk of Alzheimer's disease early in the program, which could have reduced trainees' willingness to invest effort in retraining.

There is far more research on patients with Alzheimer's disease than those with MCI, partly due to the more recent categorization of MCI, and partly due to the perceived greater needs of the more impaired population. Attempts to use traditional strategy training with Alzheimer's patients have shown some success with mild dementia (Sitzer et al., 2006), but as the disease progresses, limitations in the learning skills of impaired individuals are caused by the degeneration of cells in the hippocampal area crucial for forming new memories. As limits on new learning increase, the best approach to training changes.

For individuals with more severe forms of dementia, and particularly those in nursing homes, the interventions are more similar to those used with patients suffering from memory impairment due to head injury, stroke, and other forms of brain damage. In each case, the goal is to maximize and/or effectively utilize residual skills. These methods include reminiscence therapy, which encourages patients to practice retrieving well-known information from semantic memory (e.g., Moos & Björn, 2006); spaced retrieval, which uses a systematic behavioral cuing process to implicitly build memory traces (e.g., Camp, 2006); repetition or structured practice (e.g., Hochhalter, Stevens, & Okonkwo, 2007); engagement with simple cognitive activities involving art or Montessori sensory skills (e.g., Malone & Camp, 2007); or some form of environmental support, such as a dictaphone, written or electronic organizers, lists, or learning to create obvious visible cues. For most individuals with severe memory difficulties, "external aids are probably the most helpful compensations for the greatest number of people and are most likely to be used in the long term" (Wilson, 1995, p. 176), although it can be challenging to train memory-impaired individuals to consistently use external aids.

In recent years, an exciting approach uses spaced retrieval methods for teaching patients particular information that it is important for them to know, for example, a room number, family phone number, doctor's name, or where to find the answer to a frequently asked question (Bourgeois et al., 2003; Camp, 2006). Recall for a specific item is cued repeatedly, beginning with a very small retention interval, possibly as little as a few seconds, depending on the patient's retention capacity, and the retention interval is increased systematically over time, depending on the success of retention. The spaced retrieval method was derived from basic memory research, showing that repetition of retrieval over successively longer intervals ("expanding rehearsal") is one of the best ways to learn in episodic memory (Landauer, 1989). In addition to helping patients recall specific information (Hawley & Cherry, 2004), the technique has also been used successfully to teach safe behavior and reduce behavioral problems in nursing homes (Camp, 2006; Camp, Bird, & Cherry, 2000). The success of this method may be due to the fact that it relies on repetition-priming effects to support memory using the less-impaired implicit memory system (Cherry, Simmons, & Camp, 1999). The method also has considerable practical value as it can be employed effectively, with minimal instruction, by caregivers and nursing home staff (Camp et al., 2000).

For individuals with more severe impairments, mixed results have occurred with traditional training programs. Research on MCI with traditional interventions shows promise, although this is a relatively new area of research (Belleville, 2008). Memory training has had some success with early Alzheimer's (Mimura & Komatsu, 2007; Sitzer et al., 2006), thus there is promise for intervening with MCI and possibly reducing the risk of future decline for MCI trainees. New approaches for this at-risk group might examine the benefits of programs that combine memory training with medications known to facilitate cognitive function in dementia (Yesavage et al., 2007) or combine strategy training with retraining of beliefs (West et al., 2008). For the most impaired group, those with Alzheimer's disease, or some other form of dementia, the more successful programs emphasize some kind of environmental support, regular use of residual cognitive skills, or techniques such as spaced retrieval that afford the opportunity to teach specific important information to individuals with limited new learning potential (Caltagirone et al., 2005).

Conclusions and Future Directions

We have reviewed current research and trends in memory aging, with a focus on explanatory models and mechanisms. There is intense interest in the field at present in identifying predictors of normative and non-normative memory aging, with concomitant efforts directed at preventing, slowing, and modulating the negative effects of neuropathological processes—as well as societal-cultural stereotypes—on memory ability in old age. Investigations of neurogenesis in the hippocampus and other aspects of the aging brain's plasticity at the molecular level (Jessberger & Gage, 2008) offer new possibilities for understanding the limits and potential of memory in late life. Research on the role of emotion and the amygdala in regulating and supporting episodic memory also suggests that this is relatively new and promising territory for understanding the affective mechanisms that control memory functioning in adulthood and old age (Allen et al., 2005) and, therefore, the possibility to exploit them in the service of memory.

Some evidence suggests that emotional memory is preserved in older adults and boosts declarative memory in the same manner as for younger adults (Denburg, Buchanan, Tranel, & Adolphs, 2003). The new generation of multifactorial memory training programs, reviewed in this chapter, has begun to incorporate positive affective instructional components with promising results (see West et al., 2005). The extent to which emotion may wield protective effects against failing memory abilities in older adulthood is not known. Some studies have found preserved emotional memory even in patients with Alzheimer's disease (Moayeri, Cahill, Jin, & Potkin, 2000), but other studies report that this preservation does not, in fact, boost subsequent memory recall in AD patients (Hamann, Monarch, & Goldstein, 2000). Zanetti et al. (2001) have shown that using techniques based on procedural memory abilities can be used to improve activities of daily living in individuals with mild to mild-moderate AD. Moreover, as reviewed earlier in this chapter, spaced-retrieval techniques have been shown to improve recall and simple memory associations in cognitively impaired individuals (Cherry et al., 1999). The success of such techniques can be attributed to the relative sparing of implicit memory processes in both normal aging and early stages of AD. Thus, research on those systems that are relatively spared in late life (e.g., emotion, implicit memory, procedural/skilled memory, semantic memory) will continue to inform and likely benefit ongoing intervention-based and memory-training research efforts.

Where will research on memory aging go next? Perhaps Jane Austen knew more about memory aging than we give her credit for. As she pointed out so eloquently in *Mansfield Park*, memory is rather enigmatic. At one level, contemporary memory researchers are still searching for elusive clues, according to one recent review (Dixon, Rust, Feltmate, & See, 2007). Dixon and colleagues challenge us to consider older adults' goals and how best to optimize memory functioning in late life. They point out that those goals should be realistic and personalized and, in the case of memory improvement, tailored to individual needs, abilities, and aspirations (see Buschkuehl et al., 2008; West et al., 2008, 2009). Although researchers will continue to investigate speed/accuracy dimensions of memory ability in adulthood, new studies of the personal function, purpose, and pleasure of remembering are emerging alongside more basic research programs. Austen would undoubtedly approve.

REFERENCES

Allen, P. A., Kaut, K. P., Lord, R. G., Hall, R. J., Grabbe, J. W., & Bowie, T. (2005). An emotional mediation theory of differential age effects in episodic and semantic memories. *Experimental Aging Research, 31,* 355–391.

Alzheimer's Association. (2008). 2008 Alzheimer's disease facts and figures. *Alzheimer's and Dementia, 4,* 110–133.

Amieva, J., Letenneur, L., Dartigues, J. F., Rouch-Leroyer, I., Sourgen, C., D'Alchée-Birée, F., et al. (2004). Annual rate and predictors of conversion to dementia in subjects presenting mild cognitive impairment criteria defined according to a population-based study. *Dementia and Geriatric Cognitive Disorders, 18,* 87–93.

Andrewes, D. G., Kinsella, G., & Murphy, M. (1996). Using a memory handbook to improve everyday memory in community-dwelling older adults with memory complaints. *Experimental Aging Research, 22,* 305–322.

Anschutz, L., Camp, C. J., Markley, R. P., & Kramer, J. J. (1987). Remembering mnemonics: A three-year follow-up on the effects of mnemonics training in elderly adults. *Experimental Aging Research, 13,* 141–143.

Apostolova, L. G., Dutton, R. A., Dinov, I. D., Hayashi, K. M., Toga, A. W., Cummings, J. L., et al. (2006). Conversion of mild cognitive impairment to Alzheimer disease predicted by hippocampal atrophy maps. *Archives of Neurology, 63,* 693–699.

Arai, H. (2005). Current concept and future research directions of mild cognitive impairment. *Psychogeriatrics, 5,* 83–88.

Aslan, A., Bauml, K-H., & Pastotter, B. (2007). No inhibitory deficit in older adults' episodic memory. *Psychological Science, 18,* 72–78.

Bagwell, D. K., & West, R. L. (2008). Assessing compliance: Active vs. inactive trainees in a memory intervention. *Clinical Interventions in Aging*, *3*, 371–382.

Bailey, H., Dunlosky, J., & Hertzog, C. (2009). Does differential strategy use account for age-related deficits in working-memory performance? *Psychology and Aging*, *24*, 82–92.

Baldi, R. A., Plude, D. J., & Schwartz, L. K. (1996). New technologies for memory training with older adults. *Cognitive Technology*, *1*, 25–35.

Ball, K., Berch, D. B., Helmers, K. F., Jobe, J. B., Leveck, M. D., Marsiske, M., et al. (2002). Effects of cognitive training interventions with older adults: A randomized controlled trial. *Journal of the American Medical Association*, *288*, 2271–2281.

Baltes, P. B., Freund, A., & Li, S-C. (2005). The psychological science of human ageing. In M. L. Johnson (Ed.), *The Cambridge Handbook of Age and Ageing* (pp. 47–71). New York: Cambridge University Press.

Baltes, P. B., & Schaie, K. W. (1974). Aging and IQ: The myth of the twilight years. *Psychology Today*, *10*, 35–40.

Baltes, P. B., & Schaie, K. W. (1976). On the plasticity of intelligence in adulthood and old age: Where Horn and Donaldson fail. *American Psychologist*, *31*, 720–725.

Bandura, A. (1997). *Self Efficacy: The Exercise of Control*. New York: Freeman and Co.

Belleville, S. (2008). Cognitive training for persons with mild cognitive impairment. *International Psychogeriatrics*, *20*, 57–66.

Belleville, S., Gilbert, B., Fontaine, F., Gagnon, L., Menard, E., & Gauthier, S. (2006). Improvement of episodic memory in persons with mild cognitive impairment and healthy older adults: Evidence from a cognitive intervention program. *Dementia and Geriatric Cognitive Disorders*, *22*, 486–499.

Berry, J. M. (1999). Memory self-efficacy in its social cognitive context. In T. M. Hess & F. Blanchard-Fields (Eds.), *Social Cognition and Aging* (pp. 69–96). San Diego: Academic Press.

Berry, J. M., & West, R. L. (1993). Cognitive self-efficacy in relation to personal mastery and goal setting across the life span. *International Journal of Behavioral Development*, *16*, 351–379.

Berry, J. M., West, R. L., & Dennehey, D. M. (1989). Reliability and validity of the Memory Self-Efficacy Questionnaire. *Developmental Psychology*, *25*, 701–713.

Best, D. L., Hamlett, K. W., & Davis, S. W. (1992). Memory complaint and memory performance in the elderly: The effects of memory-skills training and expectancy change. *Applied Cognitive Psychology*, *6*, 405–416.

Bherer, L., Kramer, A. F., Peterson, M. S., Colcombe, S., Erickson, K., & Becic, E. (2006). Testing the limits of cognitive plasticity in older adults: Application to attentional control. *Acta Psychologica*, *123*, 261–278.

Birren, J. E., & Botwinick, J. (1955). Age differences in finger, jaw, and foot reaction time to auditory stimuli. *Journal of Gerontology*, *10*, 430–432.

Birren, J. E., & Schroots, J. F. (2006). Autobiographical memory and the narrative self over the life span. In J. E. Birren & K. W. Schaie (Eds.), *Handbook of the Psychology of Aging* (6th ed., pp. 477–498). Amsterdam: Elsevier.

Bischkopf, J., Busse, A., & Angermeyer, M. C. (2002). Mild cognitive impairment—A review of prevalence, incidence and outcome according to current approaches. *Acta Psychiatrica Scandinavica*, *106*, 403–414.

Bissig, D., & Lustig, C. (2007). Who benefits from memory training? *Psychological Science, 18*, 720–726.

Bottirolli, S., Cavallini, E., & Vecchi, T. (2008). Long-term effects of memory training in the elderly: A longitudinal study. *Archives of Gerontology and Geriatrics, 47*, 277–289.

Bourgeois, M. S., Camp, C., Rose, M., White, B., Malone, M., Carr, J., et al. (2003). A comparison of training strategies to enhance use of external aids by persons with dementia. *Journal of Communication Disorders, 36*, 361–378.

Brayne, C. (2007). The elephant in the room—health brains in later life, epidemiology and public health. *Nature, 8*, 233–239.

Brehmer, Y., Li, S-C., Straube, B., Stoll, G., von Oertzen, T., Muller, V., et al. (2008). Comparing memory skill maintenance across the life span: Preservation in adults, increase in children. *Psychology and Aging, 23*, 227–238.

Bröder, A., Herwig, A., Teipel, S., & Fast, K. (2008). Different storage and retrieval deficits in normal aging and mild cognitive impairment: A multinomial modeling analysis. *Psychology and Aging, 23*, 353–365.

Brooks, J. O., III, Friedman, L., Pearman, A. M., Gray, C., & Yesavage, J. A. (1999). Mnemonic training in older adults: Effects of age, length of training, and type of cognitive pretraining. *International Psychogeriatrics, 11*, 75–84.

Bruscoli, M., & Lovestone, S. (2004). Is MCI really just early dementia? A systematic review of conversion studies. *International Psychogeriatrics, 16*, 129–140.

Buchler, N.E.G., & Reder, L. M. (2007). Modeling age-related memory deficits: A two-parameter solution. *Psychology and Aging, 22*, 104–121.

Burns, A., & Zaudig, M. (2002). Mild cognitive impairment in older adults. *The Lancet, 360*, 1963–1965.

Buschkuehl, M., Jaeggi, S. M., Hutchinson, S., Perrig-Chiello, P., Dapp, C., Muller, M., et al. (2008). Impact of working memory training on memory performance in old-old adults. *Psychology and Aging, 23*, 743–753.

Busse, A, Bischkopf, J., Riedel-Heller, S. G., & Angermeyer, M. C. (2003). Mild cognitive impairment: prevalence and predictive validity according to current approaches. *Acta Neurologica Scandinavica, 108*, 71–81.

Cabeza, R. (2001). Cognitive neuroscience of aging: Contributions of functional neuroimaging. *Scandinavian Journal of Psychology, 42*, 277–286.

Cabeza, R. (2002). Hemispheric asymmetry reduction in older adults: The HAROLD model. *Psychology and Aging, 17*, 85–100.

Caltagirone, C., Bianchetti, A., Di Luca, M., Mecocci, P., Padovani, A., Pirfo, E., et al. (2005). Guidelines for the treatment of Alzheimer's disease from the Italian Association of Psychogeriatrics. *Drugs & Aging, 22*, 1–26.

Camp, C. J. (1998). Memory interventions for normal and pathological older adults. In R. Schulz, G. Maddox, & M. P. Lawton (Eds.), *Annual Review of Gerontology and Geriatrics, Vol 18: Focus on Interventions Research With Older Adults* (pp. 155–189). New York: Springer.

Camp, C. J. (2006). Spaced retrieval. In D. K. Attix & K. A. Welsh-Bohmer (Eds.), *Geriatric Neuropsychology: Assessment and Intervention* (pp. 275–292). New York: Guilford Press.

Camp, C. J., Bird, M. J., & Cherry, K. E. (2000). Retrieval strategies as a rehabilitation aid for cognitive loss in pathological aging. In R. D. Hill, L. Bäckman, & A. S.

Neely (Eds.), *Cognitive Rehabilitation in Old Age* (pp. 224–248). New York: Oxford University Press.

Carver, S., & Scheier, M. F. (2001). *On the Self-regulation of Behavior.* Cambridge, UK: Cambridge University Press.

Cavanaugh, J. C., Feldman, J. M., & Hertzog, C. (1998). Memory beliefs as social cognition: A reconceptualization of what memory questionnaires assess. *Review of General Psychology, 2,* 48–65.

Cavanaugh, J. C., & Green, E. E. (1990). I believe, therefore I can: Self-efficacy beliefs in memory aging. In E. A. Lovelace (Ed.), *Aging and Cognition: Mental Processes, Self-awareness, and Interventions* (pp. 189–230). North Holland: Elsevier Science Publishers B.V.

Cavanaugh, J. C., & Perlmutter, M. (1982). Metamemory: A critical examination. *Child Development, 53,* 11–28.

Cervone, D., Artistico, D., & Berry, J. M. (2006). Self-efficacy and adult development. In C. Hoare (Ed.), *Handbook of Adult Development and Learning* (pp. 169–195). New York: Oxford University Press.

Chalfonte, B. L., & Johnson, M. K. (1996). Feature memory and binding in young and older adults. *Memory & Cognition, 24,* 403–416.

Chasteen, A. L., Bhattacharyya, S., Horhota, M., Tam, R., & Hasher, L. (2005). How feelings of stereotype threat influence older adults' memory performance. *Experimental Aging Research, 31,* 235–260.

Cherry, K. E., Simmons, S. S., & Camp, C. J. (1999). Spaced-retrieval enhances memory in older adults with probable Alzheimer's disease. *Journal of Clinical Geropsychology, 5,* 159–175.

Chodosh, J., Reuben, D. B., Albert, M. S., & Seeman, T. E. (2002). Predicting cognitive impairment in high-functioning community-dwelling older persons: MacArthur studies of successful aging. *Journal of American Geriatrics Society, 50,* 1051–1060.

Chopard, G., Pitard, A., Ferreira, S., Vanholsbeeck, G., Rumbach, L., & Galmiche, J. (2007). Combining the Memory Impairment Screen and the Isaacs Set Test: A practical tool for screening dementias. *Journal of the American Geriatrics Society, 55,* 1426–1430.

Chua, E. F., Schacter, D. L., & Sperling, R. A. (2009). Neural basis for recognition confidence in younger and older adults. *Psychology and Aging, 24,* 139–153.

Cipriani, G., Bianchietti, A., & Trabucci, M. (2006). Outcomes of a computer-based cognitive rehabilitation program on Alzheimer's disease patients compared with those on patients affected by mild cognitive impairment. *Archives of Gerontology and Geriatrics, 43,* 327–335.

Cook, S., & Marsiske, M. (2006). Subjective memory beliefs and cognitive performance in normal and mildly impaired older adults. *Aging and Mental Health, 10,* 413–423.

Craik, F.I.M. (1994). Memory changes in normal aging. *Current Directions in Psychological Science, 3,* 155–158.

Craik, F.I.M. (2008). Memory changes in normal and pathological aging. *Canadian Journal of Psychiatry, 53,* 343–345.

Craik, F.I.M., & Bialystok, E. (2006). Cognition through the lifespan: Mechanisms of change. *Trends in Cognitive Science, 10,* 131–138.

Craik, F.I.M., & Byrd, M. (1982). Aging and cognitive deficits: The role of attentional resources. In F.I.M. Craik & S. E. Trehub (Eds.), *Aging and Cognitive Processes* (pp. 191–211). New York: Plenum Press.

Davis, H. S., & Rockwood, K. (2004). Conceptualization of mild cognitive impairment: A review. *International Journal of Geriatric Psychiatry, 19*, 313–319.

Denberg, N. L., Buchanan, T. W., Tranel, D., & Adolphs, R. (2003). Evidence for preserved emotional memory in normal older persons. *Emotion, 3*, 239–253.

Derwinger, A., Stigsdotter Neely, A., & Bäckman, L. (2005). Design your own memory strategies! Self-generated strategy training versus mnemonic training in old age: An 8-month followup. *Neuropsychological Rehabilitation, 15*, 37–54.

Derwinger, A., Stigsdotter Neely, A., Persson, M., Hill, R. D., & Bäckman, L. (2003). Remembering numbers in old age: Mnemonic training versus self-generated strategy training. *Aging, Neuropsychology, and Cognition, 10*, 202–214.

Desrichard, O., & Kopetz, C. (2005). A threat in the elder: The impact of task instructions, self-efficacy and performance expectations on memory performance in the elderly. *European Journal of Social Psychology, 35*, 537–552.

Devanand, D. P., Pradhaban, G., Liu, X., Khandji, A., De Santi, S., Segal, S., et al. (2007). Hippocampal and entorhinal atrophy in mild cognitive impairment. *Neurology, 68*, 828–836.

Dixon, R. A., & Hultsch, D. F. (1983). Structure and development of metamemory in adulthood. *Journal of Gerontology, 38*, 682–688.

Dixon, R. A., Hultsch, D. F., & Hertzog, C. (1988). The Metamemory in Adulthood (MIA) Questionnaire. *Psychopharmacology Bulletin, 24*, pp. 671–688.

Dixon, R. A., Rust, T. B., Feltmate, S. E., & See, S. K. (2007). Memory and aging: Selected research directions and application issues. *Canadian Psychology, 48*, 67–76.

Dunlosky, J., Hertzog, C., & Powell-Moman, A. (2005). The contribution of mediator-based deficiencies to age differences in associative learning. *Developmental Psychology, 41*, 389–400.

Elderkin-Thompson, V., Ballmaier, M., Hellemann, G., Pham, D., & Kumar, A. (2008). Executive function and MRI prefrontal volumes among healthy older adults. *Neuropsychology, 22*, 626–637.

Elliott, E. S., & Lachman, M. E. (1989). Enhancing memory by modifying control beliefs, attributions, and performance goals in the elderly. In P. S. Fry (Ed.), *Psychological Perspectives of Helplessness and Control in the Elderly* (pp. 339–367). North Holland: Elsevier Science Publishers B.V.

Erber, J. T., Abello, S., & Moninger, C. (1988). Age and individual differences in the immediate and delayed effectiveness of mnemonic instructions on performance. *Experimental Aging Research, 14*, 119–124.

Erickson, K. I., Colcombe, S. J., Wadhwa, R., Bherer, L., Peterson, M. S., Scalf, P. E., et al. (2007). Training-induced plasticity in older adults: Effects of training on hemispheric asymmetry. *Neurobiology of Aging, 28*, 272–283.

Fernandes, M., Ross, M., Wiegand, M., & Schryer, E. (2008). Are the memories of older adults positively biased? *Psychology and Aging, 23*, 297–306.

Ferri, C. P., Prince, M., Brayne, C., Brodaty, H., Fratiglioni, L., Ganguli, M., et al. (2005). Global prevalence of dementia: a Delphi consensus study. *Lancet, 366*, 2112–2117.

Floyd, M., & Scogin, F. (1997). Effects of memory training on the subjective memory functioning and mental health of older adults: A meta-analysis. *Psychology and Aging, 12*, 150–161.

Flynn, T. M., & Storandt, M. (1990). Supplemental group discussions in memory training for older adults. *Psychology and Aging, 5*, 178–181.

Fratiglioni, L., & Wang, H-X. (2007). Brain reserve hypothesis in dementia. *Journal of Alzheimer's Disease, 12*, 11–22.

Gabrieli, J. D. (1998). Cognitive neuroscience of human memory. *Annual Review of Psychology, 49*, 87–115.

Gabryelewicz, T., Styczynska, M., Luczywek, E., Barczak, A., Pfeffer, A., Androsiuk, W., et al. (2007). The rate of conversion of mild cognitive impairment to dementia: Predictive role of depression. *International Journal of Geriatric Society, 22*, 563–567.

Gardiner, M., Luszcz, M. A., & Bryan, J. (1997). The manipulation and measurement of task-specific memory self-efficacy in younger and older adults. *International Journal of Behavioral Development, 21*, 209–227.

Gaskill, P. J., & Murphy, P. K. (2008). Effects of a memory strategy on second-graders' performance and self-efficacy. *Contemporary Educational Psychology, 29*, 27–49.

Gatz, M. (2007). Genetics, dementia, and the elderly. *Current Directions in Psychological Science, 16*, 123–127.

Gaultney, J. F., Kipp, K., & Kirk, G. (2005). Utilization deficiency and working memory capacity in adult memory performance: Not just for children anymore. *Cognitive Development, 20*, 205–213.

Gluck, M. A., Myers, C. E., Nicolle, M. M., & Johnson, S. (2006). Computational models of the hippocampal region: Implications for prediction of risk for Alzheimer's disease in non-demented elderly. *Current Alzheimer Research, 3*, 247–257.

Godbolt, A. K., Cipolotti, L., Anderson, W. M., Archer, H., Janssen, J. C., Price, S., et al. (2005). A decade of pre-diagnositc assessment in a case of familial Alzheimer's disease: Tracking progression from asymptomatic to MCI and dementia. *Neurocase, 11*, 56–64.

Gratzinger, P., Sheikh, J. I., Friedman, L., & Yesavage, J. A. (1990). Cognitive interventions to improve face-name recall: The role of *personality* trait differences. *Developmental Psychology, 26*, 889–893.

Guarch, J., Marcos, T., Salamero, M., Gastó, C., & Blesa, R. (2008). Mild cognitive impairment: A risk indicator of later dementia, or a preclinical phase of the disease? *International Journal of Geriatric Psychiatry, 23*, 257–265.

Hall, G. S. (1904). *Adolescence: Its Psychology and Its Relations to Physiology, Anthropology, Sociology, Sex, Crime, Religion, and Education.* New York: Appleton.

Hall, G. S. (1922). *Senescence: The Last Half of Life.* New York: Appleton.

Hamann, S. B., Monarch, E. S., & Goldstein, F. C. (2000). Memory enhancement for emotional stimuli is impaired in early Alzheimer's disease. *Neuropsychology, 14*, 82–92.

Hamuro, A., Isono, H., Sugai, Y., Torii, S., Furuta, N., Mimura, M., et al. (2006). Behavioral and psychological symptoms of dementia in untreated Alzheimer's disease patients. *Pscyhogeriatrcs, 7*, 4–7.

Hasher, L., Chung, C., May, C. P., & Foong, N. (2002). Age, time of testing, and proactive interference. *Canadian Journal of Experimental Psychology, 56*, 200–207.

Hasher, L., & Zacks, R. T. (1988) Working memory, comprehension, and aging: A review and a new view. In G. H. Bower (Ed.), *The Psychology of Learning and Motivation: Advances in Research and Theory* (vol. 22, pp. 193–225). San Diego, CA: Academic Press.

Hastings, E. C., & West, R. L. (in press). The relative success of a self-help and group-based memory training program for older adults. *Psychology and Aging.*

Hawley, K. S., & Cherry, K. E. (2004) Spaced-retrieval effects on name-face recognition in older adults with probable Alzheimer's disease. *Behavior Modification, 28,* 276–296.

Head, D., Rodrigue, K. M., Kennedy, K. M., & Raz, N. (2008). Neuroanatomical and cognitive mediators of age-related differences in episodic memory. *Neuropsychology, 22,* 491–507.

Hertzog, C., Dixon, R. A., & Hultsch, D. F. (1990) Relationships between metamemory, memory predictions, and memory task performance in adults. *Psychology and Aging, 5,* 215–227.

Hertzog, C., Dixon, R. A., Hultsch, D. F., & MacDonald, S.W.S. (2003). Latent change models of adult cognition: Are changes in processing speed and working memory associated with change sin episodic memory? *Psychology & Aging, 18,* 755–769.

Hertzog, C., & Hultsch, D. F. (2000). Metacognition in adulthood and old age. In F.I.M. Craik & T. A. Salthouse (Eds.), *The Handbook of Aging and Cognition* (pp. 417–466). Mahwah, NJ: Lawrence Erlbaum Associates.

Hess, T. M., Auman, C., Colcombe, S. J., & Rahhal, T. A. (2003). The impact of stereotype threat on age differences in memory performance. *Journals of Gerontology: Series B: Psychological Sciences and Social Sciences, 58B,* P3–P11.

Hess, T. M., & Hinson, J. T. (2006). Age-related variation in the influences of aging stereotypes on memory in adulthood. *Psychology and Aging, 21,* 621–625.

Hill, R. D., Sheikh, J. I., & Yesavage, J. A. (1987). The effect of mnemonic training on perceived recall confidence in the elderly. *Experimental Aging Research, 13,* 185–188.

Hirshbein, L. D. (2002). The senile mind: Psychology and old age in the 1930 and 1940s. *Journal of the History of the Behavioral Sciences, 38,* 43–56.

Hochhalter, A. K., Stevens, A. B., & Okonkwo, O. (2007). Structured practice: A memory intervention for persons with dementia. *American Journal of Alzheimer's Disease and Other Dementias, 21,* 424–430.

Horn, J. L., & Donaldson, G. (1976). On the myth of intellectual decline in adulthood. *American Psychologist, 31,* 701–719.

Horn, J. L., & Donaldson, G. (1977). Faith is not enough: A response to the Baltes-Schaie claim that intelligence does not wane. *American Psychologist, 32,* 369–373.

Hultsch, D. F. (1969). Adult age differences in the organization of free recall. *Developmental Psychology, 1,* 673–678.

Ishikawa, T., & Ikeda, M. (2007). Mild cognitive impairment in a population-based epidemiological study. *Psychogeriatrics, 7,* 104–108.

James, L. E. (2004). Meeting Mr. Farmer versus meeting a farmer: Specific effects of aging on learning proper names. *Psychology and Aging, 19,* 515–522.

James, L. E., Fogler, K. A., & Tauber, S. K. (2008). Recognition memory measures yield disproportionate effects of aging on learning face-name associations. *Psychology and Aging, 23,* 657–664.

Jessberger, S., & Gage, F. H. (2008). Stem-cell–associated structural and functional plasticity in the aging hippocampus. *Psychology and Aging, 23,* 684–691.

Jonker, C. J., Geerlings, M. I., & Schmand, B. (2000). Are memory complaints predictive for dementia? A review of clinical and population-based studies. *International Journal of Geriatric Psychiatry, 15,* 983–991.

Jopp, D., & Hertzog, C. (2007). Activities, self-referent memory beliefs, and cognitive performance: Evidence for direct and mediated relations. *Psychology and Aging, 22,* 811–825.

Kail, R. (1986). Sources of age differences in speed of processing. *Child Development, 57,* 969–987.

Kail, R. (1991a). Developmental change in speed of processing during childhood and adolescence. *Psychological Bulletin, 109,* 490–501.

Kail, R. (1991b). Processing time declines exponentially during childhood and adolescence. *Developmental Psychology, 27,* 259–266.

Kail, R., & Park, Y-S. (1994). Processing time, articulation time, and memory span. *Journal of Experimental Child Psychology, 57,* 281–291.

Kausler, D. H. (1994). *Learning and Memory in Normal Aging.* San Diego, CA: Academic Press.

Kausler, D. H., & Puckett, J. M. (1980). Adult age differences in recognition memory for a nonsemantic attribute. *Experimental Aging Research, 6,* 349–355.

Kawas, C. H., & Corrada, M. M. (2006). Alzheimer's and dementia in the oldest-old: A century of challenges. *Current Alzheimer Research, 3,* 411–419.

Kensinger, E. A., Brierley, B., Medford, N., Growdon, J. H., & Corkin, S. (2002). Effects of normal aging and Alzheimer's disease on emotional memory. *Emotion, 2,* 118–134.

Klempin, F., & Kempermann, G. (2007). Adult hippocampal neurogenesis and aging. *European Archives of Psychiatry and Clinical Neuroscience, 257,* 271–280.

Kliegl, R., Smith, J., & Baltes, P. B. (1989). Testing-the-limits and the study of adult age differences in cognitive plasticity of a mnemonic skill. *Developmental Psychology, 25,* 247–256.

Kramer, J. H., Mungas, D., Reed, B. R., Wetzel, M. E., Burnett, M. M., Miller, B. L., et al. (2007). Longitudinal MRI and cognitive change in healthy elderly. *Neuropsychology, 21,* 412–418.

Labouvie-Vief, G. (1976). Toward optimizing cognitive competence in later life. *Educational Gerontology, 1,* 75–92.

Labouvie-Vief, G. (1977). Adult cognitive development: In search of alternative interpretations. *Merrill-Palmer Quarterly, 23,* 227–263.

Lachman, M. E., Andreoletti, C., & Pearman, A. (2006). Memory control beliefs: How are they related to age, strategy use and memory improvement? *Social Cognition, 24,* 359–385.

Lachman, M. E., Weaver, S. L., Bandura, M., Elliott, E., & Lewkowicz, C. J. (1992). Improving memory and control beliefs through cognitive restructuring and self-generated strategies. *Journal of Gerontology, Psychological Sciences, 47,* 293–299.

Landauer, T. K. (1989). Some good and bad reasons for studying memory and cognition in the wild. In L. W. Poon, D. C. Rubin, & B. A. Wilson (Eds.), *Everyday Cognition in Adulthood and Late Life* (pp. 116–125). New York: Cambridge University Press.

Levy, B. (1996). Improving memory in old age through implicit self-stereotyping. *Journal of Personality and Social Psychology, 71,* 1092–1107.

Lindenberger, U., Marsiske, M., & Baltes, P. B. (2000). Memorizing while walking: Increase in dual-task costs from young adulthood to old age. *Psychology and Aging, 15,* 417–436.

Lineweaver, T. T., Bergner, A. K., & Hertzog, C. (2009). Expectations about memory change across the life span are impacted by aging stereotypes. *Psychology and Aging, 24*, 169–176.

Lott, I. T. (1982). Down's syndrome, aging, and Alzheimer's disease: A clinical review. *Annals of the New York Academy of Sciences, 396*, 15–27.

Lustig, C., Hasher, L., & Zacks, R. T. (2007). Inhibitory deficit theory: Recent developments in a "new view." In D. S. Gorfein & C. M. MacLeod (Eds.), *Inhibition in Cognition* (pp. 145–162). Washington, DC: American Psychological Association.

Mahncke, H. W., Connor, B. B., Appelman, J., Ahsanuddin, O. N., Hardy, J. L., Wood, R. A., et al. (2006). Memory enhancement in healthy older adults using a brain plasticity-based training program: A randomized, controlled study. *Proceedings of the National Academy of Sciences, 103*, 12523–12528.

Malone, M. L., & Camp, C. J. (2007). Montessori-based dementia programming: Providing tools for engagement. *Dementia, 6*, 150–157.

Mariani, E., Monastero, R., & Mecocci, P. (2007). Mild cognitive impairment: A systematic review. *Journal of Alzheimer's Disease, 12*, 23–35.

Matsuda, H. (2007). Progress in neuroimaging of Alzheimer's disease. *Psychogeriatrics, 7*, 118–124.

Mattson, M. P., & Magnus, T. (2006). Ageing and neuronal vulnerability. *Nature, 7*, 278–294.

McCoy, K. (2004). *Understanding the Transition from Normal Cognitive Aging to Mild Cognitive Impairment: Comparing the Intraindividual Variability in Cognitive Function.* Unpublished doctoral dissertation, University of Florida.

McDaniel, M. A., Einstein, G. O., & Jacoby, L. L. (2008). New considerations in aging and memory: The glass may be half full. In F.I.M. Craik & T. A. Salthouse (Eds.), *The Handbook of Aging and Cognition* (3rd ed., pp. 251–310). New York: Psychology Press.

McDonald-Miszczak, L., Gould, O. N., & Tychynski, D. (1999). Metamemory predictors of prospective and retrospective memory performance. *Journal of General Psychology, 126*, 37–52.

McDowd, J. M. (1997). Inhibition in attention and aging. *Journals of Gerontology: Series B: Psychological Sciences and Social Sciences, 52B*, P265–P273.

McDowd, J. M., & Craik, F.I.M. (1988) Effects of aging and task difficulty on divided attention performance. *Journal of Experimental Psychology: Human Perception and Performance, 14*, 267–280.

McKitrick, L. A., Friedman, L. F., Brooks, J. O., III, Pearman, A., Kraemer, H. C., & Yesavage, J. A. (1999). Predicting response of older adults to mnemonic training: Who will benefit? *International Psychogeriatrics, 11*, 289–300.

Meguro, K. (2007). Community based measures for managing mild cognitive impairment: The Osaki-Tajiri Project. *Psychogeriatrics, 7*, 132–136.

Miller, L.M.S., & West, R. L. (in press). The effects of age, control beliefs, and feedback on self-regulation of reading and problem solving. *Experimental Aging Research.*

Mimura, M., & Komatsu, S., (2007). Cognitive rehabilitation and cognitive training for mild dementia. *Psychogeriatrics, 7*, 137–143.

Moayeri, S. E., Cahill, L., Jin, Y, & Potkin, S. G. (2000). Relative sparing of emotionally influenced memory in Alzheimer's disease. *Neuroreport: For Rapid Communication of Neuroscience Research, 11*, 653–655.

Mohs, R. C., Ashman, T. A., Jantzen, K., Albert, M., Brandt, J., Gordon, B., et al. (1998). A study of the efficacy of a comprehensive memory enhancement program in healthy elderly persons. *Psychiatry Research, 77*, 183–195.

Moos, I., & Björn, A. (2006). Use of the life story in the institutional care of people with dementia: A review of intervention studies. *Ageing and Society, 26*, 431–454.

Morris, J. C., & Cummings, J. (2005). Mild cognitive impairment (MCI) represents early-stage Alzheimer's disease. *Journal of Alzheimer's Disease, 7*, 235–239.

Naveh-Benjamin, M. (2000). Adult age differences in memory performance: Tests of an associative deficit hypothesis. *Journal of Experimental Psychology: Learning, Memory, and Cognition, 26*, 1170–1187.

Neupert, S. D., Almeida, D. M., Mroczek, D. K., & Spiro, A., III. (2006). Daily stressors and memory failures in a naturalistic setting: Findings from the VA normative aging study. *Psychology and Aging, 21*, 424–429.

Neupert, S. D., Mroczek, D. K., & Spiro, A., III. (2008). Neuroticism moderates the daily relation between stressors and memory failures. *Psychology and Aging, 23*, 287–296.

Nilsson, L-G. (2003). Memory function in normal aging. *Acta Neurologica Scandinavica, 107*, 7–13.

O'Brien, L. T., & Hummert, M. L. (2006). Memory performance of late middle-aged adults: Contrasting self-stereotyping and stereotype threat accounts of assimilation to age stereotypes. *Social Cognition, 24*, 338–358.

Old, S. R., & Naveh-Benjamin, M. (2008a). Differential effects of age on item and associative measures of memory: A meta-analysis. *Psychology and Aging, 23*, 104–118.

Old, S. R., & Naveh-Benjamin, M. (2008b). Memory for people and their actions: Further evidence for an age-related associative deficit. *Psychology and Aging, 23*, 467–472.

Palmer, K., Fratiglioni, L., & Winblad, B. (2003). What is mild cognitive impairment? Variations in definitions and evolution of nondemented persons with cognitive impairment. *Acta Neurologica Scandinavica, 107*, 14–20.

Park, D. C., Gutchess, A. H., Meade, M. L., & Stine-Morrow, E.A.L. (2007). Improving cognitive function in older adults: Nontraditional approaches. *Journal of Gerontology: Psychological Sciences, 62B*, 45–52.

Park, D., Lautenschlager, G., Hedden, T., Davidson, N., Smith, A., & Smith, P. (2002). Models of visuospatial and verbal memory across the adult life span. *Psychology and Aging, 17*, 299–320.

Peng, F. (2003). Is dementia a disease? *Gerontology, 49*, 384–391.

Perlmutter, M. (1978). What is memory aging the aging of? *Developmental Psychology, 14*, 330–345.

Peters, J., & Daum, I. (2008). Differential effects of normal aging on recollection of concrete and abstract words. *Neuropsychology, 22*, 255–261.

Petersen, R. C., & Bennett, D. (2005). Mild cognitive impairment: Is it Alzheimer's disease or not? *Journal of Alzheimer's Disease, 7*, 241–245.

Petersen, R. C., Roberts, R., Knopman, D. S., Geda, Y., Pankrantz, V., Boeve, B. F., et al. (2008). *The Mayo Clinic Study of Aging: Incidence of Mild Cognitive Impairment.* Paper presented at the 2008 International Conference on Alzheimer's Disease, Chicago, IL.

Petersen, R. C., Smith, G. E., Waring, S. C., Ivnik, R. J., Kokmen, E., & Tangelos, E. G. (1997). Ageing, memory, and mild cognitive impairment. *International Psychogeriatrics, 9*, 65–60.

Petersen, R. C., Smith, G. E., Waring, S. C., Ivnik, R. J., Tangalos, E. G., & Kokmen, E. (1999). Mild cognitive impairment: Clinical characterization and outcome. *Archives of Neurology, 56*, 303–308.

Ponds, R.W.H.M., & Jolles, J. (1996). The abridged Metamemory in Adulthood (MIA) Questionnaire: Structure and effects of age, sex, and education. *Psychology and Aging, 11*, 324–332.

Poon, L. W., Walsh-Sweeney, L., & Fozard, J. L. (1980). Memory skill training for the elderly: Salient issues on the use of imagery mnemonics. In L. W. Poon, J. L. Fozard, L. S. Cermak, D. Arenberg, & L. W. Thompson (Eds.), *New Directions in Memory and Aging: Proceedings of the George A Talland Memorial Conference* (pp. 461–484). Hillsdale, NJ: Lawrence Erlbaum Associates.

Rahhal, T. A., Hasher, L., & Colcombe, S. J. (2001). Instructional manipulations and age differences in memory: Now you see them, now you don't. *Psychology and Aging, 16*, 697–706.

Rapp, S., Brenes, G., & Marsh, A. P. (2002). Memory enhancement training for OA with mild cognitive impairment: A preliminary study. *Aging and Mental Health, 6*, 5–11.

Rasmusson, D. X., Rebok, G. W., Bylsma, F. W., & Brandt, J. (1999). Effects of three types of memory training in normal elderly. *Aging, Neuropsychology, and Cognition, 6*, 56–66.

Raz, A. (2006). Individual differences and attentional varieties. *Europa Medicophysica, 42*, 53–58.

Rebok, G. W., & Balcerak, L. J. (1989). Memory self-efficacy and performance differences in young and old adults: The effect of mnemonic training. *Developmental Psychology, 25*, 714–721.

Rebok, G. W., Carlson, M. C., & Langbaum, J.B.S. (2007). Training and maintaining memory abilities in healthy older adults: Traditional and novel approaches. *Journal of Gerontology: Psychological Sciences, 62B*, 53–61.

Rebok, G. W., Rasmusson, D. X., Bylsma, F. W., & Brandt, J. (1997). Memory improvement tapes: How effective for elderly adults? *Aging, Neuropsychology, and Cognition, 4*, 304–311.

Rendell, P. G., Castel, A. D., & Craik, F.I.M. (2005). Memory for proper names in old age: A disproportionate impairment? *The Quarterly Journal of Experimental Psychology A: Human Experimental Psychology, 58A*, 54–71.

Richie, K., Artero, S., & Touchon, J. (2001). Classification criteria for mild cognitive impairment: A population-based validation study. *Neurology, 63*, 115–121.

Ronnlund, M., Nyberg, L., Backman, L., & Nilsson, L-G. (2005). Stability, growth, and decline in adult life span development of declarative memory: Cross-sectional and longitudinal data from a population-based study. *Psychology and Aging, 20*, 3–18.

Royall, D. R. (2005). Mild cognitive impairment and functional status. *Journal of the American Geriatrics Society, 54*, 163–165.

Rozzini, L., Chilovi, B. V., Conti, M., Bertoletti, E., Delrio, I., Trabucchi, M., et al. (2007). Conversion of amnestic mild cognitive impairment to dementia of Alzheimer type is independent to memory deterioration. *International Journal of Geriatric Psychiatry, 22*, 1217–1222.

Salmon, D., & Hodges, J. R. (2005). Introduction: Mild cognitive impairment—Cognitive, behavioral and biological factors. *Neurocase, 11*, 1–2.

Salthouse, T. A. (1991). Mediation of adult age differences in cognition by reductions in working memory and speed of processing. *Psychological Science, 2*, 179–183.

Salthouse, T. A. (1993). Speed mediation of adult age differences in cognition. *Developmental Psychology, 29*, 722–738.

Salthouse, T. A. (2006) Mental exercise and mental aging. *Perspectives on Psychological Science, 1*, 68–87.

Salthouse, T. A., & Babcock, R. L. (1991). Decomposing adult age differences in working memory. *Developmental Psychology, 27*, 763–776.

Schaefer, S., Krampe, R., Lindenberger, U., & Baltes, P. B. (2008). Age differences between children and young adults in the dynamics of dual-task prioritization: Body (balance) versus mind (memory). *Developmental Psychology, 44*, 747–757.

Schaffer, G., & Poon, L. W. (1982). Individual variability in memory training with the elderly. *Educational Gerontology, 8*, 217–229.

Schooler, C., & Mulatu, M. S. (2001). The reciprocal effects of leisure time activities and intellectual functioning in older people: A longitudinal analysis. *Psychology and Aging, 16*, 466–482.

Scogin, F., & Bienias, J. L. (1988). A three-year followup of older participants in a memory-skills training program. *Psychology and Aging, 3*, 334–337.

Scogin, F., Prohaska, M., & Weeks, E. (1998). The comparative efficacy of self-taught and group memory training for older adults. *Journal of Clinical Geropsychology, 4*, 301–314.

Scogin, F., Storandt, M., & Lott, L. (1985). Memory-skills training, memory complaints, and depression in older adults. *Journal of Gerontology, 40*, 562–568.

Sepe-Monti, M., Pantano, P., Vanacore, N., De Carolis, A., Bianchi, V., Antonini, G., et al. (2007). Vascular risk factors and white matter hyperintensities in patients with amnestic mild cognitive impairment. *Acta Neurolgica Scandinavica, 115*, 419–424.

Shing, Y. L., Werkle-Bergner, M., Li, S-C., & Lindenberger, U. (2008). Associative and strategic components of episodic memory: A life-span dissociation. *Journal of Experimental Psychology: General, 137*, 495–513.

Sitzer, D. I., Twamley, E. W., & Jeste, D. V. (2006). Cognitive training in Alzheimer's disease: A meta-analysis of the literature. *Acta Psychiatrica Scandinavica, 114*, 75–90.

Skrajner, M. J., & Camp, C. J. (2007). Resident-Assisted Montessori Programming (RAMP™): Use of a small group reading activity run by persons with dementia in adult day health care and long-term care settings. *American Journal of Alzheimer's Disease and Other Dementias, 22*, 27–36.

Sliwinksi, M. J., Hofer, S. M., Hall, C., Buschke, H., & Lipton, R. B. (2003). Modeling memory decline in older adults: The importance of preclinical dementia, attrition, and chronological age. *Psychology and Aging, 18*, 658–671.

Small, S. A. (2001). Age-related memory decline: Current concepts and future directions. *Archives of Neurology, 58*, 360–364.

Soederberg-Miller, L. M., & Lachman, M. E. (1999). The sense of control and cognitive aging. In T. M. Hess & F. Blanchard-Fields (Eds.), *Social Cognition and Aging* (pp. 17–41). Academic Press: San Diego.

Spaan, P.E.J., Raaijmakers, J.G.W., & Jonker, C. (2005). Early assessment of dementia: The contribution of different memory components. *Neurobiology, 19*, 629–640.

Spencer, W. D., & Raz, N. (1995). Differential effects of aging on memory for content and context: A meta-analysis. *Psychology and Aging, 10*, 527–539.

Stadtlander, L. M., & Coyne, A. C. (1990). The effect of goal-setting and feedback on age differences in secondary memory. *Experimental Aging Research, 16*, 91–94.

Stebbins, G. T., Carrillo, M. C., Desmond, J. E., Turner, D. A., Bennett, D. A., Wilson, R. S., et al. (2002). Aging effects on memory encoding in the frontal lobes. *Psychology and Aging, 17*, 44–55.

Stein, R., Blanchard-Fields, F., & Hertzog, C. (2002). The effects of age stereotype priming on the memory performance of older adults. *Experimental Aging Research, 28*, 169–181.

Stigsdotter, A., & Bäckman, L. (1989a). Comparisons of different forms of memory training in old age. In M. A. Luszcz & T. Nettelbeck (Eds.), *Psychological Development: Perspectives Across the Life-span* (pp. 397–408). North Holland: Elsevier Science Publishers B.V.

Stigsdotter, A., & Bäckman, L. (1989b). Multifactorial memory training with older adults: How to foster maintenance of improved performance. *Gerontology, 35*, 260–267.

Stigsdotter Neely, A., & Bäckman, L. (1993a). Long-term maintenance of gains from memory training in older adults: Two 3 1/2 year follow-up studies. *Journal of Gerontology: Psychological Sciences, 48*, P233–P237.

Stigsdotter Neely, A., & Bäckman, L. (1993b). Maintenance of gains following multifactorial and unifactorial memory training in late adulthood. *Educational Gerontology, 19*, 105–117.

Stine-Morrow, E.A.L., Miller, L.M.S., & Hertzog, C. (2006). Aging and Self-Regulation in Language Understanding. *Psychological Bulletin, 132*, 582–606.

Stine-Morrow, E.A.L., Parisi, J., Morrow, D., Greene, J., & Park, D. (2007). An engagement model of cognitive optimization through adulthood. *Journal of Gerontology: Psychological Sciences, 62B*, 62–69.

Stine-Morrow, E.A.L., Shake, M. C., Miles, J. R., & Noh, S. R. (2006). Adult age differences in the effects of goals on self-regulated sentence processing. *Psychology and Aging, 21*, 790–803.

Stine-Morrow, E. A., Soederberg Miller, L. M., Gagne, D. D., & Hertzog, C. (2008). Self-regulated reading in adulthood. *Psychology and Aging, 23*, 131–153.

St. Jacques, P. L., Dolcos, F., & Cabeza, R. (2009). Effects of aging on functional connectivity of the amygdala for subsequent memory of negative pictures: A network analysis of functional magnetic resonance imaging data. *Psychological Science, 20*, 74–84.

Talassi, E., Guerreschi, M., Feriani, M., Fedi, V., Bianchetti, A., & Trabucchi, M. (2007). Effectiveness of a cognitive rehabilitation program in mild dementia and mild cognitive impairment: A case control study. *Archives of Gerontology and Geriatrics, 44*, 391–399.

Touchon, J., & Portet, F. (2004). Mild cognitive impairment: Evaluation and prospects. *Psychogeriatrics, 4*, 137–138.

Troyer, A. K., Murphy, K. J., Anderson, N. D., Moscovitch, M., & Craik, F.I.M. (2008). Changing everyday memory behavior in amnestic mild cognitive impairment: A randomized controlled trial. *Neuropsychological Rehabilitation, 18*, 65–88.

Tulving, E. (2004). How many memory systems are there? In D. A. Balota & E. J. Marsh (Eds.), *Cognitive Psychology: Key Readings* (pp. 362–378). New York: Psychology Press.

Turner, M. L. & Pinkston, R. S. (1993). Effects of a memory and aging workshop on negative beliefs of memory loss in the elderly, *Educational Gerontology* 19: 359–373.

Unverzagt, F. W., Kasten, L., Johnson, K. E., Rebok, G. W., Marsiske, M., Mann-Koepke, K. M., et al. (2007). Effect of memory impairment on training outcomes in ACTIVE. *Journal of the International Neuropsychological Society, 13,* 953–960.

Urakami, K. (2007). Prevention of dementia. *Psychogeriatrics, 7,* 93–97.

Valentijn, S.A.M., Hill, R., Van Hooren, S.A.H., Bosma, H., Van Boxtel, M.P.J., Jolles, J., et al. (2006). Memory self-efficacy predicts memory performance: Results from a 6-year followup study. *Psychology and Aging, 21,* 165–172.

Valentijn, S.A.M., van Hooren, S.A.H., Bosma, H., Touh, D. M., Jolles, J., van Boxtel, M.P.J., et al. (2005). The effect of two types of memory training on subjective and objective memory performance in healthy individuals aged 55 years and older: A randomized controlled trial. *Patient Education and Counseling, 57,* 106–114.

Verhaeghen, P. (1999). The effects of age-related slowing and working memory on asymptotic recognition performance. *Aging, Neuropsychology, and Cognition, 6,* 201–213.

Verhaeghen, P. (2000). The interplay of growth and decline: Theoretical and empirical aspects of plasticity in intellectual and memory performance in normal old age. In R. D. Hill, L. Bäckman, & A. S. Neely (Eds.), *Cognitive Rehabilitation in Old Age* (pp. 3–22). New York: Oxford University Press.

Vernhaeghen, P., Geraerts, N., & Marcoen, A. (2000). Memory complaints, coping, and well-being in old age: A systemic approach. *The Gerontologist, 40,* 540–548.

Vernhaeghen, P., & Marcoen, A. (1996). On the mechanisms of plasticity in young and older adults after instruction in the Method of Loci: Evidence for an amplification model. *Psychology and Aging, 11,* 164–178.

Verhaeghen, P., Marcoen, A., & Goossens, L. (1992). Improving memory performance in the aged through mnemonic training: A meta-analytic study. *Psychology and Aging, 7,* 242–251.

Verhaeghen, P., Marcoen, A., & Goossens, L. (1993). Facts and fiction about memory aging: A quantitative integration of research findings. *Journals of Gerontology, 48,* P157–P171.

Verhaeghen, P., Vandenbroucke, A., & Dierckx, V. (1998). Growing slower and less accurate: Adult age differences in time-accuracy functions for recall and recognition from episodic memory. *Experimental Aging Research, 24,* 3–19.

Werner P. (2000). Assessing the effectiveness of a memory club for elderly persons suffering from mild cognitive deterioration. *Clinical Gerontologist, 22,* 3–14.

West, R. L. (1986). Everyday memory and aging. *Developmental Neuropsychology, 2,* 323–344.

West, R. L., Bagwell, D. K., & Dark-Freudeman, A. (2005). Memory and goal setting: The response of older and younger adults to positive and objective feedback. *Psychology and Aging, 20,* 195–201.

West, R. L., Bagwell, D. K., & Dark-Freudeman, A. (2008). Self-efficacy and memory aging: The impact of a memory intervention based on self-efficacy. *Aging, Neuropsychology, and Cognition, 15,* 302–329.

West, R. L., & Berry, J. M. (1994). Age declines in memory self-efficacy: General or limited to particular tasks and measures? In J. D. Sinnott (Ed.), *Interdisciplinary Handbook of Adult Lifespan Learning* (pp. 426–445). Westport, CT: Greenwood Press.

West, R. L., & Crook, T. H. (1992). Video training of imagery for mature adults. *Applied Cognitive Psychology, 6,* 307–320.

West, R. L., Dark-Freudeman, A., & Bagwell, D. K. (2009). Goals-feedback conditions and memory: Mechanisms for memory gains in older and younger adults. *Memory, 17,* 233–244.

West, R. L., Dennehy-Basile, D., & Norris, M. P. (1996). Memory self-evaluation: The effects of age and experience. *Aging, Neuropsychology, and Cognition, 3,* 67–83.

West, R. L., & Thorn, R. M. (2001). Goal-setting, self-efficacy, and memory performance in older and younger adults. *Experimental Aging Research, 27,* 41–65.

West, R. L., Thorn, R. M., & Bagwell, D. K. (2003). Memory performance and beliefs as a function of goal setting and aging. *Psychology and Aging, 18,* 111–125.

West, R. L., & Tomer, A. (1989). Everyday memory problems of healthy older adults: Characteristics of a successful intervention. In G. C. Gilmore, P. J. Whitehouse, & M. L. Wykle (Eds.), *Memory, Aging, and Dementia: Theory, Assessment, and Treatment* (pp. 74–98). New York: Springer.

West, R. L., Welch, D. C., & Thorn, R. M. (2001). Effects of goal-setting and feedback on memory performance and beliefs among older and younger adults. *Psychology and Aging, 16,* 240–250.

West, R. L., Welch, D. C., & Yassuda, M. S. (2000). Innovative approaches to memory training for older adults. In R. D. Hill, L. Bäckman, & A. S. Neely (Eds.), *Cognitive Rehabilitation in Old Age* (pp. 81–105). New York: Oxford University Press.

West, R. L., & Yassuda, M. S. (2004). Aging and memory control beliefs: Performance in relation to goal setting and memory self-evaluation. *Journal of Gerontology: Psychological Sciences, 59,* 56–65.

Westmacott, R., Freedman, M., Black, S. E., Stokes, K. A., & Moscovitch, M. (2004). Temporally graded semantic memory loss in Alzheimer's disease: Cross-sectional and longitudinal studies. *Cognitive Neuropsychology, 21,* 353–378.

Willis, S. L., Tennstedt, S. L., Marsiske, M., Ball, K., Elias, J., Koepke, K. M., et al. (2006). Long-term effects of cognitive training on everyday functional outcomes older adults. *Journal of the American Medical Association, 296,* 2805–2814.

Wilson, B. A. (1995). Memory rehabilitation: Compensating for memory problems. In R. A. Dixon & L. Backman (Eds.), *Compensating for Psychological Deficits and Declines* (pp. 171–190). Mahwah, NJ: Lawrence Erlbaum Associates.

Wingard, J. A. (1980). Life-span developmental changes in mnemonic organization: A multimethod analysis. *International Journal of Behavioral Development, 3,* 467–487.

Wingfield, A., & Kahana, M. J. (2002). The dynamics of memory retrieval in older adulthood. *Canadian Journal of Experimental Psychology, 56,* 187–199.

Wolinsky, F. D., Unverzagt, F. W., Smith, D. M., Jones, R., & Wright, E. (2006). The effects of the ACTIVE cognitive training trial on clinically relevant declines in health-related quality of *life. Journals of Gerontology: Series B: Psychological Sciences and Social Sciences, 61B,* S281–S287.

Woolverton, M., Scogin, F., Shackelford, J., Black, S., & Duke, L. (2001). Problem-targeted memory training for older adults. *Aging, Neuropsychology, and Cognition, 8,* 241–255.

Yamaguchi, H. (2007). Alzheimer pathology during the past 100 years. *Psychogeriatrics, 7,* 109–113.

Yesavage, J., Hoblyn, J., Friedman, L., Mumenthaler, M., Schneider, B., & O'Hara, R. (2007). Should one use medications in combination with cognitive training? If so, which ones? *Journal of Gerontology: Psychological Sciences, 62B,* 11–18.

Yesavage, J., Lapp, D., & Sheikh, J. I. (1989). Mnemonics as modified for use in the elderly. In L. W. Poon, D. C. Rubin, & B. A. Wilson (Eds.), *Everyday Cognition in Adulthood and Late Life* (pp. 598–611). New York: Cambridge University Press.

Yesavage, J. A., & Rose, T. L. (1983). Concentration and mnemonic training in elderly subjects with memory complaints: A study of combined therapy and order effects. *Psychiatry Research, 9,* 157–167.

Yesavage, J., Sheikh, J. I., Friedman, L., & Tanke, E. (1990). Learning mnemonics: Roles of aging and subtle cognitive impairment. *Psychology and Aging, 5,* 133–137.

Yesavage, J. A., Sheikh, J. I., Tanke, E. D., & Hill, R. (1988). Response to memory training and individual differences in verbal intelligence and state anxiety. *American Journal of Psychiatry, 145,* 636–639.

Zanetti, O., Zanieri, G., Giovanni, G., Vreese, L. P., Pezzini, A., Metitieri, T., et al. (2001). Effectiveness of procedural memory stimulation in mild Alzheimer's disease patients: A controlled study. *Neuropsychological Rehabilitation, 11,* 263–272.

Zarit, S. H., Cole, K. D., & Guider, R. L. (1981). Memory training strategies and subjective complaints of memory in the aged. *The Gerontologist, 21,* 158–164.

Zarit, S. H., Gallagher, D., & Kramer, N. (1981). Memory training in the community aged: Effects on depression, memory complaint, and memory performance. *Educational Gerontology, 6,* 11–27.

Zimmerman, T. D., & Meier, B. (2006). The rise and decline of prospective memory performance across the lifespan. *The Quarterly Journal of Experimental Psychology, 59,* 2040–2046.

Index

About the Editors and Contributors

John C. Cavanaugh received his BA in psychology from the University of Delaware and his MA and PhD in psychology from the University of Notre Dame. He serves as chancellor for the Pennsylvania State System of Higher Education. Previously, he served as president of the University of West Florida, Provost at the University of North Carolina at Wilmington, and in various faculty and administrative positions at Bowling Green State University, the University of Delaware, and the Medical College of Ohio at Toledo. He was an American Council on Education Fellow at the University of Delaware. He is a fellow of the American Psychological Association, the Association of Psychological Science, and the Gerontological Society of America. He has published numerous books, chapters, and articles on topics in cognitive aging, gerontology, information technology, and higher education.

Christine K. Cavanaugh received her BS in business management from the University of Maryland, and her MBA (specialization in organizational development) and EdD (specialization in virtual learning environments) from the University of West Florida (UWF). Among her several professional certifications are Senior Professional in Human Resources (SPHR) and a Certificate of Completion from the Economic Development Institute. She is director of Training and Professional Development for the Division of Development and Alumni Relations at The George Washington University. Previously, Dr. Cavanaugh served as director of Human Performance Technology and as director of University-Community Engagement. Previously at

UWF, she served as interim director of Research and Sponsored Programs, assistant to the Associate VP for Research, interim director for Extended Credit Instruction, and associate director of the Haas Center for Business Research and Economic Development. In 2004–2005, she was an American Council on Education fellow at Spring Hill College in Mobile, Alabama. Dr. Cavanaugh has extensive teaching experience in many delivery modes (including fully online) and has written and presented on several topics in business, economic development, military linkages, and higher education. She has obtained well over $1 million in externally funded grants and contracts.

Stefan Agrigoroaei is a postdoctoral fellow in the Lifespan Developmental Psychology Lab at Brandeis University. He received his Doctorate in 2007 at University of Savoie, Chambéry, France. His general area of interest covers the antecedents of memory beliefs and their influence on cognitive performance. In his dissertation, "The decrease of memory self-efficacy in the elderly: Relationships with cognitive, affective and socio-cognitive factors," he proposed a multifactorial model that takes into account different sources of variation (i.e., cognitive decline, affective and health level, age stereotypes) in order to understand changes in memory self-efficacy.

Jason C. Allaire is an assistant professor of psychology at North Carolina State University. His research interests center on the real-world cognitive functioning of older adults, antecedents of individual differences in elders' basic cognitive functioning, modifiability of the aging mind, and short-term intraindividual variability in cognitive functioning.

Carrie Andreoletti is assistant professor of psychology at Central Connecticut State University where she teaches lifespan development and adult development and aging. She is codirector of the Adult Development and Gerontology Laboratory, and her research focuses on the content and consequences of age stereotypes as well as personality and emotion across the life span. She earned her PhD in social and developmental psychology from Brandeis University.

Jane Berry is associate professor and chair of the Department of Psychology at the University of Richmond in Richmond, Virginia. Berry completed her BA, MA, and PhD at Washington University in St. Louis and a postdoctoral fellowship at the University of Michigan. Her research focuses on memory self-efficacy as cause and consequence of memory aging; the structure of memory and metacognition in adulthood; and most recently, self- and other-perceptions of memory and aging, including Alzheimer's disease.

Fredda Blanchard-Fields is chair of the School of Psychology at the Georgia Institute of Technology. She received her undergraduate degree in psychology from the University of California at Los Angeles and her doctorate in developmental psychology from Wayne State University. She is a fellow of the American Psychological Association, the Association for Psychological Science, and the Gerontological Society of America and has held several leadership positions in these societies. She is editor of *Psychology and Aging* and has published widely in cognitive aging and cognitive neuroscience, with a focus on social cognition and aging. She has served on numerous review panels for the National Institutes of Health.

Soyoung Choun Soyoung Choun, MS, is currently a doctoral student at Oregon State University who is studying personality mechanisms for stress-related growth.

Alissa Dark-Freudeman is an assistant professor at the University of North Carolina in Wilmington. Dr. Dark-Freudeman completed her MS and PhD at the University of Florida. Her research examines the relationship between possible selves, self-regulatory beliefs, psychological well-being, and behavior related to memory performance and health.

Kate E. Daugherty is a doctoral student in the Department of Human Development and Family Studies at Iowa State University. Her research interests include successful aging and spousal influence on factors influencing health behaviors.

Diane L. Filion is associate professor and chair of the Department of Psychology at the University of Missouri—Kansas City. Her research focuses on the use of psychophysiological measures, especially measures based on the eyeblink reflex, to study low level attentional processes. She has applied her work in attention to the study of attentional changes in aging, attentional deficits in schizophrenia, and most recently to examining the role of attentional filtering in the regulation of emotion.

Brandi Hall is currently a master's student at Oregon State University who is completing her master's thesis on personality and caregiving.

Erin Hastings currently is a doctoral candidate in developmental psychology at the University of Florida (UF). She completed her MA in psychology at George Mason University. Ms. Hastings is a trainee in the Network for Biobehavioral and Social Research and Training in Aging at UF and was the recipient of the Cluff Award for Aging Research in 2009. Her interests include aging, memory beliefs, and memory training.

Karen Hooker is currently professor of human development and director of the Center for Health Aging Research at Oregon State University. Her prior positions were at Syracuse University and Duke University as a postdoctoral fellow. She earned her PhD in human development and family science at the Pennsylvania State University, her MA in psychology at the College of William and Mary in Virginia, and her BS in psychology from Denison University in Ohio.

Tara L. Johnson is an assistant professor of psychology at Indiana University of Pennsylvania. Her research program addresses how married couples collaborate on everyday problems.

Margie E. Lachman, PhD, is professor and chair of the Department of Psychology and director of the Lifespan Developmental Psychology Lab at Brandeis University. Her research focuses on how self-regulatory processes and beliefs such as the sense of control are related to memory, physical activity, and health in adulthood and old age. Dr. Lachman served as editor of the *Journals of Gerontology: Psychological Sciences* from 2000–2003, and she edited two volumes on midlife development. She received the Distinguished Research Achievement Award from the American Psychological Association, Division on Adult Development and Aging in 2003.

Courtney Lee is a graduate student and teaching assistant in the master's program in psychology at the University of Richmond. Her research interests include how the self-serving bias varies across domains in adulthood and old age; memory, mild cognitive impairment (MCI), and Alzheimer's disease (AD); and personality and positive aging.

Mary M. Lewis is a psychologist with Senior Life Consultants, Inc., in Dublin, OH, providing assessment and psychotherapy to older adults in long-term care facilities and retirement communities. She is also adjunct faculty at Columbus State Community College and received the CSCC Distinguished Teaching Award for 2007. She received her PhD and a graduate certificate in gerontology from the University of Akron, and she completed a geropsychology internship from the Malcom Randall VA Medical Center. She has authored and coauthored several articles and book chapters on older adults, spirituality, end-of-life issues, and dementia.

Jennifer A. Margrett is an assistant professor in the Department of Human Development and Family Studies at Iowa State University. Her research program focuses on everyday cognition and functioning throughout adulthood, particularly as impacted by contextual factors such as support from social partners.

Joan M. McDowd is professor and associate director for research at the Landon Center on Aging, University of Kansas Medical Center. Her research interests focus on attention in both healthy aging and age-related neurological deficits such as stroke, Parkinson's disease, and Alzheimer's disease.

Jessica Richmond Moeller is currently a graduate student at the University of Akron in the counseling psychology doctoral program. She received her master's degree in clinical psychology from Radford University in 2006. Her research interests include end-of-life care and decision making, quality of life in individuals living with HIV/AIDS, and long-term effects of childhood victimization. She has authored and coauthored several articles and book chapters on end-of-life issues. In 2008, she received the Association for Death Education and Counseling Cross-Cultural Student Paper Award.

Soo Rim Noh is a doctoral candidate in the Department of Educational Psychology and a student member of Beckman's Human Perception and Performance group at the University of Illinois. Her research focuses on age differences in discourse processing, in particular to how aging affects the ability to understand narratives.

Rick J. Scheidt, PhD, is a professor of lifespan human development in the School of Family Studies and Human Services at Kansas State University in Manhattan, Kansas. After earning his PhD in social psychology from the University of Nebraska-Lincoln, he trained in human aging at the Ethel Percy Andrus Center at the University of Southern California. His research focuses on environmental gerontology, with particular emphasis on aging in small rural communities. In addition to his contributions to several editorial boards, he has authored and coedited numerous journal articles and books on environment-aging theory and research.

Benyamin Schwarz, PhD, is a professor in the Department of Architectural Studies at the University of Missouri-Columbia. He received his bachelor's degree in architecture and urban planning from the Technion, the Institute of Technology of Israel, and his PhD in architecture from The University of Michigan with an emphasis on environmental gerontology. His research addresses issues of long-term care settings for older adults in the United States and abroad. Dr. Schwarz has been the editor of the *Journal of Housing for the Elderly* since 2000. He is the author and editor of several books and other publication on environment and aging.

Matthew C. Shake is an assistant professor in the Department of Psychology at St. Bonaventure University. He received a PhD in educational psychology from the University of Illinois. His research focuses on age differences in language comprehension, relying on eye-tracking to examine the moment-to-moment processes underlying the resolution of ambiguity.

Elizabeth A. L. Stine-Morrow is a professor in the Department of Educational Psychology and a member of Beckman's Human Perception and Performance group at the University of Illinois. Her research focuses on cognition and the capacity for learning through the adult life span.

Sarah R. Weatherbee is a doctoral student in the lifespan developmental program at North Carolina State University. Her research interests focus on cognitive aging, with a particular emphasis on elders' everyday cognition, cognitive interventions, and short-term variability in cognitive performance. Recently, she published results from a study examining the clinical utility of an everyday cognition measure.

James L. Werth, Jr., is professor of psychology and director of the Radford University PsyD Program in counseling psychology. He has contributed to approximately 100 publications, including several books and special journal issues, primarily on end-of-life issues, HIV disease, suicide, and professional ethics. He is also a licensed psychologist who provides pro bono counseling services. He has received recognition from the Ohio Psychological Association, Society of Counseling Psychology, and American Association of Suicidology.

Robin West, professor of psychology, has been conducting research on memory and aging for over 30 years, with an emphasis on memory beliefs and factors that enhance memory ability in the later years. Dr. West completed her MA and PhD at Vanderbilt University and did postdoctoral work at the Aging and Development Program at Washington University in St. Louis. In the Department of Psychology at the University of Florida since 1987, Dr. West has served as the department Graduate Coordinator, director of the Center for Gerontological Studies, and associate director of the Institute on Aging.